Foreword by Michael
Sunday Times No. 1 Best S

CHANGE YOUR STORY

December 2023

Escape from a job you hate and create a career you love - on purpose

CAROLYN PARRY

WISDOM PUBLISHING

Change Your Story

First edition published and printed in the United Kingdom 2023.

A CIP catalogue record of this book is available from the British Library.

ISBN (Hardcover):	978 1-7395432-0-4
ISBN (Paperback):	978-1-7395432-1-1
ISBN (eBook):	978-1-7395432-2-8
Imprint:	Wisdom Publishing
Cover design:	Matthew J Bird
Typesetting:	Matthew J Bird

For further information about this book, please contact the author at:
https://www.wisdompublishing.co.uk/

Dedication

To my long-suffering husband and soul mate of almost four decades, Rhys, thank you for supporting me on my journey through life, work, and writing this book - the words 'thank you' are not enough, but it is finally time to book that holiday now!

To my grown-up children, Katie and Tom, for exemplifying what life is like when you follow your bliss and create a working life you love. I am so proud of who you both are and what you have each achieved already.

To my "weekend daughter," Rhianon – I finally did it, even if it took a while! Thanks for nudging me from time to time to do it!
I am so glad I have.

For my grandchildren, Anwen and Elliot, and for those grandchildren yet to arrive on Planet Earth, I hope this helps you to create a lasting working life you love for as long as you want one when the time comes.

To everyone reading this, I hope it inspires you to find your purpose and serve it.

My love to you all.
October 2023.

CONTENTS

PART TWO: DEVELOPING YOUR STORY

PART THREE: ACHIEVING YOUR STORY

PART FOUR: APPENDICES

FOREWORD

It was 1989 when I had the realisation. I was 22, and for the previous six years, I'd been in a job that I didn't love. Worse still, that job came with a huge obligation; it was a family business: W Heppell and Sons Ltd roofing contractors. And I was one of the sons.

Since I was knee-high to a scaffolding pole, I'd been programmed that I would join the family trade. When Dad retired, my brother and I would take over the business. As a kid, this seemed like a great idea. After all, my dad loved his job, and he was brilliant at it! Bill Heppell was Chairman of the National Federation of Roofing Contractors; he trained the British Roofing Team (who won the world championships) and wrote the fixing manuals for the slate manufacturers. He was a rockstar of the roofing world.

Aged sixteen, I left school on Friday, joined the family firm on Monday, and by Tuesday, I'd made a discovery. I didn't want to be a roofer. So why did it take six years before I did anything about it? Simple. I convinced myself I enjoyed being a roofer (great tan in the summer). As much as I admired my father and, in some ways, wanted to be like him, the truth was I hadn't ever taken the time to think about what I really wanted to do. And most crucially, how I was going to do it. It certainly wasn't roofing, yet I was destined to do this for the next 50 years.

The saying goes, "When the student is ready, the teacher appears". In September 1989, my teacher showed up. Allan Percival was a youth worker I'd known since my early teens. Through a strange set of circumstances, (he saw something in me that I hadn't spotted), I was offered a once-in-a-lifetime chance. This was an opportunity to drastically change my career and my life. In one step, I was going to go from being a roofer to managing the charity involvement of the National Garden Festival, Gateshead, 1990. You couldn't take a larger sideways step.

This was my defining moment. Through working on this project, I became involved with fundraising, and as a fundraiser, I met many highly successful people. This took my path into the world of personal development. I loved it!

Thirty plus years later, my job is to teach people how to be brilliant. Every day, I wake up and pinch myself – I'm paid to do what I love.

If you're lucky, you too can have a job or a career like this. If not, then, as happened to me, your teacher has arrived. You're holding it right now. Dive into these pages and discover from Carolyn what needs to change in your story and how to rewrite it.

You spend half your waking hours and a third of your life at work. Doesn't it make sense to find something that inspires you and helps you to inspire and serve others, too? It may be a cliché, but it's true… *When you find a job you love, you'll never work another day in your life*. Open your mind, be inspired, and let Carolyn show you how.

Michael Heppell

INTRODUCTION & HOW TO USE THIS BOOK

A call to action

The Covid pandemic represents the first global wake-up call since the Second World War in the 1940s, causing millions of us to consider what truly matters. For many, it highlighted what is missing from our lives if we are to feel fulfilled, happy, and able to live to our full potential. While multitudes of people made changes to their lives as part of the Great Resignation, Great Reset, and Quiet Quitting as an attempt to recover from burnout, many others are still seeking answers to questions that continue to linger in their hearts and minds.

The pandemic not only caused us to question why we are here but also gave rise to the start of the second wake-up call, which is affecting every professional around the globe. The technology revolution driven by Generative AI and Large Language Models represents both the single biggest opportunity and threat of our lifetimes. Just as our 18th Century relatives witnessed the advent of the Industrial Revolution and its repercussions on jobs and communities, we are currently living through similar and revolutionary times as Industry 5.0 heralds the era of the human-machine interface. We see its impact daily as the work of professionals in every sector is either being re-engineered because of technology or is increasingly being lost to it at a time when employer and employee pockets are under ever greater pressure due to a pandemic and sadly war-informed cost of living crisis.

Many of the cultural, social, and work norms that have been in place for the last 50 years have either been eroded or have simply disappeared as society and communities alike become increasingly secular, fragmented, and disadvantaged - something exacerbated as technology-driven hybrid/ homeworking becomes the new way of life. The traditional concept of a career for life often passed on by well-intended but out-of-touch parents is also outdated, while the very meaning of career has changed beyond all recognition. As the Career Development Institute, the professional body for the sector, states, career now "describes our journey through life, learning, and work. We need actively to develop our careers to make the best of them. This process of career development takes skill as well as knowledge, and the right attitude. Individuals need to work on their career development skills throughout their lives... A 'positive career' will mean something different to everyone, but it will typically include being happy with the way you spend your time, being able to make a contribution to your community, and being able to have a decent standard of living."

Amidst all this change, our need as human beings to belong and feel fulfilled has never been more keenly felt. More people than ever are unhappy at work and are simply grinding their way through every day, often feeling trapped by the golden handcuffs of salary and high mortgages, in the hope that something better will turn up, but not really knowing how to make that happen.

Yet change is possible, as the eight extended stories in this book illustrate. Each of them shows how the individual concerned has consciously chosen to change their story by following a path less travelled and journey to a place of purpose and meaning that makes sense to them.

As we live in increasingly uncertain times, the days of being able to rely on the state or employer to provide our inner sense of well-being and stability are fading, so having a strong sense of inner career purpose is invaluable. It provides an intrinsic clarity of direction and focus like no other. That sense of purpose that is unique to you provides your own unique guiding north star that enables you to navigate through ambiguity and stay on course doing work that matters to you, even when external circumstances shift. When challenges arise, knowing "why" you are doing something can be a powerful motivator to persevere and push forward. A strong sense of purpose also fosters resilience and enables you to bounce back from setbacks when your efforts have a deeper meaning or purpose behind them. Having clarity about why you are here provides a filter for making choices, too, so you can prioritise opportunities and challenges that align with your core values, abilities, and long-term vision.

Rather than being rigid and fixed, a clear purpose will help you to pivot and adapt your path through life, while remaining aligned with your overarching mission. A clear and balanced sense of purpose creates a strong sense of fulfilment. It provides the perfect antidote to stress and burnout and creates a strong sense of bond and connection with others who share the same purpose. When we have a long-term vision, it helps us to keep perspective that enables us to overcome immediate obstacles rather than getting bogged down in them.

There is something magnetic and magical that happens when someone operates and speaks with clarity of purpose around an ultimate concern they have. As the stories in this book illustrate, that clarity of purpose is seen and heard by others and attracts opportunity and collaboration. Most importantly of all, in an increasingly changeable world that focuses on skills, having clarity of purpose gives us a sense of stability, a true reason to get out of bed every day, and helps our mental and physical well-being and happiness. It is up to us to decide what story we want to write to represent our lives. We can choose to settle for what comes our way, or we can choose to engage actively in writing it ourselves by leaning into who we really are and understanding what difference we are here to make.

The philosophy behind this book is simple. We all have the gift of a life, and at least in the first /developed world, the chance to choose how we want to spend it. If we opt to squeeze the metaphorical juice out of it by being clear about what matters, we can make the most out of our potential in a way that enables us to look back and say, "It was worth the ride. I mattered, and I made a difference." At the end of the day, isn't that what life is about?

How to use this book

Change Your Story distils almost 25 years of working with early-stage and established professionals of all ages and backgrounds in the context of a constantly and rapidly changing economy. The book uses my resulting INSPiRED research-proven, framework, model, and planner to help you take control of your working life. Using a problem-based lens on career choice, INSPiRED also aligns with the CDI's career development framework, and its six learning areas, and will enable you to develop the skills and mindset you need so that you can: "grow through life, explore possibilities, manage your career actively, create opportunities, balance life and work, and see the big picture." Structured in three parts, the first four chapters of this book are designed to help you understand your story so far. Chapters five to eight will help you to develop your story in a new, purpose-led direction. The final chapter (nine) shares strategies for success and well-being, so that you can create and live the working life you want by getting out of your own way and without burning out.

This book uses storytelling as a means of helping you to gain personal insights and learn effectively. It uses eight stories originally captured as interview-based episodes for my ***Change Your Story*** podcast. Storytelling is an ancient tradition that has helped humans learn to thrive from others' experiences over the centuries. As researchers have found, stories resonate because they convey information and values effectively in a way that engages the brain emotionally. This emotional engagement enhances memory retention, which can help us in the future. The power and magic of stories lie in their ability to help us hear the calls to change and find glimmers of inspiration from others, so we can navigate our own way forward. You will recognize those calls and glimmers in the stories of Vicki, Natalie, Meeta, Julia, Cathy, Chris, Mel, and Steve as they tell their stories of how they responded to these in their own words. Their words have only been edited for grammar and sense, where necessary, so that you can hear their individual voice, journeys, challenges, and experiences clearly and firsthand. If you don't enjoy reading stories, then you can always skip straight to the activities that follow each story.

The activities are designed to help you puzzle out who you are, what you have to offer, and what sort of working life you want to create. The INSPiRED Career and Life Planner serves as a one-page tool included in ***Change Your Story***, which will help you capture key learning from each of the activities in one place. There are two copies of the planner tool in this book, one at the front to use for making rough notes, and one at the back so you can keep a final version and refer to it regularly. You can also access a digital copy of the planner by visiting www.careeralchemy.co.uk/free-reader-planner-tool.html. The planner will help the brain to make sense of all the different components. As you will see, there is a light bulb symbol and question at the end of the activity for you to reflect on any insights you have had as a result.

The world is full of opportunities disguised as problems that are waiting for us to work with others to solve them. The biggest problems are those encapsulated in the United Nations Sustainable Development Goals (SDGs). They include hunger, poverty, health, and other universal challenges. You can read more about them and the primary careers and roles that relate to them in the appendices. Although they have a conceptual end date of 2030, the reality is that many will simply not be achieved by then due to their complexity. So, they offer longevity as 'ultimate concerns' around which to base your career purpose if you truly relate to them.

Once you have read the stories and worked through the activities in this book, you will be able to use what you have learned and the INSPiRED Career and Life Planner as tools to change your story whenever you need to, so you can create and enjoy the working life that inspires you – on purpose.

Change Your Story has been designed using proven processes to help you take control of your career so you can create the working life you want. That said, no book can possibly take into account every element of an individual's personal circumstances. Sometimes when we go through change, it can feel a little unnerving and it helps to talk things through, particularly if you have any doubts about your next steps. So, if you need a good career conversation and coaching support to help you move forward, please get in touch either with me or another suitably qualified and experienced career development practitioner. We all love to help.

Enjoy your voyage of discovery towards a purpose-driven life.

MY INSPIRED CAREER AND LIFE PLANNER

Who am I already?

Who do I want to be or become?

What are my strengths, talents and skills? Where are they best served and most wanted?

What do I want to be known for?

Who do I want to spend my work time with?

What life do I want to live?

What fascinates me?

Where do I want to spend my work time?

What direction am I headed in? What's my goal?

PART ONE:

UNDERSTANDING YOUR STORY

IDENTITY

1. IDENTITY: WHO AM I?

THE IMPACT OF NATURE, NURTURE, AND EXPERIENCE

Sometimes, it takes time to know who you are and be your true self, in a world full of other people's influences, noise, and challenge.

Vicki Rushton is a vibrant and energetic athletic woman in her late thirties with a big mop of curly brown hair and an accent that nods towards her Manchester roots. Her dad worked in the retail sector, while her mum ran bars in Hale. Her parents divorced when Vicki was relatively young. She gained a new stepdad and a new sibling every year until there were thirteen of them, and Vicki's mum became a stay-at-home mother.

As the eldest daughter, Vicki spent much of her childhood looking after siblings, which she found entertaining and challenging in equal measure. Despite the challenges, the family had a strong work ethic, which Vicki copied, making the most of every opportunity she came across from age 11 onwards.

"We used to have a newspaper shop on the corner directly opposite our house, and I've got an older brother who was my absolute idol. I loved him to bits, and he got a paper round. I started going with him. We had horses, which then naturally led to all sorts of opportunities. Ben used to go down and help down at the Pony Club, and wherever Ben went, I tended to follow. The same chap that ran the Pony Club also had a company that did horse-drawn carriage weddings, and I would then go and help out with them usually on a Saturday and a Sunday, most weekends."

When Vicki was approaching her teens, Vicki's mum struggled to cope as the family swelled and developed some mental health issues. So, Vicki dropped out of school at 15 to help support her and help her siblings. "I quite enjoyed school when I was there… I got quite good grades. My main subjects were food, technology or design technology, and PE. They were quite active, hands-on, but just family life and home life became quite disrupted at a time when I needed to knuckle down."

Vicki left school at 15 to care for the family. She met her first boyfriend around the same time and ended up pregnant at 16 with her daughter Jess. She explains, "Home life became really quite difficult, and I moved away at 16, bought my first house with Jessie's dad… had Jess. I think I felt older at 16 than I do these days. I think all that early responsibility, being self-reliant, and I never thought too hard or fast about a great deal of things.

"When Jess was four months old, I found myself a job in retail at the Perfume Shop in the Trafford Centre. So, I owned 50% of the house back then when you could get a hundred percent mortgage and bought my first house for £23,000. Long gone are those days when my mortgage was £110! It was so much easier - I went from looking after 11 siblings to one child… and from caring for a six-bedroom house to a two-bedroom house. It was a dream. I did actually rid myself of a lot of responsibility and could focus on myself at that time. And to do that at such a young age, I think, has made me the stronger individual that I am today, for sure."

Unfortunately, the relationship with Jess's dad broke down. Vicki explains, "As you get a little bit older and you reflect a little bit more, that relationship, I suppose, was an escapism from the situation I was in at home. But I was allowing behaviours that kind of I didn't want in the first place - I jumped straight out of the pan straight into the fire type of scenario. Then it was just me and Jess."

Vicki then met her next partner, who was completely different.

Unfortunately, life threw Vicki another curved ball that would test her in every way possible. She found out she was pregnant with her second child, Oliver, but all was not well, "We found out there were complications, and that Oliver was going to be disabled in some way. They offered me an amniocentesis so that I could wrap my head around it. To be honest, I was so disassociated from it. And I think that was something that I learned from a young age.

"They said that it could either be dwarfism or it could have been another condition where he wouldn't survive much past birth. And at 20 weeks pregnant, my emotions couldn't deal with it, and I just rolled with the pregnancy. At 30 weeks, they did a scan, and they were leaning more towards it being dwarfism, but they said, "It's looking like he's got full cleft lip and palate. He'll need full face reconstruction", and that, oh, it was just too much for me even to bear."

Vicki used strategies from her childhood to help prepare herself for what was to come and deal with the challenges of looking after a very sick baby, which led to some very unintended consequences. She explains her thinking at the time, "It was a case of, *"Right, okay, how am I going to look after this child? I'll deal with it."* But it became an "it" rather than a "him," which now, reflecting on it, was quite sad. I developed these coping strategies from such a challenging childhood. It has made me extremely resilient. I don't look back and resent any of that anymore. I see it as a blessing, and it has shaped me in the way that I think today."

When he was born, Oliver was diagnosed with dwarfism and was taken to special care because he had breathing difficulties. At this point, Vicki described it as feeling like a job, and her work ethic kicked in.

"Oliver came home after three weeks, and in SCBU (Special Care Baby Unit), they give you training in resuscitation. Never did I think I would need to use this. Within a couple of hours, he stopped breathing. So, I did breath and massage, and he came back, and that was fine. And within the coming weeks, this happened 20 to 30 times a day for about three weeks.

"One day, I couldn't revive him and rang an ambulance. What started as an emergency admission led to her son being in hospital for just short of a year, during which time Oliver had a tracheostomy and was being fed via a nasogastric tube. With a child at home and one in hospital, times were tough.

"We had a period where he got so ill, he had full organ failure. At the time, I was just going through the motions. And I became really practical in my mind. The day that Oliver had full organ failure, I'd been at the hospital with him solidly for two weeks. And I needed to go and see Jess because she has been neglected."

What happened next was a pivotal moment for Vicki and Oliver. Just as she returned to SCBU after seeing Jess, he flat lined.

"Each team that was supposed to be caring for him, we had Ear Nose and Throat (ENT), respiratory and General Medical, none of them were picking him up. They were thinking it was somebody else's responsibility, and he ended up in intensive care for ten weeks.

"The day that that happened, I didn't get angry, but I wanted answers, and I pulled together this massive multi-professional meeting. I wanted everybody there.

"The only question I had at that time was, "If he had died, what would you say to me?"

"And it was the only question I asked. I just put it on the table, and the room was silent.

"And I remember quivering and shaking being 21, coming to terms with the fact that he was a dwarf, that he had all of these challenges that I was having to give him resuscitation 20 to 30 times a day, and kind of feeling unheard. And for the first time, as drastic as that was, I felt heard. I felt seen for the first time in life and realized that these people in this room are people that I would hold in such a high regard. You know, they were so highly educated, they're meant to know their job. We looked to them to save people where they can. And yet I felt in that instance that I'd been failed, that my son had been failed, and that I was his only voice. And for the first time, I felt I had a voice, and that was the only question I put to them."

The power Vicki found in that moment was not just life-changing for her son but for her, too as she explains, "My confidence just - just grew. I felt like I could talk to anybody, and I became powerful for him, so I became his advocate, but bizarrely, even though he was a little person, and he couldn't talk, and he was fighting for his life in that moment, he gave me so much.

And when I reflect on that, I would say that's a massive, pivotal moment for me to realize that these other people, they're just people. Yes, they're highly educated in their field, but yet, unless we come together and we communicate effectively, nothing really happens, and nothing really changes."

Vicki's ability to find and stand in her power was to go on to be a key force in the rest of her life choices.

* * * *

Despite supporting a very sick son, Vicki continued to work at the Perfume Shop, was promoted to a senior sales role, and took every training course she could. By this point, Vicki discovered she was pregnant with her daughter Faye.

"I felt as if I was doing really well. And I remember when Oliver was in hospital, and he'd just come out of intensive care. At the time I was obviously on maternity. He was like seven months old, and my manager at the time was saying, "Vic, it doesn't look like you're going be able to come back."

Vicki pleaded with her boss to let her keep her job and offering to switch to part time hours. Vicki's manager told Vicki that she wasn't being very realistic and that was challenging for her to hear particularly because she gained so much from working. Vicki made her case to be able to return, "I need something for myself. This is really tiring. I'm knackered. But you go to work, and you chat with your friends, you actually offload a lot of your internal stress. And you go home, and you feel as if you've achieved and you've been a part of a team, and when the team succeed, you succeed."

Vicki finally did some more thinking and made a decision, "I remember the day that I had to resign. I don't get upset. I don't get emotional. I remember Oliver going into intensive care, and I didn't cry, and everybody around me was crying, and I was like, *"Am I just a void of emotion?"* But it was a coping strategy, but the day I had to resign from work..."

Having to resign had touched a deep nerve, which came from her childhood, as she explains, "There was always a stigma around my mum.

There were a lot of things that people would say about me being from a large family and my mum not working. I was so scared of the stigma. We were stigmatized as a large family, and then [I was] stigmatized for being a 16-year-old mum. And then I thought, *"Oh, I can't be jobless as well. Absolutely not."* So that was a really emotional day for me. But it had to happen because my son, my children needed me at that time, and I did have to make that sacrifice where it was their needs over mine." Eventually, Oliver was well enough for Vicki to take him home with a tracheostomy, which stayed in place until he was three and a half, and he continued to be fed by gastric tube. She continued to liaise with 22 consultants.

Life took on a different rhythm and shape due to Oliver's needs, and they were largely house-bound or hospital-bound for nearly four years due to his oxygen dependency, but they made the best of it as Vicki explains, "Anywhere we went, he'd have crowds of people, either in fits of laughter and for a little chap that couldn't talk and could only sign, or people would be in bits, but they absolutely adored him everywhere we went."

They continued to be supported by the team in the hospital, the hospice, and community nursing, who all adored Oliver, and another opportunity came their way, as Vicky explains, "We were approached by ITV once the new super hospital in Manchester had been built. They wanted to film our journey." Once again, Vicki's ability to say yes to an opportunity kicked in and she and her son's story was shown on TV.

Shortly after being filmed and leaving the hospital, Oliver stopped breathing again, leading to another short hospital stay and another operation. Finally, surgeons removed his tracheostomy, and Oliver's journey to learning how to speak began leading to another pivotal moment for Vicki as his mother, as she explains, "I remember there was a day when he said something that he hadn't said before, I hadn't heard before. I remember thinking, "Oh, I can be your mum. And it was really emotional for me because I'd been his carer. I was scared to get close to him."

By this time, Oliver was four, and now that his health had stabilised, Vicki felt it was time for a new chapter as she fought to have a sense of identity, connection, and normality for her and the family. She explains what was going on, "My partner at the time didn't cope very well with the situation with Oliver. I didn't have a family to lean on. The relationship with my mum had broken down. I didn't speak to my siblings. My dad lived in Wales. I was living in Manchester, and the voice in my head sometimes was so strong, and I just wanted to be like everybody else up in the morning and go to work. I'd worked from such a young age. It gave me independence, you know, kind of even just the financial side of it, the connection with people. It was a really isolating time with Olly because people didn't know what to say. They didn't know what to do, so they avoided me. I definitely did lose my identity by not working for sure."

Oliver also had asthma, and Vicki had noticed that his breathing and quality of life were much better when they visited her dad in North Wales. She also wanted to give her children a slower pace of life and more opportunities to be outdoors like she had had growing up. So, she made the decision to move to North Wales with her children. She rented a house there, sold her house in Manchester, and explained the move to her children as an adventure.

The reality of moving to live in Wales was a culture shock. Whereas her experience living in a city was that people did not interact with others, she found the opposite to be true, living in a rural part of Wales, as she explains, "People do talk and take time, and then the neighbours would come out and say hi. Everybody stops. They have a chat. It's a totally slower pace of life - not the people in the city aren't friendly, it's just that everybody gets on with their own thing, whereas it's far more community-based here. So, everybody does want to get to know you because you're part of their community. I think that's the reason I've stayed."

From the children's perspective, the timing was perfect. Oliver was becoming stronger. Vicki was able to arrange to move some of his care to Wales, keep those in Manchester on an open-door access basis, and arrange school nurse support. Meanwhile, Faye was starting nursery, and Jess was coming up to 10, the ideal age to pick up Welsh as a language. As Vicki reflected, "We were here six weeks, and then the children went to school. So, straight away, I gained my life back in a way that I'd never had before.

All of a sudden, I had this newfound freedom."

* * * *

Shortly afterwards, a chance encounter at the school gates with another mum, Becky, who was doing a university Access course, piqued Vicki's curiosity about whether she could get back into education or not, and stuck fast. She realised that without much education, she was limited and started asking herself questions: *"How am I going to package myself? I've got no education. I'm just a mum."* And I found those words leaving my mouth quite often and not seeing my own value. I couldn't see what other people could see. A lot of people would say, *"Wow, how amazing. You've done all these things with Oliver. You've trained yourself to be a nurse."* But for me, I didn't feel I was achieving anything. I was just Mum."

She realised that the shadow of a child with health care needs hanging over her was unlikely to make her the most attractive job applicant. So, she made an appointment to meet one of the course lecturers. Vicki found a good welcome waiting for her, as she explains, "She was unbelievably enthusiastic and passionate, and warm, and just had this energy, and I thought, I think this is what I need to be around. So, I thought I could tie that in with the kids. It's school hours, and kind of see how this goes. So, I just signed up, again, not thinking too hard or fast about it. I jumped on the course, and then they said, *"You can get your GCSEs as well. If you do them alongside this, it's not going to cost you anything else"*. I had no idea what I wanted to do; I just wanted to be a part of something and start to find value in myself."

Some hard work and determination led to her gaining her GCSEs and passing her Access to HE course, and as her thoughts turned to the future, she came across a Design and Technology Teaching course at Bangor University. "I thought, *"Oh, teaching that'd fit around the kids. And I used to love design technology, and I absolutely love baking. Oh, all these things are all ironing. Yeah, go on, we'll give it a go."*

Vicki applied and then received an invitation to go for an interview at the university and was offered a place on the course, even though she didn't have a portfolio. When she arrived, Vicki's confidence in her ability as a mature student and her sense of direction started to weaken, as she explains. "There were all these young students with their parents, and I just turned up with my mobile phone and car keys. I thought, *"Oh no, I'm in the wrong place."* And for the first time in my life, I felt old. I'd always felt too young to have done everything that I'd done. And I was like, *"Oh, the identity crisis has started all over again."*

That sense of imposter syndrome remained with her throughout her studies at Bangor University. Yet, she went on to complete her course in product design and engineering with qualified teacher status. She reflects on what that meant, "You had to learn product design and then learn how to teach product design. My logic in doing so was it would give me the most amount of employability at the end of the course, and I did the first semester. I was having a really, really bad identity crisis with my age and my anxiety. I did start to struggle. So, I deferred for the rest of that year, deciding, *"Am I doing the right thing? Why does it feel so off?"* And focused on being a mum, finding myself. I did a lot of soul-searching. I'm beginning to understand myself. Something I'd never, ever done before. You know, it was a lot." Vicki recalled the saying in entrepreneurship circles, which summed up her approach to life.

"You jump off the cliff and build a plane on the way down. That's kind of bizarrely the way that my coping strategy is. I tend to kind of run headlong into things and say yes, and then just deal with it. However, I felt really out of my depth and really under-prepared. I was learning how to learn, which to some might sound bizarre. I was struggling with that more than anything else. It felt like everybody else knew what they were doing, and yet when they were talking to me, my answers to their answers were, like, polar ends apart. Our thought process was like, miles off, and I didn't feel like I fitted. So, I deferred and then tried to understand, *"Why do I feel like I don't fit in? What do I have to offer? What am I bringing?"* And I did start to reflect and thought, *"You know what, actually, Vic, stop. Stop this. Stop this nonsense. You've got loads to offer. And you know what? Your thinking might not be the same as theirs, but that might be your key. That might be your golden nugget. You don't have to be like them."*

Despite her gut feeling that design was the thing for her, she committed to the teaching side of the course when she returned the following September. She soon discovered that she struggled with the structured approach that came with teaching, having had such an unstructured life. "It was throwing me into this space that just felt too restrictive. It was so foreign. I committed for the first year to teaching. I went and did a placement and knew after two weeks that it wasn't for me." She started to listen to herself and decided, *"I'm going to follow my passion. I'm going to reduce my employability and just follow design, but I will give it my everything."*

She recognised that this scattergun approach had become focused on something she loved, which she had first discovered as a child, as she explains, "When I was younger, I was always passionate about decorating the house. I used to mither my mum, *"Can I decorate the house?"* And I remember decorating my bedroom when I was about nine or 10, and I just loved how things could go together, and there was no rule for that. You get a bit of this, and you get a bit of that, and you smash it together, and you stand back, and you have a look. And it's either an absolutely amazing marvel or a car crash on a wall. There is no rule until you hit a sweet spot. And then that is the rule." For Vicki, design meant freedom of expression.

While Vicki was studying for her degree, her then-husband got into restoring paraffin stoves and would often go off and purchase bits and pieces. One day, when Vicki commented about his lack of success in buying items, he challenged her to have a go herself, so she did. Vicki picks up the story. "I went with £200, and I bought some stock, and then I popped it on eBay, and a few other platforms and the first item I bought was £40, and I sold it for £250. And then it just blew up from there. And the next thing, I had a website and an antiques and reclamation salvage business. What started as a hobby became a wholesale project. I had my own business, three kids, a degree, and a husband who wasn't amazingly supportive." One thing led to another, and Vicki decided to leave her husband during her degree. She explains, "I just realized that we'd grown apart, and that was the challenging part for me in year three."

As part of her business module, she needed to find a problem to solve as part of learning business planning. Having gained a taste for business and realising that there is no point in design if you have a product that can't be sold, she started work on developing a business plan. Driven by her strong sustainability ethic and love of old furniture, she created a scheme to prevent beautifully crafted old furniture from being thrown into landfills by making it contemporary so that its craftsmanship could continue to be appreciated. She dropped some modules to fit it in with her studies, salvage business, and being a mum and graduated with a 2(i). Vicki explains what it meant to her. "To be fair, I would've been happy to come out with a third. It wasn't about the grade. I felt as if I got so much value from that course. I was amazed by what I'd learned. You know, I'd be having a conversation with somebody, and I'd be referencing a book. For me, leaving school at 15 with very, very, very basic education and not coming from a house of academics or when I was kind of reciting textbooks and things that I was learning, sometimes I'd catch myself and, yeah, starting to be proud of myself in those little instances, that was a win for me. I didn't need the accolade at the end, to be honest. At my graduation ceremony, I was presented with an award for entrepreneurship by Santander and £1000 to do with what I wish, whether it's to start my business or just to say well done." What came next for Vicki was something totally unexpected.

* * * *

Vicki picks up the story, "I had a really big wobble. Anxiety kicked in. Depression." I was like, *"Have I made rash decisions? Have I chosen to separate and throw my life into chaos, thinking I can do it all?"* I'm finding myself in that awful territory again where I'm a young single mum of three. Me and my own mum don't speak. And she had several marriages, and I was like, *"Oh, no! It's like history repeating itself."* For about two months, I really was struggling mentally and emotionally. It's like I'd gone from the high of the high, you know, winning this award, finishing this degree. I'd reached the peak, and then I had no idea how on earth to get down. I couldn't see a path; [I] just got lost. And I went back to that crisis of what do I have to offer? *"Okay, great. You've got this piece of paper that says you can design, but you're not a designer. It says you are an engineer, but you're not an engineer. You've got no experience in it."* It's like, *"Oh, I did a couple of modules at uni,"* and this was like the self-talk, and it became really negative."

Somehow, amid her massive dose of imposter syndrome, Vicki found a way forward despite the dialogue in her head. "In that negative self-talk, I was like, *"You didn't even give teaching a good crack. You didn't try it; you just thought it didn't align with you at that time"*. And I thought, *"Right, okay, do you know what? Let's not sit here and mope."* And I just decided that I was going to ring an agency for teaching, and I thought, you know, *"Go and give it a crack. Go and spend some time there, but without the pressure of university; just go in and be in a classroom. See if you've still got the power to manage a classroom"*. So, I did that for about six months. And I was at high schools, I was at primary schools, and it was nice and without the pressure. And it was something that I could see I had a natural ability to do, but it still didn't light me up inside. It wasn't self-led. It was still structured. My passion had become about business. I reflected on what I decided to design as my final year product versus what everybody else had and the fact that I'd started to run my own business. I ended up giving my business to my husband. And yeah, it became quite chaotic. I ended up moving out of the house and sold everything I owned. I just needed a fresh start. I needed to cut it all off. And that's what I did."

This latest fresh start allowed Vicki to hear her inner voice more clearly and follow her instincts, which helped her move forward again as she explains, "I started to put my energy and my focus back into my passion. And I started to lead by my gut, not my head, not even my heart. I was just like, *"Does this feel right? Yes, right. Do that."* It's an urge. I feel uncomfortable in myself when I'm doing something that doesn't align with me. And when I move towards the thing aligning with me, all that tension disappears, and everything comes naturally. I feel comfortable. The people around me their energy towards me is different. It's warm. It's creative, it's vibrant, it's colourful, it charges me up. Even just thinking about it now, I feel charged when I gravitate towards the things that serve me. I've never really understood energy. "The insights Vicki gained from learning to follow her intuition made a world of difference to her mental well-being and outlook on life. "I didn't kind of know that I was allowed to go and follow my gut. But this sense of feeling and really tapping into it, it's exactly that. It's quite freeing. It happens naturally, and it stops my mind from getting fuzzy because my gut's telling me to go over there and do it. And by not being fixed, it almost protects me from getting too bogged down with making too many mental decisions. And in doing that, I was able to let go mentally. The depression went away. The anxiety went away. And it was if I like this today, I'm going to do this today. And if my feelings change tomorrow, there'll be something else. I've got value to add to wherever it is that I go."

Vicki had discovered that when she trusted her gut, it took her to places she loved, whereas when her intellect kicked it and started to challenge her instincts, it took her to places she didn't enjoy. Having the ability to think like this enabled Vicki to make more aligned decisions about the direction she wanted in her career. After six months of teaching and despite getting great feedback, she knew it was not for her, and it was time for another change, as she explains, "I felt as if we'd lost sight, like education is merely the transfer of knowledge. And it doesn't matter how that happens, as long as it happens safely, but it's about inspiring people to find their passion."

That was the element that was missing for Vicky.

* * * *

Before Vicki had taken up the teaching role, she had been in touch with a local charity for some employability support, including help with her CV writing. Just as she started thinking about the work she wanted to do, opportunity knocked once again, and Vicki received a call out of the blue from Tom, the Project Manager there. He said, "Are you still looking for work? My path has changed, and I'm looking to leave. And I just wondered, would you be interested in this role? I think you'd be perfect for it. You've got the right attitude, non-judging, open to all people, really diverse. You'd bring a great energy. I'm just letting you know that the post is there, and it's down the road. It works great with the kids. What do you reckon?"

Vicki realised the value of what Tom was proposing, recognising that she was good at managing projects and had good energy to bring to the role. She applied for the job. She made it onto the interview list and started to think about how she was going to prepare for it as she explains, "I was thinking, *"You know, I'm sick of kind of trying to fit this mould that I'm assuming is there."* So, I just went in. I'm just having a kind of chit-chat. They were asking me questions, and I felt just relaxed. I answered openly, with no expectations. I just thought, *"I'll give it a whirl,"* you know? And if they feel that I align with the job, great. If not, I can continue, and something will come along." Vicki recalled the panel's comments at the end of her interview. At the end of the interview, they said, "You're perfect for the job. We'll offer you the job right now. Would you like to take the job?" And yeah, I started there a week later."

* * * *

Vicki's ability to show up as her authentic self and be a natural born connector was to stand her in good stead again not long afterwards when she was having a conversation with the owner of the local gym. He asked her whether she was missing the antiques and reclamation salvage business.

"I said, "I do, but with the children and what have you, it takes you away from home quite a lot. You've got to go and find these beautiful pieces that you're going to transform, and it's just not aligning with me now." Local blacksmith and business owner and gym goer Gerallt Evans overheard the conversation and joined in and said, "What is it you do?" So, I said, "Oh, I used to do antiques, reclamation salvage, and so on and so forth."

Serendipity led to Vicki meeting Gerallt again shortly afterwards. She had sold an old workbench online to someone who said a friend of his would be in touch to arrange collection. "So, the guy rings, and I was like, I'm sure I know that voice. That's really bizarre. And it was Gerallt. And he was like, *"Oh, you selling all of this? What's happening?"* So, I explained about the life changes. And then we just got chatting, exchanged numbers, and kind of dipped in and out a little bit here and there. Then, when Covid struck, I was still working, and he was passing by outside the building where I worked on his way back from looking at a job in Chester, and he just pulled over, and he is like, "You should pop in sometime and come and have a look at my place." He said, "You know, you mentioned that you were interested in business and kind of looking at structures. I reckon you'd have a field day in our place."

A subsequent visit to the workshop shortly afterwards led to Vicki making suggestions about improving the space, as she explains "Within two days, he sent me pictures, and he'd taken down this dividing wall, and he'd moved the steel rack to the left-hand side and created so much more floor space. And he is like, "Do you want to come back next week and have a look at something else? This is how we do jobs. Can I record them any better?" And I was like, "Oh, this is really fun. Yeah, because I was making suggestions, and he was implementing them, and it wasn't taxing, but it was where I could take all of this theory that I'd learned, and he became a Guinea pig."

A few weeks passed, and in June 2020, Vicki had another call from Gerallt. “He said, "I've just done a phone call about converting a tram for ZIP World. Now, I can't take on the whole project. I think you'd be perfect for it. They need to turn this tram into, um, like a working kiosk. They want a pizza oven in there, a bar, a coffee machine. Do you fancy collaborating on it? Well, obviously, my answer as always is, "Yeah, why not?" "Great. We'll go to the site and have a look at it tomorrow. And they want it done in six weeks."

Once again, Vicki's inclination to say yes to opportunities came to the fore. "We both walked away and looked sideways at each other, and we were like, "Six weeks and Covid and the whole world's ground to a halt." And we were like, "Yeah, all right, we'll do it. Yeah." And we did!”

Things snowballed from there. Gerallt asked Vicki to help him out with his admin work and the business structure and to go along to client meetings, so he could spend more time in the workshop based in the heart of the North Wales mountains, where he and his team fuse the ancient craft of blacksmithing with state-of-the-art technology to create unique pieces that are not only beautiful but practical.

When Vicki joined the business, it was just Gerallt and two apprentices. She became a director and 50% shareholder in the business in June 2021. By April 2023, they had become a team of six and are building a new state-of-the-art, twice the size workshop due to open in late 2023 so they can expand further.

As part of their expansion, Vicki set up work experience opportunities for students from Bangor University as a way of paying back the difference the course made to her. The company is now certified to BSEN 1090, enabling it to construct and use up to 15 stories of structural steel.

"We were being approached about lots of different jobs. We ended up tag teaming on many of them and turning up at site. So, from completing the job of the tram and then some smaller jobs and commissions that Gerallt had going on towards the end of that year, I was putting in systems and processes in the company, helping him get up to date with all his invoicing, et cetera. January Zip World were opening a site down in South Wales in Rhigos, their Tower site, and asked me would I spend ten days designing a new bar to fit out their new F and B (food and beverage) building?"

When faced with the most significant commission Vicki had ever encountered, she gave her usual entrepreneurial answer of saying yes and then finding out how to deliver afterwards. "I was like, do you know what? "Why not talk me through it. What needs to be there? You know, what are you thinking? Do you want something that's heritage? Do you want something that's modern? Have you got something within the brand?" And they were like, "No, we want something that harks to the site". And I spent a couple of hours walking around looking for inspiration, there's a giant coal rig there, and thought, "Why don't we recreate that rig inside the building and make it into a bar?" And they were like, "Great, can you execute it in eight weeks?" I was like, "Oh, not one of these again"! And we did it! Zip World is just such fast pace, and we just keep responding."

What enables Vicki to thrive in this environment is her love of how design creates an external expression of somebody and offers freedom of expression. She explains why she loves it so much, "I design for the people and understand how they might not understand themselves. I'd like somebody to understand me like I don't understand me, because people see things in me that I don't see. And design enables me to do the same for them. When I was buying antiques and reclamation salvage, I remember buying a gate and remember paying £50 for the gate, and I sold it for £650. Now it's not the monetary value, but that gate must have been 200-300 years old. It was wrought iron, it had been painted so many times and I managed to strip the paint off, it was just such a beautiful, beautiful item. We're in a culture of fast fashion. Everybody wants it cheaper. They want it faster. They want it to look great, whereas I'm more of the notion I would love to be making items that outlive me. And I would love to think that we are creating something that could either be passed down through the generations or people look at our items the way that I looked at that gate, just [seeing] that it was made with love, it was made with passion, and it was made to stand the test of time. It's not damaging the environment; it's not going to landfill. You don't just see it. You feel it. You know when you see beautiful architecture, or somebody's taken great pride in furnishing the house. Yeah. I want to be a part of that journey for other people."

Vicki continues to design and work with the team to build everything from tailor-made gates that will tell stories for multiple lifetimes, to staircases that look like they have been there for hundreds of years, unique bar and restaurant metal fabrication, signage, balconies - and other largescale projects. She picks up the story, "We recently built the world's first subterranean crazy golf world - 220 tons of material. [The question is] how do you get that from surface level to 400 feet underground through a load of cabins and chambers? I talk a lot about collaboration, but none of this is possible without contractors, the building contractors, structural engineers. Zip World have got an amazing team - absolutely fantastic to work with. And once you've all kind of come together and get your heads together with a common goal, it's amazing what can be achieved."

At a talk for Bangor University at their design conference, Vicki shared the secret of their success. "I just talked about the power of yes. You don't really have to know in the beginning, just say yes, it's an opportunity and you don't have to have it all figured out to say yes. Just say yes and then work it out. I hadn't been so self-aware that this is what I do, but now I am self-aware. Your curiosity drives that as well. The curiosity to find a way to make something work."

* * * *

Vicki created her identity from what she described as a chaotic start and went from surviving to thriving by finding her voice and being curious. She discovered and learned to follow her energy and passion for design engineering. She has finally found a space and place where she could become her authentic self, working as a successful company director and business owner.

For Vicki to do that, she needed to understand her natural self, use some lessons and insights from her childhood, and put significant life experiences to work. All of these have shaped her into who she is today.

* * * *

A QUESTION OF IDENTITY: WHO AM I?

Our identity develops from the moment we are born. It comprises a mix of innate personality i.e., our nature, blended with the nurture we receive from those around us, particularly in our formative years, and augmented and informed by memorable experiences.

We have the gift of a life that we can choose to use in service of whatever calls to us. We just have to decide what we want to serve and who we want to become.

Here are three activities for this section. Completing them will help you gain deeper self-understanding and awareness so you can decide whom you want to become as Vicki did.

* * * *

ACTIVITY 1: YOUR NATURAL SELF: PERSONALITY

Understanding who we are naturally, our innate personality, helps us make more informed choices about what we want to do with our lives. We all have a sense of who we are intrinsically, but truly understanding who we are and describing ourselves to others can sometimes be quite tricky.

Personality tests offer a good starting point to give us insights and helpful language to explain who we are. They are based on traits i.e., habitual patterns of behaviour, thought, and emotion. One easy place to explore different personalities is via Truity, which offers several personality tests online. These provide high-level insights with the option to pay for more in-depth analysis if you wish to. They include:

- **The Big Five,** a highly respected Five Factor model (also known as the Big Five). It shows you what your profile is across 5 major dimensions of personality: Openness, Conscientiousness, Agreeableness, Extraversion, and Neuroticism. It is widely considered the most robust way to describe personality differences and is the basis of most modern personality research.
- **The Enneagram,** a system of personality that describes people in terms of nine personality types, each with its own core set of motivations, fears, strengths, and opportunities for growth. Truity's Enneagram assessment helps you identify your primary Enneagram type and reveals your core motivations, fears, and drivers at work, home, and in relationships,
- **DISC** is used by over one million individuals, businesses, and organisations annually. The DISC model helps people understand their drivers and behaviours in the workplace. The model classifies behaviour using four primary styles: Drive, Influence, Support, and Clarity. When everyone on a team takes the assessment, employees and managers get a common framework to view each other - unlocking a host of "a-ha" moments to guide decision-making, communication, and teamwork, and
- **the TypeFinder®** for the Workplace lets you quickly and conveniently assess your team. Based on the 16 personality types created by Isabel Briggs Myers, the TypeFinder® for the Workplace provides an efficient and accurate assessment of your team's personality preferences. It will help you to understand your unique work style, explore your strengths and weaknesses, and see how your personality type drives your approach to leadership, teamwork, change management, and communication.

The MBTI inventory is one of the most common personality tests that help identify a person's personality type, strengths, and preferences. Probably the world's most used psychological instrument, it is based on Swiss psychologist Carl Jung's theories, developed by mother and daughter Katherine Briggs and Isabel Myers. The test looks at four elements: our natural energy and whether it comes from within or from others; how we prefer to process information from either a big picture perspective or if we focus on using details and facts and experience to solve problems; whether we make decisions from the logic of our heads or are led by the values of our hearts; and if we like to be organised and prefer our activities to be planned or prefer to keep our options open and be spontaneous.

As well as using Truity tests, I also signpost clients to the 16Personalities Test, a free online test that has also been taken by millions of people in the UK alone. It has over 90% accuracy and comes with several pages of explanation.

One note of caution: given that we are all as unique as our fingerprints, it is important to note that personality types are preferences, not prescriptions, usually based on self-perception. We all need to resist the temptation to allow ourselves to be put in a particular personality box type, which could restrict our thinking and growth. This is important because neuroscientists now believe that our natural selves or personality may not be as totally fixed as first thought because of neuroplasticity - our brain's ability to change its physical structure due to learning.

Whichever test you take, you should give yourself around 15 minutes or so and somewhere quiet to complete it. You may like to complete both TypeFinder and 16Personalities for comparison. Sometimes, two different sets of explanations can help us understand better. Once you have taken the test(s), spend some time using what you have discovered to help you answer these questions:

So, what is your 16Personalities or TypeFinder personality type?

Based on your personality type and reading the description(s) provided, what top 3 – 5 keywords describe you best? Make a note of them below with a good example of each quality in action.

How did you feel during and after each of the examples you identified? What does this tell you about you? Make a note here.

So, what is your biggest light bulb moment about your personality?

* * * *

ACTIVITY 2: YOUR NURTURED SELF: LESSONS FROM CHILDHOOD

While personality is a crucial part of who we are, it is not the whole story. As Aristotle, the ancient Greek philosopher, knew, and subsequent early childhood research has confirmed, the first seven years of a child's development are highly influential in how they develop into adults.

Like Vicki, the context and way you lived and were nurtured, or not, during your formative years will impact who you are now. Family norms, values and expectations, the abundance or scarcity of money, the location and style of housing, clothing, and possessions, nutrition and exercise, people, communities and friendships, and the activities you became involved with all played a fundamental part in your development.

So did the culture and conversations, the lifestyle you had, including activities you may have taken part in such as meals out, trips to the pub or the country club, holidays, being in nature, attitudes towards health, exercise, and the quality of the food you ate. In addition, family perspectives and expectations around work and study, the arts, success and happiness, and openness to risk versus a desire for safety and security, all combine with these other aspects to inform who you are today. You will have innately accepted some of these influences and rejected others as you develop.

Being aware of how your background has influenced how your identity has developed will help you decide how you want to shape your future identity.

As you saw, Vicki's upbringing taught her a strong work ethic, resilience, a sense of responsibility, the beginnings of her love of design, and how to identify and say yes to opportunities. Ultimately, although she disliked it, the impact of the perceived stigma she felt as a single mum provided the rocket fuel to help her be successful on her terms.

So, how did your childhood influence who you are today?

The following activity will help you gain key insights into how your childhood has helped create who you are today too. Please note: if you had a challenging childhood and need support to look back, you may benefit from this activity with a suitably trained adult. Here are some themes to explore:

VALUES AND INFLUENCES FROM CHILDHOOD

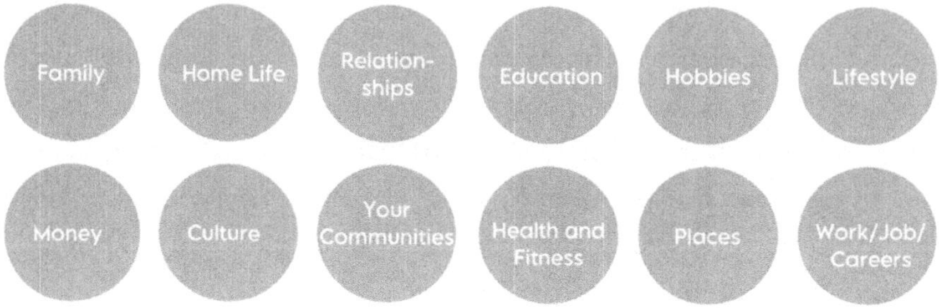

Look at each of the themes in the circles in turn and think back to your childhood. How have they influenced who you have become today? Make a note of what you discover:

What five influences from your childhood do you value most?

What values and beliefs that you hold today stem from your childhood?

When you think back to your childhood, what three influences from your childhood do you value the least?

So, how has your childhood shaped who you are today?

What is your biggest light bulb moment about how you were nurtured?

* * * *

ACTIVITY 3: YOUR EXPERIENTIAL SELF: THE IMPACT OF SIGNIFICANT MOMENTS

Life is full of highs and lows. Although we all have multiple experiences every day, we usually only remember experiences that affect us in some way, either positively or negatively. These are what Dr Morris Massey, the sociologist and marketing professor, called Significant Emotional Events. They are events we can recall vividly and impact and shape our identity and choices. Sometimes the most negative experiences are what the World Health Organization classes as Critical Incidents. These events are outside everyday experiences, are sudden and unexpected, and include physical and emotional loss that may involve the perception of a threat to life. If you have experienced severe events, please ensure you get the support you need to move on from them.

The highs provide magic moments to keep in our storehouse of memories for when they are needed and offer us clues about what we value or have overcome. The lows of life's more challenging moments help us to learn valuable lessons so that we can grow if we choose to. Either way, we win. As the former activist and leader of the Indian Independence Movement, Gandhi said, "Strength does not come from winning. Your struggles develop your strengths. When you go through hardships and decide not to surrender, that is strength." Vicki's clear description of the moment she found her voice advocating for her sick son is one example of how a challenge developed her strength in the most difficult circumstances.

Our reactions to the significant experiences we have in life, both good and bad, contribute to who we are today and often inform our choices. Identifying and reflecting on the important highs and lows that have happened to you in your life and career will help you identify recurring patterns and themes and recognise the impact of magic and challenging moments on your life and choices. It also enables you to identify the seeds of a future career direction that often lay hidden in a difficult moment and can serve as a call to action, as in Vicki's case. Ask yourself if any difficult moments could link to a career theme. If it does, create a list of possible careers and add it.

In this activity you will learn how to use a life graph (see following page) to reflect on the significant highs and lows that have happened to you so far. To do this, map out a timeline of your experiences from birth to now and plot those experiences according to how positive or negative they were for you.

Score positive experiences between one and ten, where ten is the highest. Score negative experiences between -1 and -10, where -10 is the lowest.

Completing this activity will help you understand your behaviour and choices, learn lessons from the past so you can leave the unhelpful emotions behind, and help you make informed decisions about your future.

If you prefer, you can storyboard it, create a song, or act it out if one of these approaches is your best learning style. Whichever option you use, there are some questions for you to reflect on once you have completed the activity.

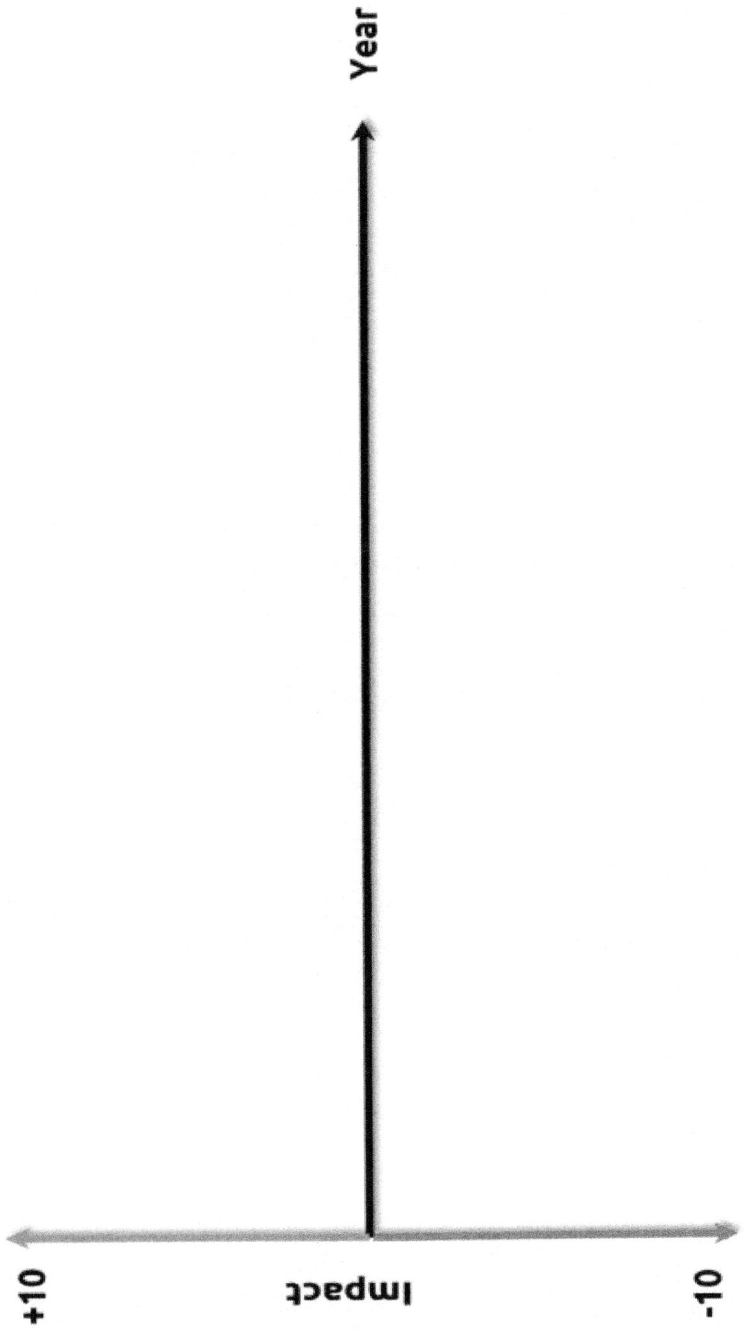
Year
Impact
+10
-10

What are your top three magic moments? Why do they matter so much? What do they represent for you? Make a note of what they are and your reactions here.

What are your three most impactful negative moments? What has each of them taught you that is helpful?

Now create a second graph on the next page to chart your career highs and lows and answer the following questions. These will help you to identify recurring patterns and see the influence of your past on your present and future success.

Once again, ask yourself the same questions. What are your top three magic career moments? Why do they matter so much? What do they represent for you? Made a note here.

What are your three most impactful negative moments? What has each of them taught you that is helpful? Again, make a note of your thoughts here.

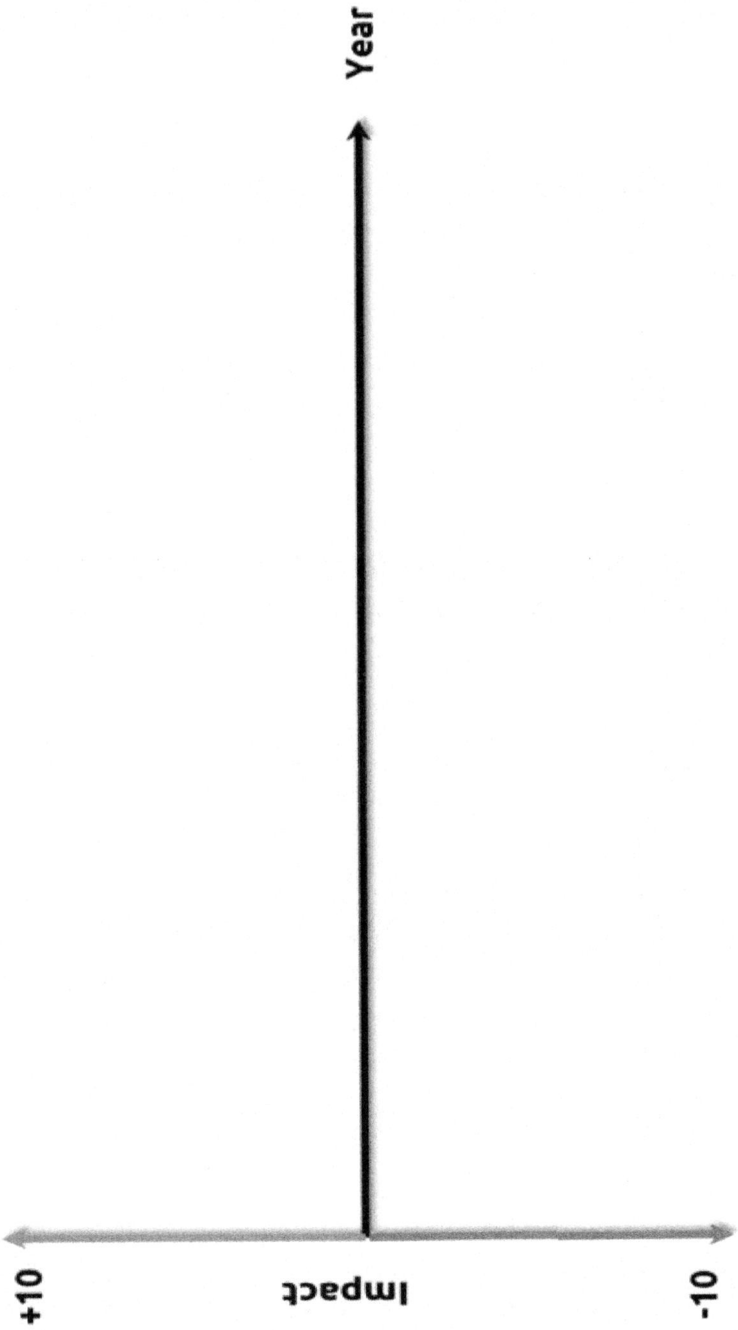
Year
Impact
+10
-10

Now that you have explored significant emotional experiences in your life and career, you may find it helpful to compare the two together so you can answer the final question in this activity.

What is your most significant light bulb moment about your career and life graphs and how they have contributed to your identity?

* * * *

CONSOLIDATING YOUR LEARNING FROM THIS CHAPTER TO ANSWER THE QUESTION:

WHO AM I?

The activities in this chapter have been designed to give you insights and clarity into your natural self and personality, your nurtured self, and your experiential self.

Now it's time to capture what you have learned about your identity in your INSPiRED Career and Life planner. Take the significant keywords you have identified in this chapter and add them to the Identity box highlighted in the diagram that follows, using the planner at the front of this book.

Then, use a second copy of the planner, at the back of the book, to record a sentence in answer to the first half of the question in this chapter:

"Who am I?"

We will return to answer the second half of the question, **"Who do I want to be or become?"** at the end of the book.

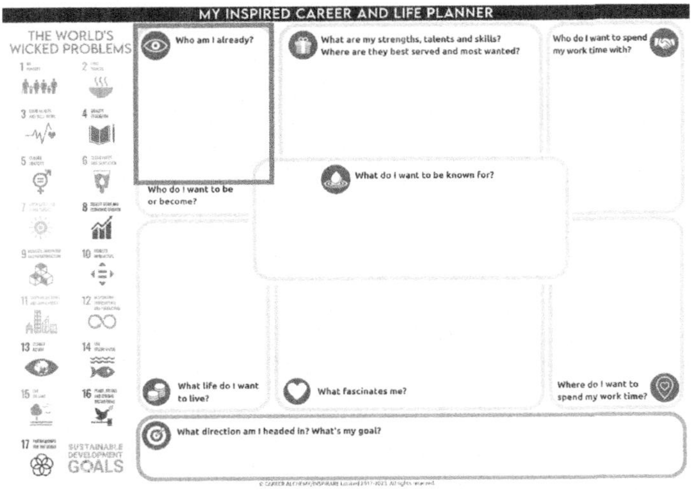

Remember you can download a digital copy of the planner tool from here: www.careeralchemy.co.uk/free-reader-planner-tool.html

* * * *

NEEDS & WANTS

2. NEEDS & WANTS: WHAT LIFE DO I WANT TO LIVE?

SUCCESS, HAPPINESS, AND VALUES IN ACTION

Choosing to live life on your own terms will bring you deep and immeasurable joy and freedom from others.

By her own admission, Natalie Williams's childhood was idyllic. Now in her forties, she grew up in Bryn, a close-knit village community in South Wales, a rural village nestling in the hills near Port Talbot. Her father was the only breadwinner at the time. Her mother often tells the story of how when they decided to have a child, they decided she would stay home and bring her up while Natalie's father worked. Natalie's father worked at Ford's in Bridgend, a twenty-minute drive away, and he was often away. Her parents were always very politically aware. Her father was in the Trade Union and was often involved in strikes. Her mother taught union studies during Natalie's teenage years. So, politics was always a theme of her childhood.

"I was always very interested in what was going on in life, and how that affected people. My father worked the line in Ford's - trade unions striking that kind of thing. What was justice? What was social justice? So yeah, the environment and the sort of discussions that we had as a family did affect what I studied at school, what I studied at university, and probably the pathways that I took early on in life and how it affected my decisions to change my career later on in life."

When it came to A levels, Natalie had an aptitude for languages, which she found easy and enjoyed studying, so she chose French and German. She also really enjoyed History and chose that as her third subject. “I think it came from my interest in the world, what happened before, how it affected how we are today.”

While it may have seemed an easy choice, it wasn’t. Natalie explains, “I had to sacrifice one of my favourite subjects, art, which I had done for GCSE. We had a fantastic teacher, Ms. Sian Samual Thomas. She was so ahead of her time. You know, we did so many different kinds of things. It wasn't just drawing or painting. We did textiles. We did ceramics. I absolutely enjoyed myself.”

I was told, "You'll never get into university with an art A Level, it's a soft subject. If you want to go to university, you have to demonstrate academic and intellectual rigour. So, when I couldn't take it, or I was advised not to take it for A levels, I was quite disappointed.”

While she enjoyed her A Levels, her choice was clearly informed by values and perceived wisdom and logic held by many parents. Those values centred on the need to get a good job to be safe and secure in life. Natalie still recalls feeling some emotion attached to the conversations.

“The emotion was fear. I know a lot of parents are fearful for the futures of their children. They want their children to do well, be safe, be secure, don't have to worry about anything. And that was very present when I was young, I felt it, and it was passed on to me. So, I was fearful of not getting qualifications, not getting a job, and that kind of thing.”

Having put what she enjoyed doing dutifully to one side, Natalie had selected her options based on those values. She studied diligently. The question of which university, and what to study came up, and the impact of talking politics around the table and her father being in a trade union came into play.

“I remember when I was doing my German A level, there were four elements - reading, writing, speaking, and listening. And for my speaking part, I spoke to the guy about politics. Oh, I was there talking about the Labour Party, all these kinds of things.”

Inevitably, that interest in politics, combined with her high academic ability, did inform her choice of degree. She went on to study for an undergraduate degree in International Politics in a world-leading department at Aberystwyth University. The university is situated in the town of the same name on the beautiful Welsh coastline of Cardigan Bay in the county of Ceredigion (Cardiganshire), with a population of some 77,000 people. Again, the theme of safety and security played a part in her choice of where to study.

"I went to Aberystwyth because I'd been to Aberystwyth on holidays for the past 20 years before then, so I felt safe in Aberystwyth." Having secured top A Level grades, she started her university degree the year after her mother had graduated as a mature student aged 41.

"It was a great, great degree to have, exploring why things happen in the world - not just the what, but the why. And obviously, we'd look at the different theoretical approaches. I was probably still looking for the answers. You know, why the world is as it is? What makes the world tick? I had the best education. It wasn't just the knowledge of facts and what happened, it was the ability to think critically. it always surprised me when I would speak to other people who had done different degrees how I wouldn't say they weren't thinking critically, but they would accept things in society and not question them."

She had enjoyed her undergraduate degree and done well, so she decided to stay in Aberystwyth to continue studying. She signed up to do a master's in international theory.

"It was only a year. It was very intense, very enjoyable, and a completely different experience from my undergraduate degree. I think I had a bit more fun during my master's... I was starting to develop in myself as well."

* * * *

The end of her master's led to another moment of choice.

"After my master's, I didn't know what to do in life. I just had no clue. I think when I left my art behind, the idea of what I was passionate about, I wasn't sure because I was still so very much thinking of safety and security, and I still didn't know what job or career I wanted. So, [I said to myself], "*Right, what shall I do?*" I still had questions I wanted to ask and answers I needed. So, I did a Ph.D., and this Ph.D. was based on something that I had done in the final year of my undergraduate degree, where I had the chance to work for four months for an MP in Westminster.

"At the time I was working with the MP, they were looking at this international investment treaty. It was a global international investment treaty where, really, they wanted to take down all these barriers so multinational corporations could do as they wanted across countries, but it didn't materialize. So, I was really looking into the reasons for the failure of this agreement.

"What I had done when I was 20 years of age still impacted me when I was doing my Ph.D. That was a great three years… it was very, very tough, very, very challenging. Doing a Ph.D. is brutal. You get torn to shreds, and that's where the grit and determination come in to carry on in the face of that criticism. It's not always constructive, either. Sometimes it can be very, very, very brutal. I know a lot of people come out of doing a Ph.D. feeling completely exhausted. I was mentally, you know. It's not for the fainthearted, but something I'm very glad I did, because it's given me some very important skills that I still have today… It's the ability to push through when the going gets tough. It was a case of push through, don't give up, every failure is a learning experience, that kind of thing. It was just that grit and determination. It just stands you in good stead for a lot of things in life. You don't realize it at the time, but now I thank goodness that I did it."

* * * *

Having gained her Ph.D. and with multiple higher-level qualifications under her belt, it was time for Natalie to get her first professional job. Because she had seen what politics was like close up in Westminster, she knew that this was not the route for her, but otherwise, once again, she was unclear what to do. She had learned to use the same value-based lens to make the choice she had learned growing up.

"Because this idea of having a passion and pursuing it really was knocked out at such a young age in favour of pursuing something safe and secure, I just didn't know what to do, and I felt safe in Aberystwyth. So, I began working for a minority language unit in the university, where my initial role was to organize an international conference, so that was my first job there."

Although it wasn't her dream job for life, it did enable her to build a bank of skills, including being organised, time management, and meeting deadlines. Once that contract ended, she became a researcher in the department on another short-term contract. The work gave her the chance to develop more useful skills which would prepare her for her next move.

* * * *

She became a Lecturer in her old department, International Politics, a role which she found challenging almost immediately. She explains, "I realized straight away that teaching is not my forte. I was very, very impatient. I wasn't teaching my specialized subject. I was teaching a lot through the medium of Welsh, and because, at the time, the department wanted to improve its Welsh language provision, you were asked to teach anything and everything. So, a lot of the time, I was just one step ahead of the students with what I was teaching them. There's a lot of stress... to learn quickly, teach something, and teach students that maybe they weren't interested, and no, it just wasn't for me. The main reason that I stopped teaching ultimately was because I realized that to become an academic, you have to be so passionate about your subject area. You have to live and breathe it because being an academic is highly pressurized. You have to love it. I didn't love it, I hated it. Although I was into politics, I loved asking questions about the world. Ultimately, it wasn't my... it didn't set me alight to the extent that I could make it my life, that I could endure the stresses of the job for it.

"Fear is what drove me to the secure path. But the security, if it's not in an area that you want to be in, ultimately will lead to unhappiness. And the idea of pursuing something that made me happy, I thought, "*Well, that's a bit decadent - happiness. You know, we don't do happy - we do safe, secure, working hard.*" That's what I'd had all my life. The pain was so intense, and I just…, despite being told, be safe, be secure... I just couldn't do it. And I think when you get to that stage, anything is better. So, I thought, "*No, I have to leave.*" I stayed there for about a year. I quit my job in the January. I left without another job to go to. That was my first sort of taking a risk in life."

* * * *

Universities are normally structured in a particular way. Departments are run by Departmental Heads and individual departments are grouped into faculties. Each faculty is led by a Dean, who has a team of support staff.

Driven by her ongoing desire for security, what came next provided an opportunity for Natalie to put everything she had learned about academia by that stage to good use. She explains what happened next, "I applied for another job at the university. This was, at the time, an administrative job in the Dean's Office. I got the job and started three weeks later. So, you could say, "Well, you dodged a bullet there, Natalie. You had an easy time. You were lucky the job came up", but it did. And yeah, I found myself another job.

"It was when Aberystwyth University was applying for degree awarding powers, so they needed an extra pair of hands. So, I was doing a lot of the administration, the report writing for that. And it was fantastic. I loved it. It was a project where you had to gather bits and bobs and make it all into a coherent document."

What sounded like doing a Ph.D. felt like one to Natalie as she remarks, "It did… but without the pressure, without the need to meet your supervisor every couple of weeks and think, "*Oh my goodness, what the hell are they going to say about my latest chapter now?*" because it's brutal. So, doing the reports for the degree awarding powers was much more enjoyable. It was a fun project. Of course, people were commenting, but it wasn't to the degree that you get, and it wasn't for the same purpose as a Ph.D. I thoroughly enjoyed myself."

Her hard work was noticed by the Academic Secretary responsible for ensuring the university follows all of the academic regulations. He told Natalie there was a job coming up in the University's Academic office and that they would like her to think about applying.

Located on the seafront at the time, the Academic Office acted as the administrative hub of people that ensured the university followed its academic standards and regulations so that the university could guarantee that it was offering degrees of the appropriate standard. Natalie decided to apply, was successful, and ended up working there for around five years.

"In a way, we were the policeman of the university, and there was often... well, probably still is a lot of tension between academics and people in the academic office because, you know, rule breakers, they want to do what they want but they can't. They have to follow the rules, so there was always a lot of tension, which was sometimes quite funny. It was a lot of banter, so that was great. It's a beautiful place. I can even see my office now.

"At the time, the Graduation Office was part of the Academic Office, and I worked with a lovely lady called Olwen Daniels. She was one of the most fantastic bosses I ever had - a pleasure to work with. I worked with her on graduation ceremonies. She was the Secretary of the University Council and Senate at the time, so I was shadowing her. And then, when she retired, I think it was 2010, I took over her post as the Academic Registrar, so I was then responsible for organizing the University Council, the Senate, and graduation. There are a lot of committees involved - a lot of minute writing. Yeah, and boredom started to set in.

"It was mind-numbing. Absolutely mind-numbing. But again, it was safe, secure, very well paid. I had a lovely office overlooking the sea and fantastic people to work with. But the pain was there again. It really was. I could start to feel it. I was coasting. It was easy, comfortable, and paid well, but I was coasting. I was not happy, but it was safe and secure, but I wasn't happy with it, and I wasn't happy with the easiness of it. I wanted the challenge, and the ability to take on a challenge and to be resilient throughout the challenge was still in me. That's why I found the job after that particularly dull and uninteresting. I couldn't get any form of growth in my job, creative or anything. I felt completely stunted. Although it was an easy, safe life, I was told, "Yes, this is what you need; this is what you want." When you've got the need or the want for more, it's absolutely crucifying, you know?"

* * * *

A year or two into the Academic Office role, as her sense of boredom and a lack of challenge grew, Natalie's love of art and innate drive to do something creative rose to the surface once again. She found solace in art and creativity, a form of oxygen to her. She explains how she felt, "Leaving something behind you that you love leaves a trace. I didn't realize at the time that it had. I thought I'd buried it. I was totally mentally focused on my A levels, making sure I got into a good university to get a good degree so I could get a good and safe job. I thought I buried this creative side to me. But I never really had because when life got difficult or boring, to use a simple word, I would turn to creative pursuits.

"It was in 2010 or 11 that certain things were happening in my life. The job I had was completely uninspiring. Life was not going as I wanted it to. "Oh, I need something else in my life. I need some more stimulation," Where did I turn to? The creative side of life. That thing that I had left behind when I was 16 years of age, this creative flair started to come out again and came flooding back in a way that I couldn't stop.

"I'd always been passionate about jewellery. My mother is a very creative person as well, and she was making jewellery. I'd always loved jewellery as a child. For me, it was like being a princess when you could doll yourself up in all these glamorous pieces. So, I started dabbling as well, and it was very, very basic stuff, anything made with beads, bracelets, that kind of thing. But then I started adding gemstones to necklaces and earrings. But it was still very basic stuff at the time, and I did that for a couple of years. I then got divorced, and I had to park it to one side."

* * * *

In 2013, an opportunity came Natalie's way once again. Aberystwyth University had decided it wanted to open a branch campus in Mauritius. Natalie was working with the Pro Vice-Chancellor on partnerships with other UK and international academic institutions. The focus was on offering the university's degrees locally or recruiting students from international partners to study in Aberystwyth. The Mauritius campus initiative was also part of the remit, so Natalie took on the role of the administrative head of the project.

"I visited Mauritius in 2014. We went to see the partners we were going to work with. At that time, I didn't think I would end up there at all. I thought, "*What an island! Wouldn't it be lovely to work here?*" Then, later on in the year, it transpired that one of the posts they needed was a Quality Assurance Manager. Well, that was what I was doing in Aberystwyth. I was recently divorced. I thought, *"Do you know what? I need an adventure in life."* I've been in Aberystwyth for 20 years. I've tried different jobs. None of them have satisfied me, really, or the ones that did had ended. "Yes, let's move to a tiny island, the size of Ceredigion, on the other side of the world!" So, I applied for the post. I got the job. I moved there in August 2015. "I needed something totally different. The population there at the time was 1.2 million. You could sense that it was a lot more densely populated, but it was a tiny, tiny island, boiling hot, then downpours of rain. I was absolutely scared witless - I won't lie! I was absolutely freaked out by it.

"But again, it's this drive in you, and I've often thought of it. It's something in your soul that will propel you. No matter what is going on in your head. Your head can be all over the place telling you all sorts of things, but the drive in your soul overrides it, and no matter how scared you are or how much it goes against so many things you've learned, you can't stop it. You can feel yourself going forward, and that's what I did. And I found myself in Mauritius."

* * * *

Like Vicki, Natalie has also learned to lean into herself by following her gut instinct, as she explains, "I once heard someone say or read something: you can never suppress who you really are. And people from all walks of life do it. Everybody has a public mask, or they pretend to be something they're not. But it will always come out. It will always come out - even your mind will tell you why you shouldn't do something.

"But the body never lies. The mind is a powerful tool, and the mind has caused me a lot of problems in taking this path or that path, but ultimately, the soul or the body, or however you want to call it, will always win, and that's why now whenever I want to make a decision, I listen to the physical sensations that I get and, it's a new way of thinking. It's not how I was brought up.

"I was brought up to override all that, to focus on what you should do in life. I'm not saying I've got rid of that completely because I haven't, but I work on that now. I listen to my body and my inner soul a lot more. And when I can sense the physical urge, I was once told that when you want something, your body will literally push you forward. And then when you don't, you will recoil, and that it happens. It happens. That's my inner compass these days, and that's what I work from."

Although Natalie still listens to her intellectual intelligence, nowadays, she leans into her emotional intelligence much more and knows how to recognise it.

"I get a sense of excitement and like electricity traveling through my body, and when I know that that sensation is there, I know it's the right thing. And it'll bring a smile to your face. Now, in my younger days, I would get it, but I would say to myself, *"Oh, don't. Ignore it. Ignore it. It's nothing. It's nothing. Quick, focus mentally, logically, on what you've been told you need and want in life."* Now, I listen to my intuition and ask a few logical questions, so I'm not totally just going off on one, but it's a lot more balanced now than it ever was. It comes from here - in the heart. A lot of people find it in their stomach, the solar plexus. For me, it always comes from the heart.

"My earlier programming of security, safety, that is still there. I still feel fearful, thinking, *"What if, what if, what if?"* But now I trust myself more. I trust life more. I'm not as fearful of life anymore because in the last, I don't know, say, seven years, I have gone on such a transformative journey.

"It's been a rollercoaster in personal development, and the image that always comes to my mind is climbing a vertical rock face constantly for seven years. You know, I spent so many years languishing. That's how I felt, you know, moving from one job to another that I didn't enjoy.

"I had no passion, or I didn't think I had a passion. I'd spent so many years doing that, that I hadn't grown. I'd stunted my growth purposefully to be safe and secure, so I hadn't grown. So, once I took off the shackles, as it were, moved to Mauritius, oh my goodness. I experienced a lifetime in those five years. The things I experienced were absolutely crazy, good, and bad. But I would always be thankful because it was just the delayed personal growth that I needed."

* * * *

Not long after she had arrived, her fear of coasting and lack of clarity rose to the fore again. This time, Natalie started asking herself questions about her career and decided to invest in one-to-one coaching with me through the INSPiRED career and life coaching programme, which is the basis for this book. She got to know and understand herself better. Her confidence grew, and she decided to test an idea for a business. She explains why, "A lot of personality traits came forward, one of which was that I was very self-determined. I could take control and take charge, and I had this creative side. So, it wasn't long after that that I set up my business side by side with my work at the university. I did the jewellery part-time. My contract was to end two years after I went to Mauritius, but they extended it for a year because there was a change of circumstances at the university."

Natalie also developed her ability to lean into herself when deciding to make the leap from the safety of working in the ivory towers of a university to the uncertain world of self-employment. "It felt like the thing to do. Again, I had a huge argument; I wouldn't say it was a discussion because it was a huge argument between my head and my heart. Again, the heart was pushing me forward. The head said, *"Oh my goodness, you are absolutely crazy. No job security".* My parents were again, well, not so much my mother, my father, "Oh my goodness, I can't believe you're leaving such a secure, well-paid job." So, all the old stories were still there, but this time, the urge there was just too much, and nothing was going to stop me. None of the fear stories. Nothing. Nothing stopped me.

"My contract ended in the August, and I'd already planned six months before this is what I was going to do. I was going to take voluntary redundancy, I'd saved up some money...and when I finally finished my post there with the university, I took the ultimate leap and started my own business in a foreign country - as you do! And yeah, it was the best decision I've ever made.

"I could never have started my own business in my twenties. The fear would've been too much, but the fear was still there. But this time, I thought, *"I either go for it now, or I never will."* I think I was 40 at the time, and many people would say, "Oh, you're too old for this, that, and the other. I thought to myself, *"You know, I'm 40 years of age. I feel young, I feel healthy. Let's do it".* I did think, *"Oh, why is it only happening now? I should have done this years ago."*

"I did beat myself up a bit because, *"Oh, look at all these years you've wasted. Only now you've found your passion."* But what I'd realized is... everything, everything I had done before then, had given me all the skills I needed. It had given me all the personal development time I needed to be able to do this at the right time.

"So, in a way, I'm glad I didn't follow my passion. I'm glad that I went through a challenging Ph.D., that I had those years of boredom. But yes, I did develop the skills because absolutely everything put me in the right place at the right time to do what I'm doing now."

* * * *

As a value, freedom was so important to Natalie that it even featured in the name she chose as she explains, "When I started making jewellery before, part-time back in Aberystwyth, it was called Natalie Adele Jewellery, because those are my names. I thought, *"No, do you know, I want something snappy that means something, that sounds pretty."* So, the word that kept coming to my mind was freedom. I thought, *"Oh, freedom. Yeah. Okay. That is not very pretty."* So, I looked up online different ways of saying freedom in different languages. So, I was looking through them all, and I looked through the word 'liri'. It's Albanian for freedom. I thought, *"Do you know what, I'm going to use that. It's such a pretty word. It encapsulates what I am finally feeling in life, what I now know is important."* I spent all these years not feeling free but rather very drained because of the stories I've been told, and I've been telling myself. Now, I actually feel this freedom. This jewellery business reflects that freedom, let's call it freedom, in a lot prettier word."

With the benefit of working for twenty years and her newfound sense of freedom, Natalie began to see changes within herself as she battled through the challenges of starting a business as she explains, "I saw myself change in that I was just pushing through all the fears, all the doubts, all the stresses. You know, a challenge would come up, and rather than giving in, I just pushed through, pushed through, pushed through. But I think that had always been there, you know. With a Ph.D., ... it messes with your mind. It affects your self-esteem. One minute you're up. One minute you're down, dependent on the comments of other people. It's so competitive ... but you push through because it's what you want to do.

"And I thought that had gone from me because I just sort of languished for a while. Yes, I discovered it when I started working in Mauritius, but it was there with a vengeance when I started my own business because starting the company in Mauritius was... I could have had numerous heart attacks. (Mauritius) is so old-fashioned, the hoops, the bureaucracy. It was absolutely crazy. And I had a three-month deadline in which to complete my application and get a successful application. It came in two days before the deadline, two days before Christmas, because I wanted to travel home for Christmas. Oh, my goodness. But I did it... and it's just this dogged determination. The passion and the want, and the knowing that this is what you've always wanted. You're not going to give up this, especially at my age."

* * * *

Two and a half years on, Natalie has seen her business grow and develop. Natalie and the brand both firmly embody her love of freedom and creativity. Several other values also shine through her work. She loves the variety and challenge of self-employment while still following customer-led opportunities, which enable her to run a highly creative, innovative, and environmentally friendly business. "People say to me, "So what do you do for a living?", and I default to say jeweller, but I'm not a jeweller. Yes, I make the jewellery, but I'm the business owner. And the skills you have to have to be a successful business owner are completely different from a jeweller. You know, I could be a jeweller employed by someone, and again, that could be quite monotonous. You are just given the design, and you make it. But to be a business owner, I have to pull on all the skills that I have developed over the 20-odd years of my career to make it a success. Where I'm at, I've seen my old traits coming through, which you think you've buried, but no... they're just growing and growing, and they're getting you to where you want to be."

Natalie outlines what she is doing now, "Most of my work at the moment is focused on recycling people's jewellery. I have limited-edition collections because the focus of my jewellery is creating high-quality, limited-edition jewellery. The reason behind it was to empower women to feel free to express themselves, and a lot of my pieces make quite a statement. You feel you're making a statement when you're wearing them of who you are. So, there's the limited-edition collections. And there's bespoke pieces.

"The main work that I do is recycling jewellery that people have inherited, or they've had sitting in their jewellery box for, I don't know how many years. And I came across that, quite by accident, really. A couple of years ago, when I moved back to Wales, an old school friend of mine got in touch, and her mother had just died. And she said, "I'd like a ring with my mother's birthstone and my birthstone, and it's so fantastic, but I've also got this wedding ring of my Gran's." So, I had this idea, "Why don't I create you a trilogy? Your mother's birthstone, yours on either side, and your Gran's, so you've got three generations of women in one ring?" And since then, it's just absolutely taken off.

"People love the idea of reusing what they have. It's environmentally friendly. It can bring the cost down, especially when we're talking about gold and diamonds. But they're also getting this highly personalized service where they get something made for them. And it enables me to be highly creative because I'm looking at everything individually. It's not mass production, it's looking at individual pieces, but I still have to be a businesswoman about that, so I can marry my creative side but still use the skills to be a businesswoman… the cost, the customer service, all that kind of thing. So, it is really the perfect marriage between my creative side, but the organisational, managerial sides, and the skills that I've developed over the last 20-odd years."

* * * *

While Natalie has loved aligning with her key values of freedom, creativity, variety, and challenge because of her business, she has recognised one of her other core values, as she explains, "I like to take charge to work for myself. I love the fact that I can do that now. I think that's probably one of my core values - the fact that I can dictate my timeframe and what I do. I'm a very self-driven, so it's not like, *"Well, I can work for myself, and I can lounge about doing nothing."* Yeah, I can work for myself, and I can set my timetable because I know sometimes when you work in employment, if it's not stimulating you, you can be very bored. And I have a lot of energy. So, the energy that I have helps me to cope with the challenges and the stresses and to be able to drive it forward. And I would never, ever change it for the world. You know, it's stressful. Sometimes it's scary, it's very scary. But ultimately, it feeds what I am, somebody who needs that challenge, and it makes you feel alive. I remember certain points during my employed career

I would think I just felt dead inside and there was nothing worse. There's nothing worse than feeling dead inside. So, I would rather the challenges and the stresses, I'd rather it because it gives you the sense of life."

* * * *

Natalie also realised that she needed to take a hard look at her work-life balance and make some changes, as she explains, "It's something I have to work very hard on. I used to work seven days a week. But I realized that was leading to burnout, but I'd never, ever change it for the world. I would never change it for the monotony, the "security" in inverted commas of an employed position.

"Before Christmas (2022), as you can imagine, it was crazy. I had orders left, right, and centre to get ready. I was working 12 hours, seven days a week. And I said to myself, *"Right, I'm going to take time off over Christmas, at least a week."* I didn't do that. Okay, I put my tools down, but I was still advertising. I was still dealing with client communications, and I didn't take enough time off work. So, when January rolled around, I was still feeling the stress of it, and really, I just had to take a step back and say, *"Look, if you're going to carry on this, you know you are going to burn out."*

"I was on the way to not enjoying life and just had to force myself to spend some time planning. How was I going to work, compartmentalising my days, sectioning my days? What was I doing on certain days? Making sure that Sunday was completely free, that I didn't speak to any clients because these days, everyone's on WhatsApp and Messenger. They expect an answer straight away. You have to have that mental space from it. And, so far this year, I have stuck to it.

"I've been pursuing more hobbies, albeit only one day a week. But now, I feel that's a good balance. Some people say, "Well, if you enjoy doing it, you can do it all the time." Well, that's not actually true because it's still very mentally and physically demanding, and the body just needs a rest. You can enjoy doing anything, but if it's a physical and mental effort, you just need to do something completely different.

"It's taken me a while and especially when your business is growing and growing. You think, *"Oh, if I take my foot off the pedal now, it could all collapse."* So, you always just want to keep going while the going's good, you know? But no, I've taken my foot off. I don't respond to client communications at certain times. I've not seen any change. A friend of mine said, "Clients will always challenge your boundaries. They don't care if you burn out. They just want their jewellery then and then.

"Yes, I'm always wanting to meet their deadlines, but ultimately, you do have to look after your health because, without it, and I know it sounds trite and as I've got older, it's something I do appreciate, you know you need your health for everything. I see so many people without it. And that's one thing I never want to be without. So, I don't want to put myself in a position where I'm physically and mentally unable to carry on because I enjoy it. But you do have to care of yourself in the process, because when you're enthusiastic and want to do it, there is this, *"I've got to keep going."* No, no. You have to pull back."

Natalie's new life as both a business owner and luxury jewellery designer has given her a new lease of life and a working life she loves, as she explains, "I'm in control of my own life to a lot more degree than I was. Before, I had abdicated all my power for the illusion of safety and security. I realize now it is an illusion because a job could be lost at any moment. Just under a restructuring programme, you could be moved. I didn't want to put my future in anybody else's hands.

"I wanted to be in control of my life. Okay, it's a lot more precarious, you could say, but it gives you that impetus to do something about it. I didn't like just sitting back and doing nothing or doing very little in my job. And when I say do very little, something that wasn't that challenging, maybe. I didn't like the fact that how I felt was dictated by outside forces that I couldn't control.

"Now, yes, some things external to me do still affect me, but I can change how I react, and, you know, I can move my focus. So now I ..., I feel alive. I'm finally living. I feel I have grabbed my fears and previous programming by the throat and said, *"Okay, I know you're there. I'm not going to listen to as much."* My inner voice is a lot stronger. I can trust myself. My inner voice and soul have guided me very well so far. *"Thank you, fears. Yes, you are trying to protect me, but you can calm down now. I know I've got this."* It's such an invigorating feeling. Now, I'm feeling all the feelings, you know, the excitement, the fear, the adrenaline, whereas before, it was just so flat because I was so wedded to this idea of safety and security, and I had abandoned what I actually wanted. But, as I said, and it's going to come out and it came out with me with such force, and it still does now, and yeah, I love it. I absolutely love it."

* * * *

As Natalie discovered, we can all be captains of our own ship, and being in charge of determining our own life outcomes is empowering. As she also found, it can sometimes seem a little scary if you are unsure what it is you want or whether you can achieve it. This fear-based discomfort springs from our desire to avoid threats and keep safe.

The problem with keeping safe is that we don't grow. Making career and life choices based on other people's well-intended but sometimes misinformed values can lead to pain and misery, as Natalie's story illustrates so well. While she was taught to value safety, security, and intellect, she craved challenge, creativity, variety, and being in charge of her destiny. Revisiting her values enabled her to identify why her life felt so wrong and to discover what she wanted. Growth comes from aligning our unconscious with our conscious and our emotional intelligence with our intellect. Once Natalie identified her values and put them to work, she created a working life that genuinely reflects who she is. Little wonder this has made her both happy and successful on her terms.

Allowing these to emerge and respecting them will lead us to live our best life. We all have dreams hidden within us, yet often, we are not fully conscious of what we really desire as a life. Completing the following activities will help you to do the same.

* * * *

A QUESTION OF NEEDS & WANTS:
WHAT LIFE DO I WANT TO LIVE?

Each of us gets given the gift of life. Yet, we all tend to sleepwalk through it rather than truly living it deeply and fully – unless we get a wake-up call. Until someone proves otherwise, we are all only going this way once.

We all have another gift – that of free will. That means we can create our own lives as we see fit. It's hard to imagine anything sadder than reaching the end of your life and realising that it could have been so much better if only you had dared to live the life you really want. You have the right and ability to choose how to spend your life so you can live without regrets and enjoy a life that is fulfilling and full of happiness.

So, what sort of life do you want to live? The three activities that follow are designed to help you become clear about the life you want to create.

ACTIVITY 1: CREATING A LIFE WELL LIVED

In 1938, Harvard University began one of the longest and most comprehensive studies of human development ever conducted. The study, now led by Professor Robert Waldinger, follows the lives of two cohorts of men: those remaining from the original group of 268 Harvard men, and now including their children, and 456 disadvantaged, non-delinquent inner-city youths who grew up in Boston and their children.

The study shows that several factors contribute to a happy and healthy life. These include:

- **Good relationships**
  The happiest and healthiest participants are those with strong and supportive relationships that provide a sense of love, support, and belonging. Those relationships can help provide purpose and a way to manage better and recover from stress.

- **Resilience**
  Having the ability to bounce back from setbacks is another crucial factor for happiness and health. Resilient people can cope with stress and adversity healthily. Learning lessons from challenging times can help us to build our resilience.

- **Healthier lifestyle choices**
  People who make healthier lifestyle choices, such as eating a healthy diet, exercising regularly, limiting alcohol consumption, and avoiding smoking, are more likely to be happy and healthy.

The study also highlighted several other findings:

- **The impact of early childhood experiences**
  As you may have discovered in the previous chapter, these can have a lasting impact on us, shaping our personalities, relationships, and health.

- **Life is not a straight line**
  The study charts the ups of life when we are happy and healthy and the downs of life when we struggle. It serves as a reminder that some days it rains on us, while on other days the sun comes out, which is a normal part of life.

- **We can change our lives**
  The study also showed that there is always time to make changes that will improve our lives. Even if we have had a difficult childhood or made bad choices, we can still create a happy and healthy future for ourselves.

We gain positive emotions by spending time with loved ones, doing things we enjoy, and practising gratitude. When we challenge ourselves with new activities, setting goals, and focusing on the present moment, it helps us to find a sense of flow and achievement. Being supportive and compassionate, and communicating effectively gives us better relationships with the people we choose to spend time with, making us feel good. When we connect our values, helping others, and pursuing goals that are important to us, it gives us a sense of meaning.

Most of us will say with authority that we want to be happy and successful - and mean it. But if we aren't clear about what we mean, the likelihood of achieving our desires is slim. When it comes to happiness, there are two types, according to American academics Cassie Mogilner, Sepandar D. Kamvar, and Jennifer Aaker. They studied the emotions reported on in 12 million personal blogs and undertook additional research to understand what happiness means. What they discovered is that it is not fixed and instead shifts systematically throughout an individual's lifetime.

As their research showed, there are two types of happiness:

- **hedonistic happiness,** a fleeting enjoyment based on a life of pleasure, which is more related to excitement, and
- **eudemonic happiness**, which is more related to peacefulness and provides a deeper, more meaningful setpoint, which is much longer lasting. It occurs when we use our strengths to contribute to something in the world which is more significant than we are.

So, what does happiness and success mean to you?

Now that we have explored what makes a life well lived, now is the moment to get clear what happiness and success mean to you. Having clarity about what you want will help you create it and recognise it.

Let's start with happiness. Use the space below to draw or write your ideas about what happiness means to you. What examples can you give to support this?

Now, consider in the space below what success means to you. Again, what examples can you give to support this?

Now that you have become clear about what success and happiness each mean to you, it is worth reviewing them together to check for any inconsistencies. Do they sit comfortably together or not? If not, why is this the case, and how do you change your definitions so they work better together? Note your final descriptions in the space below to anchor what you want to create in your working life.

To me, happiness is:

To me, success is:

Now that you have completed the activity, what is your most significant light bulb moment about what success and happiness mean to you?

* * * *

ACTIVITY 2: WORK-LIFE FIT

Work is currently central to most of our everyday lives. On average, we spend around two-thirds of our waking hours in paid employment and will continue to do so unless universal basic income is introduced for all, or we win the lottery. With state retirement ages being pushed back, we will all spend around 50 years of our adulthood working – so we need to ensure it works for us. Work also connects with and impacts the various common areas we all have: family/partner, social and friends, health and fitness, money, spirituality, and personal growth, as the diagram below shows:

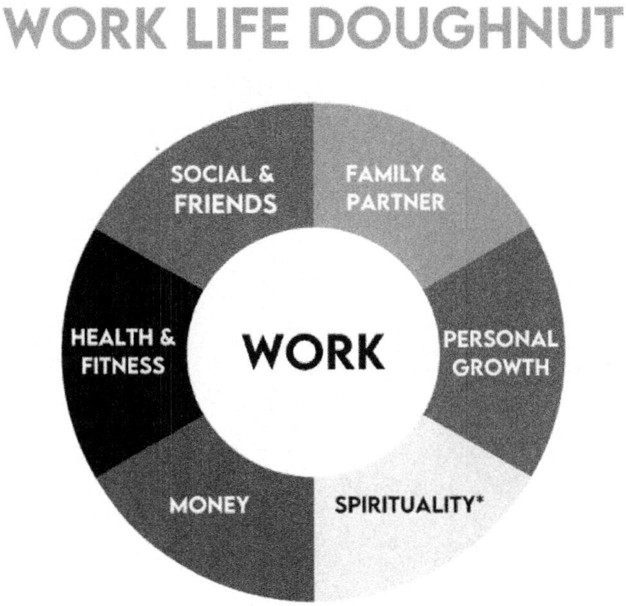

*(*Spirituality means whatever it means to you. For some, it means religion or something greater than ourselves, while for others, it could even mean community, nature, or Mother Earth).*

Putting work in the centre of our lives for a moment, as in the work-life doughnut diagram, helps us to make informed choices so that our life works for us, not against us. For instance, if health and fitness are important themes to you, think about how you can fit them easily into your working day, for instance, by choosing a job near a gym or one which supports hybrid/home working. That way, you can incorporate it into your life easily. The same philosophy of ensuring you have the time and access to what's important to you will make you feel happier and get more out of life.

So how do you want work fit with the rest of your life?

Look at each outer segment of the doughnut and ask yourself: "What matters most to me in each of these areas?" Make a note of your ideas for each element. Choose the most essential ideas overall and note the top five in order below.

For my career/work/job to enable me to create the life I want, it needs to give me:

1.

2.

3.

4.

5.

6.

Now that you have thought about it, what is your most significant light bulb moment about how you want work and life to fit?

* * * *

ACTIVITY 3: VALUES AT WORK

Values are the considerations that we believe are important in life. They act as a lens through which we view ourselves and the world and make our choices in life. They guide our thoughts, feelings, and behaviour and, over time, form our personal map of the world, helping to develop our self-esteem, fulfilment, and resilience.

Values matter because they help us to live a meaningful and fulfilling life. They give us a sense of purpose and direction. Values can help us move towards something we want or away from something we don't want. They also help us to make decisions, solve problems, and deal with difficult situations. When our values are aligned with our actions, we feel good about ourselves and our lives. We feel like we are making a difference in the world. However, when our values are not aligned with our actions, we may feel guilty, ashamed, or regretful.

There are many different types of values, but some of the most common include:

- ***Core values:*** these are the fundamental values that we hold dear and would never compromise on, no matter what. For example, some people have core values such as honesty, integrity, kindness, compassion, respect, responsibility, and fairness.

- ***Personal values:*** these are the values that are important to us on a personal level. Our culture, our upbringing, and our own experiences may influence them. For example, some people might have personal values such as family, friendship, and education.
- ***Social values:*** these are the values that are important to a particular society or culture. They may be reflected in that society's laws, customs, and norms. For example, some social values in the United States might include freedom, equality, and democracy, while in France, they may include liberty, equality, and fraternity.

Values can help us stay true to ourselves and make choices we can be proud of. Values also matter because they help us to build relationships. When we share similar values with others, we have a foundation to build strong relationships. We can trust, communicate openly, and support each other in achieving our goals. Finally, values matter because they help us to live a meaningful life.

When we live by our values, we feel a sense of purpose and fulfilment. We know we are making a difference in the world and feel good about ourselves.

Psychologist Abraham Maslow developed a Hierarchy of Needs through his observations of human behaviour and his own experiences. He was influenced by the work of other psychologists, such as Kurt Goldstein and Henry Murray, who also believed that human motivation is complex and multifaceted.

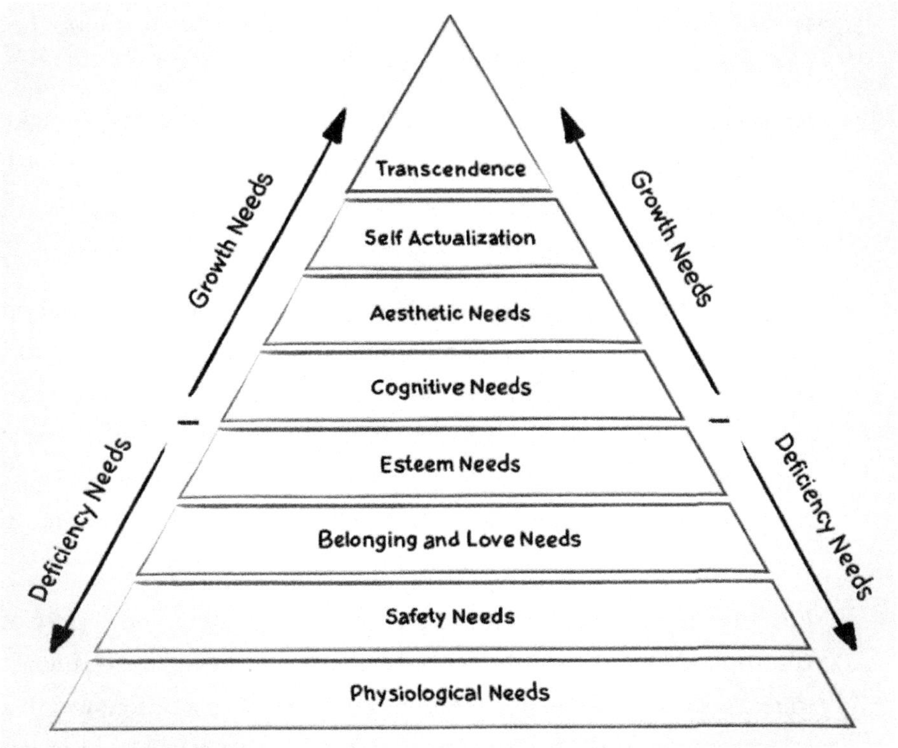

Maslow's Hierarchy of Needs © Adobe Stock by dizain

While psychologists would dispute Maslow's original philosophy that we need to meet each level of the model before we progress, his extended 8-part Hierarchy of Needs model above provides a helpful way to recognise our various needs in life and work.

Maslow identified our D-needs (Deficit Needs) as those elements that we need as a baseline, while our B-needs (Beneficial Needs) are those which bring us happiness, fulfilment, self-actualisation, and ultimately transcendence where our focus is on helping others.

Here's how each of these levels relates to your working life.

- ***Physiological needs:*** include food, water, shelter, and clothing. When these needs are not met, it can be challenging to focus on anything else. In a career context, this could mean ensuring you have a job that pays enough to meet your basic needs.

- ***Safety needs:*** include security, stability, and protection. When these needs are unmet, it can be hard to feel safe and secure in your work environment. In a career context, this could mean finding a job with a good benefits package, such as pensions and health insurance.
- ***Love and belonging needs:*** include social interaction, intimacy, and acceptance. When these needs are unmet, it can be challenging to feel connected to others and to feel like you belong. In a career context, this could mean finding a job that allows you to interact with people regularly. Most jobs contain some element of this, and there are some roles which are customer-facing or teaching where this is even more critical.
- ***Esteem needs:*** include self-respect, respect from others, and a sense of accomplishment. When these needs are unmet, it can be a challenge to feel good about yourself and like you are making a difference. In a career context, this could mean finding a job that allows you to use your skills and talents to achieve your goals and make a positive impact on the world.
- ***Cognitive needs:*** include the need for knowledge and understanding. When these needs are unmet, it can be difficult to feel challenged and like you are growing. In a career context, this could mean finding a job that helps you to learn new things, solve problems, and think critically.
- ***Aesthetic needs:*** include the need for beauty and harmony. When these needs are unmet, it can be challenging to feel at peace and like you are surrounded by beauty, order, or balance. In a career context, this could mean finding a job that allows you to work with art, music, or nature or that will enable you to create something beautiful or orderly.

- ***Self-actualisation needs:*** include finding meaning and purpose. When these needs are unmet, life can feel hollow and lacklustre, and there is a sense of going through the motions. In a career context, self-actualisation could mean finding a job that you are passionate about and that you believe makes a difference in the world. It is about doing work where you are supported to be true to yourself so you can experience fulfilment and satisfaction through using your talents and skills. It enables you to develop your potential significantly.
- ***Transcendence needs:*** include connecting with something larger than yourself, such as a higher power or a sense of purpose. When these needs go unmet, it can be difficult to feel fulfilled and like your life has meaning. In a career context, this could mean finding a job that supports you to help others, make a difference in the world, or connect with something larger than yourself.

Another psychologist who studied human motivation and leadership, David McLelland, developed a theory around the human need for achievement, affiliation, and power, which we will explore in more detail in Chapter Six when we look at relationships. Known as the acquired needs theory, these needs are developed over time through our experiences and culture. The three needs are not interdependent, and we all have different levels of each need. Thinking about these needs alongside Maslow's will help you to know what is important to you so you can create a more satisfying and fulfilling life.

Our needs become very strong values that are very important to you. Understanding individual work values is the cornerstone of good career choice, so time spent thinking about the next question is a wise investment in ensuring you know what you want and need at work.

So, when you think about career/work/job, what matters to you?

Using a separate piece of paper, write down every element that occurs to you (aim for short phrases of no more than four words). Now rank these in order of importance to discover your top 8 work values.

1.

2.

3.

4.

5.

6.

7.

8.

Now ask yourself:

What would cause me to leave an organisation?

If it is not already on your list, add it as your 9th value. Check the order and amend it appropriately to clarify what matters to you.

9.

The Life Values Inventory test provides a structured way to double-check that you have identified everything that matters to you. It only takes ten minutes or so to complete. If you take the test, consider how the results could relate to your future career. Use what you learn to check your nine values above for completeness.

What is your most significant light bulb moment about what you want from your career/job/work?

* * * *

CONSOLIDATING YOUR LEARNING FROM THIS CHAPTER TO ANSWER THE QUESTION:

WHAT LIFE DO I WANT TO LIVE?

Now that you understand what happiness and success mean to you, how you want your life and work to fit, and what your work values are, it's time to capture what you have learned about your identity in your INSPiRED Career and Life planner. Add the significant keywords you identified in this chapter into the Needs and Wants box highlighted in the diagram below, using the planner at the front of this book.

Then, use a second copy of the planner to record a sentence in answer to the question for this chapter:

What life do I want to live?

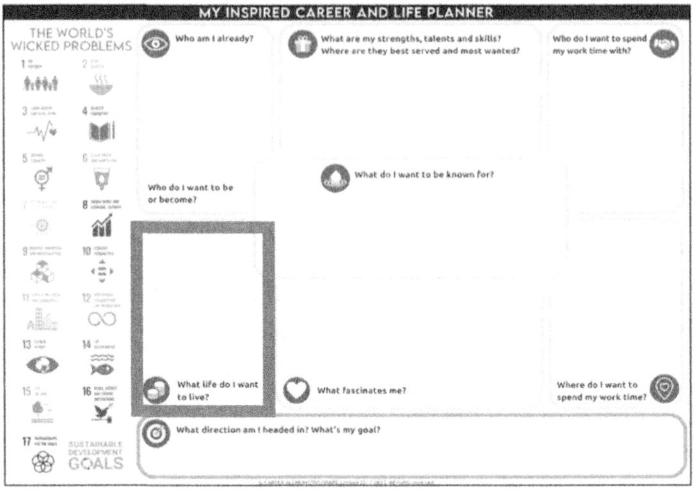

Remember you can download a digital copy of the planner tool from here: www.careeralchemy.co.uk/free-reader-planner-tool.html

* * * *

STRENGTHS, TALENTS, & SKILLS

3. STRENGTHS, TALENTS, & SKILLS: WHAT ARE MY STRENGTHS, TALENTS, & SKILLS? WHERE ARE THEY BEST SERVED, & MOST WANTED?

IDENTIFYING CHARACTER STRENGTHS, DISCOVERING NATURAL ABILITIES, NURTURING SKILLS

When you play to your strengths, do what you love doing, and commit to learning with an eye to the future, unique opportunities will come your way.

Now in her early forties, Meeta Thareja's generosity of soul and spirit shines out the moment you meet her. Born and raised in North India alongside her three sisters, she is the daughter of an Army father and an enterprising mother who has been a role model for her, teaching her the value of a curious mind and bold spirit. What started as a lively community-based lifestyle as an Army child abuzz with social events changed when they moved to Punjab, where Meeta spent most of her youth. She explains, "We moved to Punjab to be closer to our ageing grandparents. But at the time, Punjab was in the grip of violence and terrorism. It was a drastic and a scary change of environment for all of us." At one point, Meeta's father was posted away, so her mother was left raising the three children on her own. She recalls how her mother responded, which would make its mark on Meeta later. She explains, "We had no help, limited financial resources, and my mum had severe health challenges at the time. But she decided to pursue a long-held dream of establishing a nursery school. This was a time that few women worked in India, leave aside run their own entrepreneurial ventures. My mother ended up running one of the most successful schools in the city for 25 years."

Meeta and her twin sister, particularly, found the new environment challenging, as she explains, "Suddenly we went from this happy social life into this new world where everything was quiet and isolated. You couldn't go out in the evenings or go out on your own. It was a bit of a traumatic change for all of us. Any change is hard, but this was another level. To add to it, we went into a school environment that was hostile and unpleasant. All I wanted to do was get out of there." Combining her love of community gained in her early childhood with her natural ability to connect with people from all different backgrounds, Meeta found her route out by taking an entrance exam for a hotel management course. As she puts it, "I made it, and I found my escape, and that's how I ended up studying hotel management and working in the hotel industry."

She gained a BSc in Hospitality and Hotel Administration from the Institute of Hotel Management in Chandigarh, which she graduated from in 2000, with the highest academic scores in all three years during her course. She was presented a Gold Medal for academic excellence by the Indian Ministry of Tourism later the same year, something she and her parents are very proud of. She was one of 15 students to be selected for Post Graduate Management Programme in Service Management at the Oberoi Centre of Learning and Development, regarded as one of Asia's top institutions for hospitality education and a benchmark for international excellence in the hotel industry. During this 2-year programme Meeta worked and lived in New Delhi, Mumbai, Kolkata, and Jaipur, gaining valuable experience at different business and luxury hotels owned by the Oberoi Group. After completing her management training in 2002, she was appointed Service Manager at The Oberoi New Delhi, where she was responsible for all aspects of customer experience, including measuring, reporting, and managing customer service, revenue and profitability and a team of 30 staff and supervisors.

Although the hours working in the sector were long and the work physically demanding, there was another reason why she felt like she didn't fit in the hotel industry as she recalls, "Hotels are a made-up world that is beautiful and where you as part of it are taught to strive for and seek perfection. I valued what it taught me - the discipline, the eye for detail and that quest to exceed expectations in whatever you do. However, I felt disconnected from the reality of where I wanted to make a difference in a deeper way." Based on her own foundational childhood experiences and a need for a more significant intellectual challenge, she realised she needed to do something more purposeful, but it was unclear what that could be. Although she had no idea what to do next and didn't realise it at the time, Meeta had very transferrable skills and experience, which would help her to change direction into a sector that was booming.

* * * *

As often happens, her new direction came from talking to her friends to see what other avenues were open to her, as she explains, "I think I was quite fortunate because that was the time when the tech boom was just starting to happen in India. All the big brands were starting to make their presence felt. The world had just realised the potential of the Indian market. So, you had every major technology brand setting up big offices in India." A friend helped her to find an opportunity with marketing communications firm 20:20 Media, which focused solely on the tech sector. Meeta explains, "The projects that I worked on were about how you make the tech story relatable to an ordinary person in India – the impact that technology could make on lives – from digital cameras to mobile phones to computers."

For the next year and a half, she worked on marketing development, PR, and direct customer engagement for companies like Adobe, Sony Ericsson, and Intel. Then, at the start of 2006, another challenge appeared on the horizon. At a time when she was going through some difficult times personally, she became Head of Communications for India for business process and technology services provider Xchanging, where she set up the marketing communications function with the aim of raising the company's profile in India. She also worked as part of the leadership team to deliver their first phase of growth, helping them to change from being a back-office centre to a service organisation, working with clients across Western Europe. She found quite a contrast between the two organisations as she explains, "I went from working with an Indian firm in consulting roles with multiple brands to working on one multinational company and building that one brand from scratch during a very high growth phase. It was really exciting connecting with people from a whole host of different nationalities and backgrounds. I've been very fortunate that every change in my career has led me to such diverse people and operating environments. It sharpens your ability to grasp new ideas and makes you more adaptable." Meeta is clear about what enables her to get on in organisations, "The most important thing, I think, is an ability to understand people. That's where my hospitality training served me well and has continued to do so because ultimately, you're dealing with people, so it's about being perceptive and being wholly committed to being of service." For Meeta, putting other people and that diversity of need and service orientation at the heart of whatever she does comes as naturally to her as breathing – a sign not just of her hospitality training but of her natural talent and ability to understand others intrinsically.

We all sometimes need someone to support us, too. Though Meeta's work was going well, other areas of her life were not going so smoothly, as she explains, "I had these massive storms of adversity going on in my personal life, with my father's health and in my relationships as well. So, it was quite a difficult time. But I had people around me who not only supported me but did not allow any of that to get in the way of fulfilling my potential at work. Those couple of years facing that situation at Xchanging and the challenges in my personal life taught me one very simple lesson - reaching out to the person who sits next to you, being helpful to your colleagues, relating to people as people, and supporting them through their tough times is your purpose. It is a straightforward way of living a life of purpose. You don't have to look very far to make a meaningful contribution to a life. It's often the person in front of you." During this period, Meeta's career acted as an anchor through all the troubled waters of her personal life. "I had the financial wherewithal to look after myself and to do the things that I needed to do. And with that financial independence also comes options. And second, it helped me not to get swallowed up by everything that was happening around me. My career and my job were definitely my anchors at that time and always have been. I would say my career has been one of the most rewarding parts of my life."

In 2008, Meeta was promoted to a new role that required a work visa, as she explains, "It came about quite mystically. Xchanging had just listed on the London Stock Exchange, and by virtue of all the action in the India market for the company, I had been working quite extensively with the founder and chief executive, David Andrews. An opportunity opened up in London to set up a global PR infrastructure for Xchanging, and David asked if I would like to take on the role. Although it was all quite out of the blue, the timing of this opportunity was perfect, and I decided to take it on."

Meeta's philosophy on life and opportunity is simple, as she explains, "I believe that every thought, word, and action impact our bank account of good fortune, which we are either building up or depleting. So, when something like this comes about – the right opportunity at the right time - you just say, *"All right, I must be doing something right with my bank account of good fortune."* The job was in the UK, so the change was big, as she explains, "It was unnerving, yet quite exciting, unnerving because I had never strayed far from my family, and I'm very attached to them, but also because I had never experienced living in a different country. It was also exciting because I knew the people I'd be working with. I knew the teams and had a few friends here, so that gave me a bit of comfort. The first thing I did as soon as I landed was to get in touch with the local Buddhist community and two days later, I was sitting together having a cup of tea with this fellow-Buddhist who would become one of my dearest friends. So, I had people like that around me quite quickly, which made me feel quite at home in London."

She spent the next four years working in London as Head of Group Public Relations, leading communication initiatives across Europe, the US, and Asia and working at Board level, engaging stakeholders, and building compelling narratives around business priorities. She also managed CEO communications, industry analyst relations and led change messaging for all M&A (mergers and acquisitions) activity. Meeta's recollections of that period are insightful, "I was quite young and inexperienced. I would say I was a lot bolder than I am today, 15 years on. There was a lot to learn about the business and how it is done in the UK. Culturally it was very different. This was a pre-Google and social media world, and you had to learn the cultural nuances through observation and very often through mistakes. But I was fortunate - there were just amazing people around me who helped and supported me, including David, the CEO, who mentored me in a lot of ways and helped me find my feet."

Part of the secret of Xchanging's rapid growth as a private company was the application of a methodology that David Andrews had developed. Now four years into her role as Head of PR, Meeta picks up the story, "We really wanted to see if this methodology could be repurposed for smaller organisations, so that they could grow and could scale in the same way that Xchanging and some of the businesses that Xchanging supported had too. So, we set about rejigging this methodology with David's blessings. Unbeknown to Meeta when they first started working on it, this methodology would signal a change in her career direction and take her closer to her earlier ambition of doing purposeful work that could help smaller businesses grow and thrive. She explains how it came about, "We landed our first management consulting project with the University of East London. I had never been trained as a Management Consultant. I didn't know how consultants dealt with clients and what were the unspoken codes of conduct. So, I just relied on what I knew about dealing with people – be perceptive, strive to do your best, and exceed expectations. That first project was really hard, but we did our best. We didn't quite tell how well we were doing or not. Somewhere in my mind I thought that once this project was over, it might be better to give this up and find something easier to do.

However, we received glowing reviews for our work from the University's Board, especially about how they found our approach a refreshing change from other management consultancies they had engaged in the past. We were asked to come back to do some more work with them. And that's when we realized we had to set up a company if we wanted to do more." In March 2012, after six and a quarter year with Xchanging, Meeta followed in her mother's footsteps and set up her own company, MetaValue, working with another director.

* * * *

Meeta certainly felt the stretch that all start-up directors experience, but once again, she saw what could have felt like an insurmountable blow as a gift and a blessing that helped her to learn, as she explains, "If you are willing to apply yourself to a challenge, you become unstoppable. It's all about willingness – what you determine to do or not. And that gives me courage to try anything new. I still get the jitters every time I start a new project. but you've got to challenge your fears and find your way forward. I believe it makes you a creative problem solver and ever more resourceful."

MetaValue quickly established itself and received European start-up support through the 'Make it Global' programme for women-led start-ups. The organisation's reputation as a strategy and growth consultancy that supported organisations and social entrepreneurs to unlock their full potential grew quickly. MetaValue became one of the leading suppliers to the Cabinet Office on two flagship programmes supporting the development of innovative new models for delivering public services. The company now had set itself a clear mission – to be an antidote to austerity. In 2014, Meeta's success was recognised when she became one of six entrepreneurs in the UK nominated as Asian Woman of Achievement that year. Over the next ten years, Meeta and her co-director worked with universities, business accelerators, local and central government, and the European Regional Development Fund to support over 300 start-up SMEs and innovation projects, developing toolkits and guides along the way.

Meeta is clear about what she gained from her work, "The most rewarding part was working with different businesses, different people, and on a whole variety of projects. I absolutely loved that. It was intellectually rewarding and truly spurred my growth as a person and a professional. I don't think working for one organisation would have allowed me such opportunities for growth."

Remembering the benefit she gained from David's support, and as someone who always puts people at the heart of what she does, Meeta looked to the organisations she was working with for opportunities to give back. In 2016, she became an Independent Advisory Member of the British Army's Defence College of Logistics, Policing and Administration, serving for almost three years. She joined the Advisory Board of auticon UK, a firm she is as passionate about today as when she first joined their advisory board in 2016. She explains why, "Auticon is a really inspiring organisation and the first IT consulting firm in the world to exclusively employ autistic technology professionals as consultants. Autism is still quite misunderstood in society. As a result, many autistic people find it difficult to enter into the job market and to sustain employment. Auticon is working to change the conversation about neurodiversity and to help organisations become neuro inclusive" Meeta became Chair of the Advisory Board in November 2020. Little did she know then, but auticon would become even more important in her life in a few years.

Because of her involvement in the Inclusive Economy Partnership, a Number Ten Downing Street initiative, and pre-cursor to the levelling up agenda, Meeta was invited to join the Advisory Board of another social enterprise she was working with in October 2018. The match between her ongoing ultimate concern to do work in areas that provide an antidote to austerity and the work they do was crystal clear. An award-winning charity, Money A+E works on financial inclusion for some of the hardest-to-reach diverse ethnic communities by providing money education and advice to adults and young people from disadvantaged communities across the UK. Some five years on, Meeta is now their Advisory Board Chair. Meeta's belief in the value of the work they do is palpable, "The brilliant thing about how they operate is that the money mentors who guide and support other people going through financial difficulties are people who've gone through those difficulties themselves, and who therefore understand where the system fails them. It's all about providing that compassionate human-to-human support that helps people not just out of their immediate financial difficulties but also equips them for a future free of financial troubles."

Meeta's authenticity and immense empathy for others run deep within her and are informed by her beliefs as a practising Buddhist, something she encountered for the first time at 19. Meeta explains, "We all seek a sense of direction, an ideal to orient ourselves toward. My Buddhist practice guides who I am as person, how I approach people and situations, what I do and what I don't. Buddhism teaches that all life has an inherent potential for good. We can all tap into that potential through taking actions to help others and creating value in whichever situation we find ourselves in. When we are tapping into that highest potential of our lives, we quite naturally bring forth the courage, compassion, and wisdom necessary to transform any negative circumstance into a source of growth and benefit. The point of this is not just to become happy ourselves, but also take action in society and make the world a better place for everyone."

In May 2018, another opportunity to make a difference came Meeta's way when she was invited to become a strategic adviser to another social change project she supports called EmpathyLab. Founded by social justice entrepreneur Miranda McKearney OBE, the team is made up of academics, librarians, and business professionals who experiment lab-like to build children's empathy, literacy, and social activism using high-quality literature. EmpathyLab programmes are now in 120 libraries and 40 schools in the UK, are supported by leading publishers, and have reached over one million children.

Meeta continued to enjoy the blend and variety of Board work supporting other social impact organisations while delivering projects for her clients at MetaValue. One day in late 2021, a conversation with Kurt Schöffer, the Group Chief Executive of auticon, who she had known for many years, presented her with another opportunity, which she couldn't refuse. He asked her to consider stepping down from being Chair of the Advisory Board of auticon UK so she could become Chief People and Social Innovation Officer instead. Meeta takes up the story, "Kurt said, "We'd rather have you on the inside than the outside and just advising us because there's so much that needs to be done, and we think you can do those things. I wasn't prepared for the conversation, but my immediate instinctive response was "Yes"." For Meeta, yes was the only answer, as she explains, "I knew the company well. I knew the ambitions well, and as an organisation, it sits in this sweet space between making a social impact while being a commercially sustainable, financially successful business. And I like the challenge of that. Auticon's work speaks to my ambitions, my values, and what I want to do with my life. For me, the question was not about whether I would like to work with them. The question for me was, "Would I like to be part of what they are trying to do?" And for me, the answer was, "Hell, yes." As part of the Advisory Board, I had been closely watching the growth of the company and could see the tremendous potential and the impact that Auticon can make. I had run MetaValue for ten years by that point and enjoyed every moment of it. I never ran my business for the sake of running my own business. MetaValue had started because we were trying to bring an idea to life. So, there wasn't ever any egotistical attachment to it. I took a lot of pride in what I had built and had always been driven by the joy of the work we did. I think that attitude served me well because if you're not attached to any egotistical view of yourself, you are a lot nimbler. You are a lot more responsive to what life has to offer you. MetaValue was simply the result of me trying to do something different and do something bigger than what I had done before and to pivot a career, which up to a point had been quite focused on marketing, market development, and communications, to get into the areas which are really at the heart of business."

Having successfully achieved that and built a business, Meeta was presented with an opportunity that really appealed to her continued inner call to do purposeful work. She was ready to pivot into auticon, albeit with a bit of apprehension about what she might miss as an ex-business owner, as she explains, "There was no other way that I could do the job at auticon without my ten years at MetaValue. Every day, I was working on a different set of challenges, and I was parallel tracking lots of things, from projects to accounts, and I enjoy that variety in my work. So, my apprehension was that I didn't want to be pigeon-holed into one area. I was transparent about my concerns as we discussed my role with the auticon Group Board. But we are at such a stage of growth and development, and I believe, not just for my role, but for any role at auticon, it's up to you how big and interesting, and how varied you make your job. I believe this is true for most jobs. You can be entrepreneurial and show initiative or you can sit back and say, "My job description says I can only do this, so don't ask me to do that." Not being one to sit back, and with the opportunity to develop people and continue to innovate, the role suited her well as she explains, "I'm thrilled that it turned out the way it did, and I don't feel any different than I did when I was running MetaValue. We work in a space which I would say is the hottest sector to be in. Technology is a fast-paced, fast-growing sector, and that speaks to me. Auticon is the largest autistic-majority company in the world, and 80% of our staff are neurodivergent. I think autism is the most ignored dimension of diversity, with too few organisations talking about it enough, and that's true of society, too. So, for me, the opportunity with auticon represents a powerhouse combination of technology, neurodiversity, and social and business impact, and it is such an exciting challenge to have."

As an allistic Asian woman, Meeta has some clear views on diversity and equity, "I think the biggest change for me is in how we think about diversity – it's such a hot topic these days. As an Asian woman working in London, you are used to being in the minority, and now suddenly, you are in an environment where you are a minority, but in a slightly different way. Diversity is not just some people having it better than others or some people being supported to have a better work experience or a better experience in society and communities. Diversity is about equity so that everybody has the same experience. When you start to improve things for somebody who thinks differently or operates differently, you make it better for everyone."

"The first time I started to understand Neurodiversity was when I joined the auticon UK board. I started to learn about the benefits that different thinking styles can bring to an organisation. Society so far has had fixed views on who can and who cannot contribute to an organisation or to society at large. Neurodiversity describes the idea that people experience and interact with the world around them in many different ways; there is no one "right" way of thinking, learning, and behaving. Our neurological differences, including conditions such as autism, ADHD, dyslexia, and others, are natural variations of the human brain. It is estimated that 15% of the global population have a neurodivergent condition. But limited awareness and understanding of neurodiversity leads to stigma, discrimination, unequal opportunities, and unfair treatment of neurodivergent individuals.

"We know that autistic people often have cognitive strengths such as: attention-to-detail, sustained attention, heightened imagination and creativity, superior autobiographical memory and instinctive analytical abilities in trend spotting or pattern recognition. This makes them particularly well-suited for careers in science, technology, engineering, and mathematics (STEM). Despite many autistic people being talented, qualified, and keen to work, in the UK, only 22% of autistic people are in any form of meaningful employment. And of those in employment, a vast majority are under-employed in jobs that they are over-qualified or over-skilled for.

"On the other hand, there are enormous skill gaps and talent shortages in the tech sector that are increasingly difficult to fill. Data from governments and experts alike show that these shortages will only become more acute in the next decade. It is estimated that by 2030, the demand for skilled workers will outstrip supply, resulting in a global talent shortage. Yet employers today are unable to tap into this gifted talent pool of autistic professionals. We want to create meaningful careers for technology professionals who are on the autistic spectrum and create a more inclusive world. Auticon is Championing neurodiversity - challenging stereotypes and biases. We don't want to only change perceptions but also showcase the benefits of neurodiversity. Ultimately, we want to help build a more equitable and vibrant society where all individuals have the opportunity to thrive, no matter who they are and how they think."

The experience of joining a neurodiverse organisation has been profound. Meeta explains, "I feel a big shift personally in how comfortable I feel in being my authentic self at work and outside. In hospitality, I was trained to be a certain kind of person - smile, be outgoing, talk to people, and engage with the world around - all things I do naturally. I now realise how some of those expectations from your workplace can be so uncomfortable for so many people. I did wonder when I joined auticon if I needed to something different to fit in. It's been a learning process, and what I've learned is that I can be my authentic self if I'm okay to meet people where and as they are. So rather than expecting everyone to match my energy or enthusiasm levels, I have learned to recognise and accept that some people are not designed that way and that's completely fine. So, working somewhere that encourages you to be your authentic self, where you are encouraged to be okay to be just as you are, has made me a lot more relaxed. People can be how they are, and I can be how I am, and that takes the stress out of your day. That is such a big contributor to my well-being."

The importance of well-being as a theme for Meeta, as well as her willingness to play her part in fostering more diversity and inclusion, features in the latest opportunity that came her way in August 2023. Meeta was appointed Chair of the Board of Trustees for the newly created music education charity, West of England Music, and Arts (WEMA). A spin-out from three different local authorities with 160 staff that deliver 50,000 hours of music learning annually, WEMA is the largest provider of music education and therapy for young people and adults in the region. As Meeta notes, it offered her the chance to help them "work as a charity with the heart of a charity and the mind of a business" and reflects her ability to be both business-savvy and people-smart, an essential skill and mindset and philosophy, particularly as technology rapidly reshapes the landscape of both work and society.

Looking to the future, Meeta has a clear view of what's needed for organisations and for us as individuals. "Things are evolving very fast, and there's clearly a need for more tech talent for roles in AI, cyber and data science, and analytics, but it's more than that. It's not just about what's coming from the world of tech but also how people are responding to tech innovations and what they're embracing or dismissing. The pace of innovation and change means that anyone in the workforce today needs to continually adapt and upskill for this changing landscape.

"We can also already see that there is not just a disruption of skills, but a disruption of attitudes. I remember 20 years ago, in my early twenties, you related to your workplace in a very different way. There was a very different set of things that you were evaluated on and what you considered valuable in a job. That is changing now, and I think the biggest change will be in attitudes and the need to be curious and open to learning and reskilling. We already know that analytical thinking, creative thinking, and resilience are the top-rated skills, and this trend will only continue. My constant guiding principle is to learn, apply that learning, reskill, learn, apply, reskill, and repeat. I find this makes work experience and one's professional life, in general, a lot more enriching."

Meeta's constant curiosity, learning, and upskilling are part of how she keeps a sense of control in a world full of rapid change. She explains, "The world looked very different before COVID compared with what it looks like now in October 2023. So, how do you navigate that volatility? How do you have a sense of being grounded with so much flying around you and at such top speed? For me, that comes from that simple sense of purpose. I ask myself, "*Why am I here? What's my mission? What's the unique contribution that I want to make to the world today? However small, however big.*" I think that keeps me grounded and helps me approach each day with a sense of purpose. I feel grateful for the work I have done so far and the work I do now. It is great to wake up each morning knowing that what I'll do today will make a dent somewhere and make this world a better place. I may not be able to solve all the problems of the planet, but at least today, I'm doing my bit, and that gives me peace."

* * * *

Growing up in austerity with a hostile environment while witnessing her own mother's courage in following her dreams despite her frailties, gave Meeta a meaningful context in which to develop her character strengths of courage, bravery, honesty, and fairness. And she saw firsthand the value and satisfaction of helping others get on in life. Over time, all those formative years and experiences would transmute into a personal sense of calling and her mission to live a purposeful life. Time in hospitality taught her the benefit of hard work, learning, connection, and teamwork, which she combined with her natural and innate social intelligence to help her learn effectively about business and finance. Moving into a marketing agency meant she was able to understand the importance and power of effective communication, a skill and mastery she brought to bear in her work with large and small organisations alike. Sometimes, we have a sense of where we are headed and what we need to do to progress in the right direction. For Meeta that meant getting right to the heart of business and a decade of self-employment taught her the value of continuing to work across a blend of different sectors to inform her thinking enabling her to make her own unique contribution.

In an increasingly AI technology and skills-driven world, her commitment to curiosity-led learning and reskilling not only helps her to future-proof her work but also means she can enjoy the journey and contribute meaningfully to the things she cares about.

The following activities will help you to be clear about your strengths, talents, and skills now and develop a watchful eye for what's needed in the future.

* * * *

A QUESTION OF WHAT I HAVE TO OFFER:
WHAT ARE MY STRENGTHS, TALENTS, AND SKILLS? WHERE ARE THEY BEST SERVED AND MOST WANTED?

We all have a different blend of strengths, talents, and skills, which are unique to who we are. When we spend our lives being true to who we are and undertaking activities that come naturally to us and that we are good at or predisposed to do well in, opportunity has a funny habit of finding its way to us - if we are aware and open to it. When this happens, we can grow and fulfil our potential – if we choose to take it.

So, what can you offer already, and what do you need to develop to future-proof your working life? The following three activities will help you to become clear about that and start to explore who and where they can make the most difference.

ACTIVITY 1: EXPLORING CHARACTER STRENGTHS

We have already looked at personality, which the Cambridge Dictionary defines as: "*the type of person you are, shown by the way you behave, feel, and think.*" Personality is different from character. The Cambridge Dictionary defines character as: "*the particular combination of qualities in a person or place that makes them different from others.*" Very often, we speak about character as if it is just one thing, but a person's character is made up of lots of different strengths, and we all have different profiles of strengths. If we understand our character and its strengths, we can build on them, so they act as firm foundations for our working lives.

As academics Chris Peterson, Ph.D., and Professor Martin Seligman pointed out in 2004 in their book "Character Strengths and Virtues: A Handbook and Classification," we become better and progress more effectively if we focus on the positive rather than the negative aspects of ourselves – and when we do this, we experience a more meaningful, successful, and happy existence.

The study of character strengths started in the early 2000s when Peterson and Seligman led a team of 55 scientists to study character more scientifically, researching world religions, philosophies, and psychology in search of agreed-upon virtues. The insights gained from the study led to a classification of positive traits in human beings.

Once the classification work was complete, a ground-breaking personal strengths test, the VIA Survey, was designed specifically to measure these 24-character strengths in individuals. Since then, and at the time of writing, over 25 million surveys have been taken around the world, and VIA (Values in Action) continues to fuel the advancements of character strengths science through its activities.

The authors define character strengths as *"positive traits - capacities humans have for thinking, feeling, and behaving in ways that benefit oneself and others. Specifically, they are the psychological ingredients for displaying virtues or human goodness.* " Virtues are defined as *"core characteristics valued by moral philosophers and religious thinkers."*

In total, there are six virtues and 24-character strengths, as shown in the chart which follows:

THE VIA CLASSIFICATION OF STRENGTHS

WISDOM	COURAGE	HUMANITY
• Creativity • Curiosity • Judgement • Love of Learning • Perspective	• Bravery • Perseverance • Honesty • Zest	• Love • Kindness • Social Intelligence
JUSTICE	**TEMPERANCE**	**TRANSCENDENCE**
• Teamwork • Fairness • Leadership	• Forgiveness • Humility • Prudence • Self-Regulation	• Appreciation of Beauty & Excellence • Gratitude • Hope • Humour • Spirituality

Each of us has what the authors call "signature strengths," which come more naturally and easily to us; other "phasis strengths," which we use in situations where they are needed; and "lesser strengths," which we either use less or less often. In Meeta's case, her curiosity and love of learning give her wisdom and currency, while her spirituality and social intelligence create opportunities and meaningful challenges for her, which she uses her courage to transcend.

So, what are your strengths?

You can find out your strengths by taking the free VIA Character Strengths Survey on the VIA Institute of Character website (www.viacharacter.org/). It will take you around 10 -15 minutes and give you a headline report with the option of paying for a more detailed insight report.

Once you have completed the test and read your results, make a list of your top five strengths, and find an example of each of them in action. Then, list your three least used strengths and consider whether you need to develop them. If you do, then identify what steps you can take to strengthen them and make a note of these actions.

Now that you have completed the activity, what is your most significant insight about your character strengths?

* * * *

ACTIVITY 2: DISCOVERING YOUR NATURAL TALENTS

Each of us is also gifted in our own unique and vital way. The trick and the challenge are to discover what makes us unique and to understand how to use that gift to help others or something that calls to us. This activity will help you to identify your very own superpower.

We are all familiar with concepts such as IQ (Intelligence Quotient) a term first used in Germany in 1902 to measure intelligence, which was later developed by the educational psychologist Binet to measure intelligence in a specific educational context. Later, the concept of EQ (Emotional Quotient) was introduced as a way of measuring our ability to measure how emotionally intelligent we are.

In addition to IQ and EQ, there is another area related to intelligence, which is equally essential when it comes to developing our abilities and how individuals use them to create solutions to problems. In the 1970s and 80s, developmental psychologist Howard Gardner, now Professor of Cognition and Education at Harvard University, began working with children of different ages, talents, and backgrounds. He observed that a child's ability in one area did not necessarily predict their ability in others. He also worked with brain-damaged patients who had strokes or other brain lesions. He found that the location of the lesion was important in determining which abilities were lost and which were spared. This led him to study human development in different cultures and the specialized regions of the brain and develop what has become known as his Theory of Multiple Intelligences, which has had a major influence on the world of education.

Originally published in his book, *"Frames of Mind, The Theory of Multiple Intelligences,"* Gardner's theory posits that, health permitting, everyone can develop multiple intelligences because of their individual genetic and experiential factors. Further, Gardner states that everyone has a distinct intellectual profile, even in the case of identical twins. Though they share the same genetic makeup, they will exhibit different and distinct cognitive profiles because of the influence of their own unique experiences.

Gardner explains multiple intelligences as meaning that "rather than having a single computer, we have at least seven or eight different computers. And one computer can work well in one person, another computer can work well in another person."

Having identified the key prerequisites for a single intelligence to be identified and classified, Howard's work proposed initially that there are eight different fully developed types of intelligence, each of which is relatively independent of the others.

- **Spatial:** the ability to conceptualize and manipulate large-scale spatial arrays (e.g., airplane pilot, sailor) or more local forms of space (e.g., architect, chess player). This may mean being good at working with 3D images, sculpture, and designing objects.
- **Bodily-kinaesthetic:** the ability to use one's whole body, or parts of the body (like the hands or the mouth), to solve problems or create products (e.g., dancer, sculptor). This may mean being skilled at sports or dance, enjoying making things with your hands, having excellent physical coordination, and remembering by doing rather than seeing or hearing.
- **Musical:** sensitivity to rhythm, pitch, meter, tone, melody, and timbre. It may entail the ability to sing, play musical instruments, and/or compose music (e.g., musical conductor, singer) and being able to remember songs and melodies.
- **Linguistic (language intelligence):** sensitivity to the meaning of words, the order among words, and the sound, rhythms, inflections, and meter of words (e.g., poet, journalist). This may mean remembering written and spoken information quickly, enjoying reading and writing, debating, or giving persuasive speeches, explaining things well, and using humour when telling stories.
- **Logical-mathematical:** the capacity to conceptualize the logical relations among actions or symbols (e.g., mathematicians, scientists, accountants). This may mean having excellent problem-solving skills, enjoying thinking about abstract ideas, or conducting scientific experiments and solving complex computations.
- **Interpersonal (or social intelligence):** the ability to interact effectively with others. Sensitivity to others' moods, feelings, temperaments, and motivations (e.g., negotiator career development specialist). This may include seeing things from different perspectives and using them to create positive relationships with others and resolve conflicts.

- **Intrapersonal (or self-intelligence):** sensitivity to one's own feelings, goals, and anxieties, and the capacity to plan and act considering one's own traits. Intrapersonal intelligence is not particular to specific careers; instead, it is a goal for every individual in a complex modern society, where one has to make consequential decisions for oneself to become self-aware and understand the basis for one's own motivations and feelings.
- **Naturalistic:** the ability to make consequential distinctions in the world of nature as, for example, between one plant and another or one cloud formation and another (e.g., taxonomist). Sometimes called nature intelligence, this may include an understanding of and sensitivity towards animals, enjoying being outdoors, and having an interest in botany, biology, or zoology.

  Gardner later posited a ninth intelligence has not yet fully confirmed, in part because the neurological basis for this capacity is not yet clear, and also because it may simply be the result of amalgamating several already identified intelligences (e.g., linguistic, logical-mathematical, and the personal intelligences). However, it has undergone somewhat of a resurgence, not least in part in response to the COVID pandemic. Gardner defines this intelligence as:
- **Existential:** the cognitive capacity to raise and ponder "big questions" - queries about love, about evil, about life and death - indeed, about the nature and quality of existence.

In essence, Gardner's approach enables us to understand how smart we are in each of the various intelligences and to identify what comes most easily to us.

Meeta has powerful interpersonal and linguistic intelligence, which enable her to communicate effectively, whether with clients, employees, partners, city analysts, or fellow Board members; and in a way that means that organisations progress more effectively in their missions, whatever they may be.

So, what are you smartest at?

There are two parts to this activity. Firstly, ask yourself:

What's the thing I do so easily that I can't understand why others struggle to do it?

If you find this difficult, then ask yourself, "If I could have any problem that I could solve, almost without having to think about it, what would it be?"

Write your answer in the space below and identify the intelligence(s)/smart(s) you find easiest to use.

Rank your nine smarts (including existential) in order of ability, where 1 is the highest and 9 is the lowest in the space below.

Now you have ranked your smarts, ask yourself this question:

What are my top three smarts?

List them below with an example for each that you can use whenever you need to demonstrate your abilities.

It is also worth considering what you are least smart at and whether this is something you want to improve or if it doesn't matter. If it does, how can you develop it? Make a note of your ideas here:

* * * *

Now that you have completed the activity, what is your most significant insight about your talents or smarts?

* * * *

ACTIVITY 3: UNDERSTANDING YOUR NURTURED ABILITIES AND SKILLS

We have already seen how opportunities come Meeta's way because of the way she works with others. Her human skills and ability to see what is coming over the horizon and use that insight to react in an enterprising way by meeting people where they are, regardless of background, to make things happen is one of the main reasons why people want her on their team. The following section is designed to help you identify your skills and other qualities so you can make effective choices that reflect who you are, what you like doing, what you are good at, and what you know about.

For the sake of clarity, skills are process-oriented abilities that are learned and improved through practice, which help individuals achieve specific goals. They are not innate, but they can be developed through experience. People learn skills in one of two ways. The first way we learn skills is through experience, such as working effectively in teams while at work. These are known as soft skills and are also sometimes also referred to as power skills, common skills, essential skills, or core skills. They reflect the personal qualities and traits you and others have. The other way we gain skills is through formal instruction, such as in a classroom or via online learning, for instance, learning to code a computer. These are known as hard skills. All skills become more automatic with practice but are still closely related to knowledge. A skilled musician, for example, can play a piece of music automatically, but they still need to know the notes and the rhythm. Skills may also depend on physical abilities, such as strength and coordination; mental abilities, such as memory and reasoning; and sensory abilities, such as sight and hearing. These abilities are, to varying degrees, innate, meaning that some people are naturally better at specific skills than others.

Traditionally, recruiters have an "ask" of candidates in terms of the type of person, skills, knowledge, and experience outlined in the job description. I use a simple model and grid shown below which I developed called ASKE to help my clients understand this "ask" and identify what's required so they can apply for jobs effectively.

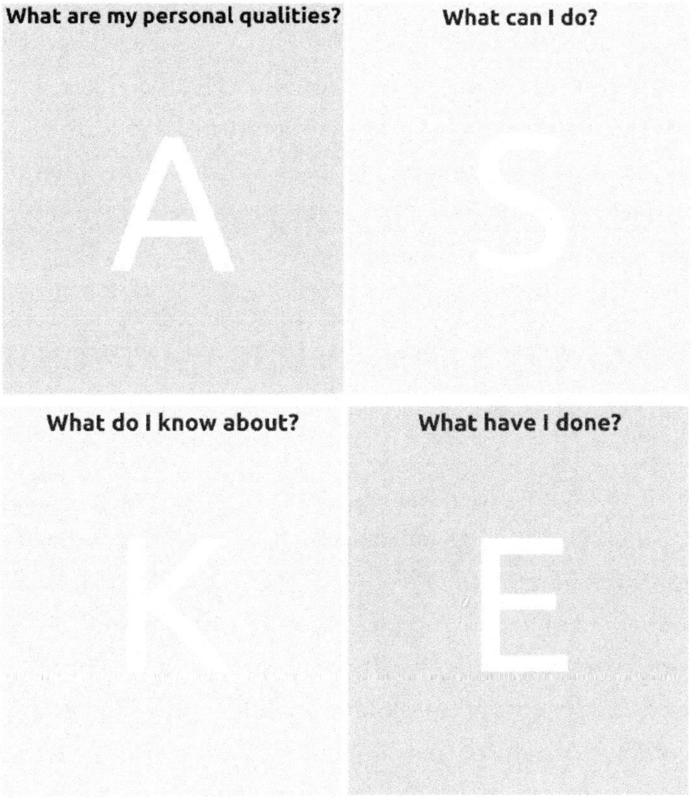

© Career Alchemy 2016 – 2023

The A of ASKE stands for Attributes. These encompass your attitude, aptitude, personality, and values and represents the "why" behind why you do something and who you are as an individual.

The S is for Skills. These represent the "how" that enables you to carry out specific tasks. Some skills are perennial such as communication, teamwork, customer service, project management, sales, marketing, analysis, and research.

The K stands for Knowledge and represents the "what" in your work. This section will be specific to formal learning in disciplines you have studied academically, and sector and role learning undertaken at work.

Finally, the E is for experience, where your attributes, skills, and knowledge come together in practice so you can learn and achieve. This section includes experiences you have had both inside and outside of work. Remember to consider the hobbies you have experienced as well, as these often contain something highly relevant but which you have not done in a work context. Side hustles also provide opportunities to learn.

As you can see in the graphic, there is a question for each of the four sections to help individuals complete the grid. These questions reflect the four sections of a typical job description.

ACTIVITY 3.1: IDENTIFYING WHAT YOU HAVE TO OFFER

If you want to be able to assess opportunities and put good applications together quickly, knowing what you have to offer provides a great foundation to your career choice. After all, if you don't understand what that is, it is very hard to convince an employer that your services offer a good return on their investment. Remember that everything you have experienced in life, education, hobbies, volunteering, and work all count when it comes to demonstrating your ability. Taking stock of everything you have to offer can lead to insights and help you to discover some golden nuggets from your past which can be really helpful in pivoting in a new direction. So, what have you forgotten about that would help you move forward? To conduct your review, create your own grid, or spreadsheet if you prefer, and spend some time considering the question for each quadrant of the grid in turn.

Once you have included everything you can think of, spend a few minutes reviewing what you have written. Identify the top 3 elements in each of the four quadrants that are most important to you and list them here. Then, add an example that demonstrates each competency in action.

My top Attributes are:

1. 2. 3.

My top Skills are:

1. 2. 3.

My top Knowledge areas are:

1. 2. 3.

My top Experiences are:

1. 2. 3.

Now consider which ASKE elements you may need to develop further to help you progress in a new direction or to a new level. Make a note of the top three elements from your ASKE analysis which need work, and write down how you are going to improve those elements:

1.

2.

3.

Reviewing and updating your ASKE Competencies Profile activity every quarter will help you revalidate what you have to offer so you can make wise choices about your next career steps. It will also enable you to create job applications more easily You may find it helpful to use a blank ASKE grid as a tool to record all the different criteria of a job or role you are interested in the appropriate segment and map your examples easily. Done properly, this will help you reach the short list more easily because your application reflects the needs of the recruiter more effectively.

Now that you have completed the activity, what is your most significant insight about your current ASKE Competencies profile?

* * * *

ACTIVITY 3.2: HOW ENTERPRISING ARE YOU?

Throughout her story, Meeta consistently demonstrates her ability to think in an enterprising way, which makes things happen. Being enterprising is "the tendency to start up and manage projects. The most enterprising people set up projects more frequently; set up more innovative projects; and are more growth-oriented, which means that they have to be opportunistic, and good at utilising resources, including human, technological, physical, and organisational resources."

People who are enterprising share many of the same characteristics as entrepreneurs. Professor Howard Stevenson of the Harvard Business School describes entrepreneurship as "the pursuit of opportunity beyond resources controlled."

Entrepreneurs choose to create and run businesses rather than work as employees. In doing so, they assume all the risks and rewards of the venture. Often seen as innovators, they are sources of new ideas, goods, services, and business or procedures. Their focus is usually on creating value and profit. Social entrepreneurs are usually focussed on introducing novel applications to help to solve community-based problems and take the risk and effort to create positive change in society through their work. There is a third context for entrepreneurial activity where individuals work as entrepreneurs inside an organisation and use their entrepreneurial skills to improve activities. These so-called 'intrapreneurs' usually work on a particular idea or project, have the resources and capabilities of the organisation at their disposal, and work without the usual risk associated with being an entrepreneur.

People often describe entrepreneurs as confident, able to delegate, determined, disruptors, independent, knowledgeable, keep an eye on profitability and building strong relationships, able to calculate risks appropriately, and able to act as the best spokespeople and advocates for their business. Typically, entrepreneurs seek to scale their business. Entrepreneurs usually depend on other people and automated systems for work without their direct involvement in product or service delivery.

People who are their own bosses and enjoy delivering specific projects for clients often refer to themselves as business owners or freelancers, depending on the work they do. According to statistics from the Office of National Statistics, in the second quarter of 2023 in the UK, there were around 2.76 million self-employed men and approximately 1.55 million self-employed women in the United Kingdom, many of whom work in particular in health and social care, education, personal services, administrative and support services and creative and media industries. There were around 4.24 million self-employed workers in July 2023, and the most likely age for self-employment is between 45 and 54. Entrepreneurial ambitions come in all shapes and sizes. Some are driven by growth, while others want more of a lifestyle business. Some are driven by necessity. Many begin as kitchen table enterprises. Whatever their ambitions, entrepreneurs lie at the heart of growth and innovation, so either being able to work effectively with them, or, better still, developing your entrepreneurial mindset, skills, and behaviours, provide some key ways to build your career over time.

In the late 80s, Dr Sally Caird, aided by Mr Cliff Johnson of Durham University Business School, undertook research following a literature review to identify the key psychological characteristics of entrepreneurs. Their research identified several vital entrepreneurial characteristics: "strong motivation, characterised by a high need for achievement and autonomy; creative tendency; calculated risk-taking; and an internal locus of control (belief you have control over your destiny and make your own 'luck')." As they put it: "People set up an enterprise because they are highly motivated (to achieve something themselves) by a good idea and will manage risks, information, and uncertainties because they believe they can set up the enterprise successfully."

The workplace of the future needs people who are enterprising and demonstrate a set of qualities that many experts assert can be learned. As a result of Caird and Johnson's research, they developed what they called *the Generalising Measure of Enterprising Tendency*. Now known as the GET2 test, it provides a way of helping people recognise their strengths through personal reflection in education and other settings. Like all such tests, results are contextual to what is happening in an individual's life at the time and to their experiences, and so are subject to change.

So, how enterprising are you?

Completing the GET2 questionnaire will help you to answer this question and will only take around five minutes. You can take the test free of charge here: www.get2test.net/get2test.html.

Using the results of the test, fill in your scores below and provide your best example of them below:

1. **Achievement**
2. **Autonomy**
3. **Creative**
4. **Tendency**
5. **Internal Locus of Control**
6. **Calculated Risk**

Remember to capture anything that matters to you in your current ASKE profile. Now spend a few minutes reflecting on which of these behaviours you want to develop further and identify how you can do this:

Now that you have evaluated how enterprising you are, what is your most significant insight from this activity?

* * * *

ACTIVITY 3.3: FUTURE-PROOFING YOUR CAREER

While employers have traditionally looked for all four elements of the ASKE equally, that approach is slowly but surely starting to change. This is due to several factors, including a push towards creating more inclusive workforces, challenges in the economy due to rapid automation, and a need for people to work in green jobs (positions in agriculture, manufacturing, R&D, administrative, and service activities aimed at substantially preserving or restoring environmental quality) in particular.

Skills-First hiring

Major recruiters are now moving towards what the WEF calls Skills-First hiring in its May 2023 Report, "Putting Skills First: A Framework for Action," produced in conjunction with PwC. This approach emphasizes evaluating an individual's skills and competencies for a job rather than traditional qualifications like degrees, prior employer, or job title requirements. Prioritising skills is not intended to ignore traditional hiring and development systems that already work but rather to enhance them so that talent can be better matched with opportunity so that businesses get the exact skills they need and access to jobs is democratised. That means that people with the right skills but without formal qualifications should be able to access quality jobs, career growth, and better earnings.

LinkedIn, the online business networking platform for professionals, now advocates a Skills-First hiring approach and has seen the effects of this change. In their "Skills-First: Reimagining the Labour Market and Breaking Down Barriers, European Highlights" report published in May 2023, they set out how this approach is already expanding the talent pool, democratising access to jobs and making the labour market and workforce more resilient. Their statistics show that this shift is working with up to 20 times more eligible workers who have been added to the employment talent pool. Women, those without degrees, and younger generations benefiting from the change are the younger generation. In the past year, members added 380 million skills to their profiles, up over 40% year over year, and certifications, including rapid acquisition of micro-credentials, are on the rise too.

One thing is for sure - skills will increasingly serve as the bridge that helps you to pivot from one role or sector to another as recruiters start to move away from more traditional requirements for relevant experience and knowledge.

So, which future attributes and skills do you need to develop to future-proof your career?

Using attributes and skills that you enjoy utilising, are good at, and that align well with who you are will help you enjoy your working week, particularly when they are used in service of a purpose that calls to you.

The following activity highlights those attitudes and skills which are becoming increasingly important in the future world of work where human skills are particularly important. Score each element on the list out of 5, where 1 is low and 5 is high, for both your ability (represented by the star) and your enjoyment (represented by the heart).

Attributes | **Skills**

Score each element out of 5, where 1 is low and 5 is high, for both ability (star) and enjoyment (heart).

Attributes	★	♥	Skills	★	♥
SELF-EFFICACY RELATED			***COGNITIVE RELATED***		
Motivation and self awareness	☐	☐	Creative thinking	☐	☐
Curiosity and life-long learning	☐	☐	Analytical thinking	☐	☐
Dependability & attention to detail	☐	☐	Systems thinking	☐	☐
Resilience, flexibility, and agility	☐	☐	***MANAGEMENT RELATED***		
			Quality control	☐	☐
WORKING WITH OTHERS RELATED			Talent management	☐	☐
Empathy & active listening	☐	☐	***TECHNOLOGY RELATED***		
Service orientation	☐	☐	Technological literacy	☐	☐
Leadership and social influence	☐	☐	AI & big data	☐	☐

Now that you have identified your star and heart rating for each shortage attribute/skill, list your top three highest scores across both in the space below, together with an example showing this competency in action:

1.

2.

3.

Now, look at your lowest scores. Do you need to take any steps to develop these to future-proof your career? If so, make a note of what you need to work on and how you plan to improve it in the space below.

What is your most significant light bulb moment now about the skills and attributes you have already and need to develop so you can future proof your career?

* * * *

CONSOLIDATING YOUR LEARNING FROM THIS CHAPTER:

"WHAT ARE MY STRENGTHS, TALENTS, AND SKILLS? WHERE ARE THEY BEST SERVED AND MOST WANTED?"

Now that you have explored your strengths, talents, and skills in a changing economy, it's time to capture what you have learned in your INSPiRED Career and Life planner. Add the significant keywords you identified in this chapter into the Strengths, Talents, and Skills box highlighted in the diagram which follows, using the planner at the front of this book.

You may not be able to fully answer the second question about where your strengths, talents, and skills are best served and most wanted yet – that's normal, and the following two chapters will enable you to answer this fully. Just keep the question in mind as you read on.

Once you have added the keywords to your planner at the front of the book, remember to use your second copy at the end of the book to record a sentence in answer to the question for this chapter:

"What are my strengths, talents, and skills? Where are they best served and most wanted?"

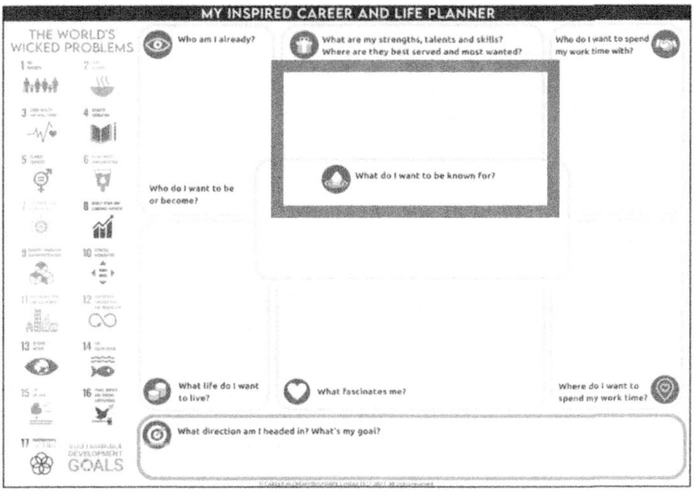

Remember, you can download a digital copy of the planner tool from here: www.careeralchemy.co.uk/free-reader-planner-tool.html

* * * *

PASSION, CURIOSITY, & INTERESTS

4. PASSION, CURIOSITY, & INTERESTS: WHAT FASCINATES ME?

FOLLOW WHAT ATTRACTS YOU TO DISCOVER YOUR BLISS AND FLOW

Those who find happiness and success do so because their passion ignites their lives and illuminates their way.

A rebellious child full of energy and curiosity, Julia grew up in the heady years of Thatcher's Britain in the 80s near Camberley in Surrey. Part of the commuter belt of the southeast of England and close to the Royal Military Academy, Sandhurst, the town nestles in the heathland and pine woods that form part of Surrey Heath. Like many at that time, Julia had ambitions to become a hot-shot businessperson and also felt a pull in a different direction. Julia explains, "I grew up in the period of saving the whale, and I think those campaigns really hit me. I actually did some work experience when I was a teenager for the Worldwide Fund for Nature as it was then. I was interested in conservation and the environment, even though I was a Thatcher child."

At that point, the pull to develop a business career proved to be the stronger of the two themes, and she set off for Hull, as far as she could get from Camberley, and studied for a degree in Management Science. It was a very mathematical degree focussing on operations analysis, though she still felt a tussle between management science and conservation. She explained, "It came to a head when I was at university, and I thought, this is really important. I think that we were just on the verge of banning whaling… So, I had heightened awareness of these sorts of issues at the time".

By the time it came to graduating in 1991, Britain had hit a deep recession, and like many graduates, Julia found herself unemployed as no one was recruiting in the sector she had trained for. As Julia puts it, "It wasn't until later years that I thought my degree could actually have been really useful in terms of environmental protection because it's all about using resources effectively. A lot of the maths could have been used to really help companies use less energy, for example."

Characteristically, instead of allowing the experience of not being able to get a job to knock her confidence, she saw this as her chance to use her time productively to develop skills within the conservation sector, even if she wasn't getting paid for it. As she explains, "I had already decided by then that I wanted to work in the environmental sector. I wanted to do something to save the planet; at least, that is how I would have thought about it then. So, I went and volunteered full-time for a charity called The British Trust for Conservation Volunteers, now known as The Conservation Volunteers, as a means to learn skills." This approach would become the strategy for growth that she would use later in her career to help her develop and change direction.

Spending her time helping out at the British Trust for Conservation Volunteers proved a wise step. Julia explains why, "I loved it. I love actually doing the work that they were helping people to do. I love planting trees and building drystone walls. I've built thousands of stone steps all across North Yorkshire, and I really enjoy the fact that I've left a bit of a legacy with all of that, and then I could help other people to do the same thing in their local conservation volunteering groups." She enjoyed volunteering with them so much that she ended up taking a series of paid jobs working for them. Initially, she managed the local group's programme and then went on to run the Natural Breaks conservation working holiday programme. In her own words, "It was completely inspiring working for a charity that was doing such good work, but they also treated their staff pretty well. We had a lot of training. I had good managers. I really enjoyed it". Having been there for some seven years, Julia realised as she explains: "It was a very flat organisation, and I got to the point where there was nowhere else for me to go. I reported to one of the directors, who reported to the chief executive. I wasn't going to be able to bridge that gap, so I had to go somewhere else and do something else or remain static." Not one to let the moss grow under her feet, she chose to leave.

* * * *

What came next was intended to help her gain experience from the wider world. She explains, "I knew that I was working in a sector where a lot of other people had worked for a long time, and I thought it would be really helpful to go out into the wider world, out into the business world or the finance world, and bring some skills back into environmental management later on in my career. So, I thought that banking would be a great place to do that. I applied for jobs in accountancy and banking, actually, the sort of accountancy that's business consulting, and chose banking."

She reset her career clock and joined HSBC as a graduate trainee en route to becoming a business bank manager. Julia explains, "To be a manager in HSBC at the time, you had to have a degree in financial services, so they paid for me to do the degree. They also gave us some extra time off to do it, so within two years, I got a degree in financial services, which enabled me to be a manager in the bank." For many, managing a job alongside a degree is not easy, but Julia's love of learning meant that she enjoyed it. She explains how she balanced work and study, "I was pretty dedicated to doing it and self-disciplined. So, I set myself a number of hours each evening that I would work on the banking exams for however many days a week it was and how many hours I would work at the weekend. And that's what I did, full stop. I wanted to get it done. I wanted to learn, I wanted to progress in the bank still at that point, and I loved it. I love learning, so it suited me fine."

Another five years followed working in the bank, where she could continue learning, but ironically, there was a fly in the proverbial ointment. As Julia explains, "I found that I didn't get on very well with banking. I felt like I was a square peg in a round hole. It just didn't suit me as a career. I just knew fundamentally that this isn't where I wanted to be and where I wanted to work." As often happens to people who feel restless in their careers, that disquiet is crystalised when a significant moment occurs. In Julia's case, it was during one of the bank's staff conferences in 2004 when she heard the guest speaker on the stage say, "If you don't wake up on Monday morning and think, yes, I get to go to work today, then you're in the wrong job." The impact on Julia was clear as she explains, "I sat there, and I thought, "Oh *my goodness. Monday mornings, my stomach sinks, you know, my heart sinks, and I really didn't want to go to work*". And I thought, *"He's absolutely right. I'm not doing the right thing."* So that was the real catalyst that made me move."

* * * *

What came next was an echo from her past. The influence of Julia's childhood once again came to the fore. She explains, "I'd always wanted to be self-employed. It had been on my bucket list since I was at school, I guess going back to the Thatcher years, and I thought, *"This is my opportunity."* but I was working for one of the biggest employers in the world and taking a step straight into self-employment I didn't feel was going to work, and I didn't know what I would do anyway. So, I had a look at franchise opportunities, and I found a franchise called Expense Reduction Analysts. As soon as I looked at that and started investigating, I thought, *"This is something I can do. This is something that I would be brilliant at."* And it was a really good choice. I made the move. I quickly earned a lot of money and did very well as an expense reduction analyst, helping businesses reduce their overhead costs."

By her admission, though she may have had some doubts about it, in October 2004, she set up her franchise and quickly found that the work was fun. It also helped her to develop the skills she thought would be useful to take back to environmental work later on. She saw the work as a way of taking some of the fat out of contracts and, therefore, a useful function for society to improve things. Owning her own franchise taught her something valuable. Julia explains, "The big thing I learned was that I could be successful. When I was in banking, as I say, square peg, round hole, I didn't ever really feel like I got on like I wanted to. And stepping out into the franchise doing something that I was really good at, that I succeeded in, gave me a real confidence boost. And I loved being self-employed as well. I loved the freedom of self-employment." She put that freedom to good use.

Having always volunteered since her childhood when she used to organise fêtes to raise money for charities like Save the Children Fund, it was part of her nature. So, when she didn't have the time and space to volunteer while working at the bank, she missed it. Running her own franchise gave her back the freedom, time, and space to start volunteering again, and she joined Junior Chamber International. A global group for young active citizens, they create action and change locally for global impact. By her own admission, initially, she saw it as a good networking opportunity but soon realised that it was so much more and would once again help her to develop and grow. As Julia explains, "I loved JCI. It's a fabulous organisation, and it helps you to develop lots of skills outside of the workplace. Although I'd done some training in the bank, that's when I really started picking up my public speaking skills. I led teams, organized events, and helped other people to develop their skills and confidence as well. It's a fabulous organisation, and I was really proud to be a part of it." Eventually, Julia became President of the Leeds branch and took up a role centrally for a year as their Membership Director. She went on to become a Senator, their term for an outstanding senior leader and an honorary lifelong member.

While she was enjoying running her franchise, again at around the five year mark, she started to feel the need to move on and had her sights on moving back towards something more environment-related. She explains, "I started wanting to work on energy management and helping people reduce their costs by reducing their energy management because by this time, I was getting really concerned about climate change, and I thought it was time to weave myself back into the environmental world, and I thought I might be able to do it through the franchise. Working as a franchisee, you are pretty restricted in what you can and can't do, and I couldn't find a way to make it work the way I wanted it to work within the franchise. So, it was time for another change."

* * * *

As luck would have it, she met Mike, who was later to become her husband. Mike had worked in environmental management and sustainability for his entire career. Julia explains what happened next, "He started talking to me about energy efficiency and saving money for businesses by helping them reduce their energy consumption. And I thought this fitted really well with a cost management consultancy, but I couldn't quite fit it in with the franchise. It's the freedom again. A franchise gives you the freedom of self-employment but also restricts what you can do, understandably, because that's the model that they know works. And I couldn't quite fit the energy management idea into the franchise, but it seemed to fit really well with where I'd always wanted to go. It felt like the next step forward of going back to work in environmental protection and bringing in all of the skills that I'd learned in banking and in cost management consultancy and taking that into environmental consultancy. So that's when Mike and I went into business together into Quest For Future Solutions, and I started working as an environmental consultant." They set up Quest For Future Solutions in 2010, aptly named given Julia's own quest for something environmental up until that point, and as a focus for the journey she and Mike were now on together.

As Julia says, it may have taken her ten years, but she never took her eye off the ball. "I didn't know how I would get to it, and then I was given the opportunity. I didn't ever feel lost, in that I still felt like I was on the path back to where I wanted to go to. I just didn't know how I would make that step until the opportunity was there. But of course, I was looking for the opportunity as well."

Her enthusiasm about her new direction was palpable, "I had always had a plan, but the plan's detail was always a bit fuzzy. So, I always knew that I wanted to go back into environmental management, and I had this opportunity. Suddenly, it felt like everything fitted together, the skills that I developed in the bank helped me develop my cost management business, and those skills that I developed there would then help me also be a self-employed environmental consultant. And I was learning new skills, partly from Mike and partly from training courses to help me along the way as well, which fits with the lifelong learning idea too. It did feel a bit like coming home. It was what I'd intended to do, and I'd achieved it because I did get back into environmental protection work... I really enjoyed working with Mike. We always worked on different projects from each other within the business. I could benefit a lot from Mike's experience of working in the industry for however many decades he already had. And I could also bring in the skills I'd learned and, in fact, the confidence. I don't think I'd have been ready before then. I think I needed those years of being successful and good at something to then go into consultancy and feel like I could go into the meetings with the directors and what have you and be on a par with them and have the conversations that we needed to have. So, it was a journey that I needed to go on to get to the point I was at."

It's not every couple that can work together effectively, but clearly, Julia and Mike could. Julia explains why it worked well for them, "We could bounce ideas off each other and what have you without feeling like we were stepping on each other's toes or anything like that." At the same time, they realised that they needed to do some things apart as well. Julia takes up the story, "When we moved to Malvern, we did an awful lot of stuff together. We both agreed that it would be good for us to do some activities that weren't together. So, I joined the WI (Women's Institute) because he couldn't join it, and my activity had to be apart from him. There was something like eight WIs in Malvern at the time. It's a vibrant organisation and again, it is an organisation that I have loved being a part of... I'd only just joined this particular institute, and they said, "If we don't get a treasurer, we will have to close," so my hand went up in the air – "I can do that job." So, she joined the local WI Committee as well and went on to become an Engendering Change trainer for them. By this point, she had already taken the opportunity of being in a new place of getting involved with the Royal Society of Arts, the global network of changemakers whose aim is to enable people, places, and the planet to flourish in harmony. Although she had been a Fellow for some time, her involvement had been on a more limited basis. She became the Worcester Network Co-ordinator, organising meetings and bringing in speakers from the local membership. She also became a Fellowship Counsellor and represented fellows on the National Board.

Julia explains why she enjoys volunteering so much, "It's helped me to develop my networks more generally. When you move into a place, if you start volunteering, you can very quickly become friendly with a lot of people, and that's where you then start becoming friends with people… I've met a lot of people who have similar values to me and have a lot of fun. And so very quickly, I've made some friends in the area. I love that. I love that sense of belonging. It's not just a helper's high. I like being a part of something as well."

While continuing to juggle business and volunteering activities, Julia also kept learning to develop the consultancy activities, gaining a suite of qualifications and certifications between 2012 and 2017. These included becoming an approved trainer for the Institute of Environmental Management and Assessment, of which she was a member. She became an assessor for ISO 14001 environmental management systems, followed by ISO 50001 and ISO 9001, so she could help organisations improve their quality standards, conserve resources, including energy, and improve the bottom line. In 2017, she became a Chartered Environmentalist through the Society for the Environment.

Apart from running her own consultancy with Mike, she also spent time volunteering on the committee of the Malvern Community Forest group, working on marketing and membership. Her ability to spot an opportunity and act on it based on her "what's the worst that could happen" philosophy was to take her in a new direction. Julia takes up the story, "Mike and I bought a woodland. It was something when we first met, we both said that we'd both always wanted to own and I was a member of the Small

Woodland Owners Group on Facebook, and they said something about looking for people to write in the magazine. I've always enjoyed writing, so I said to them, "Look, I've just bought a woodland. I can write a column for you in your magazine. Why don't you take me on as a writer, and I can talk to people about the experience of owning a woodland." I really enjoyed doing the writing, and I wrote a few other bits and pieces for Transform, which is the journal for members of the Institute for Environmental Management and Assessment, and a few other bits and pieces, but I didn't have time to give it the attention that I wanted to."

She had got to a point in her environmental consultancy work where she had helped lots of businesses to improve their environmental performance, but she wasn't doing the work on the ground. Feeling that this was a missing piece she needed to address, and despite some concerns about going back into employment and its restrictions, she decided it was time to find a job. Julia applied successfully and took up a job as an environmental manager role in a construction firm. By Julia's own admission, it was not a match made in heaven, as she explains: "I should have known better. I'd spent the last 14 years talking about how I could ever have been employed and that self-employment really suited me well. And then I went back to people watching the hours that I worked, having personal development reviews, having all of the restrictions of working for a big company. Commuting! I had a daily commute into Birmingham. It took me about three hours a day out of my time getting to and from work". Clearly, this new challenge wasn't working for her.

* * * *

Sometimes, when we find ourselves in the wrong place, life has a funny way of serving up blessings disguised as disasters, and this is exactly what happened in Julia's case just as she was hitting the start of her 50s. She had a health scare. She had developed a cough, which took several months to diagnose. Meanwhile, she continued with the routine of 'eat, commute, work, commute, and sleep'. Finally, during an appointment with a consultant, whooping cough was diagnosed. Julia was unconcerned by this as she was told that the disease has no long-term implications. However, she did discover something more troubling. Julia explains, "At the consultation, I found out that what I've always thought of as small lungs was some sort of restricted pulmonary function that I have. And I said to the consultant: "Well, I'll just carry on the same as I always have with this, presumably, and it's not going to have any impact. And he said: *"Well, as you get older, you'll be susceptible to respiratory disease,"* and the world changed in an instant when he said that."

Ever one to look for the opportunity in a situation, Julia turned her thoughts to how to create a positive future. She realised that there were so many things she wanted to do with her life. One realisation was particularly important to her as she explains, "Spending half my life travelling in and out of Birmingham on a train to a job that I was struggling with was not how I wanted to spend my life. I thought to myself, *"If as I got older, I was more likely to have respiratory difficulties, I can be employed again then, if I want to be"*. It was time to make a big change in my life." So, she began writing a list of the jobs she could do next and reflected on what really mattered to her, what she could pick up easily and enjoy. She concluded as she explains, "About sixth on the list was 'adventurer'. And I just could not get past the word adventurer. I thought, *"That's what I want to do. This is the time to do something completely different. And it would give me an opportunity to write and develop my public speaking as well."* So that's what I did. I stayed in employment for another three or four months, and then moved on into a world of adventure."

Her choice of the role of adventurer had been in her head unconsciously for a while. Julia explains more, "There were various things that happened that built up to this moment. I had a friend who walked the Camino two or three years before. She went off walking for five weeks. I'd never known anybody who'd go for a five-week-long walk before. Certainly not a woman on their own. And I just thought that was amazing. And then I met somebody at work who'd cycled around the Baltic. I was thinking, hold on a second. I want to do these things. And I think it just built, and I saw more and more of these things that other people were doing and thought, *"I want more of that in my life."* Her health scare had reminded her of something she had concluded in her thirties, when her mum had sadly died, which she had forgotten in the general business of life. Life is short, and we need to live it to the full. Julia shared more about that experience, "Mum died six months before she was due to retire. So, I promised myself then that I would not wait until retirement to go out and have some fun because I didn't know that I was going to reach retirement. By that point, I was in my fifties. My mum died when she was 59. I could see those years ticking by and, and 59 getting closer and closer, and I just thought, *"I can do these things now. I'm fit and healthy. If I want to go on long walks or long bike rides or do adventurous things, I can do it now. In 10 years', time, I might not be here, or I might not be fit and healthy enough to be able to do it, so therefore, I should get moving now, and if I need to go back to work afterwards, or sit in an office, then I can do that then. Now I want to be out and about."* So, at the age of 50, she decided it was time to head in a different direction and lead a more adventurous life, which she could use to help others.

* * * *

In choosing to develop a writing and speaking career, she had her own personal fear to overcome, as she explained, "The biggest mountain to climb when it comes to writing a book is thinking that somebody might actually want to read it. Having that degree of confidence in yourself is something I think every writer suffers from sometimes. Having said that, I want to be out there doing adventurous things. I'm also an author. I spend an awful lot of time at my desk writing. And you just have those moments of thinking, *"Why am I doing this? Nobody's going to want to read it anyway. I'm not going to be able to help anybody."* I found over the years that confidence ebbs and flows, and you have to keep building it up to keep it at a high level. I think, as an author, that's one of the biggest mountains that any of us have to climb."

As Michael Heppell, best-selling Sunday Times author and motivational speaker, always says, "It's not the book you read that will change your life; it's the book you write," and that was certainly true in Julia's case. She set about writing her first book called *'The 'Me' in Menopause'*, which she self-published and describes as being more like a booklet. It provided an excellent learning opportunity and taught her the fundamentals of how to write and publish a book. Spurred on by the questions she had been asking about the life she wanted to live, she went on to write and publish what she considers to be her first successful book, *'Live Your Bucket List: simple steps to ignite your dreams, face your fears and lead an extraordinary life, starting today'*. As someone who loves a challenge and now had the renewed energy and time to devote to it, she set a three-month deadline to get it out, aided by the support of an accountability buddy to help her cope with the ups and downs as a writer. She did one other thing to make sure she got the book over the line, as she explains, "I went public ...for me, it works really well. If I've told people I'm going to do something, it will happen. So, I went public, and I told the world that I was writing a book. I went onto Facebook and LinkedIn and what have you, sent the message far and wide, and told people when I thought it would be published. I said I'd have it published by the end of June 2021. And it was published on the 21st of June 2021."

Publishing this book helped Julia in several ways as she explains, "First of all I'm selling copies of the book, so I am confident that I am helping people improve their lives because they're buying the book and hopefully, they're taking the advice that I give in that book and, changing things in their lives. It has been the basis of speaking arrangements with companies. So, they've seen that I've got a book, and they're very happy to have me come and speak to their staff." There was another benefit that Julia identified, which has stood her in really good stead as she outlines, "I think one of the biggest things it's done for me is show mainstream publishers that I can write and that I do have that self-discipline to pull everything together to a time scale and make a book happen. I don't need to do most of that if I'm working with them but knowing that they've got somebody who can pull something together, I think, gives them some confidence that I'll understand their processes as I'm going through them. They have editors working on a book, and I'll understand that that needs to be done and that I will have the discipline to get the manuscript to them by deadlines and what have you." Julia's interpretation of using her ability to self-publish to demonstrate she was a safe choice as an author from a conventional publisher's experience was correct. She was offered and took some mainstream publishing book deals, and since her first book, she has gone on to publish four more, with more on her bucket list. Her books are aimed at encouraging people, and particularly women in their 50s like her, to create a bit more excitement in their lives by walking or adventuring more widely. This reflects her ultimate concern and passion for the environment and sustainability, which runs through each of her publications.

So far, her books include her adventures walking the Malvern Hills and the Southwest Coast Path and cycling along King Alfred's Way. Her biggest adventure and challenge so far was walking the Camino de Santiago, which she has done twice, a bucket list item triggered by her friend's experience earlier. Julia explains what happened, "I walked four weeks' worth of the French route, which is the most popular route of the Camino de Santiago in June and July last year, 2022, and then I walked the last week of the Portuguese route into Santiago with my husband at Christmas. They were both completely different experiences. It felt to me when I got back after the initial four weeks like it wasn't quite over yet. And when Mike said to me: "Why don't we do a week together in the run-up to Christmas?" I just thought, *"Oh, yes"*. And at the end of that Camino, I felt a sense of closure that I hadn't felt at the end of the summer. I learned an incredible amount about myself, and I found it really helpful. It was a real confidence boost as well, the walk in the summer and then the walk before Christmas. My husband and I have always had a 10-year plan since we met each other, and it needed a bit of updating, so we spent our week redoing our 10-year plan. In contrast, the first Camino was more that I wanted to see how a pilgrimage might be different from any other long distance walk that I'd done. And I just walked with an open heart to see what happened, and something magic happened that month."

The pilgrimage had a significant and positive impact on herself and on her confidence, "It can get knocked. You don't just gain your confidence and keep it forever. When I went on this walk, there's something called the Iron Cross, the Cruz de Ferro. Some people walk towards it for four weeks before they get there... and people carry a stone with them when they're walking that represents the burden that they're going to leave at the Iron Cross. As I walked, I thought about what my burden was going to be. I carried it, but I didn't really know what it was. So, I had this stone with me, and I thought, *"I don't know what it is I need to leave."* And it was only the morning of walking up to the Iron Cross that I realised, I thought I might want to release the grief for my mother, for my mother dying young. And I got to the Iron Cross, and I thought, *"No, I don't want to release that. I want to hold that with me, keep that with me, but carry it lightly. I don't want to carry it as a burden. I want to carry it lightly with me, but I don't want to lose the grief."* And so, I looked down at my stone, and I thought, *"Well, what is this? If it's not grief for my mother, what is it that I'm leaving behind?"* And as I walked up to the cross, I realised what it was. It's that thought as a writer, *"Is anybody really going to want to read what I've written?"* It's that fear that all you are doing is wasting your time, and it's not going to help anybody or appeal to them. And so that's the thing that I left behind. And it doesn't work instantly. You don't just leave the stone behind and then think, *"Yay, I'm brilliant,"* for the rest of your life. I know it doesn't work like that. The rest of the Camino helped to build that. The people that I met, the people that I spent time with, the whole experience of it really helped me to build that confidence in myself as somebody who can help other people and do so through my writing."

* * * *

At the very heart of what motivates Julia's work is her unremitting passion for the environment. This ultimate concern was triggered by the Save the Whale campaign, which captured her curiosity in her childhood, and quickly became her guiding theme. It provides her with a lens to help her navigate her way through work and life. Placing the environment in all its senses at the heart of who she is and what she does provides Julia with the motivation to keep learning and growing and led her to discover the transformative power, joy, and connecting with others which comes from volunteering.

Sometimes, when we have a strong passion and become so embroiled in it and day-to-day life that we can lose sight of our individual passage through life. The early passing of Julia's mother provided Julia with an early reminder of how precious life is, which slowly became lost in the everyday noise of her 30s and 40s, until one day she had a wake-up call. Julia's own health challenge led her to re-evaluate what really matters to her and to realise that for her, life is an adventure to be lived fully every day rather than to be lost commuting to a work environment that simply didn't suit her. That challenge took her back full circle to her conservation days of dry-stone walling, building steps and planting trees in a different way. She found a way to turn her love of being outdoors and walking along country and coastal walks into knowledgeable and entertaining speeches and books to help guide others to live their own adventures hand in hand with the environment more fully.

When we are called to change direction for whatever reason, we are forced to choose to stretch and grow - or to settle and shrink. For Julia, settling was never an option, even though the decision to become a writer and speaker did test her self-belief and confidence. Once again, it was the power of nature and the environment walking the Camino Way that helped her to choose to back herself and her own adventures no matter what, to leave her fear behind and to continue following her passion and curiosity as an author, adventurer, speaker, and environmentalist.

We all need to find a way to make sense of our working lives based on who we are and be at peace with that. If we can identify what calls to us as our guiding theme, what researchers call our ultimate concern, and then have the courage and wisdom to listen to our inner voice regardless of what others may think, we can create our own adventure and discover the joy of doing work we love.

If you haven't already found your guiding theme, the exercises which follow will help you to do so or at least begin the journey with a glimmer to follow.

* * * *

A QUESTION OF PASSION, CURIOSITY, AND INTERESTS:
WHAT FASCINATES ME?

As we saw in Julia's case, passion is not just what she does, it's who she is and what causes her to adventure through life. She found her passion by being open and responding to what she encountered around her, whether the landscape itself or what she heard early on. While some people doubt the value of having a passion at the heart of your career, there is plenty of research which shows that having a passion is good for our happiness, success, and well-being, too.

You may already have found a glimmer of something you could be passionate about or what that is for you. Either way, completing these activities will help you understand what you want to centre your working life around as your ultimate concern. If you do so, it will make it so much easier for you to navigate your way through the complex and fast-moving world of work we are all living through and dealing with today.

* * * *

ACTIVITY 1: UNDERSTANDING PASSION AND WHAT LIGHTS UP YOUR HEART

So, what is passion? Dr Robert J Vallerand of the University of Quebec defines it as "a strong inclination toward a self-defining activity that people like (or even love), find important, and in which they invest time and energy regularly". His research identifies two types of passion: obsessive and harmonious. Whereas obsessive passion comes from a controlled internalisation and eventually goes on to control an individual, "harmonious passion" reflects an autonomous internalisation of the activity and becomes a central and defining part of who we are. As his research shows, having a harmonious passion also plays a critical role in sustainable psychological well-being. Quite simply, having a central passion for our work and lives is good for us. Julia's story, where her love of the environment and writing has turned her into an author, illustrates this perfectly.

If you think about the people, you know who are truly happy and successful, they are highly likely to have a specific passion. That passion is intrinsically rewarding and fuels their happiness and success at the heart of their lives. If you consider other famous heroes and sheroes for a moment, they too will have a passion that they have developed through hard work and determination, and which inspires their actions. So, who are your heroes and sheroes? The chances are that what attracts you to them is a shared passion for the same guiding theme. Time spent looking into the stories behind the people featured will reveal the passion which fuels them and may well provide a glimmer of your embryonic passion, too.

So, passion matters. It is often what we would do whether we get paid or not. It's the fuel which ignites careers and lives, and it's what makes organisations and the people who work in them successful and happy, too. As Gallup said in its "Where the Great Jobs Are" report, "When the hearts and minds of employees are engaged, they give more to their jobs." According to Gallup, there are three types of employees in every workplace. For ease, let's use the terms 'stars', 'sleepwalkers' and 'saboteurs'. We all know who the stars are. They are the handful of people who go the extra mile because they are intellectually engaged and care. In the UK, currently, only around one in every ten people at work are stars. Then there are the sleepwalkers, who represent just over two-thirds of people who are intellectually engaged and go through the motions every day but without feeling connected to what they do emotionally. Finally, there are the saboteurs – the one person in five who has become actively disengaged intellectually and emotionally. As a group, they were probably stars who were treated badly, so they have become disaffected and potentially disruptive, too. When intellectual and emotional connection is missing, so is success and motivation. So, the question is, how do you become a star? How do you create that deep emotional and intellectual connection with work? The answer is by finding your passion and wrapping the right skills, knowledge, and experience around it so you can't help but both love and excel at what you do.

Passion is part of something wider, too, according to Professor Angela Duckworth of the University of Pennsylvania. She describes grit as "passion and perseverance for long-term goals." Her research recognises that grit is a persistent commitment to a meaningful goal that surpasses talent or luck. Grit embodies perseverance even in the face of challenges, setbacks, or slow progress. Grit consists of six elements, of which passion is one. The other five are hope, effort, precision, passion, ritual, and prioritisation, some of which will emerge as themes later in this book. According to Duckworth, grit, together with self-control, form the two key indicators of achievement.

As Julia's story illustrates, grit and passion combined with self-control enabled her to acquire the skills and knowledge needed so she could achieve her long-held ambition to become an environmentalist and now a best-selling author. Finding her passion has led her to create a working life that gives her happiness and success.

Searching for what lights up your heart

The following exercise is designed to help you identify your ultimate concern or passion. As you approach the exercise, remember that the job for life has gone. We now live in a very different time and space, so careers can be built successfully with pretty much any passion at their heart. Rather than censoring your thoughts by looking in your rear-view mirror at what careers were like in decades gone by, keep an open mind and listen to your inner voice. It is wise for reasons which will become apparent later on. Think carefully about each idea that occurs to you and consider whether it could or could not become your work passion before you discard it; after all, you never know where it might lead!

So, what are you passionate about?

Make a list of everything you do that you are passionate about in the space below. Once you have done that, identify beside each one how it connects with your personality, values, and significant experiences from chapters one and two, as well as the character strengths, smarts, and skills you identified in chapter three. You may find it helpful to look back at the keywords on your draft INSPiRED Career and Life Planner to help with this. Doing this will help you understand at a deeper level why you care about a particular passion and where its roots lie. You may see the influence of your sheroes and heroes here, too. Your next step is to identify the top three ideas you have the most passion for as a result of this review. If you find this hard and have more than three, rating each option from 1 to 10, where 1 is low and 10 is high, will help you rank them.

1.

2.

3.

Once you are clear about your top three, consider how you could build a career around each of them. Don't discount an idea just because you can't currently see how to make a career from it but do discount it if it doesn't feel right to you. Trust your instincts!

Use the space below to record your ideas here:

1.

2.

3.

It's time to reflect on what insights you have had about what you are passionate about and make a note of that here.

* * * *

ACTIVITY 2: STIMULATING CURIOSITY

If you have yet to identify a strong passion, don't despair, it may be that you simply have not come across it yet. That's where curiosity comes in. Julia did not instantly develop a passion for the environment. Rather, the Save the Whale caught her interest, and her curiosity served as a compass, ultimately leading her to turn what captured her imagination into her passion. This took a commitment to learning. As research shows, once we become curious about something, it keeps us learning and learning effectively by triggering the release of dopamine in the midbrain, which enhances our memory by forming new neural connections. Curiosity has also been linked to helping us to stretch and develop skills. It develops people into open-minded employees who are more likely to be engaged and motivated in their work because of experiencing enhanced meaningfulness. Curiosity helps to develop what Carol Dweck and colleagues coined a growth mindset, the premise of which is based on the belief that a person's capacities and talents can be improved over time. As other research shows, curiosity is also a catalyst for personal action, aids interpersonal action and leadership, and brings organisational benefits, too. No wonder Julia continued to stretch and grow, given her inquisitive nature, openness to exploring new ideas and learning from others, creative problem solving and tolerance of change. Clearly, like passion, curiosity is also good for you too.

Finding your sweet spot

One of the byproducts of curiosity is reaching a state of what the American psychologist Mihaly Csikszentmihalyi called "*flow*", which he describes as "a state of heightened focus and immersion in activities such as art, play and work". That happens when, by following your passion and energy, work becomes play as you discover the joy of being lost in the moment. Csikszentmihalyi's work indicates that we need eight elements to experience flow: having clear goals every step of the way, getting direct, having a balance between skills and level of challenge so it is not so easy you get bored, and not so challenging it tips you into anxiety; having immediate feedback to actions; concentrating deeply on the task in hand so much so that you are not aware of distractions; being completely involved in the present moment so that the activity becomes an end in itself; having a strong sense control and free from any worry about failing; experiencing an altered sense of time so that it either evaporates or the clock seems to stands still; and finally, having no sense of self and ego, so we are no longer self-conscious. If you think about moments when you have been in flow, this may help you to discover curiosity is at the heart of it.

So, what are you curious about?

As we have explored, curiosity leads to insights and develops into career passions. In this activity, simply find up to five things you would like to learn more about. To help you, think about times when you have been in flow. What were you doing, and why did you become totally absorbed in it? Did curiosity feature in that activity? If your mind has gone blank, think about different areas of life that may interest you, including health, finance, travel, education, hobbies like art, music, dance, drama etc, volunteering, the law, politics, property and environment, computers, machines, food, animals, transport, etc. Use the space below to make a note of them.

1.

2.

3.

4.

5.

Once you have identified five things, make a note of what sparked your interest in it beside each one. Now, ask yourself which of these five you have the highest level of curiosity for, then use the space below to identify how you can build a career around it.

If you can't identify how your passion or curiosity connects with a career, use a search engine to help you find a list of careers related to that topic and research individual roles from there.

Now you have finished this section, what is your biggest light bulb moment about curiosity?

* * * *

Understanding what's needed in the future

When you are considering a change of direction, it is wise to do a little horizon scanning to understand how changes in the world of work are affecting roles and what is likely to be needed in the future. The information in this section uses both what's called Labour Market Information and Labour Market Intelligence. The former uses data, graphs, and statistics to describe the state of the labour market, both past and present, and to make future projects. Labour market intelligence is an adaptation or interpretation of labour market information. Developing your ability to use both types of LMI will help you make wise choices. It will help you understand employment trends, the structure of the labour market, how it works, and the supply and demand levels. It will also give you insight into labour market equality and diversity issues.

As the WEF Future of Jobs 2023 report indicates, up to a quarter of jobs today will change. If you are considering a career change, the last thing you want to do is to choose a career that is contracting. There is a clear demand for green jobs as the quest for achieving Net Zero and the challenges of global warming grow. The International Labour Organisation (ILO) defines green jobs as "decent jobs that contribute to preserve or restore the environment, be they in traditional sectors such as manufacturing and construction, or in new, emerging green sectors such as renewable energy and energy efficiency. Green jobs help improve energy and raw materials efficiency, limit greenhouse gas emissions, minimise waste and pollution, protect and restore ecosystems, and support adaptation to the effects of climate change."

There are three clear areas where jobs are likely to grow. Technology is obviously one of these, and there is likely to be continued growth and demand for those with specialist skills in technologies such as cloud computing, encryption and cyber security, big data analytics, artificial intelligence (including large language models, neural networks, machine learning, and natural language processing), the internet of things and connected devices, text, image and voice processing, e-commerce and digital trade, augmented and virtual reality. Blockchain, robots including drones and other types of industrial automation are gathering pace. We are also seeing AI being used extensively to automate and augment jobs.

Looking to the future, the second area of opportunity lies in areas of work where human skills are imperative. People still like to deal with people, so despite witnessing a significant shift toward the era of human-machine co-working, people-related skills are highly valued. Growth areas include people and product development, project management, sales, content development, and marketing. People are also needed in education and any guidance, counselling, and therapy work, for instance, where human qualities like empathy are particularly important. When you are looking at roles, look to see how easily they can be automated as not every role can be – there has been a national shortage of roof thatchers, for instance, for years.

The third area which always relies on people is the foundational or everyday economy. This relates to "the services, production, consumption, and social goods that sustain our daily lives". It covers sectors like retail, health, transport, trades, education, council/local government, and the other services we access daily. The everyday economy includes the care sector. As populations age, so does the demand for care. According to the United Nations World Social Report 2023, "the number of people aged 65 years or older worldwide is projected to more than double, rising from 761 million in 2021 to 1.6 billion in 2050. The number of people aged 80 years or older is growing even faster. Population ageing is an irreversible global trend. It is the inevitable result of the demographic transition – the trend towards longer lives and smaller families – that is taking place even in countries with relatively youthful populations. In 2021, 1 in 10 people worldwide were aged 65 or above. In 2050, this age group is projected to account for 1 in 6 people globally." As Age UK highlighted in its The State of Health and Care of Older People, 2023 Report, the number of vacant adult social care sector posts in England alone increased by 52% in a single year – from 110,000 in 2020/21 to 165,000 in 2021/22 with a vacancy rate of 10.7%.

Clearly, in this context, there is a need for human support, which can't be replaced by technology and is only set to grow based on current statistics.

ACTIVITY 3: SHORTLISTING ROLES OF INTEREST

Now that you have read more about how the world of work is changing, the final activity in this chapter is designed to help you create a short list of roles to explore further. If you completed the first two activities in this section, you will already have a list of things you are passionate or curious about and will want to explore roles which link to these. Now it is time to review those and any other ideas which have occurred to you so you can start to identify your future direction.

So, what interests you?

Use the space below to create a shortlist of up to five roles and/or sectors you would like to learn more about. You can always add new ideas to this list as they occur through the course of using this book.

1.

2.

3.

4.

5.

Now, write down beside each one the name of someone you know who you could speak with to find out more. Talking to people can give you a first-hand perspective of what they do in their role, though remember that this is their perspective, which may not be the same as others who do similar work, depending on whether they are a star, sleepwalker, or saboteur currently. Make sure if you do speak to others that, you explain that this is confidential so that you don't risk your current role in any way unless it is already at risk for some reason.

Researching to find out more

You will find a list of links to help you research individual roles and sectors at the back of this book. The careers-related websites outline sectors, roles, and subject-related opportunities. As you will see when you explore individual role descriptions, they usually also contain links to other similar roles. Using these links to read around related roles will help you to contextualise the opportunity and explore other related options. One of the links in the back of the book will help you explore further LMI information so you can compare salaries, demand, and the rate of churn between individual roles that interest you. You may find that the role you are interested in connects with a professional body like Julia's work as an environmentalist does, so make sure you also look at the professional body/association(s) for the sectors and occupations which interest you. Doing so will help you to gain an in-depth understanding of that area, including the latest news and research, investigate what training they may offer, and sometimes explore their job boards, too if they have one. You may choose to be self-employed like Julia is, and there are links to help you find out more about that, too.

What is your biggest light bulb moment about what's needed in the future and how your passion, curiosity and interests connect with these opportunities?

* * * *

CONSOLIDATING YOUR LEARNING FROM THIS CHAPTER TO ANSWER THE QUESTION:

WHAT FASCINATES ME?

The activities in this chapter have been designed to develop and refine your ideas about alternative careers to the ones you are currently in. There is no need to worry if you still have a small or empty list of roles/sectors you want to move forward. In the next chapter, we will be taking a different approach to the question of career choice and using a problem-solving-based lens using the United Nations Sustainable Development Goals. Meanwhile, it's time to capture what you have learned about what fascinates you in your INSPiRED Career and Life planner. Take the major keywords you have identified in this chapter and add them to the Passion, Curiosity and Interests box highlighted in the diagram below, using the planner at the front of this book.

Then, use the second copy of the planner at the back of the book to record a sentence in answer to the question for this chapter:

"What fascinates me?"

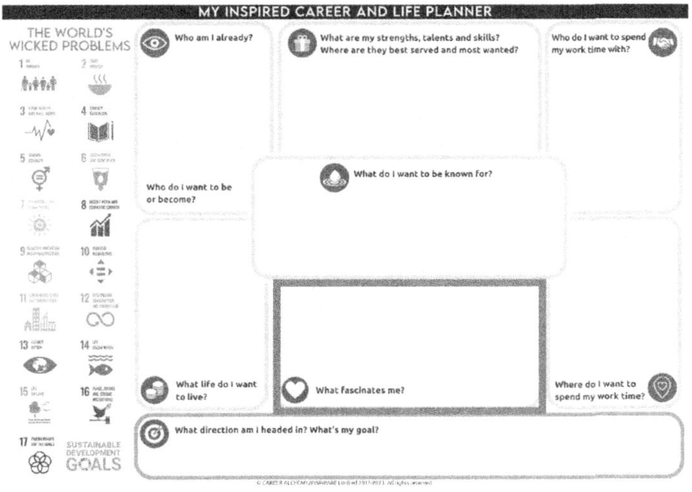

Remember you can download a digital copy of the planner tool from here: www.careeralchemy.co.uk/free-reader-planner-tool.html

* * * *

PART TWO:

DEVELOPING YOUR STORY

IMPACT, CONTRIBUTION, & PURPOSE

5. IMPACT, CONTRIBUTION, & PURPOSE: WHAT DO I WANT TO BE KNOWN FOR?

FINDING AND PUTTING MEANING TO WORK

When you find and connect your reason to your unique abilities, the path will open before you - keep walking, and opportunity will come your way.

Originally from Manchester and now in her late fifties, Cathy Presland is as warm a human being as you could meet. An only child, she was raised in Manchester by parents who grew up in relatively poor circumstances. Inevitably, their values become an essential part of the fabric of Cathy's life. Unlike most people, as Cathy puts it, "I know it's easy to look back… but to me, it looks really clear that there's like kind of thread around equality and justice and economic inequality. My mum was not an activist, but a very strong advocate for social justice and feminism in a way ahead of her generation. And at her funeral, one of my friends said to me, *"Oh, your mum was way ahead of her time. She was a kind of a woman ahead of the generation that she lived in.*" And I'd never really thought about it like that. But I think that was pretty much through everything I've done - that sense of knowing there's something fairer and a little better in the world."

Although that sense of the importance of equality was always there, it initially sat in the background when it came to making her choice as to what direction she wanted her working life to go in. Cathy grew up with a poodle she adored, so she wanted to become a vet and studied Physics, Chemistry, and Biology for A Level. Her hard work paid off, and she headed off to begin her studies at the Royal (Dick) Veterinary School, part of Edinburgh University. Sometimes, things don't work out for a reason. She found the first year a real challenge and realised the reality of too much memorisation and not enough thinking in her first year did not suit her at all. So, she changed direction and transferred to a geography degree instead. Here, once again, family influences played their part, this time due to her father's interests. It was from him that she caught her love of travelling. He had served as a soldier in the war in various places and, at one point, had been keen to emigrate, but Cathy's mother was not convinced, so they stayed in the UK. Unsurprisingly, Cathy loved her geography studies and particularly enjoyed studying the USA, thanks to an inspiring and engaging lecturer. It was also during this course that Cathy studied gender-related topics in an academic setting for the first time, an echo back to the childhood values she had learned from her mother. It was at Edinburgh that she had an early opportunity to develop her leadership skills as she was elected as President of the Students Association. It provided her with an early experience of listening to issues and challenging and negotiating solutions that made a difference for those who needed a voice and change to happen. It was also an opening into 'politics', which would become a recurring theme for her.

At the end of her first degree, she went on to complete a postgraduate certificate in economics at Birkbeck College in London and, from there, went back up north. Her destination was Glasgow so that she could continue her master's studies, this time signing up for a Master of Philosophy in Economics. A mix of economics and politics, looking at the macro picture, Cathy was a very able student and graduated at the top of her class, winning class, and year prizes. Inevitably, she needed to choose as she came towards the end of her studies what she would do next. Her choice was to give her more than just a career move.

* * * *

Cathy tells the story, "I studied gender wage equality in developing countries. And so, from that, I was looking for an overseas posting as that was the logical place to go." It was in the early days of microfinance when the Grameen Bank in Bangladesh had been pioneering a model for low-income women, although not totally new given the history of co-operatives in Britain and elsewhere. She took a post to set up a microfinance organisation for women in Swaziland against the advice of her lecturer, as she explains, "When I took that post, I was coming out of the MPhil, and one of my lectures advised me against it. He wanted me to join the World Bank. He said, "No, you shouldn't take this. You should wait for something better", but we take what's in front of us, and we make the choices that we make. It's not something that I ever think: *"Should I have waited? Would I have done something different?"* I don't think there's a right or wrong answer to that. I think we're on the path that we're on. So, that led me to Swaziland."

To Cathy, it felt right and reflected her authentic self and the values she had absorbed from her mum. She also felt another emotion, as she explains: "I was excited by the fact that it was a relatively innovative prospect. It was gender-focused... so there was that aspect to it. I don't think I felt like, *"Oh, I have to wait for a certain kind of organisation to come along"*. I wouldn't say that I had a really strong feeling it was right. But it was almost like I didn't question it. It just felt like a less conscious choice." In making that choice, Cathy saw a way of helping women create better futures through the power of micro-finance, which would enable those who did not have the legal status or financial collateral to access funds independent of their husband's funds. This would enable them to trade their way to a better life. Still in existence today, the Imbita Swaziland Women's Finance Trust is a non-profit organisation that supplies micro-finance services, business training, and support to low-income entrepreneurs, particularly women and youth. Its mission centres on promoting economic empowerment and alleviating poverty.

As well as setting up the trust with Swazi women throughout the next two and a half years or so, Cathy also held several volunteer and advisory positions in the region, including supporting the Swazi delegation in advance of the UN Conference on Women in Beijing. As well as gaining experience in the region and the topic, Cathy also went through some personal changes, as she gained a husband and then went on to have her first child whilst there.

Her next long contract overseas was to be in Namibia for NEPRU (Namibian Economic Policy Research Unit Project), a Namibian Government initiative, for whom she worked as a Senior Policy Adviser. She acted as an adviser to the World Bank-funded five-year 'Poverty Project', leading a range of donor-supported projects funded by the likes of the IMF (International Monetary Fund and the UK Department for International Development as well as the World Bank). These governmental projects included water pricing, international trade negotiations, and the UN's Human Development Index (HDI). The HDI was set up in the UN's own words to "emphasise that people and their capabilities should be the ultimate criteria for assessing the development of a country, not economic growth alone." The index measures average achievements in three key dimensions: a long and healthy life, being knowledgeable, and having a decent standard of living.

A little over three years after they first headed out to Namibia in 1995, Cathy and her family returned to the UK to take on a new role as her contract had ended. She recalls feeling a little uncertain at the end of both contracts but had a sense that things would be OK. Cathy outline why, "I've felt pretty much a trust in that it hasn't occurred to me that there isn't going to be something, and maybe it's a kind of innocent trust. And again, you're looking back, like that feels true. And I know it's a question that people ask me, "Oh, well, what if this doesn't work?" I have that sense that even if there are rocky phases, there will always be something else." As one of her line managers was to recognise and comment on later on, Cathy is not worried about having a stable job or 'career plan', and, after adapting to a change of lifestyle, the next opportunity appeared and gave her a renewed sense of purpose. This theme would come to the fore again later.

* * * *

Cathy joined the British Council in the UK as an International Development Projects Director, a role she was to stay in for another three years until 2001. She recalled what it was like as a job at the start, having previously been working in a micro fund and in a policy research position in a quasi-think tank. “I remember feeling in the British Council that the nature of the job felt as if it came with a lot of administrative work. And I felt a bit lost and not playing to my strengths. It wasn't the policy content that I relished. And so, I did go through a phase of being pretty unhappy in that job, finding my feet. *“What is this for me? What is the nature of it?”*. I don't know if I asked myself if I made a wrong decision, but for sure, at that point, it looked like I had, *“This is not really what I thought it was, and I'm not sure it's what I want to be doing at this point.”*

She realised something important, “I like to engage my brain in a thinking process. Not that that can't apply to anything, but just my particular flavour of it felt during those years, for sure, that I needed a bit of a “why” that made sense to me that I needed to be in touch with, whether it's the equality strand that we've talked about or antipoverty. So, I felt I needed to see some dots being joined in terms of what I was doing.” She saw that you could do more to effect change as part of a big organisation with more resources and the benefit of specialists in certain areas. She also realised that she valued engaging with colleagues. “I like working as part of a team. I've always absolutely loved managing staff. I mean, so many people say how much they hate it, but I loved having a team. I loved having people around me, projects, different people contributing their different pieces... I love that sense of being alive in a moment with another person. I think it's everything.” Despite her misgivings, the work she had been doing to support institutional reform in the pre-accession countries in Eastern Europe meant she was incredibly well-placed for and suited to another twist of fate.

* * * *

What came next was to lead Cathy to another role in which her spirit of adventure would place her right at the heart of another new and emerging nation once again, this time in the context of devolution. Cathy picks up the story, "My husband had a job with the government in the Northwest of England, and we were back in Manchester. And then, the office that he worked for was going to close, and he was given the choice of either going to Newport in South Wales or going to London. So, we had just had our second child by then, and we didn't know what to do. We were weighing up options, and although we didn't want to go to London, I had looked at jobs just in case. I had applied for and been offered a job with DTI, as it was then, the Department of Trade and Industry as a grade seven policy analyst. Based on that, we thought we were London-bound and then decided, *"Do you know what, this is crazy with two young children and, you know, my work is relatively well paid, but it's not super well paid. Do we want that lifestyle?"* So, we decided to take a leap of faith and moved to Newport in South Wales. And so, I approached the Government Economics Service office there and said, "Have you got any jobs?" And they said, "Well, you know, you'll have to apply." And then I met with somebody, and it turned out because I had already got a job offer with DTI, even though I never actually started with them, they could transfer me straight into the Welsh Assembly Government. So, it was a complete set of coincidences and fortune. It's funny how that happens. And you know, again, it's often not on us to necessarily know how these things will happen. So, we'd thought we were going in one direction. We decided, "You know what, we're going to go in another direction." And that sense of just turning up and saying, "This is who I am; this is what I've got. Have you got any suggestions or ideas for me?" And then the actual transfer, in that case, was something that just arose. It didn't even occur to me that it would be something relevant, but these things happen."

Cathy spent the next decade or so working right at the heart of the Welsh government in Wales's infancy as a devolved nation, where she could use everything she had learned from her earlier experience. She found herself working alongside the first ever First Minister for Wales, the universally celebrated Rhodri Morgan, who made such a massive impact on the country of Wales and politics, with a vision to open and level up opportunities for all at a stage when that term didn't exist. Cathy explained what it was like to be in the middle of history in the making, "It was really exciting, and I really enjoyed the enthusiasm and the excitement that came from that very, very early de-evolution. I think the politicians definitely contributed to that. It was, "*How can we make this work? How can we be as professional as we possibly can? How can we serve the people of Wales?*" and I think, the spirit of intellectual excitement as well. You know, "*We're not just here to implement a political agenda. We want to look at what we can do, which is evidence-based, which makes sense.*"

Cathy's love of adventure and trailblazing, what some might call her entrepreneurial spirit, meant she was in her element. She had found a blend between the importance of home and the importance of internationalism, working with Ministers on economic strategy and large funding programmes. She also formed key relationships at home and in Europe as Wales formed alliances with the other devolved administrations in Scotland and Northern Ireland and secured EU funding. By 2010, however, as the new devolved nation of Wales became more established, she began asking herself a question: "I loved my job, and I know people leave and become self-employed because they don't like what they're doing or there is a personal reason or whatever. They reach a moment when they are questioning what they're doing. I had a slightly different question to ask myself. I wondered, "*What else is there that I could do? I could do this for the rest of my career, but do I want to, or do I want to try some other things and see what else is out there?*" After spending over 20 years as a development economist and policy advisor to governments and international organisations across the globe at the highest level, her spirit of adventure would lead her in another purposeful direction.

* * * *

Cathy remembers vividly when she left the stable employment of the Welsh Government. She had been feeling her early love for being in the moment with another person that made her feel so alive, increasingly tugging at her for a while. She had done an executive coaching qualification as part of a leadership development programme, so eventually, she took a leap of faith and set up her own coaching business, running a programme she called *'World-Changers Circle'* that took five action-takers on a 6-month transformation journey. Her coaching work centred on helping leaders gain clarity, perspective, and a much greater sense of who they are. Unsurprisingly, many of her clients came from international development and the public sector. Wanting to add another string to her bow and motivated by a desire to help people who felt they had an idea they wanted to share with the world, she wrote a book called *Write! Stop Waiting, Start Writing. A Step-by-step Guide to Turn What You Know into a Book*. It became an international bestseller. She began offering online courses and mentoring to entrepreneurs and professionals who wanted to reach more people, raise their credibility, or spread their message. At one point, she had 22,000 students on her courses and, in 2014, was running a series of writing masterclasses for the Guardian newspaper. As Cathy says herself, she found self-employment "a crazy ride! At this point, I'm really glad I did it. For a while, I wasn't a hundred per cent sure... And it felt like it was missing something. I didn't know what it was. Now, years on, I wonder if sometimes those slightly less grounded or slightly rockier phases are just par for the course, and we take avenues, and we learn something, and we bring it back."

That sense of something being missing led Cathy to double down her focus on coaching. She continued to invest in courses that would enable her to deepen the coaching experience and magic of being in the moment with another person for her clients. She explains, "I feel as if there are a few of us who are in this world of really trying to understand what it is about, the human individual, the human species, what it is that makes that work... I don't think that we give enough credit that we do have self-awareness. Too often, we look for external solutions when what we need to know is already inside us... We know when we're overthinking, we know when we're not thinking enough analytically. And I think, again, particularly in sort of Western European mode of thinking, not geographically, but conceptually, that we're taught that the intuitive sense, which I think is like a preconscious...we're trained into thinking somehow that's a lesser way of thinking. And so, we trip ourselves up with attachment to our models and our evidence and not realising that we make those all up anyway." Cathy is clear that those bigger questions like, "What's it all for anyway?" and "What are we doing here?" when asked in a positive sense, are critical to helping us "elevate out of the hamster wheel".

In 2015, Cathy decided to elevate by taking on another activity alongside her coaching work. For nearly five years, she co-led the London Impact Circle, a small group of impact investors and professionals working in international development, finance, and consultancy. The Circle's aim was twofold: to provide an opportunity for deep and honest conversation to develop a more thoughtful and considered way of engaging in the impact space over the long term and to facilitate small investments. In the summer of 2018, she became a Fellow of the RSA (the Royal Society for Arts, Manufactures, and Commerce). She started volunteering as the Co-Lead for the RSA's coaching network, facilitating in-person and online events with other Fellows interested in coaching as a social contribution.

Although Cathy has no definitive answer to why she is here from a metaphysical sense, she does have some sense of what informs her why. She explains, "Part of me thinks we're all just here to live; we're all here to engage with life. I've thought about it a lot in a metaphysical sense, but also in the sense of "How can I make the most positive contribution given where I am in my career, life experience, all of those things?" And at the same time, I think the most useful thing I feel like I can offer, in a work sense and other senses as well…is shining that light and waking someone up to that sense of awareness of how they are thinking, how they are living, how they are sleepwalking almost, or walking through the world in a maze of thinking, to help people get that perspective on who they are."

For Cathy, "There is this sense of something that is conceptually so much bigger than me, that I can't possibly conceive of what it is, let alone even try to understand it with all of my very clever intellectual systems thinking… and just to accept that I don't know. I can't possibly know enough about all of the pieces and how they interrelate. And so, therefore, it makes sense to me to go forward with some sense of trust in the unknown." This is something Cathy has done all her working life. She has a sense of when she is in a space, being open to the synchronicity of an opportunity and the trust to walk forward and into it.

Cathy is clear about what matters, "Foundationally, what I see in people is an incredible ability for rebalancing and finding their way. I've had my phases. That is part of the nature of being human. And if we can somehow amplify that and turn down the doubts and the worries... and if we can shine the spotlight on that power and capacity that we've got, I think great things are possible or just a happy life...we spend a lot of hours in work. We spend a lot of mental space thinking about the hours we spend at work. And I think it's a really valuable reflection for people to go through and to do what they really want to be doing with this wild and precious life."

* * * *

It seems almost inevitable that Cathy would become a changemaker and focus on work that made a difference, even if that was not always clear. Her childhood experiences gave her a real sense of why equality from a justice and economic perspective matters so much based on her parents' experiences. Too often, we are tempted to look for external solutions to challenges we are experiencing when what we need to know is already inside us. What some may have interpreted as a blow when her original career plan of becoming a vet did not work out became the first of several occasions when Cathy was able to lean into her own sense of authenticity and calling, so she could hear her inner voice, trust herself and make choices that meant she could make a difference that was meaningful to her. Learning to trust that quiet inner voice is key. In Cathy's case, it meant that her early decision to redirect to study geography matched her spirit of adventure and desire to think and question. Perhaps more importantly, it also meant she would eventually marry her intellectual training as an economist with her undoubted passion and heart for improving gender equality and reducing poverty. In doing so, she created her own unique set of ultimate concerns upon which she would centre her career - the twenty years she devoted to working as a changemaker, combined with her unfailing belief in the power of working with people who all share the same common purpose, led her from supporting changes on the ground to working at the very heart of governments in young countries around the world, from the African continent to mainland Europe and the UK home nations.

Often, when we look back at a distance, we can join the dots and see the invisible threads that are woven together over time to create the tapestry of our own unique and meaningful working life. Sometimes, these threads come from early formative career experiences, which go on to become our ultimate concerns. Set against the backdrop of her mother's values, Cathy's time in Swaziland helped her to see firsthand the importance of empowering women to take their courage and destiny into their own hands and trade their way out of poverty. Empowering people who worked to effect social and political change became a founding thread through Cathy's work, which ultimately led to her working as a leadership coach with others working in similar spaces.

In a world full of change, the wise often look for opportunities to be right at the heart of something that is just beginning. Cathy's story shows time and time again her spirit of adventure in action, whether helping Swazi women, working with and in emerging governments with politicians and funders to create change through policies, teaching other changemakers and entrepreneurs to become authors in the early days of self-publishing, or working in the sacred and privileged space as a coach working with leadership clients who also want to change things for the better. The changes we create through working with and through others who share our same ultimate concerns to improve things for the better become our legacy.

* * * *

A QUESTION OF IMPACT, CONTRIBUTION, & PURPOSE: WHAT DO I WANT TO BE KNOWN FOR?

What is clear from Cathy's story is that she can create something a little more human in this world by helping people feel empowered. While she could have done this in any context, she did so through the lens of her two inextricably linked ultimate concerns, improving gender equality, and alleviating poverty, often working with others who shared those same concerns in government and policy-related contexts. Doing so has given her a clear sense of purpose for her work, enabling her to identify need, contribute where needed and see the difference that contribution has made both on the ground and through the implementation of policies. Ultimately, her ultimate concerns around equality, empowerment and the planet led Cathy to opportunities she was uniquely able to help with through her natural ability to empower others.

If you have not yet found your ultimate concern in earlier chapters, the activities which follow will help you to take a different approach from looking at careers in a sector and roles-based perspective. If we want to find work that is meaningful and fulfilling, focussing on which problem(s) we want to solve provides a different lens through which to make that choice. Focussing on contributing to solving the biggest and most complex problems the world is facing creates the ultimate thread for our careers – and one which has longevity for reasons which will become clear as you explore this chapter further.

* * * *

ACTIVITY 1: FINDING YOUR REASON

There is good reason to have a reason. As PwC's Global Workforce Hopes and Fears Survey 2022 showed, meaning and fulfilment-related themes form three of the top four most principal factors when considering a change in the work environment. Many of us have experienced the pain of golden handcuffs where the salary is good, but the work slowly but surely erodes our souls. That's why, as the economy focuses increasingly on skills, having a clear sense of why you do what you do becomes all the more important to help you make sense of your career and its purpose beyond generating income. Knowing why you wake up in the morning is also good for your well-being, and being clear about your why can add up to seven years to your life, as researchers studying Blue Zones, where people with the highest life expectancy have found. Having a powerful sense of purpose is the reason many who retire early have come back to the workforce, and it is also good for your career. It keeps us feel connected, engaged, and healthy. So, whichever generation you belong to, whether Gen Z, a Millennial, or a Baby Boomer, purpose matters. Purpose also shows up in career success. Earlier we looked at the concept of being a star, sleepwalker, or saboteur at work and how those who were stars cared emotionally and intellectually. Purpose is what causes them to care and gives us a sense of intrinsic motivation, which is deeply satisfying. Organisations also care about purpose much more now since the dawn of stakeholder capitalism in a global economy which needs to work for progress, people, and planet, and rise of the ESG (Environment, Social and Governance) agenda in Boards all around the globe.

So, what is purpose?

Psychologists define purpose as "an abiding intention to achieve a long-term goal that is both personally meaningful and makes a positive mark on the world." It provides the backdrop to a journey and becomes a practice rather than a destination that is personal and specific to you. Purpose gives us a sense of significance, creates meaning and focus, leads us to feel in control, gives us hope, makes us happy and is part of our growth as human beings.

As Cathy found, with purpose comes a sense of feeling alive. Her twin ultimate concerns of gender equality and poverty are two of the world's 17 biggest challenges we have today, which is what we will explore next.

Introducing the United Nations Sustainable Development Goals

The UN SDGs are a set of 17 interconnected global goals that address the most pressing challenges facing our world today. Superseding the Millennium Development Goals, the SDGs were adopted by all 193 Member States of the United Nations in September 2015 as part of the 2030 Agenda for Sustainable Development.

The goals are the most complex or "wicked" problems we all face. A wicked problem is a term Rittel and Webber used in 1973 to describe problems that are social or cultural and are difficult or impossible to solve because of their complex and interconnected nature. These problems have strong ethical, moral, political, and professional dimensions, need consensus to reach stakeholder agreement and usually have no best solution, just a better or worse alternative.

So, which goals do you care about?

As is clear from her studies onwards, and for the first 20 years, the work that Cathy felt drawn towards focused on helping to reduce poverty (SDG 1) and improve gender equality for women (SDG 5). She worked to do that through policy and other support in emerging governments, which helped to build strong institutions (SDG 16) and empower people. As her career developed, she asked what else was there for her, her work related to helping others to grow and enjoy decent work and income as individuals (SDG 8), whether through her writing venture or coaching work. These ultimate concerns became the threads that helped her identify and feel a sense of meaning and purpose in her working life. As you read earlier, serving something bigger than ourselves creates a different perspective and is an important part of well-being, success, and fulfilment at work.

Here's an overview of each of the 17 SDGs and some of their main individual challenges we need to mitigate against, according to the United Nations:

- **Goal 1 - No Poverty**
  If we continue as we are, 575 million people around the globe will still be living in extreme poverty, and only one-third of countries will have halved their poverty levels by 2030.

- **Goal 2 – Zero Hunger**
  Unless we do something about it, more than 600 million people worldwide will face hunger in 2030.

- **Goal 3 – Good Health and Well-being**
  Although things are slowly getting better, one woman still dies every two minutes due to pregnancy and childbirth-related issues, and 381 million people (almost five per cent of the world's population) have been pushed into extreme poverty by health-related out-of-pocket expenses.

- **Goal 4 – Quality Education**
  By 2030, unless we do something, 84 million children will be out of education, 300 million students will lack basic numeracy and literacy skills, and only 1 in 6 countries will achieve universal secondary school completion targets.

- **Goal 5 – Gender Equality**
  At the current rate, it will take 300 years to end child marriage, 286 years to improve legal protection and remove discriminatory laws and 140 years for there to be equal representation in leadership in the workplace for women.

- **Goal 6 – Clean Water and Sanitation**
  As things stand, in 2022, 2.2 billion people didn't have safe access to clean drinking water and lacked basic hand-washing facilities. 3.5

billion had unsafe sanitation conditions, and four-fifths of inland wetlands species have declined since 1970.

- **Goal 7 – Affordable and Clean Energy**
Currently, 675 million people worldwide live in the dark, and if current trends continue, one in four people will still be using unsafe and inefficient cooking systems by 2030. Clean energy includes solar, wind, and hydropower, created by harnessing natural elements like sunlight, air currents, and water flow to generate electricity with minimal environmental impact.

- **Goal 8 – Decent Work and Economic Growth**
Globally, one in four young people are not in education, employment and training, and 2 billion workers are in precarious jobs with no formal social protection.

- **Goal 9 – Industry, Innovation, and Infrastructure**
Currently, only 53% of the world's population uses the Internet, and 16% have no access to mobile broadband networks; the least developed countries have an industry value added per capita of $100 compared to $4,500 in Europe and Northern America. Measured by research and development expenditure, innovation is below 1% of GDP in many developing nations and is also a key focus aimed at bridging the significant disparities in technological advancement. Globally, CO2 emissions reached a record high of 36.8 billion tonnes despite global manufacturing falling back due to inflation, energy price shocks, supply disruption and global economic deceleration.

- **Goal 10 – Reduced Inequalities**
In 2022, globally, 34.6 million people were refugees, including 14,186,000 children; women became twice as likely to report experiencing discrimination as men based on their sex, and between country-inequality worsened by 3.6 per cent, the largest change in over three decades and globally.

- **Goal 11 – Sustainable Cities and Communities**
  Globally, there are currently 1.1 billion people living in urban slums. If we don't act now, that will become 2 billion in the next 30 years. Only one in two urban residents have convenient access to public transport, and three in four cities dedicate less than 20% to public spaces and streets.

- **Goal 12 – Responsible Consumption and Production**
  Globally, each person wastes 120 kilogrammes of food every year. The use of fossil fuels has nearly doubled to $732 billion due to global crises, and high-income countries leave a 24 metric tonne material footprint per head, ten times that of low-income countries.

- **Goal 13 – Climate Action**
  The rate of sea level rise around the world has doubled in the last decade, and we are rapidly reaching what experts are calling climate calamity. If we carry on as we are, temperature rises will go up by more than 1.5°C by 2035 and 2.5°C by 2100.

- **Goal 14 – Life Below Water**
  Global warming is affecting coasts and seas alike. Ocean acidification is 30% higher than in pre-industrial times. Plastic pollution stood at 17 million metric tonnes and will increase by 2 – 3 times by 2040 unless we do something about it.

- **Goal 15 – Life on Land**
  Around 100 million hectares of healthy and productive land (that's twice the size of Greenland) were degraded between 2015 and 2019, forests are being lost, and we are facing the largest species extinction event since the dinosaur age.

- **Goal 16 – Peace, Justice, and Strong Institutions**
  Some 108.4 million people were forcibly displaced in 2022, up 2.5 times from a decade ago, and conflict-related deaths rose 50% due to the war in Ukraine. In 2021, 458,000 people, 90% of whom were male, were murdered intentionally, the highest figure in 20 years, and those

under 30 found it hard to gain representation, given an average age of 51 for members of parliaments around the world.

- **Goal 17 – Partnerships for the Goals**
  Goal 17 promotes global collaboration and partnerships between governments, the private sector, civil society, and individuals to achieve sustainable development by sharing knowledge, expertise, technology, and financial resources. At the end of 2022, 37 out of 69 of the world's poorest countries were in debt distress or at high risk. Net official development assistance (i.e., loans and grants) to promote economic development reached $206 billion, up 15.3% from 2021. Of the two-thirds of people who used the internet in 2022, this included 259 million more men than women.

As the statistics above show, there is plenty of opportunity to make a difference, given the level of change needed in each goal. The appendices at the back of ***Change Your Story*** will help you explore each of the 17 challenges further. They set out the current state of play globally, outline the key challenges which affect the goal and include suggested related career options.

Of course, some career roles are common to all of the goals as they are needed in most organisations, though there may not be an individual department for some of these in small businesses. These roles include leadership and management, human resources, finance, sales, marketing, PR, operations, IT, research and development, administration, estates/facilities management, and legal/contracts. Some of these may be outsourced to external suppliers. As you consider these, make sure you also consider the impact that AI-driven automation may have on the role, as outlined earlier.

If any of these roles appeal, choosing to work in an organisation related to one of the 17 SDGs will increase your sense of purpose and commitment as you will have a clear sense of how the value of what you do connects with the big picture of the difference that you want to make.

So, what stirs your emotions?

By this point, you may well have had a light bulb moment, helping you to be much clearer about the work that will light up your soul as you look to the future. If you still have some doubts or need some more inspiration, though it's worth having a look at the stories of people who are on the Forbes 30 Under 30 list. Created ten years ago and published annually since then, the Forbes list offers a rich collection of stories of young innovators across North America, Europe and Asia working on problems that matter to them. While some people seek to make a substantial difference, it's important to remember that we all create an impact during our careers, and it is up to us to decide how big we want that to be and what that means to us. After all, we all have different paths that are unique to us. As the saying goes, we can help change the world, or we can work to change the world for one person. Both contexts create impact, and it just depends on us and whether we need to see the impact of our work directly on one individual or if we are happy for that impact to be shown as part of a collection of big-picture statistics instead.

Now that you have explored all 17 goals and perhaps found inspiration in other people's stories, it's time to identify what stirs your emotions, just as Cathy found hers. So, what do you feel strongly enough about to want to commit to working with others to create a change? What matters to you most?

To find your own why/ultimate concerns, think about:

- ✓ your values (chapter 2)
- ✓ the things you are passionate or curious about (chapter 4)
- ✓ traditional job roles that are growing (chapter 4)
- ✓ the new and emerging tech-driven opportunities
- ✓ other people's stories you know about, and
- ✓ the SDGs that you have read about in this chapter.

Now, to find your why, like Cathy did, ask yourself: "What stirs your emotions?" To do this, identify your top five themes and list them in the space below. Now rank them from highest to lowest interest, based on what you believe in enough to want to take action and influence, improve or change. It may be that, like Cathy, you have also found a couple of themes which go together in tandem, and that's fine, too.

Use the space below to write down what your ultimate concern is:

Finally, think about the insights you have had about what stirs your emotions and make a note of that here.

* * * *

ACTIVITY 2: WHAT'S YOUR CAREER PURPOSE?

As we have seen, those who have become crystal clear about their why are more intrinsically motivated and tend to get better results. This happens because they can focus on what really matters and filter out distractions quickly and easily so they can use their energy and time more effectively. People who are on the path that is right for them often also notice that opportunities seem to come to them almost magically. This is often due to their brain's reticular activating system scanning for opportunities related to their prime concerns. Some would also say that it is because they are in the right time and place for opportunities to come to them through twists of fate and serendipity as Cathy experienced. Having a clear why is great, but alone, it is not enough - you need more than that to create a working life you love truly and that is meaningful. The missing piece comes from exploring what and how your purpose takes life through being able to weave the threads of your values-driven ultimate concerns with your talents and strengths so you can create your unique career tapestry, just as Cathy did.

So, what's your career purpose?

To help you combine what you have discovered before and to ensure that it is crystal clear, it is helpful to create a focused career purpose statement. This acts like a lens through which to make good career choices. It will help you to navigate change effectively and create a sense of control and well-being. To create your career purpose statement, use the space below to answer the first question:

What contribution/difference do you want to make, and to whom or what?

How specifically do you want to do that?

Finally, using your answer to these two questions, use the space below to write your career purpose statement:

Now you have finished this section, spend a few minutes reflecting on what is your biggest light bulb moment about your purpose and make a note of it here.

* * * *

ACTIVITY 3: CREATING YOUR FUTURE STORY

As always happens at funerals, when Cathy's mother sadly died, people talked about her legacy. They noted that she was ahead of her time in wanting to make things a little fairer and better in the world. We all leave some form of legacy, whether we think of life like that or not. If we do think in this way, it can encourage us to dare to dream and really make use of the lifespan and potential we have available to us. Thinking with the endpoint in mind can help us avoid settling for less than we are capable of - if we commit our energy and effort to something we care about.

So, what do you want your life to stand for?

The last activity in this chapter uses the power of creative writing and your imagination to test out and refine what it would be like to achieve your career purpose and to make changes to your vision before you commit. To do this activity, find a quiet place where you won't be disturbed. Now, imagine it is the last day of your working life and your favourite magazine or newspaper is running a story about the legacy of your working life to share with the next generation. What would the published article say? Get as descriptive as you want to be. Make sure you write a compelling headline for it at the end. If you prefer to use art, music, or poetry to do this, that's fine too, as long as it helps you to become clear and describe your ultimate story. Avoid any temptation to self-censor and allow yourself to dream while you do this. It will help you to connect with and lean into your inner voice and wishes like Cathy learned to do.

Now that you have written/painted, or used music to describe your legacy, spend a few minutes reflecting on what you have learned from this activity.

* * * *

CONSOLIDATING YOUR LEARNING FROM THIS CHAPTER TO ANSWER THE QUESTION:

WHAT DO I WANT TO BE KNOWN FOR?

In this chapter, we have taken a problem-solving lens to help you choose your direction by looking at the world's greatest needs. We have explored why purpose matters and how to connect it with your talents and strengths to create a working life you love that matters and one that leaves a legacy you care about. Now, it's time to capture what you have learned through these activities in your INSPiRED Career and Life planner. Take the major keywords you have identified in this chapter and add them to the Impact, Contribution, and Purpose box highlighted in the diagram below, using the planner at the front of this book.

Then, use the second copy of the planner at the back of this book to record a sentence in answer to the question for this chapter:

"What do I want to be known for?"

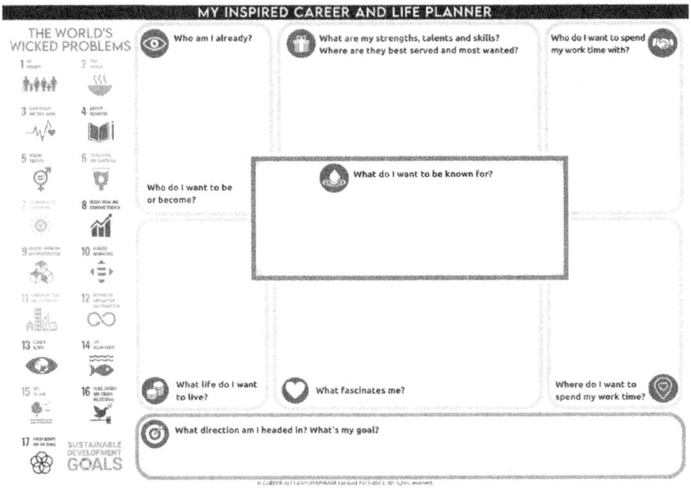

Remember, you can download a digital copy of the planner tool from here: www.careeralchemy.co.uk/free-reader-planner-tool.html

* * * *

RELATIONSHIPS

6. RELATIONSHIPS: WHO DO I WANT TO SPEND MY WORK TIME WITH?

FINDING, CONNECTING, AND GROWING WITH YOUR WORK FAMILY

When you find the right group of people to belong to, one where everyone shares the same passion and work together well, anything becomes possible.

Nestled around the harbour, the Georgian Nash-designed town of Aberaeron, with its colour-washed houses overlooking the magnificent mid-Welsh coastline of Cardigan Bay, provided an idyllic setting for Chris Jones's Welsh-speaking childhood. An only child, he spent his childhood days playing football and out on boats on fishing trips with other boys and girls, while his entrepreneurial, self-employed father ran the local Gwasg Aeron/Aeron Printers he had set up, and Chris' mother worked as a nursing sister, and later as Matron of the Aberaeron Community Village Hospital. Aberaeron was also where Chris went to school, found his love of English, and, above all, his passion for Geography. Chris explains what he was like at school, "I was a bit of a show-off and into acting and singing. And the eisteddfods[1] were big in school, obviously, and I did

1 *An eisteddfod* is a *festival with competitions for music, poetry, and other art forms. Thousands take place across Wales every year either as stand-alone events or as competitive rounds, which lead to qualifying and taking part in national eisteddfods.*

amateur dramatics, and I was always on stage. And people were always saying, "Oh yeah, Chris, he's going to be an actor. He's going to be in front of the camera." A young man with a big heart and no doubt influenced by his mother's career in nursing, he spent a couple of years volunteering as a presenter on Glangwili Hospital Radio in Carmarthen. Chris recalls the time with fondness, "I've always loved radio. It was a late-night show, and I'd just learned to drive. I remember the drive from Aberaeron out to Carmarthen, then doing this little radio show in Glangwili, and I thought it was brilliant." He took both English and Geography for A Level, along with Welsh, and headed off to university in Bangor, North Wales, where he studied media, no doubt encouraged by his hospital radio experience.

While Chris was at university, he realised what he wanted to do. "I was always interested in photography, even in school. I didn't do much in the first and second years, but in the third year, I buckled down. The third year was all about TV camera work basically, and I remember to this day, they introduced us to these cameras…huge, heavy, cumbersome things. I remember looking at it: *"Oh, okay, well, this is why I'm here. This is why I'm in university. This is what I'd like to do."* So, I used the cameras, got to know the techniques, and learned a lot about lighting and lenses and that kind of thing. It was a light bulb moment… a Eureka moment of: *"Right, this is what I want to do."*

When he graduated, Chris headed off to Cardiff, though he had never been there. He was full of confidence that he would land a job in the media quite quickly. Sometimes, things don't always go to plan, and it took Chris a good eighteen months to get his foot in the door, an experience he found soul-destroying. Finally, after months of cycling around the Bay in Cardiff, literally knocking on doors searching for media work, he got a break. He explained, "I got a job as a tea boy. It was for a sound production company called Echo Studios down in the docks, and it was fantastic because I got to know all kinds of people from every aspect of the media, and it was a great, great grounding and a great place to start. I wasn't just making tea, obviously, and it was a runner role as well, and you've heard the story of, "Go and get me a left-handed screwdriver." It was a bit like that being sent out to get all kinds of things. But I learned from the bottom up and got to know people, and I'm still in touch with some of the people I got to know back in 1987, 1988."

For the next 18 months at Echo Studios, he met people from all corners of the industry. As well as getting to grips with the industry he had dreamed of becoming part of, Chris's early experience in the industry shone a light on his natural ability to connect authentically with people as a genuine relationship builder. He got to know some of the most influential people in the broadcast industry in Wales at that time, including David Parry-Jones, Peter Walker, Patrick Hannon, and John Humphreys, who was the household face of the BBC's flagship Nine O'clock News for much of the 80s, the voice of BBC Radio 4's. Today programme for over 30 years and host of Mastermind for the best part of 20 years until 2021. One day, the four men made Chris an offer he couldn't refuse.

* * * *

Chris was invited to a meeting with David Parry-Jones, Peter Walker, and another Welsh broadcaster, Beti George. They had a question for Chris as he explains, "We're starting this new company. It's a bit different from the usual companies in Wales. It's a corporate company making corporate films and also TV documentaries. Would you like to join us?" I said, "Err, yes!" So, I got a job as an assistant cameraman. I can't stress enough how much it meant to me because that's what I wanted to do. When they offered me a job as an assistant cameraman and to learn the trade with them, I thought I was in heaven. It was absolutely wonderful. And I joined Merlin Television, first as an assistant cameraman and then cameraman, and after a while started directing and doing all kinds of things."

Chris's work was to take him all over the world over the next ten years and put him right at the heart of the action. As Chris explains, "One of the major contracts we had as a company was for the BBC and Grandstand. We used to follow the British Bobsleigh team around the world circuit. I was very lucky to travel the world following this amazing team along the world circuit, including Canada, every year." Being a follower on the circuit in the days before health and safety became such a focus, Chris had some of his own experiences of bobsleighing as the team used to let him and others have a go on their bobsleigh, too. It was in 1988 that the Winter Olympics went to Calgary. That was the year when Eddie 'the Eagle' Edward hit the headlines, competing for the first time, representing Great Britain for the first time in the ski jump. Chris witnessed another first at the Games that year when the now-famous Jamaican bobsleigh team competed for the first time, a story later captured in the film Cool Runnings. While filming the British bobsleigh team in St Moritz in 1991, Chris had an idea that would change his career dramatically.

* * * *

Forever a passionate Welshman with Wales at heart, Chris's thoughts turned to S4C, the Welsh Language TV channel, as he was filming on the slopes one day, Known as S4C. Sianel Pedwar Cymru ('Channel Four Wales') had been broadcasting since November 1982 as the first television channel explicitly aimed at a Welsh-speaking audience and was just under ten years old when Chris was filming in Saint Moritz. He had already met a few of the staff there as Merlin had been producing documentaries for them in both Welsh and English. He picks up the story, "I thought there's some great footage here for S4C, so I remember phoning someone I knew and said: "Oh, hi, it's Chris. I'm in Saint Moritz, Switzerland. There are some fantastic scenes here. Would you like me to film something and put it down the line so you can do something with it?" And they said: "Oh, yeah, that sounds like a great idea, but why don't you do something in front of the camera as an intro?" I said, "Well, I can't do that; I'm a cameraman!" "Well, just try it." I said, "Well, oh, okay." So, it was a matter of pressing the record button on the camera, running around the other side of the camera, and saying something, I don't even remember what it was, and running back again, pressing stop, then sending it down the line." That phone call was to mark the start of Chris's presenting career.

Two weeks after he got home from Switzerland, the head of presentation at S4C called Chris and invited him to come and discuss an opportunity they had in mind for him. Chris explains what they asked him when they met, “They said, "Well, we've got an opening for a presenter." And I thought, *“Oh, okay”*. "In the weather team. Do you know much about the weather?” I remember blagging, "Yeah, yeah. I'm quite interested in the weather." And not that I was at all, and I had no thoughts about going in front of the camera, but I did geography at A Level, part of which was all about meteorology. So, it came back to me.” As a result of that conversation and being able to say yes to the opportunity, even when he didn’t know what was needed, Chris was invited to join the weather presenting team of S4C. It marked the start of what was to be a 29-year career as the Welsh-speaking face of the weather in households around Wales. Having already gained extensive knowledge working behind the camera, Chris started studying for his new role and took the exams needed to become a qualified presenter in meteorology. Throughout, he remained clear about his identity as a weather presenter rather than an expert in meteorology.

Chris explains what it was like in the early days before computers, “It was quite old-fashioned. It was a magnetic map with little icons being stuck on the map and then falling off. And then it changed; everything became computerised.” For the first five years or so after he began presenting the weather, Chris also continued to work for Merlin as a cameraman, blending employment and self-employment, which was quite unusual at the time. Chris explains, “Yeah, that was quite unusual at the time because I was working for Merlin obviously as a staff member, and they didn't have to say yes, but when I went to them and said: "Listen, I've been offered this job. it won't impair anything I do for you.” It was mostly weekends and bank holidays anyway, the weather presenting, to begin with, so they said, "Yeah, absolutely no problem whatsoever".

Looking back, Chris recognised how lucky he was to have such understanding bosses and mentors, as he says, “They could see that it was something I wanted to do. And it was good for them as well to have a little bit of a connection with the broadcaster as well. So, I was working for Merlin plus being self-employed with S4C. That pressure was not sustainable, and the writing was on the wall. The sheer volume of work and travel began to take its toll. Chris explains, "In 1996, it became a bit too much, and I was never home because we were always out filming, obviously, and I was always missing birthdays and Christmases, and anniversaries. And then, as a result, my first marriage broke down. I'd become a father of two beautiful little girls by then. And I was missing a lot. I thought, *"Oh God, this is silly."* So, I just said, "Right, it's time." With that, Chris decided to go totally freelance.

* * * *

It was a scary time he would never forget by his admission. "I remember going to one of my bosses and saying, "Right, I've decided to, uh, to go freelance." And they were very, very supportive. They even actually gave me a guarantee of a certain amount of work for the next six months just to get me going, as it were." That scary moment marked the start of Chris following in his father's footsteps. Chris explains where his motivation came from, "I think that's where the entrepreneur spirit, the influence of my father came in, because obviously, he was an entrepreneur and a business owner himself, and I've had that entrepreneurial spirit, but it was somewhere there in the back of my head, even before then. So, it was a scary move, a big move, but the best move. I've always liked being in charge of my destiny." There is still one element that he struggles with even today after over 25 years of being self-employed. Chris explains, "I still can't accept even now, after all these years that when the work's not there, it's okay. It's okay that the money's not coming in because things will improve; they always do. I still get a massive lack of confidence and scary moments, but it was the best thing I did. And I couldn't work for anyone else anymore. By now, I only work with nice people. I don't want to work with idiots anymore. I've done that, and I like the fact that it's quite freeing in every way, and when the work is there, don't get me wrong, it can be wonderful, lucrative, it can be fantastic. When the work is not there, obviously, it can be quite scary. But I love that I can dip my toe into so many things. I have a so-called portfolio career, a finger in every pie. I never had that at the beginning, and I love that I can try; I might fail, but try again, and then try another thing and try another thing. Like many who run their own business, Chris has learned that things don't always work out. He picks up the story, "My wife and I had a cleaning company many years ago when my youngest daughter was tiny, purely because. somebody asked us: "Do you know a cleaner? I'm desperate for a cleaner. I said: "No, I don't know a cleaner." And then I remember asking my wife: "Why don't we start a cleaning company?" And she said, "Okay". So, we started a cleaning company, but it failed. We ran it for four or five years, but we couldn't get the staff. And that's another story. But then we started something else. So, it's all a method of being scared but not too scared that you were afraid to try, you know, and you can't be afraid of failing." As Chris found, if you look for it, failure always contains the gift of learning something that you didn't know before that helps you move forward better equipped for the future.

As anyone who has started a business knows, work-life balance can be difficult, particularly in the early days. Chris explains the challenges, "That's a tough one. I think there's a lot in me and a lot of freelancers and self-employed that you can't say no. And it's not so much now, but in the early days, I said yes to everything. And I soon realised that "Okay, if you're going to freelance, you can't do that. You've got to be a little bit ruthless with yourself and say, *"Right, unless you say no, nothing will change. Again, you'll never be home, you'll never have a successful relationship, and you'll never spend time with your kids, blah, blah, blah."* So, it took a while, but over time, as you get to know people and get to know the kind of thing you like to do, you learn to say no, or you learn to say, *"Right, not this time,"* and you learn to spend time with the family, with the kids, with your parents. It's hard. It is hard, but I think it's essential that you do so. Being freelance could be even worse than being employed by somebody you don't respect. So, it can be not easy, but I'm 58, and I've been doing this for so many years. I can say, *"Right, I don't want to do that anymore"*. Then there's a part of me saying, *"Well, okay, I've got to do it because I've got to pay the mortgage and bills like everybody else. And there's always that financial worry on your shoulders thing, right? If I don't do this, I won't be able to do this. And if I don't take that on, I won't be able to do that*". So, it's just, it's a constant battle." I asked Chris, whose voice belonged to the parrot pecking away at him. After a moment, he realised, named the parrot, and told me whose voice it was, "That's my father saying all the time: *"Why aren't you doing this?"* Because of his background, because he worked, you know, literally every hour God sent, because of running the business and starting the business from nothing. That's my father saying, *"Right, okay, well, you know how much you get paid for that and what are you going to do next and how are you going pay for this? And, you know, if you don't work, if you don't do this..."*. So, there's always Eric the parrot on my shoulder."

One of the ways Chris mitigates against failure is to spread the risk across several activities, as he explains, "I've usually got about, 4, 5, or 6 different things going on, and I love the fact that it's not just one thing. And I think that's quite important to someone like me because I need to be kept interested, and I need to have that spirit of trying if you like." His visibility as the S4C Welsh weatherman has meant that opportunities have come his way, as he recounts, "It gave me all kinds of opportunities. I presented everything from gardening programmes to fashion programmes. And then, as you get a little bit of a profile, and you get more well-known, you get invited to all kinds of things, and you get the chance to take part in quiz shows and panel shows. And then I did a bit of radio on Radio Wales, Radio Cymru. And then, I was asked to contribute to a few magazines. And they love that it's Chris Jones, the Welsh Weatherman. There seems to be a fascination with weather presenters. I'm very conscious of sounding a bit pompous that being Chris Jones the Weatherman was my life. It gave me so much, not only financially. As a profile, it gave me all kinds of opportunities to get to know people. I did interviews with Anthony Hopkins and Michael Sheen and Sian Lloyd and everyone really, purely because I was the weatherman."

Chris's work from behind the camera as a freelancer filming and directing programmes for children, gardeners, corporate videos, and sponsorship footage inevitably helped him understand what was needed when it came to presenting. It also meant that he was uniquely placed for some opportunities where his love of the media, using a camera, presenting and geography all came together. Chris tells the story, "I was invited to go walking and filming simultaneously and being paid to do it. It was incredible. So, I went to China. I went to Chile, did the Appalachian Trail, Mont Blanc in Europe, and all over Wales to present programmes about these certain charities, one of which was Velindre. It's a cancer charity, which is quite big by now. And they asked me to go to Chile first of all, and then Mont Blanc. I was filming promotional material for them as well." As the saying goes, what comes round goes round. As Chris explains, "Several years after, I did a fundraising walk in Peru for Velindre because my father-in-law had passed away with cancer, and he'd had treatment in Velindre as a lot of people do in this part of the world. That was an amazing experience as well, going to Peru to raise money for the charity that my father-in-law had benefited from, but I was still Chris Jones the Weatherman doing that, but filming as well." Chris's love of walking remained a theme that he would come back to again later on. Meanwhile, his love of presenting was to take another turn as an opportunity came up, which would remind him of his time on hospital radio in his youth at school.

* * * *

By 2016, Chris's profile had grown such that he was asked to join Swansea Sounds, the longest-running commercial radio station broadcasting across Wales and possibly the UK at that time. Chris picks up the tale, "I was asked to come on board, and I'd never done proper radio as it were, but I was given a few days of training. I thought I would press some buttons and present, and somebody else would do the leg work. But no, it was all down to me. So, it was all self-run and self-operated. So, I had a three-hour weekly show on Swansea Sounds, and they gave me carte blanche to do anything I wanted. I played any music I wanted, I loved playing new tracks, and then I had people in as guests. And then we started recording guests, and I used my list of contacts. I had well-known people. I had politicians, I had ministers, and all kinds of things. I loved every second of Swansea Sounds. It was between seven and 10 in the evening on Tuesday night, and it was a bit of a dead show before I came. And then because of the kinds of things I brought in and made it a bit informal, if you like, and brought these well-known people along, the listing figures rocketed. That was fantastic - and I loved it."

Around the same time as Chris had started hosting his show on Swansea Sounds, he got involved in another project, as he explains, "I came to know someone who had a string of shops, selling Welsh gifts and a bit of everything. So, we said, "Well, why don't we come up with a range of products and gifts with a weather theme with your logo on it." So, we came up with a logo, and then we started with weather-related mugs. We had umbrellas, aprons, tea towels, posters, and welcome mats. They went really, really well." His success with this project led him to explore another weather-related opportunity. "I came to know a company called Corgi Hosiery. Now Corgi is a very, very well-known company in the sock world if you like. And would you believe the CEO's name was Chris Jones! We met each other at some event, and we found out we had the same name. And he said, " Err, do you fancy coming on board and doing a range of socks? We're always looking for novelty, you know, fun socks." I said, "Yeah, okay, great." I came up with a few drawings on paper for five different kinds of weather to go on socks for men and ladies. There was sun and rain, snow, thunderstorms, and rainbow. I gave them to their designer, who came up with these amazing-looking designs on socks, and they were called the Welsh Weatherman Range. They still sell, not only on their website, on my website, but in shops all over the country." His socks have sold far and wide, including in South Africa, all around Wales and the rest of the UK, and Ireland. They have even been sold to famous people and politicians, including Justin Trudeau, the Canadian Prime Minister. From Chris's perspective, all was going well – until suddenly, it wasn't, and life threw him a giant curve ball.

* * * *

In 2018, Chris had been out celebrating his birthday in Aberaeron. "I remember going back to my parents' house and being unable to pass water for 24 hours. I thought to myself, *"Okay, something is wrong here."* I was in a great deal of pain and then rushed up to Bronglais Hospital and diagnosed with an enlarged prostate, which I'd never even heard of. I didn't really know what the prostate was at that time, and then I dealt and lived with that for a couple of years. Having all kinds of issues with water retention and blood in the urine affected me mentally as well because I knew I couldn't drink too much volume of anything as I'd have issues with water retention, and my confidence just ebbed away. I didn't want to socialise, didn't want to go anywhere. I knew the toilets on the M4 motorway extremely well because I knew I needed to stop, and I knew where the nearest toilet was. But after one incident then, funnily enough, coming out of Swansea Sounds, I had water retention and was in so much pain. But I remember driving to the hospital, and they said, "Right, come on, we got to do something about this." And in six weeks, I had green laser surgery in Bridgend Hospital in the Princess of Wales here in South Wales for an enlarged prostate. And it was basically reducing the size of the prostate from a very large prostate to a much smaller prostate, thereby improving the symptoms, as it were, which is great. And it worked really well. And then I went back for the check-up in six weeks, and they said, "Well, the prostate's fine, but you've got cancer cells". So, I was diagnosed then with early-stage prostate cancer, which I've still got. I have a regular PSA blood test every six or seven weeks, which is about the only test really for men to have for prostate cancer. I have an MRI every quarter, every four months, and at the moment, touch wood, it's below a certain level to do something about it. I'm on active surveillance, as many men in my position are. So, as long as you keep an eye on it and are proactive and go back and check, and check and check, then you should be okay because when the time does come, there are at least four, if not five, options to cure cancer completely."

His health was not the only challenge Chris faced. He lost the radio show he so dearly loved presenting as Swansea Sounds Radio was taken over and then closed down by a huge conglomerate based in Germany. Then, in 2020,

COVID hit, and Chris was dealt his third blow in swift succession. His services as the weather presenter for S4C were no longer required. "As well as being diagnosed with the early stages of prostate cancer, which I accept and live with, I was then, what's the word? Elbowed, pushed, bullied, I suppose, out of my weather-presenting job, which was almost, if not worse, than having prostate cancer, which sounds a bit daft but, as you can imagine, 29 years of doing the same job and then all of a sudden not doing it, it really was like losing a member of the family. And that affected me mentally. A lot of goalposts were moved, and lawyers were involved with all kinds of legal implications. And in the end, I remember my wife saying the second time I woke up in the middle of the night sweating and crying, and I thought: *"Hmm, this is not good. Uh, I've just got to let it go."* So, I remember going in and saying: "Right, if you don't want me, you don't want me. Forget solicitors. I won't get into the details, obviously, but they told me that I just didn't fit in with their plans, as simple as that, so in 2020, I lost my job as the weather presenter as well."

The combination of the three blows left their mark on Chris, and he felt the impact on the career part of his identity keenly, as he explains, "2020 was a horrible year in every way. I'm only just accepting it, to be quite honest with you. Swansea Sounds I've accepted, disappointed. Uh, the cancer, it is what it is. I can't, literally can't, do anything about it, but the weather role has taken me just over two years to accept it, that I'm not on camera anymore, that I'm not the presenter, that I'm not Chris Jones, the Weatherman, even though I'm still being asked to contribute on radio and in articles about the weather. When I was told that I wasn't part of the weather presenter's role, my self-worth just disappeared. My self-confidence disappeared. After 29 years, I was floored! *"What the hell have I been doing for 29 years? And suddenly, I'm told I'm not good enough".* So, it makes you, it makes you think, *"Okay, what have I been doing?"* And then, as I say, it really did affect my self-worth, my self-confidence. I went downhill quite fast. Yeah, in a few ways. It's still quite difficult to talk about, but I've just got to accept it. Otherwise, uh, I'll never get over it. It was part of my identity, and suddenly, it wasn't there. But as I say, funnily and ironically, I'm still known as Chris Jones, the weatherman. And I'm still getting work because of it. Maybe not in TV, but I'm getting work as an awards host for conferences, and I'm still getting work because, at one time, I was Chris Jones, the weatherman. So, I think: *"Okay, right. In that case, I must have done something right. I must be quite good. I must be not too bad for them to still think that."* It's just the employers that took that bit over maybe didn't think that, which is fine, you know."

* * * *

When we face challenges of the magnitude that Chris has faced, we have two options: capitulate and give in to the grief and emotion of the situation or take the opportunity to rebuild and come back stronger. Not one to give in to what life throws at him without a fight, Chris decided he needed help rebuilding. He explains what steps he took, "You know, men are hopeless about talking about our bits, our private bits, we don't do that - men. And men don't talk about mental health as well. But I suddenly realised, *"Well, okay, I've got to do something about this."* And I went to see a counsellor and a therapist through somebody else I knew, and I started talking to her. And oh my God, that helped. It helped so much. I suddenly realised I've got to talk, um, and I poured it out to this lovely, lovely lady who I met once a week for six, seven weeks. And by doing so, it helped me put things a little bit into perspective, thinking, *"Oh, for God, Chris, just get over it. Get over it and move on."* And I have by now, and I moved on to other things just about though, just about."

Seeking to move forward and turn both his physical and mental health challenges into something positive, Chris has become an ambassador for Prostate Cymru, hosting awards and ceremonies, staffing their event stands and organising walks to spread the word that it is essential to get checked and not leave it too late. As Chris explains, "We are trying to get across that men need to talk to each other and the experts and the nurses. Mental health has also become a big subject over the last three or four years, hasn't it, because of Covid and everything else? If you're not proactive, or if you're not the kind of person who will go and have a PSA or digital examination or anything like that, as we've heard with Bill Turnbull and a few others, if you're too busy to go and check this out, then it might be too late. That's the big message of Prostate Cymru."

During COVID, when everyone had to stay home, Chris also decided to rebuild his professional identity. He explains, "I remember sitting down and doing a lot of research and putting videos on YouTube. My wife and I were both at home, and the kids had gone by then; they'd all left because we had an empty nest and thinking, *"Right, we've got to do something. Apart from the weather, which we were still doing, there's nothing else. So, okay, what should I do?"* I thought, *"Oh, I quite fancy doing a little radio thing, a podcast."* And as simple as that, I just started my own podcast. I started in English one, first of all, and I spent a bit of money on the recording kit. I built myself a little studio and recorded once a month an English podcast called 'The Influencers' with people who I think were changing and shaping and influencing our daily lives and, you know, in every way. So, I started with domestic abuse and then LGBT and then a charity, homelessness; I did entertainment and politics and a bit of everything. And then started a Welsh language one as well because I am primarily obviously, you know, a Welsh speaker, and took advantage of Chris Jones, the Weatherman thing again, every week. And it's been going up for the last three years, and I've had over 150 guests, and it goes out on Spotify and Apple, and Google, and Webcast and all kinds of platforms. It's just an informal chat show. We have ten questions. We have a bit of a quiz. We laugh. And most people have said, *"God, that was good. You've got me talking about things I've never talked about."* One celeb came out as being gay. And he's never done that before. One lady, who's quite a well-known actress, started to break down crying because she started talking about how she lost her mother and that kind of thing. So, it was almost like a therapy session."

Anyone who knows Chris will not be surprised by this. He has a unique talent for building relationships with people and making them feel welcomed, wanted, and safe because of his genuine desire to help people in any way he can. That ability enables him to host guests, whether they are top names from the media or others who have something interesting to say. Yet, like many, he wasn't aware of his gift and talent for connecting with others until it was pointed out to him during our conversation. It left him a little surprised, as he explains, "I didn't realise I did have that skill, if, if that's the word. But I think that's what makes my one a little bit different is that I can empathise, I can sympathise, I can put people at ease." That ability to provide a safe space for people to open up to him and tell their stories has also led Chris into another activity as part of his enforced career pivot.

* * * *

As a geography lover, Chris has always enjoyed walking and not just in places like Chile, Peru, and China. Chris explains how his latest venture came about, "I live in a little place called Ogmore by Sea, a seaside village in the Vale of Glamorgan in South Wales. I'm a stone's throw from the beach, and I'm out walking every day with a dog along the cliffs and on the beach, and it's been great. So, I thought: *"Well, okay, how can I use that passion as a business?"* and I've started doing guided walks, not only in this area but in other parts of Wales as well - not just walking from A to B, that'll be boring. So, what I'm doing is trying to introduce a bit of history, a bit of well-being, a lot of food and drink, with talks plus characters. So, if, for example, we are walking along the cliffs in the Vale and there's a certain history about ghosts or pirates or monks or something like that, well, I get an actor in. They dress up as the character, and they appear on the walk, on the path as the walkers pass by. And I tell you, it makes such a difference to have that little bit of extra interest, and they keep on coming back." Chris also offers individual guided stays, where he arranges the accommodation and takes them on excursions. As Chris says, "It's an extra second string to the bow, but I love it. I love talking to people. I love walking. But it's the extra elements, and I'm supporting local businesses, supporting local pubs and food producers and coffee producers. We've been from gin distilleries to cider makers, we've been to lava bread makers, we've been cockling, so there's everything across the board."

For Chris, enjoying the natural environment around him has been another crucial factor in helping him through the challenging times of the last three years. Chris explains what has allowed him to rebuild, "Talking, walking without a shadow of a doubt and the dog. Those three things saved my life, yeah. Without sounding dramatic, they did - talking for obvious reasons, walking because the dog needed walking. It got you out of the house. It got you on the cliffs in the wind and the rain. So, they really, really helped. Walking is brilliant. It's so good for so many people in so many ways. Not only physically, obviously, but mentally, with your well-being, you get time to think. I don't walk with headphones listening to music. I don't want that. Some people do that. I mean, they switch off with that. But I want to hear everything around me, and I want to feel everything around me. So, I want to be aware, I want to be conscious of what I'm doing every second, so I don't walk around listening to music, which some people find quite strange. And the dog - I mean, my dog is my favourite child, and I got four children!"

With his love of Wales and its countryside and his profile and knowledge of marketing and broadcasting, and his contacts, it is little wonder that he was invited to go for an interview to join the Board of Keep Wales Tidy as a trustee, a role he thoroughly enjoyed, as he says, "Keep Wales Tidy have been going for quite a few years now, and they do so much amazing work: not only on beaches, and parks, and litter picking, and that kind of thing. But they try to shape the law; they try to shape government thinking in regard to plastic bags and everything from rivers to oceans to beaches. And it's been wonderful dealing and sitting down with people once a month from all walks of life and contributing as much as I think I can."

There is one other opportunity that Chris has taken up, which has also played a significant role in his well-being, and which echoes back to his childhood. "I was in my local pub hosting a night for the outgoing owners, and we had speeches, and we had a bit of music, and I made a couple of speeches and just hosted the whole thing. And then I went to the toilet as men do, and I was standing there, and the door opened, and this gentleman walked in and stood next to me, and he looked at me and, you know, "How's it going?" And he said, "Oh, you've got a good voice then, mate. Good voice. Have you ever sung? You'd be a good baritone. Come and join Bridgend Male Voice Choir. I said, “No, it's not; it's not my thing. "Well, okay, come on, we meet every Thursday night." "Okay." Anyway, I went home that evening and told my wife; she laughed and said, "Well, why don't you just go and see? You love singing.” I'd recorded - I was given the opportunity as the weatherman to record songs with well-known people here in Wales, Heather Jones especially. They're still available on iTunes, and they play on the radio. I used to sing in school; I was never a choir member. So anyway, I went along one Thursday evening thinking, *"Oh, well, you know, I'm far too young, surely"*, and as soon as they started singing, there were about 65 men in one room. Oh my God. It was almost a eureka moment again. The hairs just stood up on the back of my neck and my arms, and I thought, *"Oh! This sounds incredible."* And I was aware of male voice choirs, being Welsh. And I thought, *"Right, okay, I'll give it a go."* And that was March last year, and it's one of the best things I've ever done. I love singing what we sing. I love the camaraderie; I love the community thing of it all. I've had such a welcome. I'm nearly the youngest there. Not quite nearly, but they're a wonderful, wonderful bunch of guys. And they've got engagements and events from weddings to concerts to quite high-profile concerts. And we've done the Elvis festival, we've done the Pride march in Cardiff. We're going on tour to Cornwall and North Wales and Ireland. And I love it. So, singing again has certainly added a lot. Oh God, a lot. It's enriched my life. Even though all this nonsense has been hitting me the last few years, it has. Life has been good to me so far.”

* * * *

Chris's early experiences of growing up in what was then a rural coastal village in Wales with its people, sense of resilience, community, and pride provided a psychologically safe backdrop for Chris to grow up in. Supported by parents who were both hardworking and offered a combination of entrepreneurial spirit and caring nature, it is little wonder that Chris developed an open, engaging, and adventurous nature and was a welcome childhood companion to adventure with, whether by the sea, on it, on the football pitch or in the drama and excitement of competing in the Eisteddfods.

That childhood contained the seeds of what he later went on to do. The place where he grew up, with its rapidly changing weather systems caused by the combination of beautiful and rugged coastlines, the strong natural beauty of the sea, and the Cambrian mountains with its rapidly changing weather systems, provided the perfect reason for him to love geography. Later, it would also provide the ideal backdrop for his love of travel and walking across challenging terrains. His mother's focus on looking after others is reflected in the way he builds relationships that are underpinned by trust, authenticity, integrity, and openness, which together create a psychologically safe place for honest and deep conversation to take place. That's partly why the loss of his role shocked him, and the loss of that part of his identity left him feeling a sense of grief. His innate sense of caring is also reflected in his volunteering work, whether supporting men with cancer as an ambassador for Prostate Cymru or helping the environment as a Non-Executive Director/Trustee of Keep Wales Tidy. Together with his paid work, his activities are all external reflections of who he is intrinsically.

His early love of performing and being at the centre of it informed his university studies. It led to the lightbulb moment when he fell in love with the opportunity to be behind the camera. That entrepreneurial spirit that came from his father, combined with his sense of caring for others, which reflected his mother's view of the world, has enabled him to make lasting connections and create opportunities that help others, and which bore fruit for him, too. This entrepreneurial and caring mindset led to him becoming a familiar face on Welsh television, where the various threads of media, environment, and creating a sense of connection with others were all woven together. When you step forward and take up an opportunity that fits who you are, the path has a happy habit of opening in front of you.

Chris's innate ability to build long-lasting relationships, entrepreneurial spirit, and love of the media, geography and the environment have created his unique tapestry and backdrop to his working life. Together, they helped him to find a sense of meaning and purpose and the ability to be curious and try new things so he could endure and overcome, regardless of the challenges thrown at him.

* * * *

A QUESTION OF RELATIONSHIPS:
WHO DO I WANT TO SPEND MY WORK TIME WITH?

Even with the advent of hybrid working, you are still much more likely to be spending more time talking with colleagues and clients than you are with your significant other, so choosing who you want to work with really matters.

As Chris's story illustrates, being able to form bonds with others built on trust and respect leads to conversations that create connections, opportunity, and success. Chris is a member of several work and volunteering groups or tribes, has been employed in both large and smaller businesses, and has also been self-employed for many years. When people share similar values and unite around a common purpose, it paves the way to outstanding achievements. They say that we can go fast alone, but going far comes from working with others, given none of us are islands. If you choose which group you want to be part of well and invest in building strong and reliable relationships, you will find it easy to make new and lasting connections that enable you to help others and which will bring you benefits and opportunities, too.

The activities that follow will help you to find the best group of people and culture for you to thrive, understand how you build connections effectively so you can do that with everyone you meet, and how to work effectively with people who aren't like you so that together everyone achieves more.

* * * *

ACTIVITY 1: FINDING YOUR TRIBE

As you saw in Chapter 2, when we looked at Maslow's Hierarchy of Needs, we have a strong need to belong. As researchers Baumeister and Fuller also identified in the late 1990s, belonging is good for us. According to their research, we are wired to form social attachments quickly and react badly to existing bonds being broken. We benefit emotionally and cognitively when we have a sense of belonging, and when disrupted, it adversely affects our health and well-being. Underneath all that, our need to belong is a powerful and fundamental motivator. In other words, fundamentally, we all like to play in a metaphorical sandpit with others we know, like, and trust and with whom we share common values, beliefs, interests, and goals. So, choosing what type of organisation you want to join is, therefore, something that needs more than just surface research to be sure that you are making the right choice.

Small organisations enable staff to work across a wide number of areas and activities because there are only a few people there to do the work. This means you can gain lots of experience in various areas quickly. Large organisations offer the chance to work more deeply in one area rather than perhaps less deeply across a range, so think about what would work best for you. Bear this in mind as you read through the different sector options. This may well be nothing new for you, but it will make you think more consciously about your choices and the reasons behind them.

Private sector

The latest 2023 ONS statistics released in September 2023 show that the private sector currently employs 27.15 million people, or 83% of those employed by any organisation. According to Government statistics, at the start of 2023, around 5.6 million UK private sector businesses were operating. Just under 99.2% of these are classed as small businesses with under 50 employees. Of these, almost three-quarters of those small businesses (some 4.3 million) are micro-businesses with no employees other than the business owner. Just short of 40,000 businesses are classed as Medium Size Businesses and employ 250 people or less. Less than 8,000 businesses are classed as large-size businesses and employ more than 250 people. So, if you work in the private sector, you will much more likely work for a small to medium-sized company or run your own business rather than work for a large corporate/household name listed on the Stock Exchange. Overall, SMEs (Small to Medium Size businesses) accounted for 61% of employment and 53% of turnover at the start of 2023. In terms of sectors, the UK uses the Standard Industrial Classification of Economic Activities to categorise business activities. The wholesale and retail trade sector accounted for the highest share of both employment and turnover at 14% of all SME employment and 33% of turnover. A third of SME turnover was spread across construction (12%), Professional, Scientific, and Technical (11%) and Manufacturing (9%) at the start of 2023.

When you decide to explore a sector with a view to working in it, remember to consider the impact of automation on both a sector and the roles within it and use the links in the Appendices to help you do so. Are you happy to work for an organisation which has profit as one of its key drivers? If so, a private company is a good fit.

Public sector

It may be that you would rather focus on doing work which is not profit-related. The public sector plays an essential role in society by providing goods and services vital to all citizens' well-being. It also helps to promote economic growth and social development. It comprises all levels of government and government-controlled enterprises. It provides essential goods and services to the general public, such as: national defence, law enforcement, public education, healthcare, and infrastructure. The public sector is funded by taxpayers and does not seek to make a profit. It also includes public enterprises, which are self-financing commercial enterprises under public ownership. Examples of public sector organisations include: government departments and agencies, the Civil Service, devolved governments and their agencies, local councils and regional development organisations, NHS hospitals and clinics, schools, colleges and universities, public transportation companies, public utilities where these are in government ownership, public libraries and museums, parks and recreation facilities, local housing authorities, and public broadcasting companies. In June 2023, there were 5.87 million employees in the public sector, with the NHS being the largest employer in the UK. If you prefer working in organisations funded by tax rather than profit, then the public sector is a good option to explore.

Not-for-profit/third sector

This sector is known by various names, including the third sector, voluntary sector, not-for-profit, community, or civic sector. Figures from the NCVO show that there are just under 166,000 voluntary organisations in the UK, which in 2019/2020 contributed £20.2 billion or 1% of GDP (Gross Domestic Product). The vast majority of organisations are micro and small organisations. In total, around 1 million people work in the charity or third sector, representing about 3% of the UK workforce.

If your focus is more on creating social value rather than material wealth, then working in this sector would be a good choice.

Checking the culture out

As well as identifying what type and size of organisation you want to join, it's wise to check the different types of cultures in those you are considering joining. An easy way to do this is to spend time reading the vision, mission, and values, which are usually available on their website. You can also use sites like www.glassdoor.co.uk/ and www.b.co.uk/the-lists/ to check out what individual organisations are like from their employees' perspectives. Look out for insights into whether they walk their talk and are constructive, passive, aggressive, or controlling in style. Also, consider how your style of thinking and working would fit. You can check this further when you talk to people you know who work there and when you go for meetings or interviews.

Of course, you may decide to become self-employed, having perhaps been encouraged by the results of the GET2 test you took in Chapter 3. If this is the case, it is wise to get support from your local business, social enterprise, or charity start-up support organisations to ensure you set it up appropriately.

So, what type of tribe and organisation do you want to join?

As you have seen, it is important to choose the right size and type of organisation to join, which reflects who you are and what will suit you best so you can thrive rather than struggle. Consider what you have learned about the different types of organisation sectors - private, public and third sector (i.e., charities/not-for-profit organisations) and spend some time exploring the vision, mission, values, and culture of organisations that interest you. Once you have done that, think about what type of organisation you are drawn to and use that understanding to answer the following three questions:

What type and size of organisation do I want to work for and why?

How does this link to the impact I want to make and my values?

What would I have in common with people who work there?

Make a note of any light bulb moments you have had during this activity in the space below:

* * * *

ACTIVITY 2: BUILDING CONNECTIONS

Having strong connections enables effective communication. As the saying goes, the meaning of communication is the response you get. Chris's great strength is his ability to build relationships which are built on trust, and which create such a sense of being psychologically safe that people open up to him in ways that they wouldn't open up to others. Psychological safety can be explained as "the belief that one can speak up without risk of punishment or humiliation." Effectively, it is about whether it is safe to engage in interpersonal risk-taking in the workplace. According to researcher and author Amy Edmondson, a recognised authority on psychological safety, "In a psychologically safe work environment, employees feel that their colleagues will not reject people for being themselves or saying what they think, respect each other's competence, are interested in each other as people, have positive intentions to one another, can engage in constructive conflict or confrontation, and feel that it is safe to experiment and take risks". The benefits are felt by both individuals and organisations alike as it creates a place where ideas can be exchanged freely, and innovation, learning, and growth can occur effectively.

In the 1960s, psychologist and researcher David Mclelland developed his needs theory to explain how different people are motivated in the workplace. He identified that people are either driven by a need for achievement, power, or affiliation. The chart below shows the different elements for each of the three needs. Understanding what drives you and others will help you work more effectively with them.

WHAT DRIVES YOU?

ACHIEVEMENT	POWER	AFFINITY
• Desire to set and deliver challenging goals • Finds tasks fulfilling • Self-motivated • Likes feedback on progress • Likely to respond to financial reward linked to achievements	• Desire/need to control and influence others • Satisfaction from being in charge • Enjoys status and recognition • Likes to win arguments • Enjoys winning	• Wants to belong to a group • Gains satisfaction from quality of relationships • Wants to be liked • Dislikes high risk/uncertainty • Very co-operative

One of the reasons that Chris can achieve psychological safety with others is due to his need for affiliation with others and a desire to achieve. It also accounts partly for why he was shocked when his services were no longer required, as he no longer belonged to the group. One note of caution: the possibility of conflict between those who like power and those who want to achieve is high, especially when those in power perceive achievement by others as a threat to their status, so watch for this. Understanding what drives you will also help you know which work-related rewards will keep you most motivated, as recent research based on McClelland's theory shows. Those who appreciate affiliation will want to work in groups and appreciate respectful leadership who is warm and encouraging. Those who are achievement-driven will respond well to being rewarded financially, while those who are power-orientated will seek prestige and a car which reflects this and acts as a symbol of their status.

It was in the 1950s and 60s that an American organisation called TRACOM began to develop a new lens for understanding others. Called the TRACOM SOCIAL STYLE Model, its focus is on behaviour and provides a valuable, objective approach.

As the diagram below shows, we tend to one of four ways of behaving where we prefer to control or emote and ask or tell. Once again, Chris's tendency towards amiable behaviour is reflected in his story and reaction to people.

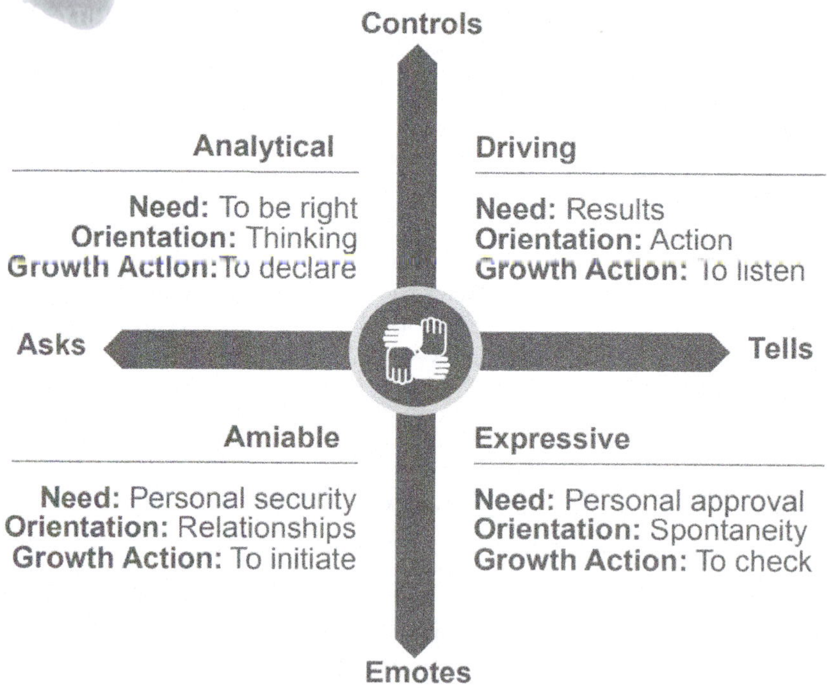

SOCIAL STYLE® is a registered trademark of The TRACOM Group and is used with permission. Learn more at www.tracom.com.

TRACOM's model encourages behavioural flexibility by helping people to understand what the underlying concern is that motivates each behavioural style, as the diagram shows.

Using the TRACOM SOCIAL STYLE Model™ as a lens to help you understand yourself first and then understand others will enable you to adjust how you interface with those who are not like you in a way which is less stressful and more effective. Of course, there is much more depth that you can go to by reading their books and taking one of their courses.

So, how effective are you at building good relationships with others?

As Chris has demonstrated, understanding others effectively is vital to creating understanding and trust so you can work together well. So, what is your communication default? Look at the four different social styles diagram and then use what you learn to answer the questions below and make a note of what you discover:

What is my behavioural type according to this model?

How do I build effective connections with colleagues?

Think about a significant and successful work connection you have built with a colleague and use this experience to identify how you develop effective connections with colleagues. Remember to outline what fundamental elements are at play to enable this relationship to build. Make a note of what helped you to interact effectively together here:

How can I build effective connections with people who are not like me? Now consider a relationship which has not gone well. What went wrong, and how could you build a better relationship with a similar person now using what you have learned? Remember to make a note of your answer below.

Now you have finished this activity, what is your most significant light bulb moment about how you build effective connections with colleagues?

* * * *

ACTIVITY 3: THE POWER OF TEAMS

We have looked at how an individual's communications behaviour is driven by their needs. Now, it's time to look at how individual behaviour can contribute to or detract from effective teamwork. In the 1970s, Dr Meredith Belbin and his team of occupational psychologists spent a period of time observing a group of executives hard at work at the Henley Business School, noting down their every move. From the resultant data, they identified what was to eventually become nine different clusters of behaviour which facilitate team progress, and Belbin Team Role Theory was born.

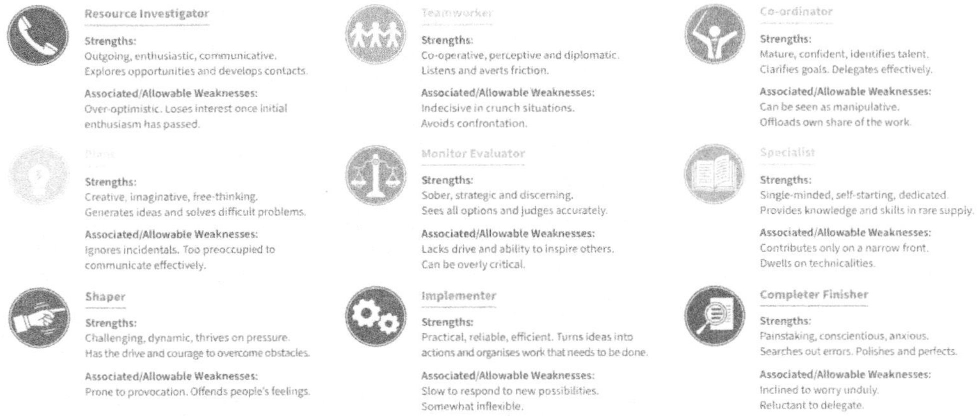

Reproduced with kind permission of Belbin Ltd (www.belbin.com)

The nine roles are either action, people or thinking-oriented, and each reflects a strength, an allowable weakness, and a non-allowable weakness specific to that role. Taking a team role profile will highlight an individual's top two or three strengths and rank the rest in order. This enables an individual to understand where their unique blend of strengths fits best in a team project.

So, let's look at the roles in more detail. When a team needs to exploit new opportunities, you need to call on the *Resource Investigator*, who will use their existing connections and create new relevant ones both inside and outside an organisation to help the project move forward. When a new idea or two and some innovation is needed, that's when the *Plant* is required. If the pace needs to pick up and decisions need to be made, this is where the *Shaper* comes into their own. If a team becomes unhappy and arguments break out, it is the *Teamworker*, who will put the kettle on and sort out concerns and worries. Where there are competing options, the *Monitor Evaluator* is in their element, and once a decision is made, it is the *Implementer* who turns the decision into workable procedures. When the team needs someone to research a subject in depth, that's where the *Specialist* gets involved, and it is down to the *Completer Finisher* to make sure that the quality of the project is good enough. Finally, all projects need someone who can bring individual talents together in a cohesive group effort, and this activity belongs to the *Co-ordinator* role.

When it comes to mitigating against individual allowable weaknesses, the Resource Investigator needs to watch that they don't run out of steam. The Plant needs to avoid being too preoccupied to communicate properly. The Shaper needs to ensure they don't offend people's feelings; the Teamworker needs to avoid being indecisive. The Monitor Evaluator needs to avoid being overly critical. The Implementer needs to be more flexible when it comes to change. The Specialist needs to avoid thinking too narrowly. The Completer Finisher needs to worry less and delegate more, and finally, the Co-ordinator needs to stop offloading their work onto others. To discover your profile and understand more about how you can use this to your advantage, you may want to take a Belbin profile test either as a standalone test or on a 360-degree basis.

Now that we have looked at team role preferences in more detail, it's time to consider your behaviour in a team. Think of a time when you worked well in a team and then use that memory to ask yourself the following question:

So, how do I work most effectively in a team?

Once you have an answer, think about a time when you worked in a team, and things did not go well. Use that memory to answer this question:

What do I need to watch for?

Of course, the great thing about Belbin's team role theory is that it is behaviour-based, and we can all learn to change and adopt new approaches when working with others.

Now that you have considered how you work with others in a team, what insights have you gained?

* * * *

CONSOLIDATING YOUR LEARNING FROM THIS CHAPTER TO ANSWER THE QUESTION:

WHO DO I WANT TO SPEND MY WORK TIME WITH?

In this chapter, we have taken a closer look at which type and size of organisation you want to work in, explored how our needs affect how we communicate with each other and considered how we work best in a team. Now, it's time to capture what you have learned through these activities in your INSPiRED Career and Life planner. Take the significant keywords you have identified in this chapter and add them to the Relationships box highlighted in the diagram which follows, using the planner at the front of this book.

Then, use a second copy of the planner at the back of this book to record a sentence in answer to the question for this chapter:

"Who do I want to spend my work time with?"

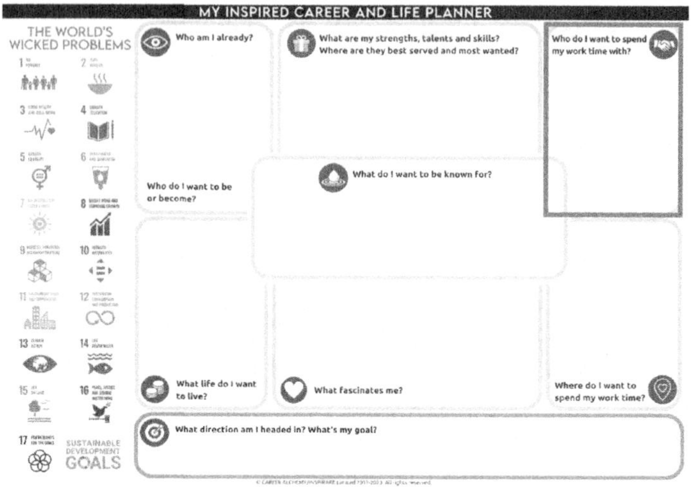

Remember you can download a digital copy of the planner tool from here: www.careeralchemy.co.uk/free-reader-planner-tool.html

* * * *

ENVIRONMENT

7. ENVIRONMENT: WHERE DO I WANT TO SPEND MY WORK TIME?

MATTERS OF PLACE, SPACE, AND EFFECTIVE WORKING

When the environment we live and work in matches who we are and what we value, our lives are enriched and conditioned for growth.

A vivacious, gregarious, and upbeat woman in her late thirties, Mel Cameron grew up as an Army child, where her parents met. Her dad was in the Royal Corps of Transport and later transferred to the Parachute Regiment, while her mum joined the Army as a nurse in The Queen Alexandra's Royal Army Nursing Corps (QARANC). They first met in England, then moved to Paderborn in Germany, where Mel was born. A few years later, they moved back to another Army base, this time in the Southeast of England in Aldershot. Although a very different childhood from many, Mel recalls it as being a great environment to grow up in, surrounded by a myriad of people from all sorts of other places and cultures.

Time moved on, eventually, her parents left the Army, and when she was eight, the family moved to Llanharan, a town in South Wales. Mel started school at Pencoed Comprehensive, near Bridgend. It was here that she did her GCSEs in French, Welsh, Religious Studies, and Art and had to choose what to do next. Mel picks up the story, "I'd always enjoyed entertainment movies as all children do. But then, as I got older, I was obviously making my choices about what I'd like to do in the future, and I was always geared towards the creative side of things. I wanted to be doing things I liked, to be thinking on my feet, and just being creative. And nothing was available in my school at that time that interested me. I did actually like school, but I did then look towards the technical college, which was in Bridgend, and immediately, as soon as I opened up the prospectus, I thought, *"That's what I want to do"*. And it was film production, media production, that kind of thing. And I thought, *"Yeah, I love that"*. With her plans for spending the next two years in Bridgend College of Further Education set and armed with a strong work ethic, which she had gained from her parents, Mel got a part-time job as soon as possible. She went for an interview on the last day at school in her school uniform. That first job was with Pizza Hut, and she learned a lot from it as she explains, "When I got my first job, I was like, *"Oh, I like this. I'm responsible. I'm in charge of my own money"*, and all that kind of thing. I got good things from it. I worked, and I met people, I made friends, and I had a good time, and I was enjoying it. So, it fired me up to want to do more. It gave me a sense of purpose as well.

"That summer, I spent most of my time there because it was a brand-new store, and we were putting our mark on it. Again, all different ages of people working there, different backgrounds. So, it was just like a time in my life when some old things were ending; even though it was a bit sad, it was all exciting because all these new possibilities and doors were opening in front of me. So, it was a brilliant time." Mel continued to work part-time at Pizza Hut for almost nine years on and off. Mel's first day at college that September was a revelation. She felt at home immediately, as she explains, "I remember the first day walking through the gates, and it felt like it was where I was meant to be. And I know it sounds so corny, but it did because it was from the no uniform to the freedom to know that I could be creative, and I was in charge of my own destiny almost. It felt like it was right. And I just loved the environment and being in that environment with people of all different ages again, different backgrounds, everybody was so different." The people reminded her of her Army childhood. She soon settled into college life, balancing study with part-time work, until the time came to consider what her next steps would be. She also managed to get some work experience, spending two weeks at BBC Wales in Llandaff, Cardiff. This gave Mel the opportunity to see what it was like working on the news, the weather, editing, and pre- and post-production, which encouraged her to keep developing her practical skills in media, even if she wasn't sure yet what direction she wanted to go in. Later on, she also did a two-week placement at Global, the radio station company in Cardiff, where she worked in the studios supporting the DJs on the admin front, prepared content for live shows, and generally helped out wherever she could.

As time went on, inevitably, conversation at college was to start turning to the future. Mel explains what happened, "I was about to turn 18. And the talk of university was starting to buzz around, with lecturers and people in college asking what I was going to do. My parents wanted to know if I would go, and I did want to go, but I didn't know what I wanted to do. At that time, I realised, *"If I'm going spend this money to go to university, I want to know that I'm doing what I want to do"*. So, my parents were okay with it, but I was a bit worried about whether delaying my entry to university was a good idea. But in the end, that is what I decided to do. And I thought I would like to travel. And that's where that journey started. And I didn't realise it would take me in a completely different direction from where I thought I would be."

It was one day when she was working at Pizza Hut that her direction became clear. "I was talking to one of my managers at the time, and I was explaining my dilemma, and I said, "I know I want to go travelling, but I want to go somewhere where they speak English because it's my first time away from home and I want to feel safe, and I want to work. I don't want to just travel". And then this manager said, "Have you heard about the Camp America thing? And I was like, no. And then, all the doors opened, and a friend and I went to London to a recruitment fair. We met lots of different camps, and I was offered a position working at a summer camp in Pennsylvania, and I was hired to teach video to the children, and I had no idea what I was getting myself into." Little did she know what impact this decision would have on her life and career.

* * * *

This was in 2002 when the internet was just being born, so Mel's insights into what it was like there were limited. She explains, "It wasn't until I arrived that I could see the size of the place and how far away I was from home. And I realised what I got myself into, and as soon as I arrived, it just felt like I was in heaven because it was just so beautiful there. When you're in the middle of nowhere, it's surrounded by a beautiful lake in the forest; it just felt like the people were all great, kind people just cared about making sure these kids had the best summer ever. And it felt like a family because the camp now is over a hundred years old. So, it'd been going for a very long time. And they knew what they were doing. They were professionals; these are all people who work with kids all year round. Their kids are gone. They've gone to camp, their grandparents have gone to the camp or met there. It's so very traditional. And I love that environment because I had a relatively small family growing up, so being part of something so big just felt amazing."

It was here that her mother's nursing activities came to the fore and gave Mel a context to draw on while working with children from 7 to 16. When the family had been living in Aldershot, Mel's mother left the Army and spent some time working in a children's home in Farnborough. Mel recalls how this helped her in the camp, "Sometimes, if my dad was posted somewhere, I would go with her to work, and I would just sit with my colouring book or whatever. But often, when we went to this place, I would interact with the children, who were from all over the place. They've been in places where there had been war, and I would help her out, or I'd play with them. And I think that kind of experience probably, I didn't realise at the time, but it resonated with me. And I think being with different people and having an open mind to different abilities or just different people, in general, was probably a seed planted quite early on."

For Mel, the experience of camp and seeing young people develop because of the experience became something that kept calling her back year after year as she explains, "When I first went, it wasn't my intention for it to go in the direction that it did. It was more of an *"Oh, I fancy going away for the summer; it'll be a good experience."* But I knew the day that the kids arrived, which was a very nerve-wracking day... and I had no clue, but I just fell into it. And I knew that I would be back the following year, but I didn't realise I'd keep going. But it just snowballed... I would recommend it to anyone because of the people you meet as well, the experiences you have, and the memories you make will really stay with you for life. I think about when I was 18 now, and I would love to be able to watch myself and see how much I've changed because I think that it taught me a lot about resilience and powering through, digging deep, and all that kind of stuff, that you don't necessarily pick up. Being immersed in an environment was something that I got a lot out of."

Initially hired to teach video and photography, she worked with children aged 7-16 and staff from all over the world. She led countless basketball games, taught 7-year-olds to use a pottery wheel and did other daily activities with them. In all, Mel went back to the same summer camp in Wayne County, Pennsylvania, for the next four summers, interspersing her time in the US with working in Pizza Hut and would return to work for the same organisation in camps for 16 summers in total, having been bitten by the camp experience bug. In those early years, as well as working in the summer camp sector in the summer and Pizza Hut outside those times, Mel realised the importance of continuing her education, so she continued to study, as she explains. "I did some part-time courses at college in the media field just to make sure that I was still studying and then started another full-time course, which was in Performing Arts. And I thought I'd try the other side of the camera this time. And I loved that." Now aged 22 and with quite a lot of experience from both the retail and camp sectors, Mel finally felt it was the right time for her to go to university. As she explains, she knew it was right, "I went to university with so much confidence in that field, and I thought, *"Yeah, I'd like to do this."* I did more performing arts with a little bit of media on the side, and I thought, *"You know what? I know I'd like to do this now. I want to have that experience because I think I loved camp so much."* Being with my friends all the time, I thought, *"University's going to be 20 times better, and I'm in the UK."* I applied to a few universities and I went to visit a couple of them. The day that I went to the university I ended up going to, walking on campus. I just knew this was the place for me because it was a stunning campus, and I loved my time at the university. Looking back, I think if I'd been younger going to university, I probably would've changed my course. Not significantly, but I would've probably gone to a more media direction because that's where my interests lay. But I would not change anything else. The university, the people. All perfect."

That was the second time when facing significant change that Mel just knew that she was in the right place based on her reaction to the physical environment. Until our conversation, Mel had never really considered her ability to make decisions that way, but now she recognises that she is very tuned into how she feels. She explains, "I can get a vibe. I felt the people around me were happy. It wasn't like I opened the door, and it was like, wow. It was spending a little bit of time there. It was beautiful, I have to say because it had a beautiful clock tower. There was grass, it was summer, and people were sitting on the grass chatting. I thought, *"I like this. I want to be somewhere where I feel like I'm in the environment. I don't want just to shut my door at the end of the day, and then that's it. I want to be absorbed, and I want to enjoy every aspect that I can."* And I did that definitely when I was there." The university campus she had fallen in love with belonged to the University of Wales, Newport in Caerleon.

The hard worker and social person she is, it didn't take Mel long to get into university life. While studying, she was an active volunteer in the Students Union. She also had several part-time jobs during her studies to fund her way through. As well as continuing at Pizza Hut, she worked in three different roles for the university. One of these was within one of the university's companies, which did outreach work aimed at opening the minds of children to higher education. Mel's performing arts and camp experience were invaluable here as she worked as a presenter, visiting schools and hosting groups on campus. She also worked as a student ambassador on university open day, answering queries, welcoming potential students, and families, and showing them around campus. Her third role used the experience she had gained at camp helping young people to settle away from home, to do the same thing for freshers starting university for the first time. She also worked throughout her course, promoting the opportunity of working overseas at summer camps to students. By now, her studies were ending, and it was time for her next chapter.

* * * *

Mel faced a dilemma, "I was very torn. I had the opportunity to stay at the university and work within the Student Union, and that was something that was proposed to me. And I know it sounds wild now because I look back and think you are no age, but I was very conscious that I was a mature student even though I was 25 or 26 or something, which is insane now. But the company that I'd worked for at the time had a marketing role, and they'd asked me if I would like to do it. Being a graduate, finding a graduate job is hard enough. And I thought, well, this is something that does interest me. And I like the sound of that. I can talk about camp; I can get people to come along. I'd had some experience at that point with interviewing, and I got to meet students, travel around, and I thought, *"Oh, that sounds quite interesting; I wouldn't mind going to visit other universities and seeing what they have to offer"*, and I was quite a confident, public speaker and I'd had experience in that." In the end, working back in the summer camp sector won, and she decided to take up the offer to become a marketing rep covering Wales and the southwest. It wasn't without its challenges; as Mel explains, "I was living in a student house share at the time as well, so it was quite difficult. It was the first time I'd had to really manage my workflow to make sure that I was getting what I needed to do, done. I did struggle with the working from home aspect because I liked the interaction with people." For someone who is as extroverted as Mel, this was to test her, though she loved the engagement with the 26 university careers services and the students she was responsible for – once she got there. "I was responsible for every university that fell in that area to promote the programme. I didn't drive then either, which made it very difficult. But thankfully lots of the people at the different universities were really helpful... I loved the face-to-face things I did with the students and working with them, I loved that."

She spent just short of the next two years working with the university careers services to organise visits, attend Freshers and careers fairs, deliver presentations and recruit applicants. By this stage, the internet had taken off, and Mel was able to develop her digital marketing skills using search engines, direct mail, and online advertising to promote the summer camp offer. She also managed a large team of recruiters who worked on the ground in the various universities. The experience of working with different careers services was something that she would later come back to later on, but not just yet. In May 2010, the company she worked for sent her to Manhattan as Office Manager for the summer in their biggest hostel in the US, where they ran a Meet and Greet service for the thousands of scheme participants that summer. Mel explains what that entailed, "The majority of people go through New York, and they have a Meet and Greet where the students would fly in, they'd have a night in a hostel, and they would have a short orientation, what to expect, that kind of thing and then they would go on their way the next day. We were based in a hostel, which was on the upper west side of Manhattan, and 15 of us worked there, and we would welcome the staff. We'd go to the airports to meet them. We'd bring them back to the hostel. Sometimes, we'd have coaches of people arriving with like a hundred people on one particular day, and people were coming from all over the UK, Europe, Australia, New Zealand, everywhere. A lot of these people were first time away from home. Some of them were scared. They didn't speak English as their first language. You were there as their person to welcome them and be a shoulder to cry on because some of them were very nervous, but on the whole, people were so excited, and we were there to pump them up and get them ready and excited, and they were arriving at all times of the day for the two months. I just loved working with the staff, and it was just a fantastic environment because a hostel has people coming from all over the world.

The people that we worked with were people who had been to camp, and they all understood what these participants were going through. I loved being there, and to get the opportunity to live and work there for two months was a dream come true. I love New York City. It's an amazing place. I don't think I slept for two months! It was fantastic, but I couldn't have done it for much longer than that. I would've had to have had a better sleep schedule, that's for sure. But it was just a fantastic opportunity." That caring gene she had acquired from her mother and the visits to the children's home came into their own.

Shortly afterwards, she headed off to the camp where she had first worked once again as she did every summer. Over time, she took on additional responsibilities, working at first as Assistant Group Head for 11-year-olds and then as Group Head for 16-year-old girls who were training to be camp counsellors, returning to the UK afterwards to continue to work in the industry. By the time she came back after camp in summer 2011 and was always eager to learn and develop, she had begun to realise that it may be time for a fresh challenge.

* * * *

Sometimes, what we seek is seeking us. By chance, an opportunity came up within the summer camp sector which would be instrumental in Mel's future direction. She takes up the story, "Whilst I was in America, I received an email letting me know that this position was available within the summer camp industry. It was less of a marketing role but more of one-to-one processing participants who were going to work overseas and doing all of the things that are involved with that, and I applied for that. I had the interview, and I found out I had the job. I had to get home and find somewhere to live because it was in Liverpool, and I had to move up there and start a new life." She started her new role as US Travel Adviser and Team Leader in the autumn of 2011 and stayed there for almost five years, continuing to go back to the US camp herself every summer until 2017.

Over time, the new role led her to manage a team of 6 staff members.

Together, they worked to ensure that the thousands of people who went to work abroad every year got the most out of their experiences. The role enabled Mel to combine her biggest passions, people, and travel, while delivering exceptional customer service, echoing the Pizza Hut training of her early days. It also taught her something else, "It cemented my thoughts of thinking that I don't know if I'll work in camping forever, but I want to work in a role where I'm supporting people because the majority of the people that we were working with were around 18 to 25 and most of them were in university... So, working in that coaching environment was something I thought, *"Oh, I like this."* And I think that's where I thought about the future and thought, *"Where can I take this maybe once I've had enough of the summer camp industry?"*

Meanwhile, as part of her desire to learn new things and help people, Mel decided to start volunteering and joined a couple of organisations in the autumn of 2015 to lend a helping hand. She also signed up to be a First Aider with St John's Ambulance, something she continued to do for another seven years, attending all sorts of events from music to sports and local fêtes. Doing so gave her a lot back, too, as she explains, "I just really liked working with people who needed support, and I enjoyed working with the team. Some of the people that I was working with were doctors, nurses, and really skilled people who were teaching me lots of great skills. So, it is just an environment that was very people focused." She also started fundraising as an Ambassador for Tŷ Hafan, the Welsh children's hospice which supports children with life-shortening conditions and their families.

In September 2016, another opportunity within the summer camp industry came her way, and she returned to work on another Camp Counsellor Program as their Special Programs Co-ordinator. This meant a move back to her roots in Cardiff, from where she supported the businesses recruitment of staff for seasonal business around the world to support cultural exchange programmes. Over the next five years, she used a combination of different experiences and knowledge in the role, including her knowledge of cultural exchange and travel, the media, video production, photography, and digital marketing, to create digital content for use worldwide across all platforms. She also managed the company's digital advertising and analytics, as well as participating in fairs and other promotional activities aimed at recruiting 18- to 25-year-olds through social media, once again working with her preferred age range.

By November 2018, with the continued theme of supporting vulnerable young people in mind, Mel signed up as a volunteer for the National Youth Advocacy Service (NYAS), a children's charity that provides advocacy and legal representation to children and adults. She trained to join the Bank of Independent Visitors, reliable adult volunteers who spend time with a child or young person in care. They provide a reliable presence in the lives of their young people and meet up monthly with them to do fun activities together and provide practical help and emotional support.

Although she had stopped going to her usual summer camps in the US by this point, as she didn't want to be away for so long anymore, she was committed to continuing to develop her ability to support young people individually. So, in the summer of 2019, she returned to the same camp she had been visiting for 17 years to spend a week working as a videographer and photographer. This time, she worked in a camp for children who had lost a parent, primary caregiver, or sibling, capturing memories as they were made there. Once back in the UK, she came back to her everyday life and its business as she focused on achieving year-end targets.

Then things changed, as Mel explains, "There was this thing called the Global Pandemic which changed everything. And at the time, it was quite scary, if I'm being honest. And I was very worried, as everybody was at the time, what would happen? Am I going to lose my job? Where am I going to go from here? As we were drawing closer to March, obviously, it was in the news, but we carried on as normal. I think a lot of people didn't expect the world to change as much as it did. And when we got to around, I would say, May 2020, working in the camping industry, I think it dawned on everybody that the summer wasn't going to happen, and that's our income, completely gone in a heartbeat, and we were placed on furlough. This thing had come out of nowhere and stopped the whole world and was stopping something that had been going on for over a hundred years, as well as everything else.

It completely took us by surprise." Although it was a massive jolt for Mel, as it was for millions of others, it gave her a chance for reflection, as she explains, "I spent a lot of time thinking about where I'm going, *"Is working in the summer camp industry, what I want to do, where am I going?"* And I thought, *"No, I'm going to have to do this now because it feels like the right time."* I took a pen and paper, and I was writing down what it was that I wanted to do and where I wanted to be. And I started just looking at different roles that were available, and all of them that I liked were around people. Over the years, I wanted to work in a university environment. I'd thought about becoming a careers advisor, but I'd looked at different avenues, and I thought, *"Well, I'm not in a position right now to be able to do that whether it was money or just time, I'm going to have to study, how am I going to do that? I live here."* So, it was, *"Maybe when I'm a bit older and I've got a bit more time, or I can save whatever, I'll do it then. That's that."* But it was always in the back of my mind, thinking, *"Oh, this is where I want to be."* One day, on furlough and knowing that redundancy was on the horizon, Mel realised the time for change had come. Mel was made redundant and was connected with specialists who could help her.

* * * *

Sometimes in life, whether due to luck or fate, opportunities align with our ambitions, as happened in Mel's case. She explains what happened next, "I was very lucky that I spoke to a careers advisor, and I told her exactly what I wanted to do, and I said, "Actually, I'd like to be doing what you are doing," and I said, "Oh, I would like to work in a university, though. That would be my ideal environment. Obviously, I need the training. If I'm going to do this, I might need to save or should I get experience first, *et cetera*". A couple of days later, at about midnight, I got this email from her, and she said, "Look at this. This is perfect". The job was at the University of Wales, Trinity St. David, with sponsorship. And the job sounded fantastic. I'd been to the university before with my previous job, and I really liked the environment. I thought, *"Oh my gosh, this is great. It's just down the road."* And then I thought, *"I'm going to go for it"*. I had an interview, and I loved the people that interviewed me. They were great and answered all my questions. They just were nice people. And it just felt right. And then, obviously, when I found out I got the position, I was thrilled because I just thought, *"This is it"*. As Mel recognised, life sometimes has a happy way of sending us a gift disguised as trouble, "Pre the interview and pre finding out that I'd had the job, it was the scariest time as anyone's ever been out of work or had the thought that they might not have that money coming in knows. It's a frightening time. But looking back on it now, it was the best thing that could have happened. It removed me from something that maybe I wasn't fulfilled from anymore. And it gave me the kick up the butt that I needed to seek out what I needed to do. And now I look back, and I think, *"Oh, it's the best thing ever because now I'm in a role that I absolutely love, and I'm working with people who are teaching me things every day."*

For Mel, all those elements of being in an environment she loves, working with people who share the same desire to help people develop and having the opportunity to learn and grow herself all came together. What she felt initially was a disaster was actually a redirect, as Mel recognises, "If I hadn't had had that conversation with that particular career advisor on that day, would I have found that job myself? I don't know. You do make it as well because you put yourself out there. Not achieving it wasn't an option. It wasn't 'if'. It was 'when', so whether it wasn't this point, it would've been in, hopefully, in another job. So, I feel like I was driven to get to where I wanted to be." In February 2021, Mel started working remotely at the University of Wales Trinity Saint David as a Trainee Careers Adviser. The conversation she had with the careers adviser was as she puts it "definitely a massive moment in my life because if we hadn't have had it, I would not be doing this now."

* * * *

As part of her career change, and alongside working with students at the university, her employer-funded her to study for a Post Graduate Diploma and MA in Career Development and Management at Coventry University. She explains how she found combining work and study as a mature student, "I thought it'd be okay studying and working full-time. But I would say that would probably have sent me into overdrive. Even though it's part-time, there are times of the year when you've got more assignments to do than others. And it's always in the back of your mind. However, I think planning your workload, being clear and starting your assignments as early as possible is advisable. I think it's doable though. If you are lucky enough to work in an industry which is related already, then that definitely helps. I kept a clear line of communication with my manager, who has been so flexible and helpful throughout the whole time, as has my team, who have been very understanding and patient, as they've been through the process too, and they understand. It's helped me because I know that if I need more time, I can speak to them and say, "Oh, you know, would you mind if I took this day or this afternoon or whatever to do the work?" Then that does help because, sometimes, there aren't enough hours in the day. But just planning it and ensuring you are keeping on top of your schedule will help the process. "I don't think I've met anyone that has not been willing to answer questions or share their life experiences, tips, and guidance, even little things like conducting interviews or working with students. It's just been a great couple of years so far.

"I've learned so much, and I'm very fortunate that I work with people who are open to sharing things with me and have been patient with me. They have also been encouraging and allowed me to bring my own skills and experiences. Being kind to yourself and giving yourself time is essential. I was never the most academic student growing up. I was very creative, and I still am. So, it's not come easy for me, the academic writing." She also found support and encouragement from her fellow learners and the lecturing staff at Coventry, though she has been glad to be able to return to the physical classroom, as she says, "Face-to-face classes are so much better! It has been really tough at times juggling work, study, and life, but it has been a great experience, and I have learnt so much! I'm looking forward to fully immersing myself in university life and taking what I've learned and pushing myself forward because I think it's given me so much enthusiasm to go out and be a careers advisor".

Once again, the environment was all for Mel to be able to thrive. She successfully submitted her dissertation in the summer of 2023. Inevitably, her choice of topic relates to her experience in the overseas summer camp and learning journey and explores how the fun of working overseas in summer camps helps young people develop the foundations for a successful career. Completing her studies as part of her career change has undoubtedly helped Mel to learn the biggest lesson of all, as she recognises, "I have a new faith in myself about what I can do. And I think that's been great for me personally, to remind myself that I can do it. I might need to take a bit more time to do things, but if you push yourself, you can achieve anything."

* * * *

Mel's story shows the inevitable impact of our childhood on our lives and choices. Her familiarity, comfort, and sense of fun, which she gained by growing up in an Army base with its vast array of people from different cultures and backgrounds, left an indelible stamp and sense of place. This experience has stayed with her throughout her life as a backdrop and has given her the ability to know when she is in the right place based on how she feels about it. Naturally outgoing, that experience enabled her to create a bond quickly with anyone she meets and also taught her the discipline to make things happen and to see them through.

Mel's big heart and desire to help people is an ultimate concern, which reflects her mother's role as a nurse and working in a children's home. That experience equipped Mel for her work in the summer camp sector, an opportunity which came from a chance conversation one day. Since then, she has helped thousands of young children to learn and grow through fun during 17 summers of working in summer camps in Pennsylvania, while spending the rest of the years back in the UK helping thousands more to experience the benefits of cultural exchanges, so they can also develop and learn lessons vital to their career success. One of the challenges of being a giver like Mel is making sure that you look after yourself and your future, too. Driven by a desire to challenge herself and learn new skills, she eventually managed to find a way of balancing helping other people to grow with her own developmental needs. Doing so equipped her to tell other people's stories and showcase the value of the opportunity. Over time, she felt the need to widen her focus beyond helping lots of people at scale. Her innate desire to make a real and long-lasting difference led her to gain the skills and insights to engage in deep conversations with those who need it, whether as a first aider, a children's hospice fundraiser or as an Independent Visitor supporting young people in the care system.

As we progress through our journey in life, we get nudges to change direction. Often, we choose to ignore them until there is no option, as in Mel's case. The circumstances of a global pandemic conspired not only to create the impetus she needed to decide to change direction but also to put her on her chosen path again due to someone else's intervention with a timely job advert. Committed to being the best she could be and despite some challenging moments, she found a way to combine doing her MA while starting to work with university students using the skills and experience she had already and finally back to working face-to-face in a place she loves.

While we witness the relentless progress of technology in the workplace, Mel's story reminds us of the importance of having a sense of place at work and feeling at home there. That enables us to contribute our best and to live enriched and fulfilling lives that charge us rather than leave us feeling depleted. For Mel, that place is in a Welsh university surrounded by young people for whom she feels a deep affinity and a burning desire to help.

* * * *

A QUESTION OF ENVIRONMENT:
WHERE DO I WANT TO SPEND MY WORK TIME?

The place we are in affects how we feel, how much we enjoy work and life, and how well we do. Some places energize us so we can recharge, while some places sap us and make us apathetic or, worse still, ill. Mel's story illustrates just how well she thrives in a place where the conditions are right for her. While she has had to work and learn remotely, as a natural extrovert, she does better and enjoys working face-to-face more. As she discovered, working from home in a student house did not suit her, whereas working in camp or on campus in a green and leafy place does. Her experiences of both have helped her to understand what she needs as an environment to thrive. One of the dictionary definitions of 'environment' is "the circumstances, objects, or conditions by which one is surrounded."

As part of a new workplace that is characterised by speed, change, and constant learning, Mel's attitude, tenacity, and commitment have helped her to understand how she works and learns best online and in person and to find ways to balance work and study. Doing so has enabled her to complete her MA and develop her practical experience of applying the theories and techniques she was learning with students so she could become an effective and qualified career development professional.

We each have our approach when it comes to where we need to be to work and live our best lives, and our own ways of being and working. The activities that follow will help you to identify and develop your preferences so you can create a working life you love every day.

* * * *

ACTIVITY 1: THRIVING IN LIFE

As we saw, for Mel to thrive in life, she needs to be in an environment which reflects her multicultural childhood experiences, where there is nature all around and young people. The place we work and live in matters, and although we can't take a photograph of how it makes us feel, we all have a sixth sense when we are somewhere, just like Mel has. In the old world of work, because we had to be in the office full time unless we were out on the road, we used to choose where we lived based on access to that work. In the new post-pandemic world of work, that is no longer the case as more of us work on a hybrid or fully remote basis. As countless news reports have shown, collectively, our mental health and well-being concerns and needs have risen to the top of our agenda, and well-being has become one of the top priorities for employers who need to ensure they attract and retain the staff they need. To thrive in life, you need more than work and a home to make you happy. As we know from exploring our needs and the work-life doughnut in Chapter Two, we need to have enough money to fund a decent standard of living and social life in a place that we can afford to live in and where we can do things that keep us healthy, connected, growing, and enriched.

To create the life we want, we need to consider how much money we actually need to sustain the lifestyle we want. Websites like Expatistan enable you to compare the cost of living both between different cities in the UK and across countries. This is a great way to understand the implications of working in one place versus another and can be important to explore, particularly if you work in the public sector, for instance, where national pay scales are used. Choosing to live somewhere that is cheaper will help you retain more of your money every month, so you have more disposable income. The same is true for those who choose to become self-employed, too. Having a reduced cost base can make all the difference between a business surviving and a business failing and a business owner, that is thriving. There are plenty of examples in the media of digital nomads and laptop entrepreneurs working remotely, spending periods travelling and exploring the world and working online from different locations around the world now that the world of work has lost some of its previous constraints.

Choosing to spend some time commuting to work if you can tolerate the thought and having to go into an office, for instance, may also bring cheaper housing and living costs. Of course, if you can work from home for most, if not all, of the week, you have even more flexibility in terms of location, as long as there is good internet coverage. For some people, living in a city is exciting and recharging, while for others, finding a town, village, country, or coastal location that suits their needs best. If you decide to move, apart from the obvious things like checking out schools if you have children, there may be other amenities which matter to you, for instance, if you need to be able to visit museums and art galleries to refresh your soul, a remote seaside location may not be ideal with poor road and rail connections may not your idea of heaven. If you need to be able to swim or run or take part in other sports, make sure you factor that into your choices, too.

There are other considerations, too, when choosing a place to live. What sort of community do you need, or is it enough to be part of a professional community? What opportunities and activities do you miss out on, or gain based on particular locations? And does it give you access to opportunities to volunteer in areas that interest you so you can both give back and grow as Mel does, or is that not important to you? The following activity will help you to answer these questions and more.

So, where do you want to create your future?

As the world of work continues to support either hybrid or full-time remote working, we have more choice and freedom than ever to create a working life we love in a place that speaks to us. This activity, with its five questions, is designed to help you identify the key elements you need to consider to create a life you can enjoy. Use the space after each question to make a note of what matters to you:

Where do I need to live to feel at my best?

Who and what do I need to be near so I can relax, refresh, and recharge?

How much do I need to earn and commute to sustain the life I want?

What sort of community do I want to live in, and why?

What opportunities are available (people, places, things) to stimulate my growth?

Now, make a note about the insights you have gained about where you need to be to thrive in life here:

* * * *

ACTIVITY 2: MY WORKING DAY

Work takes place in all sorts of different settings, from offices to factories, hospitals to schools, colleges and universities, sports halls, and arenas, in airports, garden centres, cafes, restaurants and hotels, at sea, in the air, outside, in nature or working with animals, in space, in studios, at home and in many other places. Some people appreciate the regularity of office hours and the routine of going to and from a specific space. Others need to move as they work or be outside, and everyone likes some form of variety. For some people, working at home is their idea of heaven, particularly if they can work flexibly and in line with their body clock and the demands of the rest of their life, like caring responsibilities, whether for little ones or older people. Other people like Mel appreciate being in a place of natural beauty and working in a space with people they find energising. Those who are more introverted or need time and space to think would find this tiring and need a quiet corner to work effectively. Whether you spend most of your time working from home or in the office and don't have the space and peace you need, that can adversely affect your well-being and productivity.

We also need to fit the rest of life in. We often make choices and accept jobs without thinking through the potential ramifications carefully enough and then find, to our disappointment, that we do not have the time or opportunity to take part in activities and life outside work which matter to us. Without these, our lives, health, and well-being can be lessened. While work will take up most of your time every week, it is important to remember that it is part of it and not all of it. That means consciously designing a working life that suits the rest of your life, so you get the best out of life every day.

Creating your working day

To help you understand what this is for you, spend a few minutes imagining what your ideal working day would be from the moment you wake up to the moment you go to bed. Think about where you want to live and how much travelling you want to do to get to work (if you wish to travel more than a few minutes). Imagine the type of physical environment and culture you want to work in and the self-care activities you want to be able to take part in before and after work. Write your answer in the space after the question overleaf, or if you prefer other learning modalities, you could draw it, sing it, visualise it or even act it out so you can be clear about what matters to you.

So, what is your ideal working day like?

What is your most significant light bulb moment about how you want your daily working life to be?

* * * *

ACTIVITY 3: DOING MY BEST WORK

As we explored in Chapter Four, when we are happy and working effectively, we are more productive and achieve more. When that happens, we go up the staircase of happiness rather than descending the spiral of despair. Those who succeed and achieve often do so because they have set up the right conditions to work effectively, both intellectually and emotionally. If we do this consistently, we can become a rising star at work and progress more efficiently. Given we all only have 24 hours every day to work, and we need around 8 of those to sleep, that leaves the remaining 16 hours for work and the rest of life. The more we have a hybrid or remote working approach, the more wise organisations shift their focus away from time serving and onto results. So, we need to ensure that we work in a space and in a way where we use our time at work efficiently.

A space to thrive

Being comfortable in your working environment matters for your well-being. Sometimes, buildings can cause health problems because they suffer from what has been termed Sick Building Syndrome. This can cause a range of symptoms, including headaches, a blocked or runny nose, dry or itchy skin, dry or sore eyes or throat, coughing or wheezing, skin rashes, tiredness, and difficulty concentrating. While these symptoms are familiar to many, if others in the building have the same symptoms and these get worse the longer you are there but improve after you have left the building, then it would tend to indicate that the building itself is causing these. So, if you start to experience these, it may be time to investigate a transfer to a different building or explore hybrid or remote working if possible. The call centre industry has spent millions over the last 20 years or more investigating what staff need to be happy and efficient in their working environment so they can deliver high levels of customer satisfaction. According to research by HermanMiller, innovators of design and furniture solutions in call centres and other industries, the most significant cause of office irritation is inappropriate temperature. Here, research has shown that women like a warmer temperature than men. Inadequate lighting/lack of natural light, inadequate computer displays causing eye strain, inappropriate noise, poor layout or not enough personal space, uncomfortable seating leading to back, shoulder and neck problems and depersonalised workspaces all cause employee stress.

If you have a hot desk, having some personal items that you can put on your allocated desk and headphones to help mask noise around you will help you concentrate more easily. If you are a hybrid or remote worker and miss having people around, as long as you don't have to be online in meetings, a morning or afternoon in a coffee shop with good Wi-Fi can give you a lift. If you do work from home all or most of the time, make sure you stay in touch regularly and attend meetings, so you maintain a sense of connection with colleagues and stay in the loop when it comes to developments. Avoid over or underworking a lot and use systems to help you manage deadlines and meetings. Above all, make sure you have a decent workspace and chair, which reduces back and eye problems and have some form of routine which marks the end of the day, whether that is switching off your computer or something else like changing your clothes or shoes to help your brain switch off from work.

Working remotely makes it harder to build relationships and understanding with others. Not everyone has experience of as many people from different cultures and backgrounds as Mel has, and sadly, unconscious bias is incredibly common. Where this is evident, it is often due to a lack of knowledge and understanding, so sometimes we need to help employers and others to understand and widen their thinking and knowledge. Most of the large employers are usually well versed these days in what they need to do to ensure an inclusive work environment and ensure they meet the requirements of both legislation and best practice.

The Equality Act 2010 highlights nine protected characteristics and provides legal protection in the context of age, disability, gender reassignment, marriage and civil partnership, pregnancy and maternity, race, religion or belief, sex, and sexual orientation. The Act has led to organisations creating Equality/Equity, Diversity, and Inclusion policies to ensure every individual can thrive at work. As the Chartered Institute for Personnel and Development (CIPD) highlights, informed and enlightened employers who have good EDI policies that are enacted and encourage an intersectional awareness through open and respectful cultures enable staff to experience greater well-being and social and economic benefits.

The Act also includes the Disability Discrimination Act 1996, so if you have some form of disability, and let your employer know, they are duty-bound under the Equality Act 2010 to consider any reasonable adjustment you need to access routes, toilets, equipment, and adaptive software so you can access your learning environment or working space and be comfortable there. It is always wise to check out an employer from an EDI perspective as a way of ensuring cultural fit before you join and exploring examples of good practices highlighted by The National Diversity Awards, the British Diversity Awards, and other similar events will help. Similarly, from a physical perspective, it is essential to choose an employer who is committed to ensuring the health and safety of its staff.

Maximising impact and happiness

As Mel experiences regularly when she is working with young people and students, helping others makes us feel good. Known as the Helpers High, the sensation is caused by the brain receiving a shot of dopamine, the happiness chemical. We feel a similar sensation when we complete activities and projects. Apart from the two per cent or so who are genuine super multi-taskers, almost all of us lose a significant amount of time and energy trying to multi-task all the time and our productivity dips significantly. The rest of us have our brains whirring like an overstretched computer disc until the number of tabs we have open is too many, causing our brains to suffer a dose of brain jam and crash.

As Georgetown Professor and author Cal Newport argues, we need to engage in deep work which is focused and meaningful if we are to thrive in an increasingly busy and noisy world. That means using our time and energy wisely at work so we can enjoy a greater sense of happiness and well-being because we have done a good job. Managing our time and energy wisely also gives us the resources to enjoy the rest of each day outside of work. These days, there are a plethora of technology-driven scheduling and project management tools, often using AI integration with other systems to help with this. While these can be helpful, they all fail if we don't have the right mindset to achieve what we need to do and make the right corresponding choices on how to allocate our time and energy to get us there. There are several simple but impactful techniques to use to help with this, and we will explore them now.

Understanding what you need to do, rather than what you want to do, and how long it will take you will help you to increase your productivity and, assuming the work is done well, your impact too. When we fail to plan adequately, we are, in effect, planning to fail, as the saying goes. In today's world, what is deemed urgent but not important often gets done first, and other people's priorities serve as time rustlers when their priorities and yours don't align. This is where Steven Covey's Time Management Matrix, shown below, comes into its own by asking you to categorise all your tasks using a 2x2 matrix to help you identify what is both urgent and important, what is not urgent but important, what is urgent but not important and what is neither urgent nor important - that way you can make clear progress on what counts most.

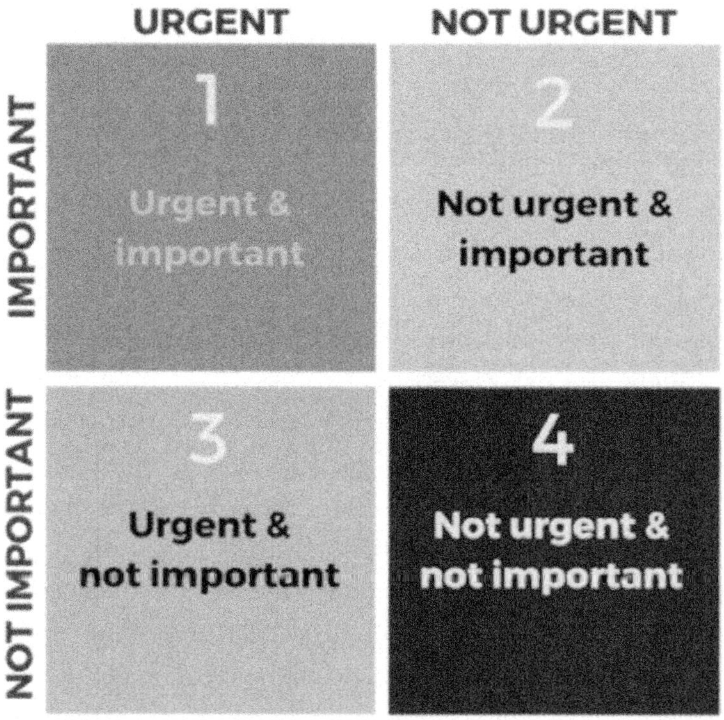

Once you have understood your priorities on this basis, there is a second model, which is helpful when allocating your time. Named after the economist Alfredo Pareto, born in 1848, the Pareto Principle or Pareto's Law helps you to recognise how much effort, energy, and time you need to devote to achieving your outcome so that it is done and good enough, rather than perfect and late.

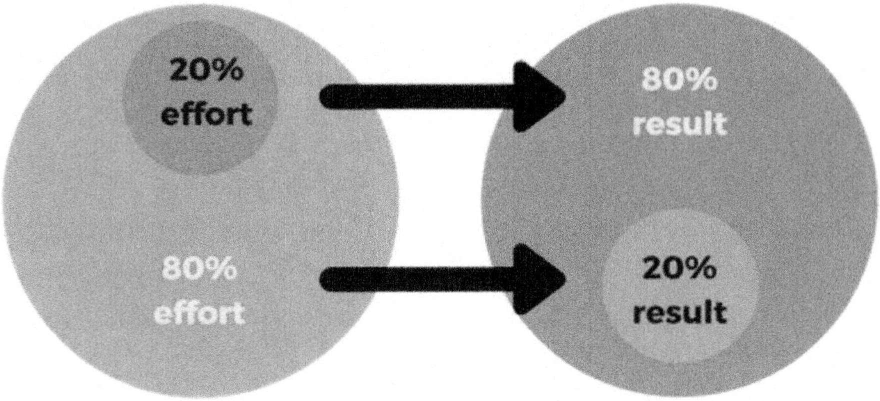

As the diagram above illustrates, the 80/20 Rule means that in any situation, 20 per cent of the work or activities deliver 80 per cent of the outcomes or results. In other words, 80% of the consequences come from 20% of the causes. If you continue past this point, you get into the land of diminishing returns, and sometimes this isn't worth doing. On the other hand, sometimes the remaining 20%, which will take 80% of the time, is significant depending on what you are seeking to achieve and the context. So, it would be best if you thought about this to help you plan and schedule your time monthly, weekly, and daily.

Those who work effectively plan how they will use their time the following day at the end of the current working day, so they start with the end in mind and measure achievements, not time. Where possible, they work according to their natural cycadean rhythms based on whether they have a morning, intermediate or evening chronotype. They work in a focused way for specific chunks of time, which allows for periods of intense focus and recovery before beginning the next activity. If you don't already do so, starting your day where possible by working on your most significant projects first rather than on other people's priorities, which have landed in your inbox, will significantly help your progress. Most emails will keep until after lunch and switching your phone to silent so you can avoid social media distraction and email alerts provides the time and peace to do both focussed work and solve problems. Planning meetings, if needed, when you have less energy, may provide a lift, and help you recover your energy and pick up important tasks again. We all need periods when we are unavailable so we can do some creative thinking in areas where we or our organisation struggle. That's how organisations progress and gain an edge. Forward thinking technology companies recognise this and often encourage staff to build that time into their days. Finally, it also helps our energy and enthusiasm if we celebrate wins each day and either record them electronically in a good outcomes folder, write them in a small notebook or on scraps of paper which you can put in a jar and keep to hand for moments when you need a lift.

So, what do you do when you work most effectively?

To recap, to do our best work, we need to ensure that both the physical conditions around us and our work strategies are set up for success. This exercise will help you understand and improve both. Think back to a time when you were highly effective in the way you worked, which led to great results. What was the context? How were you thinking and feeling? And how did you set yourself up to be successful? Use your memory of this experience to help you answer the questions below:

What do I do when I work most effectively?

Based on what you have remembered and using what we have covered earlier in this chapter, now ask yourself this question and make a note of your answer underneath:

How can I improve my effectiveness even more and conserve my energy?

What lightbulb moments have you had about your environmental needs so you can enjoy your working and non-working life? Make a note of them here.

* * * *

CONSOLIDATING YOUR LEARNING FROM THIS CHAPTER TO ANSWER THE QUESTION:

WHERE DO YOU WANT TO SPEND YOUR WORK TIME?

In this chapter, we have explored what sort of environment you need to thrive in, what your best working day would look like and considered different ways to help you get the most out of your time and energy. Now, it's time to capture what you have learned through these activities in your INSPiRED Career and Life planner. Take the significant keywords you have identified in this chapter and add them to the Environment box highlighted in the diagram below, using the planner at the front of this book.

Then, use a second copy of the planner at the back of this book to record a sentence in answer to the question for this chapter:

"Where do you want to spend your work time?"

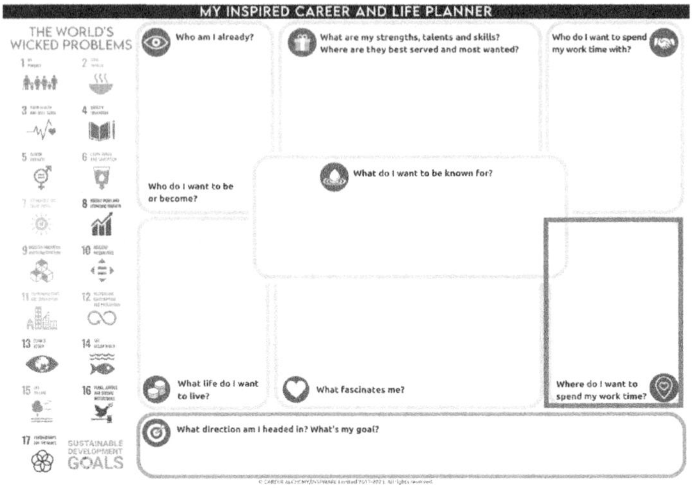

Remember you can download a digital copy of the planner tool from here: www.careeralchemy.co.uk/free-reader-planner-tool.html

* * * *

DIRECTION & GOAL SETTING

8. DIRECTION & GOAL SETTING: WHAT DIRECTION AM I HEADED IN? WHAT'S MY GOAL?

CREATING THE VISION AND MISSION THAT INSPIRES YOU

> You can either design your own life plan and enrich the world in a way that matters to you or end up doing something that matters to others instead.
> The choice is yours. Choose wisely.

Steve Keith describes himself as a cheeky northern monkey. Now just turned 40, he grew up overlooking Morecambe Bay, in the land of sticky toffee pudding, potted shrimps and mint cake, in a hamlet on the edge of Flookburgh on the southern edge of the Lake District. The village was built as a place for engineers, builders, and construction workers to live while they built the nearby airfield, so it has a strong sense of community, and it was here that Steve and his brother went to primary school. His grandfather owned a haulage company, so Steve's dad and uncle trained to be mechanics to help with the family business. It is also while doing his apprenticeship there that Steve's dad met his mum, who was working there at the time as a secretary. Once trained, Steve's dad joined the family business. Steve picks up the story, "He was one of the truck drivers, driving nationally around the UK. Me and my brother would go on trips with my dad sometimes, so there were sleepovers in the cabin and those big breakfasts with all the other truck drivers up on the A66 in the middle of winter, which was cool. When my grandfather passed, my father and my uncle took over the family business. and once my grandmother had passed, decided to shift the business more firmly into cars and automobiles rather than trucks." Like Chris Jones, Steve grew up listening to conversations about the family business around the kitchen table. When the time came, Steve headed off to Cartmel Priory School, a mixed Church of England school for 11- 16-year-olds, whose motto is "Faith and Courage". A bright lad, he did exceptionally well in his GCSEs, gaining mainly A*s and As, and then went to Barrow Sixth Form College, where he carried on down the science route, excelling in chemistry, geography, and maths at A Level. By now, it was time to decide his next steps.

He applied to university and was accepted into academically elite Russell Group member Durham University to study geography, an experience he loved, as he explains, "At the time, it was the best four years of my life. I was incredibly proud not only to get to university but to be the first person in the family to go to university and at such a prestigious university as well. It was a huge achievement. We can all pick a teacher we will remember, and mine is Mrs. Weir, my geography teacher. She was amazing, and she inspired me. She influenced my decision to go and study geography. I was very strong academically, and that influenced the opportunity to get my foot in the door in Durham. I just wanted to be happy. So, I picked the subjects that made me happy, largely because I either enjoyed them or was good at them." After three happy years at Durham coming to an end in 2004 and graduating with an Upper Second, it was time for Steve to make another decision about his future direction, "I went home that summer after I'd graduated and hadn't invested any time in exploring what I was going to do. I think there are lots of positives investing your energy into things that you enjoy, are passionate about and are good at. But I wasn't thinking about where it was taking me, so I found myself at a point where I didn't have any plans. I didn't know what I was going to do."

* * * *

A conversation with his parents led to him finding an answer, "I remember sitting and having a conversation on the patio outside with my parents, and them saying, "What are you going to do next?", and me saying, "Well, my friend Melissa's going back to do a master's, so I might go and do it as well." He wanted to continue his studies in Durham and applied for a master's in management and business. He explains his thinking at the time, "In the back of my mind, I had thought to myself, *"Well, do you know what, I have a lot of entrepreneurial influence around me, whether it's from Dad running his own business, whether it's from the moves that Mum's made since she stopped secretarial work and has become self-employed as a dog sitter, for example. My brother ran his own business as well at one point, but I've always had that influence around me*", and so I felt like I would give it a go because business was something that I teetered on the edge of whether or not I wanted to do it at A Level.

Although it was at master's level and was very demanding, the course itself was almost like an introduction to business at master's level. There were modules on accounting and finance, how to set up a business, and how to do competitor analysis. By now, Steve was heading for the end of his master's year and again had to think about his next steps. It was while going around the university's career fair that he had an idea, as he explains. "I remember very vividly the stand at the careers fair for Teach First. They had a graffiti campaign that year, and I remember looking at it and thinking, *"Oh my God, that's awful as a campaign for teaching."* Many of my family members commented whilst I was growing up and doing part-time jobs and things at university, how good I am with people and young people and whether I'd ever thought about becoming a teacher. I'd always dismissed it. I remember having a conversation with the recruiter on the stand and hearing about this fantastic opportunity. I was very nervous about going into the workplace because, at that point, I still hadn't decided what I would do next. I'd put it into more of a funnel and gone, *"Right, I love geography, but what realistically, what career can I get out of that? I will look at the business side of things because that's something I want to revisit."*

"The Teach First programme combined the two; it allowed me to spend some time in a classroom teaching a subject that I love, on a leadership development programme that would further build on the skills and knowledge from my master's. And if I'm completely honest, it bought me another two years to think about what I would do next." Research helped him to understand more about Teach First's aims as a charity, which works to address education disadvantage by placing top graduates in some of the most challenging schools in complex urban areas across the UK. Steve was accepted onto the scheme, spent the summer learning how to be a teacher and set off for Essex on the outskirts of London to start his first teaching role in September 2006.

* * * *

Despite growing up in a rural area, Steve coped well with the change, as he explains, "The school that I was placed in was on the outskirts of London. It was in zone four in Essex. I was fortunate for two reasons. They never put you into a school by yourself, so you've got somebody from your cohort to share the experience. But I was one of seven who went to my school, which was quite rare and the school needed two geography teachers. So, I was with my good friend Grace, which was great as we'd been on the same degree course at the same time but never met until we ended up in that school together in Essex." Clearly, Steve's secondary school motto of having the faith and courage to be brave had prepared him well as he recognised, "Brave is a word I'd use for it now. Back then, it was probably bonkers, stupid – other words that come with that. It encourages you to invest in yourself by throwing you in the deep end. I love learning by doing, so I think that was what I'd been missing throughout university. When I'd done my geography degree, yes, I focused quite heavily on the physical environment, but I wasn't able to afford a lot of the trips that were happening. Durham, at the time, was world-renowned for its sea level research and things like that, so there were trips that would go up to Greenland. Some were going to Gran Canaria to look at volcanoes, and I couldn't afford that. And so, I think the practical application of what I was learning didn't come out of the degree, whereas when I was doing my Master's, a lot of the case studies and my dissertation involved applying learning. Things started to click, and it didn't take me as long to process stuff and to get it. So, being told I would do six weeks of intense teacher training in the summer and then go straight into a classroom in September as a full-time teacher was great. I had 12 classes and nearly 300 pupils straight away."

As Steve found, teaching is not a soft option, "It was not an easy two years, but it was probably the two years that made me who I am because it encouraged me to start taking hold of opportunities. I've always been very curious, and it encouraged me to be more curious about a subject that I thought I knew inside out. I had to think about how you would teach very high-level concepts to someone 11 years old, for example. The best teachers are the ones that can explain very complex processes and issues. You've got to be able to get into their head and discover how they want to learn and understand them."

This ability to take something complex and make it simple would be something he would come back to later in his career. Meanwhile, he was taken by understanding how you do that and how people learn and started using that curiosity to help him understand how he can learn well and thrive, too. Primed by his own experience of growing up in an area of economic deprivation in a working-class family, Steve also saw some significant deprivation close up, including the challenges faced by asylum seekers as he explains, "I've seen these young people that get thrown into a classroom who can't speak a word of English and have just arrived in the country. They were some of my pupils. At the other end of the scale, in a classroom of 30, I'd have somebody whom I couldn't keep up with and whom I constantly had to give extension tasks to. The diversity of the pupils in front of me and the spectrum of their ability to learn was huge, and again, it was really daunting but so motivating. It was those individual interactions with the young people who didn't enjoy geography when they suddenly started to thrive at it and to come into the room and enjoy it themselves. One of my students went on to study geography at Queen Mary's University, London, and it was those moments of pride in the young people I was working with. And I loved knowing that I'd had a part in helping them to get to that point, that got me out of bed."

Getting out of bed to help others was one thing, but finding the time to look after himself was another, as an incident one evening highlighted. Steve picks up the story, "I remember working late one night, and it was just dark and miserable, and the bus that got me to the train station, then onto the tube, then got me home, only came every half an hour at the end of the school road. I could see it when it was about to set off. And so, I ran for it and managed to catch it in time, but I was dripping with sweat. I was clearly massively unfit. It was also a bus with a load of my students on, and they berated me for being so ridiculously unfit at my age. And it encouraged me to start taking my physical health a bit more seriously.

"When I was at school, I hated PE, absolutely loathed it. There was a lot of toxic masculinity around PE when I was growing up, and if you didn't play football or rugby, then you weren't considered to be a proper man. And that's still quite prevalent even within the village now. But I decided to join a gym, and me being me again, I thought, *"Well, I've got no idea what I'm doing, so I'm going to hire somebody who can show me what to do".* So, I hired a personal trainer and had lots of great conversations with them whilst they were training me, and over about six to nine months, I saw some massive gains in my fitness. I started to enjoy exercise, which had never happened before, and asking questions of my trainer, as I do with most people when I meet them, such as "How did you get to where you are in your career today?" And he showed me some of the courses that he'd done and the learner inside me just went, *"Ooh, that'd be good to do".* So, I decided to embark on a personal training diploma."

It took Steve a couple of years to complete it, and he set up a side hustle as a personal trainer, his first experience of running his own business, which he did alongside his day job as well as full-time work to bridge the gap while he pivoted from teaching into a new direction. Steve picks up the story, "One of the things that I used to get feedback on as a trainee teacher was that I didn't necessarily always teach to the test when I should be. I would rather have the light bulb moment where a young person got it rather than constantly trying to hammer learning into somebody because they've got to sit an exam. But that's maybe more to do with my own personality of wanting to be a bit disruptive and a bit of a rule breaker at times." Despite the challenges and enjoying his time teaching, he did not see himself as a teacher and decided to walk away from it at the end of the programme and the 2008 academic year. His reason was clear, "I don't think our education system is fit for purpose in many areas, particularly around geography."

* * * *

Steve felt drawn to something else within Teach First, which needed his experience as a Teach First teacher and was still related to helping develop people but in a different way. He picks up the story, "They were looking for recruiters to join the graduate recruitment team. I realised that I've got a talent for speaking to people and understanding their motivations, as well as their passions."

He spent the following year in this role as a Graduate Recruitment Officer, encouraging students to consider applying for the programme and explaining the reality of a career in teaching. "They wanted young people graduates to be very aware of the fact that this is not an easy route into teaching. It's not an easy route into any career, and to attract the right people, you have to be realistic about what you'll get when you join the workplace. It was a fantastic role, and it got me out of the classroom but kept me engaged with teaching. I was still getting those moments when I was working with young people in the classroom. I saw that spark and felt like I'd achieved something when I was going home in the evening because there'd be at least one or two graduates that day, or undergraduates, that would say, "I'm going to go and apply for this", and then would get onto the programme."

In total, he recruited over 60 graduates from a portfolio of London universities for the 2009 Leadership Development Program. Always one to contribute new ideas and suggestions, Steve was asked to review recruitment activities over the previous seven years as a project over the quieter summer period in 2009. His work helped the company but did not help him, as it meant roles would change, and he would now have to split his time between London and being back in the Northwest. So, he moved into a third role in Teach First, this time as a Leadership Development Officer, supporting 24 trainee teachers to develop their skills as reflective practitioners and leaders, visiting them in their schools and giving them teaching feedback and pastoral support. Eight months into the role and realising that the role was not right for him, he decided to change employer.

Along with several other colleagues, Steve had realised he missed the interaction with young people, so he decided it was time to go back to working in schools. In April 2010, he and his colleagues all joined vInspired as schools advisers based in boroughs. Part of the Youth Community Action Programme, launched by the government in March 2010, the initiative sought to inspire all 14- to 16-year-olds to give their time and get involved in projects and activities that would benefit 14– to 16-year-olds. Steve was given Lambeth and Wandsworth. Steve picks up the story, “I really thought I'd managed to find something that would be huge for me in my career. Three months later, about three or four days after the general election, our manager sat us down and told us that funding from the Labour Government had been withdrawn and we were being made redundant. We were going to be paid whilst there was a consultation that went on throughout that redundancy process. Then, I was made redundant. I think it was the first time I'd made a move in my career when I regretted my choice, and not because of anything through my own fault. I spent the summer of 2010 lying largely on Clapham Common and sunbathing, and I suppose ignorantly and naively at the time, thinking, *“I'll figure something out”*. I remember a friend saying to me when we'd gone to Spain on holiday at the end of the summer, "So, what are you going to do next?” And me saying, "I don't really know, and the money's running out!"

* * * *

As luck would have it, he had become good friends with someone in Clapham who worked for EY, the professional services firm and one of the

Big Four consultancies. Steve explained his predicament, to which they responded with a suggestion, "My friend who works in the graduate recruitment team at EY is looking for recruiters right now. You've done graduate recruitment. Why don't you apply to that? At least get a job for a recruitment season to get yourself back on your feet." I applied for the job and went for the first interview at this big EY office in London Bridge, a big glass building. I remember thinking, *"Is this really me? I'm going to give it a go. I'm going to embrace it. My friend has looked at my CV. I know I can probably ace this interview.* A couple of days later, I got a call from the recruiter and was rejected. As somebody who likes to self-reflect and develop, before I even had the opportunity to ask for some feedback on why they decided not to take this application forward, the recruiter said, " There's another role within the employer brand team, which sits alongside the student recruitment team, and with your schools' experience over the last four years, would you be interested in that?" And that was when I met the then head of employer brand, Jane."

"It felt like one of the hardest interviews that I've ever had in my life. Maybe it was because somebody had seen something that I hadn't seen. I remember being incredibly nervous about messing it up. When Jane offered me the role a couple of days later, she said, "There's a lot of things in me right now that are saying I shouldn't be making this offer because you've got no branding and marketing experience, and that's what I want for this person in this role, but I know I'm confident enough to say that I am happy to mentor you, coach you, develop you, and help you learn those skills. What you have that nobody else I've seen has, and that I need, is an understanding of what 14- to 18-year-olds are like, how they behave, what they're looking for. It felt like somebody had thrown an olive branch and gone, "Have a go at this. I believe in you. I think you could be amazing. I have spotted something you haven't seen". Until that point, I'd had a lot of good managers, but I hadn't had a great manager, somebody who knew how to develop people, and I'd started my career on a leadership development course; I didn't necessarily finish those two years feeling like I was a leader and it was that sense of somebody who had a huge gravitas, she achieved so much in her career, had gone, " I will help you". I spent some time before I said yes to that offer, just reflecting and looking back at everything and seeing what the role was that she'd described and said to myself, *"Do you know what, ..., if I've been waiting for something, this is it. So, it's time to grab that bull by the horns and go for it."* It felt like at that time that that penny had finally dropped. I'd gone, *"This is what I'm meant to be doing*". I'd lost a lot of confidence in myself, and it felt like somebody believed in me. So, it was very powerful in that sense as well, and it just gave me a great sense of achievement. It gave me a lot of purpose from that point forward."

It was October 2010 when Steve started his new job, which he found very overwhelming, partly due to a strong sense of imposter syndrome and the inevitable loss of confidence he had felt because he had been made redundant. He also needed to adapt to office life. He reflects on what he experienced, "I had several moments in that first few weeks where I was thinking, *"I have made the wrong choice. I am absolutely out of my depth. I should do something else.*" I felt like I was the only person because I was the first to focus on schools within the team. So, I'd been given this huge amount of responsibility. Jane had been very clear that she would give me that responsibility, but she'd also held me accountable for any decisions I made. I'd been given a six-figure budget to work with, and I was looking at it and going, *"Oh my Lord, there is so much that could go wrong here, but a lot could go well. I need to have some faith in myself.* " A few weeks later, he went to meet his new colleague, Liz, at one of the roadshows she was running in Birmingham, as part of her work running the selection and onboarding part of the schools programmes Steve had joined to support.

Things started to slot into place. Steve recalls, "We started to bounce off each other, and we sat down for a good three days after that and built out our strategy. We started to lay out the table of what recruitment for schools at EY would look like and had a vision of where it was going over the next five years because the business was demanding that. I'd always worked in an environment where you were working towards somebody sitting in an exam to get a grade as part of an annual cycle. Just that vision and that ability to see forward and go, "This is what we're working towards", that was the first time in my career where I'd had that, and it anchored me incredibly well because I had those check-in points where I could see how I was doing, but it gave me a good push all the time."

Steve continued to work hard and deliver innovative branding and marketing, and in July 2013 was promoted to Senior Employer Brand Adviser for Schools. This marked a period of significant achievement and national recognition. Steve led the EY Schools team toward winning seven prestigious industry awards and becoming rated the No. 1 professional services firm to join and one of the top industry apprenticeship employers, too. Steve recalls the moment he found out, "That was one of my career highlights. I remember it well. I was sitting with the person from the organisation that was running the ranking, wondering why we were together, and they said, "I just wanted to let you know that we're about to announce that EY has become the number one employer". I managed to hold myself together quite well in the meeting. Then, I left for my Cannon Street Office. I cried in the street, pure tears of joy. It was a chef's kiss moment for my career."

That magic moment gave Steve the continued impetus to keep pushing hard. In August 2014, his efforts were rewarded as he was promoted again to an Assistant Director level role as Employer Brand, Attraction and Selection Manager for EY Apprenticeships. Again, a raft of national awards followed every year, culminating in the Best School Leaver Programme and Best Graduate Website awards in 2017, as he and his team delivered campaigns with online reach statistics in the millions and application numbers to join the firm going through the roof.

In May of that year, driven as much as ever to succeed, he moved into a new role, this time as Marketing and Communications Lead for Apprenticeships. He took on responsibility for all marketing and communications, including employer branding, PR, and internal communications. Aware of just how influential parents and carers are in their children's career choices and to support EY's choice to move from a graduate programme to offering Level 7 apprenticeships. Steve explains what that period was like, stepping up a few gears into that assistant director role and then taking a sideways move into the marketing and comms lead for the UK for apprenticeships. "It was an opportunity. My manager went on maternity leave, and I was given all of the responsibilities that she had on top of my own. I was asked to step into her role rather than them bringing somebody in to manage above me. Again, Jane had that faith in me. Others had faith in me in the team, too. At that point as well, the apprenticeship levy was coming in, so some big changes were happening in the business, and my name had apparently been brought up in several conversations where they'd said, "We need him to lead this now. He's going to have to do it whether he is ready or not and whether you are ready for him to do it." And so, I did it. It was the magical part of the role; everything started to slot into place. There were things like the Recruitment Advertising and Design awards; we won the Best School Leaver Apprenticeship Campaign three years in a row in the early careers market. We became the number one employer for apprentices." Steve and his team launched EY's nationwide "Parental Advice" campaign, an industry first for the sector. He explains how it came about, "A lot of it was from conversations I had in regular meetings with Maggie, the UK Talent Partner there. It was great to have a senior leader interested in my work She had two teenage sons; one of them was about to do their GCSEs, and one of them was about to do their A levels, and we had this fantastic conversation about her children, about her career, about just the general early careers market and how employers needed to be supporting young people more, and the campaign, I suppose, was born out of that in many respects, because I remember going back into the office the next day and having a meeting with Jane and saying I've been given the green light by Maggie, to invest quite heavily in parents as part of our, employer branding strategy. That was a gap that we weren't addressing. And as the managing talent partner, a woman who had two children, she expected it to be filled. One of the things that I loved about working with Jane's team at EY was that anything that we did was based on research, so we knew that it was correct and that we were speaking to the people that we needed to be speaking to. It was an opportunity to engage parents in a really meaningful way to start a conversation." Once again, opportunity had knocked on his door.

* * * *

Steve continued to work hard to achieve and deliver, but he began to feel the pressure as things beyond his control had an adverse impact on his area. "There was that personal cost. I was taking a lot of risks. I was working in a recruitment market, which back then was very much like working blind a lot of the time. And that vision became very important for that because the personal cost for me was me failing. Things got too much for me. I don't necessarily think it was the pressure that got to me. I'd had my ego massaged so much and felt like I was on top of the world, and I was the expert and everything. I got the opportunity to move into a new role. It was being created for me. I was being asked to continue the work that I was doing but also lead internal comms within the business. About six months in, I found myself becoming incredibly anxious about the work that I was so confident in. At that point, as well as part of my "I'm so happy with my career and where I'm at", I had been given four weeks off work to use all of my annual leave entitlement in one go, and I'd been off to Australia with my friend Liz. I had an epiphany whilst I was out there that something wasn't necessarily right, but I didn't feel like I knew what it was." Steve came back from Australia to work in January 2017 and got into a conversation with Jane. She said, "I feel like something's different in you, and I'm not quite sure what it is. And I'm a bit concerned that it's the beginning of the end of something."

As happens in life and work, the demands of work and deadlines were pressing. Steve was effectively running his existing team and working with a second brand new team to ensure the parental guidance campaign took off and delivered the results anticipated. He recalls how he felt, "I was overstretched. I felt like anything that anybody was saying from the new team felt like they were criticising me. I became very touchy. I remember one little thing that somebody said to me and me slamming my laptop lid down and storming out of a meeting room, which was completely unlike me. Things were not good." Steve had a catch-up with Jane in June 2017,

"Jane asked me if I was OK, And I said, "Yeah, I'm fine." Then she said, "No, are you really okay?" and something unlocked inside me, and I just burst into tears in the middle of the coffee shop. Jane got up and left me there. She returned about two minutes later; she had brought my bag downstairs and said, "Go and take two weeks off. You are not okay right now. And you need to have some time to yourself." Steve came back after a break and picked up his work activities again. By this time, he had been at EY for seven years. In December 2017, Steve had another conversation with Jane, who said, " When you come back in January, I think we need to have made a decision. We need to have worked out whether or not I need to support you in tackling what's going on right now, or we need to work out an exit strategy." And she was very open and honest about that with me. 2017 was a very difficult year because it was a year where I realized that part of my career was coming to an end, and I'd suddenly gone back into that territory of, "I don't know what else I could do". Steve felt that fear of being lost came back again, but this time decided to be brave and embrace it and had another conversation with Jane; "I decided to resign. I didn't have a job to go to. I had three months' notice that I needed to work. I didn't have a clue what I was going to go and do, but I knew that I'd got a nice pot of savings."

Sometimes, things have to fall apart to make way for new beginnings, and perhaps driven ultimately by his unconscious fear of failure, Steve had burned out. He left EY and his corporate life in April 2018. His decision to step away was both brave and inevitable as he identified, "In the back of my head I said, *"Do you know what, I think now is the time in my career where I don't feel comfortable in the environment I'm in, but I know that I'm really good at what I do."* I needed to change the environment and the delivery of how I was using my skills, knowledge, and experience, and so coming back right full circle as well to my parents' background and entrepreneurship, I had decided before I'd handed my noticing that I was going to try working for myself. When people are talking about depression and anxiety and things, it can feel like you're wading through mud, you're sinking, and it was an opportunity for me to break free of that, and I felt it was the right time. I felt confident in my abilities, which would give me an edge when I was having to deal with all of the logistics and admin and everything that goes with creating a business."

Steve decided he needed some time and space to think, recharge and start planning how he wanted to move forward as a freelancer. He flew to the Philippines for a month. It was while he was there that he had another moment of insight while watching the sunset, "I've got a photo that I've used in presentations where I've talked about my career, a bottle of a well-known brand of beer and the book, 'When Breath Becomes Air' by Paul Kalanithi. It's a book about the regrets that people have about their careers, and watching the sunset over the archipelago, everything was becoming very clear. I came up with the name of the business. I was going to call it the Branding Man. It was going to be a consultancy that was delivering employer brand services for employers that wanted to target young people who were interested in apprenticeships. And it would be the start of a new chapter in my career. And that's where I went from."

* * * *

Now captain of his own destiny, albeit with a sprinkling of nervousness, Steve set up his business and started tapping into his network for opportunities. Given his profile and reputation, his services were soon in demand. He worked on a range of different activities from large and small organisations alike. These included supporting an early careers online careers platform, a parental careers advice programme, writing reports for key bodies in the sector and acting as a recruitment assessor in the public sector, something which he still does today. In May 2019, he began contributing to sector-wide activities at a professional body level and became a Member of the Institute of Student Employers Steering Committee. He continued to update his own marketing and business skills and took a podcast course as part of that. In June 2019, driven by his own sense of curiosity and a continued desire to help young people see the bigger picture of a career as a journey, Steve launched the first episode of "My Career Story" podcast, which shares individual career stories and now has over 100 episodes to date. As he discovered, it also helped him identify his strengths and development areas. Opportunity continued to come his way, including an invitation to judge the 2020 Business Book Awards.

As someone who believes in promoting diversity and as part of his own journey, Steve had also been volunteering as a role model with the LGBTQ+ inclusion charity, Diversity Role Models, since he first started his business. Steve explains why this matters to him so much, "As a gay man, I use the pronouns he, him, cisgender male, and one of the biggest regrets of my career is that when I was a teacher, I missed this huge opportunity to not necessarily be dancing around the classroom and saying "I'm gay" to all of the students. But when you're a teacher, you are essentially a role model for them as well as their teacher. And I'm not saying that out of all those 300 pupils that I taught, I could spot the kids that I thought might be LGBTQ+, but I would've liked to have been in that position where if they had been, they could have approached me; because I think back to my own experience of appreciating who I am and sharing that part of myself with everybody. I didn't come out fully until I'd finished teaching. I was 25 by that point. The year before that, I'd signed up with the LGBTQ+ inclusion charity Diversity Role Models. I'd become a storyteller for them, going into schools in London and talking to young people about my coming out story. And I was thinking to myself, there must be something here where I can add value, where I can use my experience, where I can contribute to a community that I have got so much out of over the last decade, but I've taken a lot out. I've not put anything back in."

As many of us did, the COVID pandemic caused Steve to take stock of where his business was and what was most important for him to focus on in the future. Steve explains, "When I look at it now, I'm somebody who identifies as a gay man. I am very open about my own struggles with my mental health when it comes to anxiety and depression. I am from a working-class background and the first person who attended university in my family. I realised these are the things that I want to start leaning into. And if I'm going to lean into those, it's the same kind of work. I will still be working with employers within early careers, but it's not employer branding anymore. This is diversity, inclusion, equity and belonging work. I was looking at student recruitment in general, and I'd had a lot of conversations as part of the project that I was doing with UCAS, where I'd spoken to early careers employers about what their focuses were. And everybody was talking about gender and ethnicity and nothing else when it came to diversity and inclusion. And yes, they are two huge and important focuses, but they are visible characteristics if we're talking about protected characteristics within diversity and inclusion. There are other ones like sexuality, like 'ability' as I call it rather than disability, something that I adopted from EY, and your socio-economic background, social mobility." He realised that to take the business in the direction that matters most to him, he needed to pivot and rebrand the Branding Man as Curious Consulting, so he was better placed to take up opportunities that spoke to him. Once the rebrand was complete, he set up the Queer Student Awards, an inclusive award celebration that recognises young LGBTQ+ people and the organisations and spaces that are helping them to be their most authentic selves. The initiative was not without its challenge, as Steve explains, "The first one is just the challenge around the name itself, so the use of the word "Queer". I wanted to be able to create somewhere where we could have meaningful conversations about sexuality and where we could use that as an opportunity to celebrate young people who identify as being LGBTQ + or Queer. I wanted to use the word Queer within the awards because it is a word that is being wholeheartedly embraced by young people right now. I fully appreciate, at the same time and in that same breath, that it is a very painful word for a lot of people within the LGBTQ+ community.

"I have people within my own friendship groups or older people within the LGBTQ+ community that I'm friends with that have asked me why I've used such a divisive word. I haven't used it to be divisive. I've used it because, for me, the awards are about celebrating young people. So, it goes back to what I was saying about using research throughout my career at EY within employer branding. If you are going to do something that is celebrating young people, in my opinion, you have to be using the language and the narratives that they are using, not what you would prefer to use. That in itself has presented a challenge because there have been a lot of people who have seen the work that I'm doing, wanted to know more about it, but then decided not to invest or to interact with it because I've used that word. I did have some feedback that I was trying to provoke, and to be intentionally disruptive was a piece of feedback that somebody gave me. And, you know, I put my hands in that conversation and said, "Yes, I am," because, for me, there is not enough attention being paid to sexuality in student recruitment. So, if I want to get your attention, I'm going to get your attention. And also, if we are going to talk about diversity and inclusion, we are talking about a lot of topics, whether that's going across gender, whether that's going across ethnicity, the two biggest focuses, as I've said, that are uncomfortable that people squirm in their seats about, that they don't want to admit that they hold certain views and opinions. Sometimes, you have to do things and say things that will stir the pot a little bit. So, that was one of the challenges I had with it. It's a slow burn. I still think there are a lot of people who are polite when they say no to interacting with it and come up with an excuse about budget or something like that, which is fine. I appreciate that it's a journey and that I'm bringing something to the student market that is new, and as somebody who enjoys being or trying to be the first person to do something, I appreciate that you're going to get 'Nos'."

The challenge presented by COVID meant that he ran the first awards virtually. The impact it had on those participating gave Steve the confidence to scale up and push harder. He ran a second successful awards hybrid event in Manchester in 2022, a location he deliberately chose over London to make the point about regional needs and opted to run the 2023 awards there again. At the same time, he used the mental health qualifications he had gained with his lived experience to devise and deliver workshops for employers and their recruitment teams, so they were better equipped to handle conversations around mental health and well-being when they saw a person in distress. Steve's intention was clear, "It can be quite hard to start the conversation. I was lucky I had somebody like Jane who was there for me; she'd noticed the signs, and she was equipped, and there was a power that came out of that conversation with her. If you can have a proactive conversation about mental health and encourage transparency and honesty in those conversations, you never get to the point where you have to leave."

* * * *

Inspired by the geography on his doorstep and an influential geography teacher who had inspired him, it was hardly surprising that Steve chose to study geography. When we need to make choices, they are often based on erring on the side of caution and choosing familiarity over something foreign. The Teach First advertisement, which used graffiti he saw at the careers fair, sowed an early seed, and provoked an inner desire to find out more. As a former first-generation student himself, inevitably, the life-changing work done by Teach First teachers helped him to experience and fall in love with the joy of helping others to develop in the classroom.

His experience of the sheer breadth of diversity in his classroom every day, combined with his own lack of being able to learn fully at university due to a lack of funds for field trips, was a vital part of what informed his commitment to degree apprenticeships and helping parents from less well-off areas of the UK to understand how to support their teenagers' choices effectively. That inner motivation gained from the emotion of personal understanding combined with the certainly of research enabled him to lead the creation and implementation of multi-award-winning campaigns that ensured diversity won over postcode.

As a rule breaker with a mission to help the most marginalised young people from disadvantaged backgrounds without any restrictions and set against the background of entrepreneurial parents, it was almost inevitable that Steve would opt to start his own business. Those themes, together with the challenges and lived experiences he continues to face as a gay man learning to cope with periods of mental ill health, provide Steve with his own very personal ultimate concerns. It is through those lenses that he steers his business activities with a sprinkling of courage to step outside the box and dare to be brave. Having that level of clarity about why you are doing something and what difference you want to make makes it easy to make decisions about what matters. In Steve's case, the answer is to create impactful events and workshops which help to raise awareness and improve acceptance of the LGBTQ+ community. Doing so means he can encourage and support open and meaningful conversations that change lives for the better.

* * * *

A QUESTION OF DIRECTION AND GOALS:
WHERE DIRECTION AM I HEADED IN?
WHAT'S MY GOAL?

It helps to understand how you think before you make important decisions. As we saw with Steve, he uses his emotional response to situations to shine a light on what matters to him. He listens to and trusts his intuition, particularly when he has moments of insight, and combines it with research to inform what he does next. Together, both lead and enable him to take action and commit to goals to achieve his vision of equity for all and his mission to contribute towards it.

It's now time for you to take the next step in creating the working life you want. To prepare for this, spend a little time reviewing everything you have captured on your INSPiRED Career and Life planner and also review the light bulb moments at the end of each chapter so that you can move forward confidently.

ACTIVITY 1:
STARTING WITH THE BIG PICTURE IN MIND

Having a clear sense of purpose, vision and mission that reflects your ultimate concern aligns with your values, strengths, talents and skills, and your intended goals will help you make clear and confident career choices as and when opportunities arise, or things change.

You have already identified your Purpose Statement or "Why" in Chapter 5. It provides a great starting point which will help you to create a concise vision statement that expresses an ultimate aspiration/why. Once you have done that, the next step is to create a mission statement which describes how you will work towards that. Here are my purpose, vision, and mission statements to illustrate the concepts:

My career purpose *is to help aspiring and established professionals, regardless of their context, to create their own unique career purpose confidently so that no matter how the world is changing, they can create happy, successful, and fulfilling working lives which are built on purpose and not get lost like I did.*

My vision *is a world where everyone is contributing their full potential, inspired by purpose, for the benefit of all.*

My mission *is to change how aspiring and established professionals make career choices by enabling them to create purpose-driven "careers for good" using the research-proven INSPiRED career and life model and toolkit.*

So, what's your career vision and mission?

Use the space below to help you write the vision and mission that matters to you for your career:

Once you have written it, check that you connect with it instinctively and fully. If not, review what you have written and rework/distil it so that it resonates fully with you. You may need to come back to it later to do this.

It is also a good idea to allocate time every year to check if it needs refining or altering. Doing so helps you to keep in touch with the big picture of your working life amid the noise of everyday life.

Now you have a clear purpose, vision, and mission statement, how does it feel, and what is your most significant light bulb moment from creating it?

* * * *

ACTIVITY 2: DECIDING BETWEEN JOB OPTIONS

Now that you have a clear purpose, vision, and mission statement, it's time to choose the role/job you want to do which aligns best with those statements. Making a decision can be tough, but it's also an opportunity to take control and shape your future. Let's explore how you can approach decision-making with confidence and clarity. Understanding how the brain works will help with this.

Until relatively recently, researchers had adopted a model of the brain called the Triune Brain, which was initially developed in the 1960s by Paul D MacLean. According to this evolutionary theory of brain development, three areas of the brain were particularly important, which were largely independent of each other: the basal ganglia area, including the amygdala responsible for coping with moments of high alert and generating a flight, fight, or freeze response; the limbic system which provided the seat of our emotions; and the cortex, the home of cognition and rational thinking.

More recently, researchers have developed a new understanding of how what they call our adaptive brains and how they work. In this model, emotion and cognition are interrelated functions which work together to create our human experience. As part of that experience, we focus on what matters to us and delete, distort, or generalise what is irrelevant. Our brain filters what is around us based on location, energy, language, memories, patterns, and our values and beliefs. It then creates a mental picture in our mind's eye, which informs how we feel and affects our posture. We can use that ability and our rational judgement together to help us make the most informed decisions about our future direction. The activities in this section will help you to confirm your choice using both instinctual and cognition-based decision-making techniques. If you are still undecided, now is the time for you to confirm which direction you want to go in. If you are already pretty sure which direction you want to go in, completing these activities will help to confirm your choice.

Let's start by taking a look at a more instinct-based technique. If I were to say to you, "Don't think about a blue tree", what are you picturing? As you were reading that, it is more than likely that your brain will have obligingly created an image of a blue tree in your head, yet you have probably never thought about one or seen one before. This simple activity illustrates two concepts: firstly, the brain pictures the positive before it can deal with the negative. In other words, as far as the brain is concerned, you have to picture it first before you cannot think of it! This explains why children consistently spill drinks on the floor despite being told not to by their parents, or why we do poorly in presentations or interviews because we are unintentionally picturing what we don't want. Secondly, the activity of thinking about a blue tree illustrates the power of the brain to create something which doesn't exist. This is the power of visualisation, a technique used extensively in business and sport, which builds both capability and confidence. One example of this from many comes from a University of Chicago study. Researchers explored the effectiveness of visualisation and mental rehearsal compared with court time in basketball players' ability to score penalty shots. Their study showed that while an entire month's court time led to a 24% improvement in penalty shot outcomes, mental rehearsal alone for a month led to a 23% improvement – only one per cent less effective than actual practice.

Choosing which door to go though

As well as helping to develop specific skills, the power of visualisation can also help you to decide between different options by bringing insights from your unconscious mind to your conscious awareness.

The visualisation approach tool you are going to learn I call the Doors Technique. Find a quiet time and place where you won't be disturbed so you can settle down to a place of stillness. Taking a few deep and slow breaths will help you to be in a relaxed state. Notice as you settle into that sense of being relaxed how your breathing is becoming slower and more rhythmical. Once you are ready, imagine you are standing in a big circular hallway which has several doors leading off it into rooms – the same number of doors as you have options. In your mind's eye, put a nameplate on each of the doors so it is labelled with the name of one of the different roles, jobs, or options you are considering taking, moving forward. Once you have done that, now go into each room in turn and experience that role option. Notice what you see, hear, and feel and whether this is taking you in the right direction or further away from where you want to be. If something feels wrong, work out what it is so you can identify what is worrying you and consider if it is something you want to overcome or need to avoid.

So, what did you discover by using this visualisation technique? What worked well for you, and what didn't?

Use the space below to make a note of what you felt, if anything, using the technique, what insights you gained and whether you find this an easy and natural activity to do or not.

Using an analytical approach

Having looked at a more intuition-based method, now let's explore two more cognition-based decision-making approaches. The first tool uses a weighted pros and cons approach to help you identify how close a particular role is to your own wants and needs so you can assess its suitability. The diagram below shows you what this will look like:

Job Title:			
Pros		Cons	
Element	Importance	Element	Importance
Total		Total	
What's missing/decision:			

The first thing to do is to set up a scoring system which reflects what you want (your pros). Use what you have learned about what you want through the programme to create a list of all the essential elements you require in your career/job (your pros or positive elements). These include values, sector, role, theme, purpose, location, salary, hours, opportunity, and anything else that matters to you. Give each element an importance score between 1 and 10, where 10 is very important and 1 is not at all important. Now, you need to give a score to what you don't want (your cons). E.g., a commute of more than x minutes, a pressurised environment, etc. Score each con with a negative mark, this time between -1 and -10.

Once you have done that, look at each job/role you are interested in and score it against each element on your list using the grid. Add up the score for each job and review your options based on the final scores to identify which opportunity suits you best. Finally, to ensure you have included everything that matters to you, ask yourself what may be missing and factor this into the process, too. If you complete this activity for each role/job you are considering, it will enable you to compare each equally and based on what matters to you. If, for some reason, you feel that the one with the highest score is not so appealing, think about what is causing you to be uncomfortable about it. Please spend some time identifying what is causing you to feel uncomfortable with it. It may be that you don't feel fully equipped for that role yet, which may be causing an element of imposter syndrome. Though experienced by everyone, women are more prone to this. Remember that if you can match around 75% of the job (and all of the essential criteria), then it is worth applying. It is worth doing a sense check with someone you respect to see if it is just your internal parrot being unhelpful and causing you to question your ability. It may be that you need to do some training to be in the right place to go for it. The next activity will help with identifying what you might be missing.

Once you have completed the pros and cons scoring, using the following decision-making tool will help you make a considered career choice. It uses a form of Strengths, Weaknesses, Opportunities and Threats (SWOT). It will enable you to identify present and future helpful strengths and opportunities while understanding what you need to do to mitigate against potentially harmful weaknesses and threats.

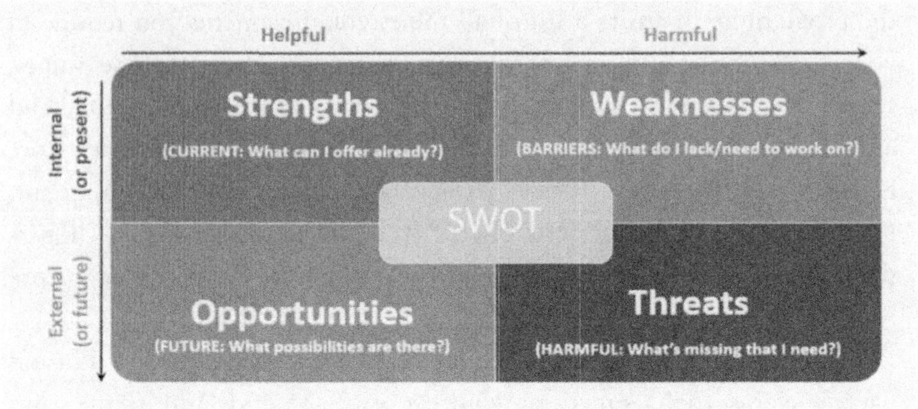

Answer the question in each of the four boxes in light of the role/job you are considering targeting.

Once you have answered the questions, make a note of what you have discovered as a result here:

So, how do you like to make decisions?

Now that you have used both instinctual and cognitive approaches to help you decide, it is helpful to reflect on the different strategies you use to make decisions so you can change your approach if you need to.

Think about a time when you had to make a small, everyday decision. How did you go about it? Did you take a long time choosing, or is it reasonably automatic? Make a note of an example and your reflections on your decision-making strategy.

What about significant, meaningful decisions? Again, think about a time when you had to make a big decision about something important. How did you make that decision? Do you use a different approach in this context? If so, why? Make a note of any difference between your different approaches here:

Finally, make a note of the role/job that you have decided to apply for in the space below:

So, what's your most significant light bulb moment about how you make decisions and the direction you have now decided to go in?

* * * *

ACTIVITY 3: SETTING YOUR BEST GOAL

Goals are what help us to stretch and grow, a crucial part of having a fulfilling life. To set your goal, review your completed planner and decide what is most important to achieve to help you move forward. If you don't set a deadline, what you want to achieve will remain an unfulfilled dream. For goals to be effective, they need to appeal on every level to our adapted brains and to our emotions. That means they need to be SMARTER goals:

S – specific, simple, and short
M –measurable, meaningful to you
A – as if it is happening now, achievable for you
R – realistic for you, with a stretch, and responsible, i.e., they do not harm people or the planet.
T – time-related, towards what you want (and for you only)
E – exciting, emotional, and evidential and include the last step needed to make it happen
R – resourced, reviewed regularly and rewarding

For a goal to be well formed and written, it needs only to use positive language, be meaningful, motivating, and believable, and contain enough detail and emotion to create a compelling picture in your mind's eye. The date at the goal's start needs to be the date that the goal is achieved with the events of the day written in the present tense. It also needs to contain the top three benefits. Once the goal is written, it needs to have the next three steps towards it, complete with a timeline so that you are committed to taking timely action.

Here's an example of a well-formed goal written by Vicky, a 53-year-old aromatherapist I worked with who wanted to grow her business and increase her income in a way which sat comfortably with her value set as a therapist.

"It is Friday, 4th November 2016, and I am in my new Angel House consulting room, which is warm, cosy, welcoming and painted in peach. I can smell the aroma of wine and nibbles and see the leaflets and discount vouchers for my aromatherapy and reflexology services. New faces from the gym surround me: the bridal shop, the hospital, the university, and my regular customers, friends, and fellow therapists. My diary is filling up, and I have just made my 8th new appointment of the day. I felt inspired, energised, and ready for action because I have found the beginning of my path to my life as a healer."

As you can see, Vicky's goal evokes a vibrant mental picture when you read it. As a result of setting this goal, she organised and ran a very successful event involving seven different therapists/colleagues, all using the shared accommodation. This has led to a series of regular "Meet the Therapists" events, increasing business for all. Vicky sold out of a new range of aromatherapy products she made to test the market at the event and set herself a new goal to explore getting them manufactured commercially.

Whenever someone writes a goal, it is essential to ensure that what they have written scores a perfect 10 in terms of appeal and level of commitment to achieving it. If it scores less than a ten, it just needs to be adjusted until it does. Often, this requires the addition of a sensory element such as colour, touch, sound, taste, or smell for it to evoke the right feeling.

So, what's the goal you need to set now?

Having read how to set a goal successfully, now it's your turn. What's the most important goal you could set to help you move forward effectively? Spend some time thinking about it and use the earlier guidance notes to help you write a compelling goal in the space below:

Now that you have written it remember to score it out of ten in terms of how appealing it is to you and how committed you are to it. If it helps you, get someone else to read it to you or record it on your phone and listen to it. If you give either element a score lower than a ten, make whatever changes you need so it is totally compelling on both fronts. Use the space below to record your final version:

Now, identify the first three steps/sub-goals you need to achieve to move towards completing this goal. Then, assign a date to them in the space below:

Maintaining focus

Now that you have set a direction for your life, keep moving forward. Make sure you read your vision, mission and goal regularly. Consider creating a vision board consisting of images and words that represent what you want to achieve and pin it somewhere where you can see it regularly.

You could also use a focus question to triage your decisions and keep you on track to achieving your vision and mission. Here's mine as an example: "*Will this opportunity or action cause significantly more people to choose their career on purpose?*" Saying yes to this question is what led me to writing ***Change Your Story***.

Use the space below to create your focus question:

Now that you have a focus question to help you stay on track, remember to add it to your vision, mission and goal document and use it very regularly. It will make a big difference to what you achieve.

Now that you have written your goal, what is your most significant light bulb moment about setting your goal?

* * * *

CONSOLIDATING YOUR LEARNING FROM THIS CHAPTER TO ANSWER THE QUESTION:

WHAT DIRECTION AM I HEADED IN? WHAT'S MY GOAL?

Congratulations on writing your goal and completing all the activities for this chapter on Decision Making and Goal Setting. Now it's time to capture what you have learned about your direction and goal in your INSPiRED

Career and Life planner. Take the significant keywords you have identified in this chapter and add them to the Direction and Goal Setting box highlighted in the diagram below. Then, use the second copy of the planner at the back of this book to record a sentence in answer to the question for this chapter:

Where am I headed? What's my goal?

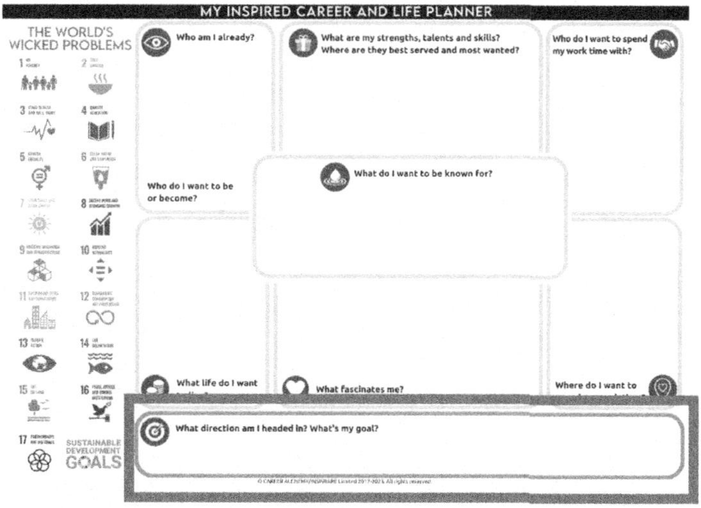

Remember you can download a digital copy of the planner tool from here: www.careeralchemy.co.uk/free-reader-planner-tool.html

* * * *

PART THREE:

ACHIEVING YOUR STORY

STRATEGIES FOR SUCCESS & WELL-BEING

STRATEGIES FOR SUCCESS & WELL-BEING: WHAT DO I NEED TO DO TO THRIVE IN LIFE AND WORK?

HARNESSING MINDSET, BEHAVIOURS, AND WELL-BEING

Squeeze the juice out of life, not to the point that the pips squeak and you burn out, but so you can say you made the most of the ride and thrived.

Congratulations on understanding and developing your story so that you now have an inspiring vision, mission, and goal for your future. You now know who you want to become and where your strengths, talents and skills are best served – the second half of the questions in Chapter One and Chapter Three. Before you move forward, it's worth spending a few minutes adding a sentence or two on these to your INSPiRED Career and Life Planner.

The question that remains now is, how do you get there easily so you can thrive in life and work? Part of that has to do with how you tell your story from now on, and part of it has to do with your thinking and strategies for success and well-being, and how you react to what comes your way.

Just as those whose stories that are shared in this book discovered, now that you are clear about what your ultimate concern is, and the difference you want to make, you will start to notice opportunities come your way much more easily.

That happens for two reasons. First, we attract them consciously because of the way we position ourselves online, for instance, on LinkedIn and other social media sites, and at meetings and conferences when we have the chance to discuss and present ideas that matter. Sharing valuable insights on topics related to what we care about that help others with similar interests will naturally attract people from the same tribe to you. Doing so will also attract those outside that tribe who need your expertise. This type of activity helps us to be seen and builds credibility and connections, which naturally lead to opportunities.

The second reason that we benefit from opportunities is due to the way our brains work. Our brains are primed to see opportunities easily because of our reticular activating system (RAS). Your RAS automatically scans the horizon through the lens of what matters to you to filter out what is irrelevant and shine a spotlight on what matters.

As you also will have noticed in the stories in this book, sometimes things go wrong, and for whatever reason, we don't get the outcome we want. This is when the wise recognise the power of redirection and the opportunity to create something better in work and life. Being made redundant is one example of how you can use the power of redirection to create a better future. If viewed that way, redundancy is not a curse but rather an opportunity to do something better. If you face some form of unwanted redirection, instead of fighting it, use the experience to turn what initially feels like a blow into something likely to be a blessing in disguise. To do that, use the simple ABC approach, which follows below to help you see a brighter future:

- ✓ **Acknowledge the emotion:** it takes around 90 seconds for emotion to wash through us, so sitting quietly with it for a moment or two and taking a few breaths as you do so will enable you to feel in control. Think of it as a wave going through your mind. You don't have to ride the wave or create a pity party; you can let it pass. Once you have done that, your brain will be in a better state to help you move forward.

- ✓ **Brainstorm your challenges to find helpful solutions:** use this approach so you can start focusing on how you can move forward with your vision and mission in mind. Ask yourself, "What could be good about this? What possibilities does this open up for me that take me closer to working on my ultimate concern?"
- ✓ **Concentrate on taking action by identifying your next steps:** do this to help you change direction, reset, and regain a greater sense of control over your future. Having worked with hundreds of people at risk of or who have been made redundant, in 99% of the cases, when they look back, they are surprisingly glad it happened, as it gave them permission to make changes and experience other adventures.

Repeat whichever steps you need to develop a sense of what to do next to move forward. That will often mean tapping into your network for help. Please remember it is OK to ask for help. Like car accidents, redundancy is widespread and increasingly driven by technology-related change. It is the post that is being made redundant. You are still a valid human being!

We all have something worthwhile to contribute. To do that to the best of our abilities means managing our mindset, habits, and well-being. The following activities in these chapters are designed to help you explore all three areas.

* * * *

A QUESTION OF SUCCESS & WELL-BEING:
WHAT DO I NEED TO DO TO THRIVE IN LIFE AND WORK?

If you are like the people in the stories you have read, you will have noticed that they either had unhelpful events or better opportunities that have redirected them to a better future. Each of the eight individuals in this book has learned to deal with fear and the negative. They embraced new opportunities because of their mindset, habits, and how they allocated their time and energy so they could be successful and thrive. Some of them had to get to the point of burnout or disease before they responded to the nudges, and sometimes shoves, of life. Others needed to grab their faith and courage in both hands to give them the fortitude to take on the challenges and opportunities they attracted or created. All of them have learned how to thrive rather than survive by managing their mindsets, adopting helpful habits to ensure they move a little closer every day to their goal, and managing their energy and well-being effectively.

* * * *

ACTIVITY 1: THE MAGIC OF RIGHT THINKING

We are all influenced by external factors which cause us to react. To operate at our optimum, we need to manage our thinking. That means we need to be aware of how we think in different circumstances. Sometimes, we react positively, and sometimes, our response is negative. As neuroscientists have identified, our brains have a primaeval negative pre-set built in, which is meant to keep us safe, but instead, it can keep our thinking small and prevent us from growing. We react more strongly to negative emotions but can train our brains to be more positive in the way we think. So, if you see your glass as metaphorically half empty instead of half full, maybe it's time to retrain it to look for the positive.

Practising self-compassion

While self-esteem is a positive evaluation of self-worth, self-compassion is a way of relating to the ever-changing experience of who we are with kindness and acceptance - especially when we fail or feel inadequate. This helps us to deal with the ups and downs of life. Self-compassion does not require feeling better than anyone else. It simply requires acknowledging the shared and imperfect human condition we all experience and treating ourselves with kindness rather than judgment, seeking connection rather than isolation and reconciling suffering in a mindful way so it can pass.

The latest research shows that one of the best things we can do for ourselves in difficult times is to give ourselves the same compassion as we would to others. Self-compassion involves offering oneself understanding and encouragement in times of distress, whether these stem from personal faults and shortcomings or challenges imposed by outside circumstances. Associate Professor at the University of Texas, Kristin Neff, has developed a model of self-compassion, which includes six elements: enhancing self-kindness, recognising common humanity, practising mindfulness, and reducing self-judgment, feelings of isolation, and overidentification with negative thoughts. Her research counters misconceptions of it being selfish or demotivating and instead shows the role self-compassion has to play in fostering a greater sense of well-being.

Everyone worries over things. The underlying reasons are simple. Sometimes, it's because we don't want to fail, we fear we aren't good enough, we want certainty or control, we want safety and comfort, or above all because we hate rejection. That fear can prevent us from moving forward effectively. What we say to ourselves and others has a power in it, and although words represent the map, not the territory, they are stacked with meanings which evoke positive and negative feelings and responses. One of the most important things we can do to achieve greater success and happiness is to mind our language and edit out the negativity of the words our own, often unhelpful internal parrot uses. As you saw when we explored the concept of Blue Tree thinking in Chapter Eight, we can set ourselves up for success or failure very easily, simply by what we say to ourselves. Many people are usually their harshest critics. We need to avoid beating ourselves up by using language such as, *"Why can't I...?"*, *"Why haven't I...?"* or *"Why aren't I ...?"* It is simply a form of self-abuse, which we all do sometimes, but does us no good at all. When under pressure, we delete, distort, or generalise our abilities negatively. While this often reflects how we feel at the time, if we check the facts, we will usually find that others do not hold the negative beliefs we have about ourselves.

The solution is to be kind in what you say to yourself and how you say it. That way, your brain can create a positive image, which leads to the right sort of action and outcome you want rather than failure. Replacing questions which begin with *"Why can't I...?"* with better-formed questions such as *"How can I...?"* will help you move forward more effectively and prevent you from being stuck.

If you find yourself stuck and suffering in moments of crisis, there is a simple but effective antidote. Just remember and relive one of the magic moments you identified in Chapter One and re-run the movie of the event in your mind's eye. Doing so will help you move from being in *a right state* into being in *the right state*. The more you learn to rebalance your emotions during the day, the more you train your brain to focus on desired outcomes, not distractions. Though a work in progress for many of us, the more you do it, the easier time you will have every day.

Being aware of how we think habitually helps us to recognise automatic behaviour and conditioned responses. As always, the power of awareness and reflection gives us the insights we need to change them and get better results. The following questions will help you to be aware of your habitual thinking patterns and enable you to change them.

So, what triggers your positive thinking?

Think of a time when you felt really positive. Relive that in your mind's eye and ask yourself what happened to make you feel so positive. What influences were there on your state of mind that caused you to feel positive? Write down the triggers which influenced your thinking in the space below the question:

What triggers my negative thinking?

Now, think of a time when you really doubted yourself. Relive that in your mind's eye and ask yourself what happened to make you feel so uncertain/negative. What influences affected your state of mind and caused you to feel that way? Again, write down the triggers which influenced your thinking here:

Now that you have identified the triggers which lead to doubt, loss of motivation and poor performance, you can use a range of different techniques to help change your thinking. One of them is to check whether what you believe to be true is actually true. The advice in Chapter Seven to collect evidence of things that go well each day will, over time, provide proof of your ability to do things well. It provides an excellent way to correct persistently inaccurate thinking and beliefs.

One other approach, developed by French psychologist Emile Coué, is to use affirmations. They are short, meaningful statements that use conscious autosuggestion to help the brain think differently. They can be big-picture or detailed in their approach. One of the most well-known is Coué's own affirmation: "Every day, in every way, I am getting better and better".

So, what affirmations can I use to change my mind set for the better? Use the space below to create one or more affirmations to help you overcome the negative triggers you identified:

For maximum impact, repeat your affirmations every morning when you wake up and every evening before you go to bed to help adjust your habitual thinking responses. You may find it helpful to write them on a sticky note and put them on the mirror in the bathroom or the fridge as a daily reminder or use a virtual sticky note on your computer or mobile phone.

Remember that we are all FAB when we are **Focused**, **Action-orientated** and **Believe** in ourselves.

So, what is your most significant light bulb moment about your mindset, and how can you change it?

* * * *

ACTIVITY 2: MAKING SUCCESS A HABIT

As well as creating and using the right mindset, it is helpful to ensure that your habits set you up for success too, so you can achieve your mission and goal. Habits develop over time and are things we do regularly and often. Our brains use habits as they are familiar and need less energy to run. While overall, they are helpful, sometimes we run habits as a strategy without remembering the reason why. Habits are triggered by a cue to begin a particular action to generate a specific outcome. This activity will help you identify which habits work well for you and which need changing. Let's start by looking at your effective habits first through this question:

So, given your goal and mission, which of your current habits work well for you?

Make a note of your top five valuable habits. Consider each habit in turn and identify what triggers you to perform the habit, what action you take, and what feeling you get from doing it. Here's an example pro forma sentence to help you with this:

When [cue/trigger] happens, I [habit] because I want [outcome, e.g., result or emotional state]. Here is a worked example.

When I receive an email from my boss, I read it as soon as possible so I can respond quickly and feel good/in control.

Now, consider what you gain from this habit and why it helps you so much. Note what you discover about your top five habits in the space below.

These are your most helpful habits, and you need to make as much use of them as possible.

So, what habits do you need to change to help you be successful?

Now, let's explore which habits are unhelpful and prevent you from being successful so you can replace them with a better approach. Completing this activity will also help you to identify the root cause/motivation behind your unhelpful habits so you can change your habits, and they can be more effective in helping you to achieve what you want. The following question will help you to identify which habits are holding you back.

Given my goal and mission, which of my current habits don't work well for me?

Knowing what does not work well for you enables you to change it. Make a list of your top 5 least valuable habits in the space below:

Now, ask yourself what you could do instead to achieve the gain you want. Consider whether you could even drop the habit totally if that seems appropriate. Remember that behind every seemingly negative outcome, there is a positive intention. So, look for what benefit is behind the unhelpful habit. These unconscious benefits often include themes such as a desire for safety, time off, the chance to recharge, avoiding conflict, or using fear to motivate you, etc., so be kind to yourself as you explore what you need to change and remember the power of self-compassion in enhancing your well-being. Use the same structure as before to break down the unhelpful habits into the three component parts of trigger, action, and outcome and make a note of what you discover here:

Now, decide if you need to stop doing that habit or change it so it is more effective. For instance, if you tend to head for food or drink when you are stressed, you may be able to improve how you feel by having a simple conversation with a loved one or playing your favourite music. The action of eating and the action of talking with someone special or playing music you love will make you feel better, but some may be less harmful to your waistline and health than others!

Make a note of what you will do differently to get the same benefit and outcome here:

According to researchers at UCL, it takes 66 days to change a habit, so once you have decided on what your new habit will be, you will need to persist at the start until the new habit replaces the old one automatically. If you reward yourself every time you use the new habit rather than the old, it will reinforce and speed up your progress to using better habits more effectively. The rewards do not have to cost money or involve food or drink and could be simple and low/no cost, e.g., more time to read a book, watch a film, or do your favourite hobby.

What is your most significant light bulb moment about your habits?

* * * *

ACTIVITY 3: THRIVING IN LIFE

We often hear people talk jokingly about how an afternoon spent in some pretty pointless meeting represents an afternoon of their life they will never get back. If any of us were to win a significant sum of money, we would take advice from experts and plan how we want to invest and spend it. Yet most people fail to consider how they want to spend the gift of life and time that we all have, often only realising its value when some form of wake-up call reminds them of their mortality. So, to thrive in life, we need to be more mindful and conscious of how we spend our time and energy, so we can get more out of it. This section contains two activities to help you get the most out of your life.

The Pizza of Life

You may remember completing the work/life doughnut activity in Chapter Two, where we looked at how to work connected with the rest of life on a daily basis. The Pizza of Life tool will help you decide how to spend your time and effort to create the life you want. Being clear on what that is will help you to get what you want out of your life and enjoy a smoother ride because you are spending your energy wisely and in pursuit of what really matters to you. Once you have decided what you want to achieve, you can use the Pizza of Life tool to slice your life according to your priorities. It gives you a big-picture view so you can monitor and review your progress and your direction of travel in life. Here's the Pizza of Life I use with my clients.

**Spirituality means what it means to you. For some, this means religion, or something greater than ourselves, while for others it could even mean community.*

Like any pizza, you can cut it up into as many slices as you like to reflect what's important to you, though typically, you may want to restrict it to six or seven. It may well be hard to manage many more than that, and who wants a life full of lots of really thin slices anyway?! You can either decide on how many slices you want to have and create your own version, or you can use the version below. Whichever option you go for, give each slice a score between 0 (the centre of the pizza) and 10 (the outside of the pizza) by colouring in an appropriate amount. Doing this will help you see how smoothly your life is running and identify areas where it needs more work to be as full of flavour as possible.

When you have done this, make a note of your answers to the following questions in the space below them:

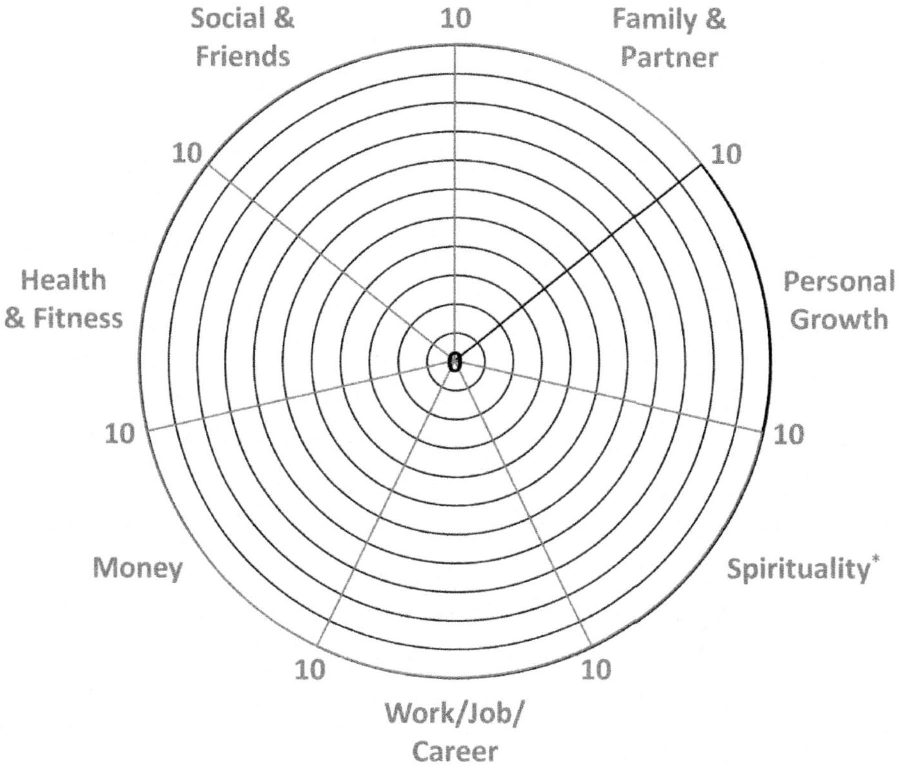

**Spirituality means what it means to you. For some, this means religion, or something greater than ourselves, while for others it could even mean community.*

What three slices of the Pizza of Life do I need to work on?

What changes can I make to improve these slices, so they taste great?

What is your most significant light bulb moment of your Pizza of Life, and how will you use it?

* * * *

Achieving and maintaining health and well-being

The World Health Organization defines health as "a state of complete physical, mental and social well-being and not merely the absence of disease or infirmity". If we want to thrive in life, we need to pay attention to how we look after ourselves every day and how we manage stress. Stress comes in two forms: eustress, which energises and motivates us, and destress, which depletes us and can make us ill. The trick is to identify what causes the negative stress and take steps to change it. There are also steps we need to take to help us to thrive. When we are tired, we are less able to handle stress. According to experts, adults need at least seven hours of sleep a night and a lack of sleep causes levels of anxiety and stress to rise. According to statistics from Mental Health UK, one in every four people has experienced a mental health problem, and just over one in ten people (that's eight million adults) are currently suffering from anxiety disorder. Given that experts estimate that we are made up of between 50 and 75% water, keeping hydrated is also important, not least as there is clear evidence that when we are dehydrated, it causes our anxiety levels to rise. Similarly, drinking too many drinks with caffeine in them can also cause anxiety levels to rise. Many of us turn to something sweet when we are feeling stressed, but that doesn't help either.

According to researchers at Harvard, a sugar rush can mimic a panic attack. If we can avoid eating processed food and, in particular, food which is high in sugar, we will experience fewer highs and lows of blood sugar and less anxiety. As we know, exercise causes the brain to experience happiness chemicals such as dopamine, which also helps to counter anxiety. If we make small changes to our lives, choices, and habits and increase the amount and quality of sleep, we can drink more water, reduce caffeine, and sugar, and do a few more steps every day, we can help ourselves to feel better.

Using gratitude as an antidote to anxiety

In addition to practising self-compassion, another tool which helps us to reduce stress and enjoy life more is the practice of gratitude. One of the world's leading experts on gratitude, Robert Emmons, defines gratitude as an affirmation of what's good in the world and the gifts and benefits we receive every day from others and life, which exist outside of us. Emmons' work shows that, psychologically, the practice of gratitude, even though in a simple way like saying 'thank you', brings many benefits. It helps us t' enjoy enhanced well-being and positive emotions and reduces anxiety, depression, and comparison with others. It increases our resilience in adversity and the transitions of life. It helps us to live a more meaningful life of constructive activity, which helps us to grow because we are more alert, alive, awake, and more open to learning. As a result, we experience more joy, pleasure, contentment, hope, optimism, pride, and happiness. Physically, experiencing gratitude helps us to have more robust immune systems, less concern about aches and pains, and lower blood pressure, so we get better sleep and feel more refreshed when we wake up, are more able and inclined to exercise, and take better care of our health. Gratitude also brings social benefits and makes us more helpful, generous, compassionate, outgoing, and forgiving, resulting in more friends to whom we can show and express gratitude and praise and feel less isolated and lonely.

From a career perspective, practising gratitude makes us better managers who praise more easily, are less impatient, and are better decision-makers. That leads to lower staff turnover, stress, and better work-related mental health. Gratitude also helps us find meaning in our work and gives us a stronger sense of spiritual connection, should we choose to explore it. Social psychologist Barbara Fredrickson has identified gratitude as one of the top ten emotions which helps us to be more in tune with others, while gratitude is one of the 24 character strengths identified by the VIA Institute and features strongly in Meeta's life and story in Chapter Three.

Learning the practice of gratitude, therefore, brings many benefits and has been used successfully in helping those in stressful roles, like healthcare workers, to recover from burnout. If we can harness these benefits and use them to reduce stress and anxiety, then burnout is much less likely. The more grateful you are, the more you attract things to be grateful for, not least because your brain is looking for them. When you practice gratitude, it engages the brain regions linked to social and moral cognition, reward, and value judgment, such as the anterior cingulate and medial prefrontal cortex. It induces the hypothalamus, influencing metabolism, stress, and behaviour, and increases levels of the happy hormone and neurotransmitter dopamine. It also improves self-worth, compassion, and interpersonal relationships, counteracting negative interactions with positive feedback.

Developing gratitude as a habit

A great way to start your day and create the right frame of mind is to ask yourself, "*What am I grateful for already this morning?*" If you can, spend ten minutes at lunchtime every day going for a slow and rhythmic mindful walk or walking meditation in a park or garden. Notice the feeling in your feet on the ground as you walk. This type of walking brings you into the present with a heightened sense of awareness, so you can notice the beauty of nature around you. When you see little things that make you smile, it lights up your brain and wires it for happiness over time. As Chris discovered in Chapter Six, walking brings both mental and physiological benefits. These include increased blood flow, circulation and blood sugar levels, improved digestion, lower anxiety, and improved sleep. It is often when we are in this state of heightened relaxation that we gain significant insights, which can help us solve the challenges we are dealing with. Yoga is also helpful as an activity to bring you to being here in the moment, as is meditation, either in silence or achieved by listening to ambient meditation music.

Before bed, spend some time journalling about your day. Ask yourself, "*What three things am I grateful for today?*" If you face unwanted challenges, asking yourself, "*What could be good about this experience? How could it help me?*" will enable you to find the gift disguised as a problem.

Journalling is a powerful tool that transmutes our experiences, thoughts, beliefs, and desires into language in a way which helps us to make sense of and understand ourselves and grow. As research has shown, as well as cultivating gratitude, journalling offers a range of other benefits, including lower anxiety and depression, improved memory and immune function and is used to aid recovery from trauma. In an era where we usually spend hours hunched over a computer, there is something comforting in using a pen and cursive writing to reflect and grow. It also aids brain development in the areas of thinking, language and working memory by stimulating brain synapses and synchronicity, leading to increased comprehension and participation. The following activity is designed to stimulate your gratitude muscle. Before you start, notice how you feel. Then answer the following questions:

So, what are you grateful for in your life?
Make a list of ten elements and explain why.

Who do you need to say thank you to?
Write a sentence or two which expresses your gratitude to them. If you prefer, draw a picture, or write a poem or piece of music instead.
Notice how you feel now after that activity. Do you feel different, and if so,

how? Use the space below to make a note of what you discover.

Looking back over activity 3, what is your most significant light bulb moment that you need to do to achieve and maintain your health and well-being?

* * * *

CONSOLIDATING YOUR LEARNING FROM THIS CHAPTER TO ANSWER THE QUESTION:

WHAT DO YOU NEED TO DO TO THRIVE IN LIFE AND WORK?

The activities in this chapter have been designed to equip you with the mindset, habits, and well-being strategies to help you be successful and thrive. Spend a couple of moments reviewing what you have discovered while reading this chapter, so that you can answer the following final question that will help you change your story for the better.

What is your most significant light bulb moment of the strategies you need to adopt to thrive in work and life?

* * * *

Moving forward in life is about having the right mindset and strategies to help you grow so you can achieve your goals, ambitions, and potential. I hope that the INSPiRED Career and Life approach has given you the clarity of direction, confidence, and motivation to create and develop the working life you want because you have found your ultimate concern. If you ever find yourself going off track during the rest of your career, revisiting the questions in this planner and the relevant chapter exercises will help you identify what is wrong and find a way to fix it.

When it comes to responding to unforeseen change in your life, you have the power to accept it, refuse it, revolt against it, or create something new.

Choose wisely – you have one life with which to make a difference to something you care about.

I hope that your ultimate concern provides the rocket fuel for you, your talents, and your skills so you can make your unique contribution in a way which lights you up, fills you with joy and serves the world for as long as you choose to do so.

Enjoy the ride of your life.

PART FOUR:

APPENDICES

Section Source: The Sustainable Development Goals Report 2023: Special Edition by Jennifer Ross, Content Services Unit/Department for General Assembly and Conference Management

For more information visit: www.un.org/sustainabledevelopment/

WHAT DO YOU CARE ABOUT ENOUGH TO WANT TO CHANGE IT FOR THE BETTER?

This section contains an overview of each of the goals and their challenges and includes a list of the primary career roles related to the individual goal.

As you read through each of the goals, make a note of what interests you and spend some time reflecting on why that specific goal or role appeals. Consider what gives you a sense of progress. Some people need direct feedback from their actions, so they choose to be working on the ground at a tactical level, while others prefer to work at a strategic level. Which is true in your case, or would you prefer a blend?

Remember that in Chapter Five, we looked at some career roles like leadership and management, human resources, finance, sales and marketing, operations, IT, research and development, administration, estates/facilities management, and legal work that are standard functions in most organisations who are working on a specific SDG, depending on their sector and size. In that chapter, we also explored how connecting your why, a theme you care about, with a function that suits you will provide you with long-lasting meaning and fulfilment. Remember that the key to creating this type of working life is to find an intersection between who you are, what you can offer, what attracts you and specific opportunities to make a positive difference.

This section explores each of the SDGs, and includes key definitions, outlines the current state of play globally, some of the root causes and issues which lie at the heart of an individual goal and addressing, and lists details of some related primary job roles. Given the complexity of the SDGs as wicked problems, please bear in mind as you investigate further that there is a significant level of interrelatedness between individual goals, which will inevitably lead to some level of duplication of roles overall.

Each goal includes space for you to note your insights from reading about the goal and contains links to help you investigate further and improve your understanding of what the work entails:

- UK: https://www.prospects.ac.uk/job-profiles
- US: https://www.onetonline.org/ (use the occupational keyword search tool)
- Europe: https://eures.ec.europa.eu/index_en
- Use https://www.careeralchemy.co.uk/understanding-job-market.html to help you compare jobs and understand key labour market information.

* * * *

THE SUSTAINABLE DEVELOPMENT GOALS REPORT 2023: SPECIAL EDITION- UNSTATS.UN.ORG/SDGS/REPORT/2023/

(***Abbreviations:*** *Least Developed Countries (LDCs), Landlocked Developing Countries (LLDCs) and Small Island Developing States (SIDS)*)

SDG 1: NO POVERTY

"End poverty in all its forms everywhere."

Being able to enjoy an adequate living standard is a fundamental human right. Addressing poverty is one of the most complex challenges of all time and requires a multi-faceted approach to end poverty in all its forms around the world.

Key factors which cause an individual to experience greater poverty include:

- **Changes to the Economy:** economic downturns reduce job opportunities and increase living costs, pushing vulnerable groups into deeper poverty.
- **Under/unemployment:** insufficient income from joblessness or underpaid positions makes covering basic needs challenging, perpetuating poverty.
- **Lack of Education:** limited education restricts access to well-paying jobs, increasing economic hardship risks.
- **Lack of House/Insecure Housing Tenure:** unstable housing leads to stress, impacting mental and physical well-being and job stability.
- **Disability and Ill Health:** disabilities increase medical costs and limit job opportunities, exacerbating economic challenges.
- **Ethnicity:** discrimination against certain ethnicities limits job and education opportunities, inducing economic instability.

- **Location:** living in resource-limited or high-cost areas can trap individuals in poverty due to reduced opportunities.

JOB ROLES RELATED TO ALLEVIATING POVERTY:

Aid and Relief

✓ **Program Managers** oversee implementing programmes to improve access to food, health, and other support, including creating sustainable livelihoods. They work with staff to ensure that programmes are effective and that they are reaching the intended beneficiaries.

✓ **Humanitarian Aid Workers** provide immediate relief to prevent extreme poverty and starvation in regions affected by conflict, natural disasters, or other crises.

✓ **Healthcare Workers** ensure people are healthy, they can work and lift themselves out of poverty. Good health is closely linked with economic productivity.

Economic and Financial Development

✓ **Economists** can help design policies that promote economic growth, redistribute income, and provide opportunities for the poor. They work in areas such as economic development, poverty research or policy analysis and can also analyse the root causes of poverty and recommend solutions.

✓ **Trade and Investment Specialists** work towards fairer trade systems. Trade policies can significantly impact poverty levels, especially in developing countries.

✓ **Microfinance Specialists** provide small loans and other financial services to nascent entrepreneurs in developing countries in particular and to low-income individuals and businesses, which help to uplift communities out of poverty. They also work with clients to develop business plans and to track their progress.

- ✓ **Social Entrepreneurs** set up and run businesses which contribute to reducing economic inequality, improving social justice and increase environmental sustainability.
- ✓ **Fundraisers** raise money to support the work of the organisation. They work with donors to secure funding, and they develop and manage fundraising campaigns.
- ✓ **Sustainable Agricultural Specialists** help improve agricultural productivity, diversify crops, and promote sustainable farming. Since many of the world's poor are farmers, specialists who work in this area can make a significant impact.
- ✓ **Fair Trade Advocates** work to ensure that farmers and workers in developing countries receive a fair price for their products. This can help to improve their standard of living and reduce poverty.
- ✓ **Business Advisers** provide information, support, coaching, advice and guidance to individuals and companies from start up to help to grow, scale up, change, or diversify their business model.

Social Welfare, Community & Housing Development

- ✓ **Social Workers** support and help people and communities struggling with poverty, homelessness, and other social issues. They can work in various settings, such as government agencies, non-profit organisations, and schools.
- ✓ **Development Workers** work with NGOs, international organisations, and community groups to implement poverty alleviation projects in areas like education, health, and infrastructure.
- ✓ **Community Development Workers** help communities bring about social change and improve the quality of life in their local area. They help people to develop leadership skills, advocate for their needs, and build stronger communities.

- ✓ **Housing Officers and Managers** support individuals to become successful tenants in local authority and housing association properties.

Education, Training & Jobs

- ✓ **Educators**, from teachers to policymakers, can make a difference. Education is another one of the primary tools to break the cycle of poverty.
- ✓ **Trainers** provide training to individuals and organisations on poverty-related topics, such as microfinance, business development, and community organising.
- ✓ **Careers Development Professionals** provide education, information, advice, and guidance to help people understand themselves, their motivations, and their abilities so they can make appropriate choices about their education, training, and work.

Environmental and Urban Planning

- ✓ **Environmental Scientists** work to mitigate the impact of climate change, which can exacerbate poverty, especially in vulnerable communities.
- ✓ **Urban Planners** ensure that urban environments are sustainable, inclusive, accessible and provide opportunities for all. As more people migrate to cities, this work is critical.

Policy, Research, & Advocacy

- ✓ **Researchers** help guide policy and practice through their research on poverty dynamics, interventions, and the effectiveness of various programmes (including in trade unions).
- ✓ **Civil Servants** support various government activities, including housing, health and social care, and business.
- ✓ **Policymakers** work in government or influential positions to develop and shape policies that directly address poverty, such as social safety nets and tax policies.

- ✓ **Local Government Officers** enact local government policy and ensure that local services are delivered efficiently and cost-effectively in areas in this context, such as education, health and social care, housing, and transport.
- ✓ **Legal Experts** work on land rights, labour rights, and other areas to ensure the impoverished are protected and can access opportunities.
- ✓ **Advocates/Activists** campaign for policies that target poverty alleviation, whether through grassroots movements or working for more prominent NGOs, play a critical role.

You may also find it helpful to look at roles included in a related SDG that interests you. The following websites will help you explore these and other roles in more detail:

- UK: https://www.prospects.ac.uk/job-profiles
- Use https://www.careeralchemy.co.uk/understanding-job-market.html to help you compare jobs and understand key labour market information
- US: https://www.onetonline.org/ (use the occupational keyword search tool)
- Europe: https://eures.ec.europa.eu/index_en
- More about SDG 1: https://www.un.org/sustainabledevelopment/poverty/

CONSOLIDATING YOUR LEARNING FROM SDG 1 – POVERTY:

What is your biggest light bulb moment about SDG 1?

* * * *

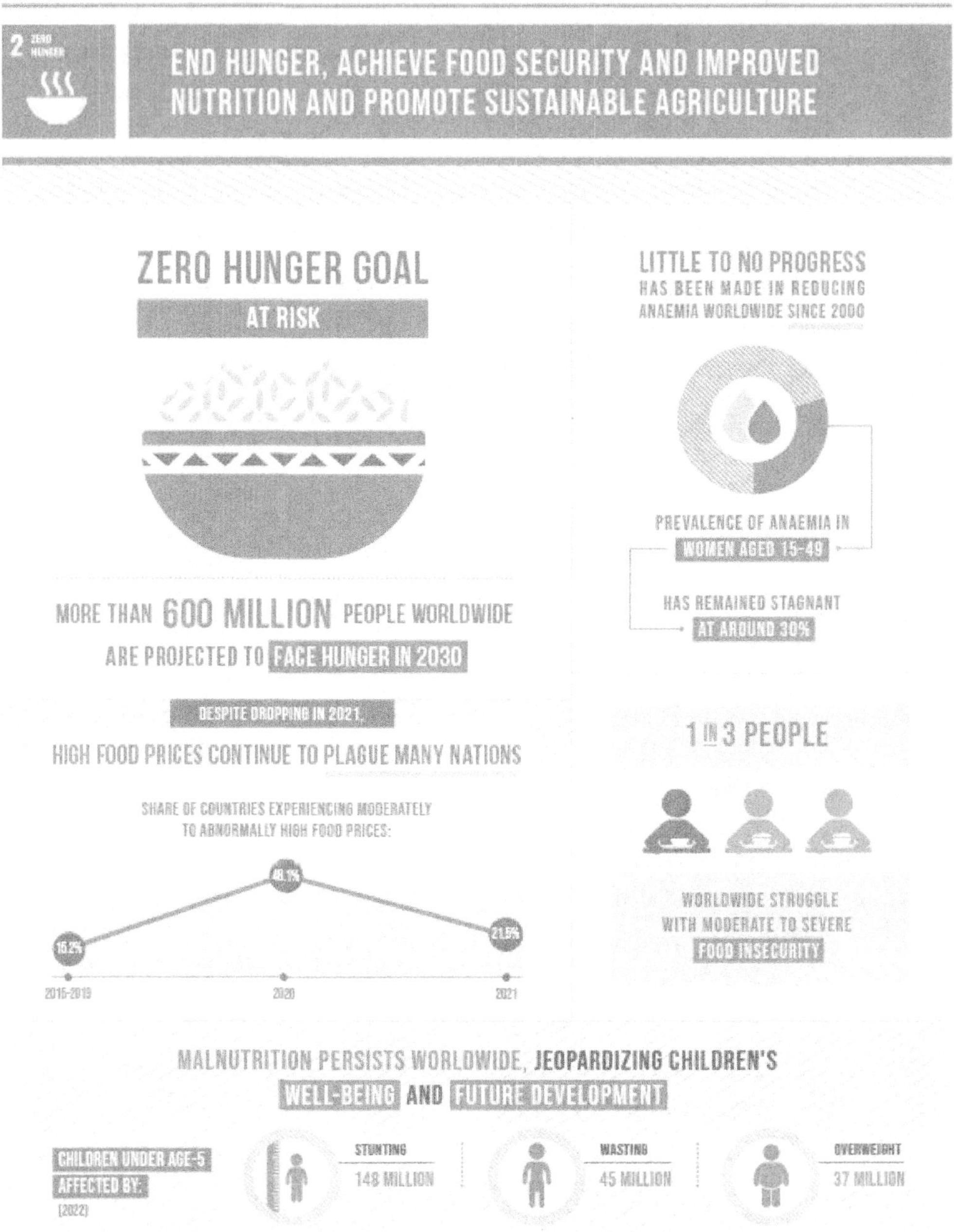

THE SUSTAINABLE DEVELOPMENT GOALS REPORT 2023: SPECIAL EDITION- UNSTATS.UN.ORG/SDGS/REPORT/2023/

SDG 2: ZERO HUNGER

"End hunger, achieve food security and improved nutrition and promote sustainable agriculture."

SDG 2 aims to end hunger, support rural development, achieve food security and improved nutrition, and promote sustainable agriculture.

Key factors which cause an individual to experience hunger and food insecurity include:

- **Poverty:** limited financial resources prevent individuals from purchasing enough food or accessing nutritious meals.
- **Unemployment:** lack of a stable income due to unemployment often leads to food insecurity.
- **Food Prices:** high food prices can make it difficult for low-income households to afford adequate and nutritious food.
- **Conflict and Warfare:** displacement, destruction of infrastructure, and disrupted supply chains due to conflicts can severely restrict access to food.
- **Natural Disasters:** floods, droughts, hurricanes, and other natural disasters can destroy crops and food supplies.
- **Poor Agricultural Practices:** over-farming, use of inappropriate techniques, or lack of access to modern farming practices can reduce crop yields.

- **Land Ownership Issues:** inability to own or access land for farming can hinder food production for individual families or communities.
- **Climate Change:** changing weather patterns can affect crop yields and increase the frequency and intensity of extreme weather events that damage food sources.
- **Lack of Infrastructure:** poor road networks, inadequate storage facilities, or lack of refrigeration can lead to food loss and restrict access to markets.
- **Health Issues:** illness or disability can prevent individuals from earning a livelihood, leading to food insecurity. Additionally, malnutrition can exacerbate health issues.
- **Lack of Education:** individuals without education might lack knowledge about nutrition or farming techniques that can ensure food security.
- **Economic Shocks:** sudden unexpected expenses, such as medical emergencies or loss of assets, can strain household budgets, affecting their ability to purchase food.
- **Discrimination and Social Inequalities:** discrimination based on gender, race, ethnicity, or social status can restrict access to resources and opportunities, leading to food insecurity.
- **Displacement and Migration:** people who are forcibly displaced from their homes, whether due to conflict or environmental factors, may lose their means of food production and face difficulties accessing food in unfamiliar locations.
- **Trade Policies:** policies that impact the prices of agricultural commodities or restrict the free movement of goods can affect food availability and affordability in certain regions.
- **Food Speculation:** speculation on food commodities in global markets can drive up prices, making food unaffordable for many.

- **Wastage:** significant amounts of food are wasted globally, from the production stage to retail. This reduces the overall availability of food.
- **Macroeconomic Factors:** economic downturns, inflation, and other broad economic factors can reduce purchasing power and increase the risk of food insecurity.
- **Cultural or Social Norms:** in some societies, cultural practices or beliefs might influence food distribution within households, making some members more food-insecure than others.
- **Lack of Social Safety Nets:** in the absence of welfare programmes or community support systems, vulnerable individuals may be more exposed to food insecurity.

JOB ROLES RELATED TO ALLEVIATING HUNGER AND FOOD INSECURITY INCLUDE:

Sustainable Agriculture and Farming

✓ **Agricultural Scientists/Researchers** engage in research to improve crop yields, resist pests, or adapt to climate change.

✓ **Agricultural Economists** research and analyse economic aspects of agriculture, such as production, distribution, and consumption.

✓ **Climate Change Specialists** design adaptive and mitigating strategies needed to help agriculture reduce its contribution to climate change while ensuring it is as productive as possible.

✓ **Agri-tech Developers** develop technologies, tools, or apps that can help improve agricultural yields, predict diseases, or streamline farming operations.

✓ **Agricultural Extension Workers** operate on the ground to train farmers in modern agricultural practices and technologies.

- ✓ **Farmer and Sustainable Agronomists** cultivate food using environmentally friendly, economically viable, and socially just methods.
- ✓ **Business Consultants** advise agricultural enterprises on market trends, business strategies, and sustainable practices.
- ✓ **Microfinance Officers** provide small loans or grants to farmers or communities to invest in agricultural ventures or food production.
- ✓ **Fishery Specialists** work on sustainable fishery practices to ensure that aquatic life is preserved, and communities have food and jobs.
- ✓ **Forestry Specialists** promote sustainable forestry practices, which can be integral to local food systems in certain regions.
- ✓ **Urban Farmers or Community Garden Coordinators** promote local food access and initiatives, which grow food locally.
- ✓ **Agricultural and Food Policy Analysts** analyse and advise on policies to ensure food security and sustainable agricultural practices.
- ✓ **Biodiversity Conservationists** ensure farming practices promote biodiversity, given its importance in resilient and sustainable food systems.
- ✓ **Land Rights Advocates** work to ensure that farmers and indigenous communities have rightful access to the land they depend on.

Nutrition and Food Safety

- ✓ **Development Aid Workers** help communities in crisis with immediate food aid and long-term strategies to improve food security.
- ✓ **Nutritionists/Dietitians** offer expertise on diet to combat malnutrition and ensure populations have access to nutritious food.
- ✓ **Food Safety and Quality Inspectors** ensure the food produced meets health and safety standards, reducing the risk of foodborne illnesses.

Infrastructure, Logistics and Operations

- ✓ **Supply Chain and Distribution Specialists** oversee the logistics of getting food from farms to tables, aiming to reduce wastage and ensure efficiency.

- ✓ **Water Management Experts** help design sustainable irrigation and water conservation methods to meet the significant need by agriculture for freshwater of agriculture.
- ✓ **Food Bank Managers** oversee the operations of a food bank to provide emergency food to people in need.
- ✓ **Food Distributors** work with food banks and other organisations to distribute food to people in need.
- ✓ **Food Waste Reduction Specialists** work to reduce food waste in the food system.

Education, Employment, and Training

- ✓ **Rural Development Specialists** advocate for and implement strategies to uplift rural communities where much of the world's farming occurs.
- ✓ **Educators/Trainers** develop and train the next generation of professionals in agriculture, nutrition, and food security or create public awareness campaigns.
- ✓ **Financial Education Instructors** develop financial literacy by providing instruction in areas such as budgeting, saving, and investing.
- ✓ **Debt Counsellors** help individuals to develop a plan to manage and reduce their debt.
- ✓ **Life Skills Instructors** provide instruction on life skills, such as cooking, cleaning, and time management.
- ✓ **Parenting Educators** provide instruction on parenting skills.
- ✓ **Health Educators** provide instruction on health topics, such as nutrition and exercise.

- ✓ **Careers Development Professionals** provide education, information, advice, and guidance to help people understand themselves, their motivations, and their abilities so they can make appropriate choices about their education, training, and work.
- ✓ **Job Centre Advisors and Employability Coaches** help people find work by providing job search advice, CV and interview skills, work experience, training, financial support, and personal support.

Economic Inequality

- ✓ **Charity Officers** work on policy, projects and with individuals to alleviate wide-ranging challenges, including housing, equality, and food.
- ✓ **Housing Specialists** work to facilitate successful tenancies by supporting tenants in local authority and house association homes.
- ✓ **Community Organisers** work with communities to develop and implement economic development initiatives.
- ✓ **Welfare Rights Advocates** help individuals navigate the welfare system and represent them in their interactions with the welfare system to ensure they get the appropriate benefits.
- ✓ **Social Workers** provide case management and other services to individuals and families struggling with economic hardship.
- ✓ **Solicitors** provide expert legal support and advice on a range of personal and commercial issues, including employment and housing rights.
- ✓ **Economic and Social Policy Researchers and Analysts** analyse data, study economic trends, formulate theories, and provide insights to guide decision-making on economic and social policies and organisational strategies.

Health and Well-being

- ✓ **Occupational Therapists** provide practical support to help people overcome barriers caused by illness, trauma, disability, ageing or accidents that limit their independence.

✓ **Health Psychologists** work with patients to help them respond to and manage the psychological and emotional aspects of illness.

✓ **Disability Advocates** represent individuals with disabilities in their interactions with the government and other entities.

✓ **Counsellors** help people to identify problems in their lives, helping them to reflect on what is happening to them and consider alternative ways of thinking and being.

These are just some of the many career options that can contribute towards Goal 2 of the SDGs. As in the last SDG section, as wicked problems, the goals are interlinked, and this list is by no means exhaustive, nor is it intended to be. It is designed to get you thinking about which areas interest you.

You may also find it helpful to look at roles included in a related SDG that interests you. The following websites will help you explore these and other roles in more detail:

- UK: https://www.prospects.ac.uk/job-profiles
- Use https://www.careeralchemy.co.uk/understanding-job-market.html to help you compare jobs and understand key labour market information
- US: https://www.onetonline.org/ (use the occupational keyword search tool)
- Europe: https://eures.ec.europa.eu/index_en
- More about SDG 2: https://www.un.org/sustainabledevelopment/hunger/

Remember, the key to finding your ultimate concern is to find an intersection between who you are, what you can offer, what attracts you, and opportunities to make a positive difference.

CONSOLIDATING YOUR LEARNING FROM SDG 2 - HUNGER:

What is your biggest light bulb moment about SDG 2?

* * * *

THE SUSTAINABLE DEVELOPMENT GOALS REPORT 2023: SPECIAL EDITION- UNSTATS.UN.ORG/SDGS/REPORT/2023/

SDG 3: GOOD HEALTH AND WELL-BEING

"Ensure healthy lives and promote well-being for all at all ages."

The third of the Goals focuses on ensuring healthy lives and promoting well-being for all at all ages by ensuring global access to expert, funded health care and support locally. The targets under this goal cover a wide range of health-related challenges, from improving maternal and child health and family planning to combating diseases and addressing non-communicable illnesses through programs and new medicines, and include reducing drug, alcohol, and tobacco abuse, as well as health risks from environmental hazards. Health is one of our fundamental human rights.

Key factors which cause an individual to experience greater health and well-being needs include:

- **Genetics:** an individual's genetic makeup can predispose them to specific health conditions, including heart disease, diabetes, and specific cancers.
- **Age:** older adults are more prone to chronic diseases, disability, social isolation, reduced physical ability, and other age-related health concerns.
- **Gender:** both women and men have unique health needs and risks. Women, in particular, face challenges related to reproductive health, mental health, and violence.

- **Race and Ethnicity:** people of colour often encounter more significant health and well-being needs, especially concerning chronic diseases, mental health, and environmental hazards.
- **Socio-economic Status:** lower socio-economic status can cause greater health risks due to limited access to healthcare, poor housing, exposure to environmental hazards, and lack of nutritious food and education.
- **Environment:** exposure to pollutants, unclean water, or unsanitary living conditions poses significant health risks.
- **Mental Health:** disorders like stress, depression, anxiety, PTSD, and others can have profound effects on overall well-being and physical health.
- **Traumatic Experiences:** trauma, whether from abuse, war, natural disasters, or other sources, including accidents and fires, heightens health and well-being needs.
- **Lifestyle Choices:** smoking, excessive alcohol consumption, unhealthy eating habits, and lack of physical activity are leading causes of various health issues.
- **Access to Healthcare:** limited access to affordable and quality healthcare can exacerbate health issues.
- **Cultural and Social Norms:** certain societies or cultures may stigmatise health conditions or inhibit seeking medical assistance.
- **Education:** inadequate education about health and well-being can result in poor health decisions and unaddressed health issues.
- **Occupation:** risky jobs can expose individuals to harmful substances, physical challenges, or psychological strain.
- **Substance Abuse:** dependencies on drugs, alcohol, or other substances can cause numerous health problems.
- **Social Relationships:** while positive relationships can boost well-

being, isolation or harmful relationships can adversely affect mental and physical health.

- **Chronic Illnesses:** diseases like diabetes, hypertension, and autoimmune disorders require constant attention and management.
- **Disabilities:** both physical and mental disabilities can amplify health and well-being needs, frequently demanding specialised care.
- **Geographical Location:** living in remote or underserved regions can limit access to healthcare, proper nutrition, transportation, employment, and other essential services.

JOB ROLES RELATED TO ALLEVIATING HEALTH AND WELL-BEING CHALLENGES:

Medical Professionals

- ✓ **Doctors** work as general practitioners and specialists (e.g., paediatricians, gynaecologists, cardiologists, infectious disease specialists) to help prevent and cure illnesses.
- ✓ **Nurses and Nurse Practitioners** provide primary and speciality health care.
- ✓ **Midwives** specialise in childbirth, postpartum, and women's reproductive health.
- ✓ **Dentists and Oral Health Professionals** focus on oral health and hygiene.

Public Health Professionals

- ✓ **Epidemiologists** study patterns and causes of diseases and injury in humans.
- ✓ **Health Educators** educate people about behaviours promoting wellness.

- ✓ **Health Administrators** manage public health services and systems.
- ✓ **Community Health Workers** provide support and assistance within specific communities or populations.

Mental Health Professionals

- ✓ **Psychologists and Psychiatrists** offer therapy, diagnosis, and treatment for mental health issues.
- ✓ **Counsellors and Therapists** assist people with emotional and psychological challenges.
- ✓ **Social Workers** support individuals and families dealing with various challenges, including health-related issues.

Healthcare Research

- ✓ **Medical Researchers** investigate ways to improve health outcomes, create medications, or develop medical procedures.
- ✓ **Biostatisticians** use statistics to interpret, analyse, and summarise medical and public health data.

Health Technology and Informatics

- ✓ **Health Informaticians** specialise in the efficient and secure use of information to advance health objectives.
- ✓ **Biomedical Engineers** design equipment, devices, and software used in healthcare.

Pharmaceutical Careers

- ✓ **Pharmacologists** study and develop drugs to treat diseases.
- ✓ **Pharmacists** dispense prescription medications to patients and offer expertise on safe use.

Health Advocacy and Policy

- ✓ **Health Advocates** work on promoting health policies, resources, and education.
- ✓ **Health Policy Analysts** analyse, recommend, and implement health policies.

Environmental Health Professionals

- ✓ **Environmental Health Officers** address environmental factors affecting public health, such as water quality and pollution.
- ✓ **Occupational Health and Safety Specialists** ensure workplace environments are safe and healthy.

Nutrition and Fitness

- ✓ **Dietitians and Nutritionists** offer guidance on proper eating habits and nutrition plans.
- ✓ **Physical Therapists** assist patients in improving movement and pain management.
- ✓ **Fitness Trainers** promote physical well-being and exercise.

Global Health Careers

- ✓ **Global Health Consultants** work on health challenges that span across countries and regions.
- ✓ **Field Medical Officers** offer medical support in international settings, often in crisis or development scenarios.
- ✓ **Health Communication and Journalism** professionals work to communicate health news, research, and challenges to the public.
- ✓ **Alternative and Holistic Medicine** specialists work in roles as chiropractors, osteopaths, acupuncturists, and naturopathic doctors.

These are just some of the many career options that can contribute towards Goal 3 of the SDGs. Remember that as wicked problems, the goals are interlinked, and this list is by no means exhaustive, nor is it intended to be. It is designed to get you thinking about which areas interest you.

You may also find it helpful to look at roles included in a related SDG that interests you. The following websites will help you explore these and other roles in more detail:

- UK: https://www.prospects.ac.uk/job-profiles
- US: https://www.onetonline.org/ (use the occupational keyword search tool)
- Europe: https://eures.ec.europa.eu/index_en
- More about SDG 3: https://sdgs.un.org/goals/goal3
- Use https://www.careeralchemy.co.uk/understanding-job-market.html to help you compare jobs and understand key labour market information.

CONSOLIDATING YOUR LEARNING FROM SDG 3 – HEALTH AND WELL-BEING

What is your most significant light bulb moment about SDG 3?

* * * *

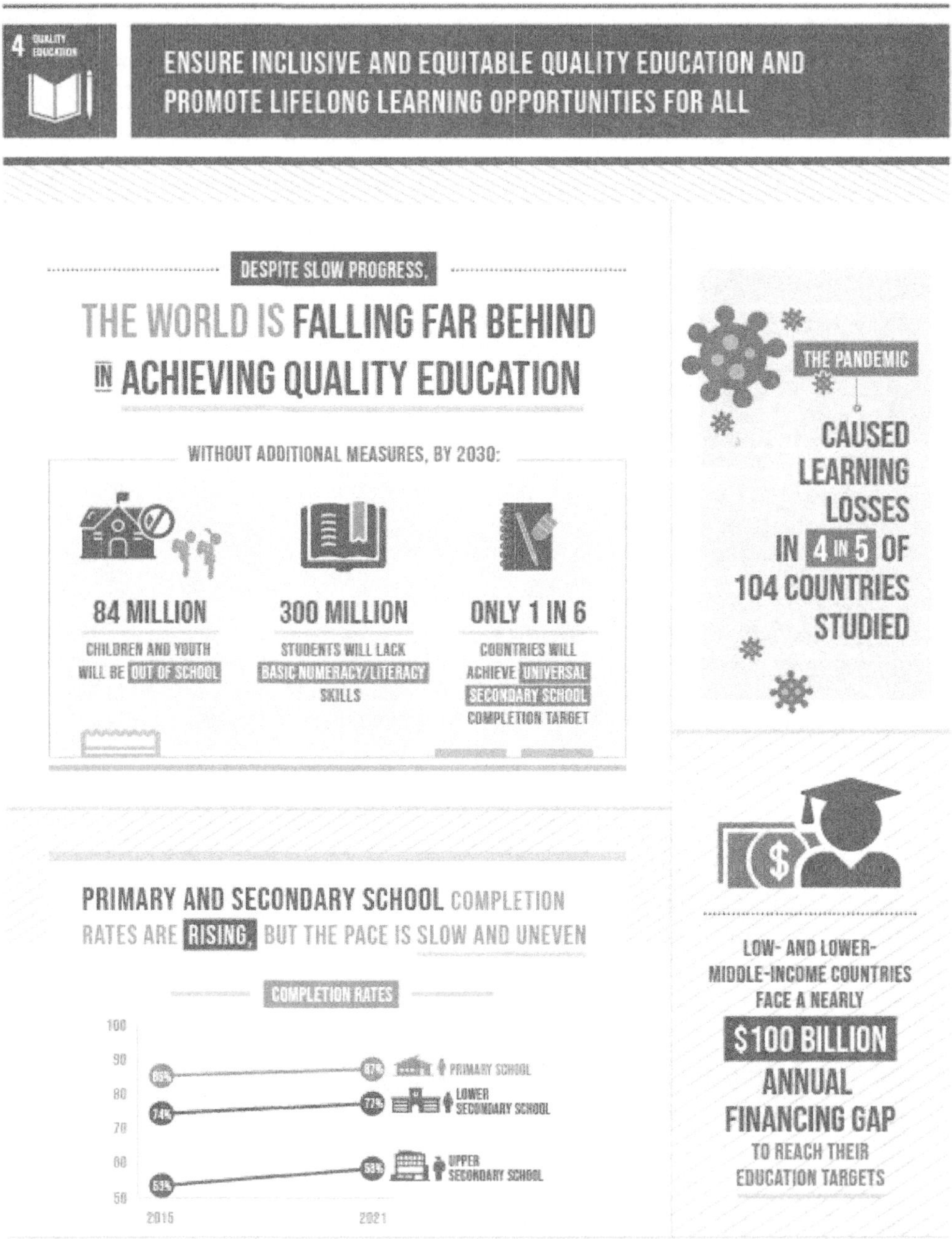

THE SUSTAINABLE DEVELOPMENT GOALS REPORT 2023: SPECIAL EDITION- UNSTATS.UN.ORG/SDGS/REPORT/2023/

4 QUALITY EDUCATION

SDG 4: QUALITY EDUCATION

"Ensure inclusive and equitable quality education and promote lifelong learning opportunities for all."

SDG 4 aims to provide equitable, quality education for all, focusing on lifelong learning without discrimination. Key objectives include ensuring universal access to free primary and secondary education by 2030, promoting early childhood development, and facilitating affordable higher education. The goal also focuses on enhancing job-relevant skills among youth and adults, promoting gender equality in educational settings, and integrating sustainable development principles into education. As the world continues to adopt technology and AI at an ever-increasing rate, gaining a quality education becomes all the more important to ensure individuals can progress on to developing the higher-level skills needed for today's global economy.

Key factors which cause an individual to miss out on the benefits of quality education include:

- **Poverty:** limited financial resources can make schooling unaffordable, from tuition fees to the cost of books and uniforms.
- **Geographical Barriers:** in rural or remote areas, the distance to schools can be a major hindrance to regular attendance.
- **Conflict and Instability:** wars and civil unrest can lead to school closures, reduced quality, and even risks to student safety.

- **Cultural Norms:** in some societies, cultural or religious beliefs may discourage education, particularly for girls or specific ethnic or social groups.
- **Lack of Infrastructure:** poorly equipped or understaffed schools can severely limit educational quality and outcomes.
- **Language Barriers:** non-native speakers or minority language speakers may face difficulties in understanding and integrating into the educational system.
- **Disabilities:** lack of facilities and trained staff to accommodate students with disabilities can prevent them from receiving quality education.
- **Health Issues:** chronic illnesses or poor health can lead to frequent absences from school, affecting academic performance.
- **Early Marriage and Child Labour:** in some places, young people - often girls - are married off or have to work, curtailing their educational opportunities.
- **Quality of Teaching:** inadequate training of teachers can result in poor delivery of education, making schooling less effective and engaging.
- **Gender Discrimination:** unequal treatment based on gender can prevent girls from accessing the same educational opportunities as boys.
- **Curriculum Relevance:** outdated or irrelevant curriculum can disengage students, leading to high dropout rates.
- **Socioeconomic Status:** children from wealthier families generally have access to better educational resources and extra-curricular activities.
- **Parental Involvement:** low levels of parental education or engagement can affect a child's educational attainment.

- **Mental Health:** psychological issues like anxiety or depression can impact a student's ability to focus and excel in academic settings.
- **Systemic Inequality:** discrimination based on ethnicity, religion, or social class can lead to unequal educational opportunities.
- **Political Factors:** government policies and investment in education can significantly affect its quality and accessibility.

KEY JOB ROLES RELATED TO GOAL 4:

Teaching and Instruction

✓ **Early Childhood Educators** focus on the foundational years of a child's education.

✓ **Primary and Secondary School Teachers** teach basic subjects like math, science, languages, and more.

✓ **Tertiary Education Lecturers/Professors** specialise in advanced and specialised topics in colleges and universities.

✓ **Adult Education Instructors** provide education opportunities for adult learners, often focusing on vocational skills, literacy, or continuing education.

Education Administration

✓ **School Principals** manage the operations and resources of schools.

✓ **Deans and Academic Administrators** oversee academic departments or entire institutions in higher education.

Special Education

✓ **Special Education Teachers** work with students who have a range of disabilities.

✓ **Therapists** work in roles such as occupational or speech therapists, supporting students with specific needs.

Curriculum Development and Instructional Design

- ✓ **Curriculum Developers** design, evaluate, and update the educational content.
- ✓ **Instructional Designers** create educational experiences, often for online or hybrid learning environments.

Educational Technology

- ✓ **EdTech Developers** create tools and platforms to enhance digital learning.
- ✓ **Educational Technologists** implement and manage tech solutions in educational settings.

Educational Research:

- ✓ **Educational Researchers** investigate effective teaching methods, learning processes, and educational outcomes.
- ✓ **Psychometricians** design and analyse assessments and tests.

Education Policy and Advocacy

- ✓ **Education Policy Analysts** research and recommend educational policies.
- ✓ **Education Advocates** promote educational rights and access, often focusing on underserved populations.

Counselling and Guidance

- ✓ **School Counsellors** assist students with academic, personal, or career challenges.
- ✓ **Career Counsellors/Advisers** provide guidance on career choices, often in high schools, colleges, or vocational institutions.

Educational Training and Development in Corporates

- ✓ **Corporate Trainers** offer training programs to employees.
- ✓ **Learning and Development Managers** oversee employee training and professional development in organisations.

Library and Information Science

- ✓ **Librarians** manage resources and services in public, academic, or specialised libraries.
- ✓ **Archivists** preserve and catalogue historical documents and materials.

International Education

- ✓ **International Educators** work in global education settings, perhaps teaching abroad or coordinating international student programmes.
- ✓ **Education Consultants for International Development** focus on improving education systems in developing countries.

Non-formal and Community Education

- ✓ **Community Educators** provide learning opportunities outside the formal school system, often focusing on community development, health, or civic education.
- ✓ **Museum Educators** design and deliver educational programmes in museums, zoos, or similar settings.

These are just some of the many career options that can contribute towards a quality education, SDG Goal 4. Remember that as wicked problems, the goals are interlinked, and this list is by no means exhaustive, nor is it intended to be. It is designed to get you thinking about which areas interest you.

You may also find it helpful to look at roles included in a related SDG that interests you. The following websites will help you explore these and other roles in more detail:

- UK: https://www.prospects.ac.uk/job-profiles
- US: https://www.onetonline.org/ (use the occupational keyword search tool)
- Europe: https://eures.ec.europa.eu/index_en

- More about SDG 4: https://sdgs.un.org/goals/goal4
- Use https://www.careeralchemy.co.uk/understanding-job-market.html to help you compare jobs and understand key labour market information.

CONSOLIDATING YOUR LEARNING FROM SDG 4 – QUALITY EDUCATION

What is your most significant light bulb moment of SDG 4?

* * * *

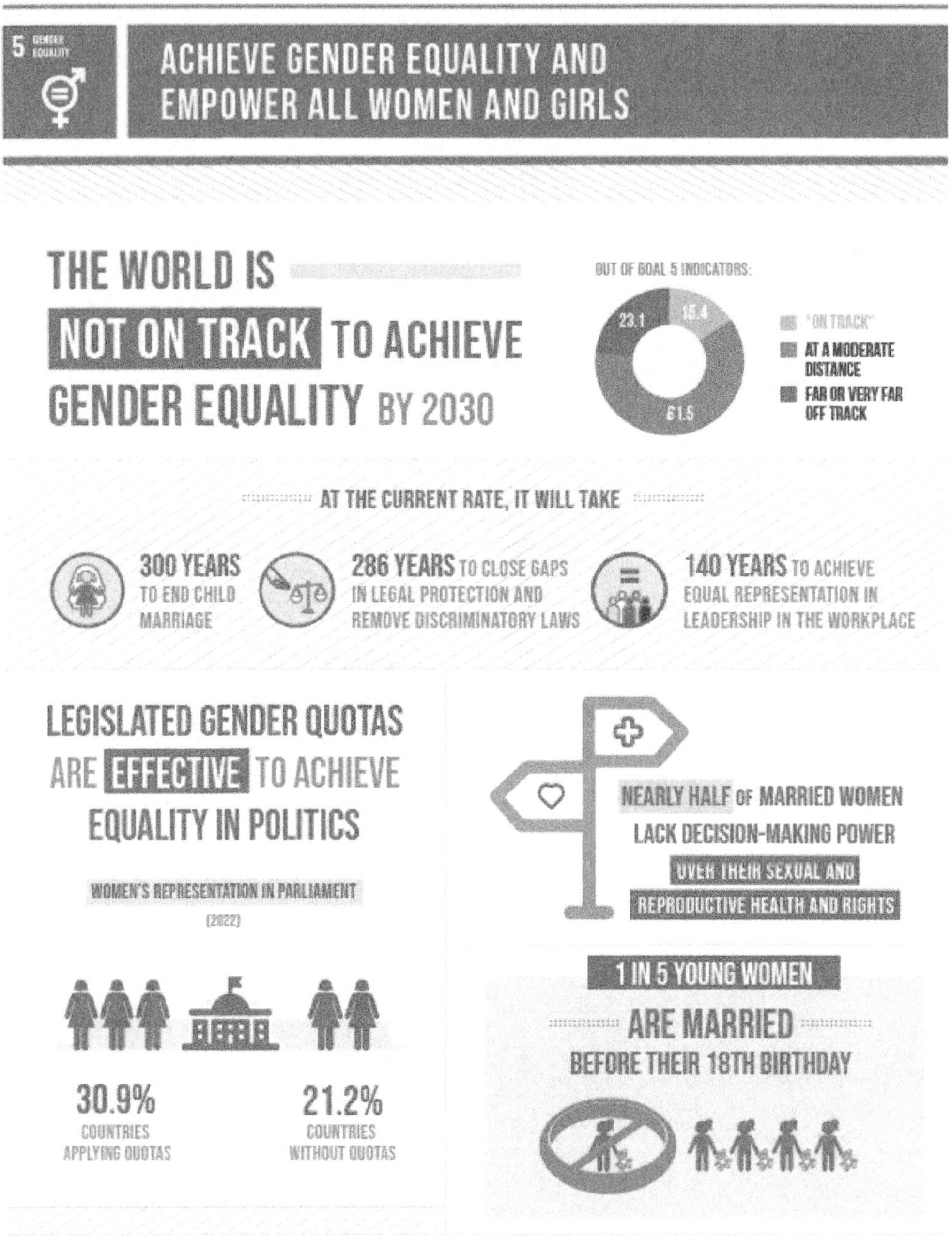

THE SUSTAINABLE DEVELOPMENT GOALS REPORT 2023: SPECIAL EDITION- UNSTATS.UN.ORG/SDGS/REPORT/2023/

5 GENDER EQUALITY

SDG 5: GENDER EQUALITY

"Achieve gender equality and empower all women and girls."

The fifth SDG aims to achieve gender equality and empower all women and girls by 2030. It targets a broad spectrum of issues, including ending violence against women, eliminating harmful practices like child marriage, ensuring women's full participation in leadership and decision-making, and guaranteeing equal opportunities for education, employment, and health care. Being treated equally is a fundamental human right.

While the language and primary focus of this goal take a male and female gender binary approach and places high emphasis on addressing issues traditionally associated with women's rights, the principle of "leaving no one behind" is foundational to all SDGs, which therefore includes marginalised communities like the Lesbian, Gay, Bisexual, Transgender (LGBT) community. This has been reflected in this overview.

Key factors which cause an individual to experience gender equality needs include:

- **Cultural Barriers and Gender Discrimination:** deep-rooted societal norms and gender discrimination act as significant roadblocks to achieving gender equality, including lack of childcare provision, paid family leave and help with other caring roles they undertake.

- **Economic Disparities and Inequality:** women are often relegated to unequal, low-wage, non-STEM jobs and have limited access to economic resources such as land, credit, and financial services. They lack affordable childcare and decent flexible working provision for women working at all levels.
- **Political Underrepresentation and Lack of Representation:** women are significantly underrepresented in decision-making roles across sectors like politics, business, and civil society.
- **Violence and Exploitation:** various forms of violence against women and girls, including trafficking, sexual, and psychological abuse, persist despite global initiatives.

KEY JOB ROLES RELATED TO ALLEVIATING GENDER EQUALITY CHALLENGES:

Advocacy and Activism

✓ **Gender Equality Advocates/Activists** work at grassroots levels to promote gender rights, often within NGOs or community-based organisations.

✓ **Campaign Managers** oversee campaigns focused on gender equality, women's rights, or related causes.

Policy and Governance

✓ **Gender Policy Analysts** research and recommend policies that address gender disparities.

✓ **Gender Advisors in Government** provide input on policymaking from a gender perspective.

Research and Academia

- ✓ **Gender Studies Professors** teach and research gender issues in academic settings.
- ✓ **Researchers/Specialists in Gender Issues** focus on topics like gender-based violence, women's economic empowerment, etc., often for think tanks or NGOs.

Legal and Human Rights

- ✓ **Women's Rights Lawyers** advocate for women's rights in legal systems, either through direct representation or through pushing for legal reforms.
- ✓ **Gender Equality Officers in Human Rights Organisations** focus on gender-specific challenges and rights violations.

Development and Humanitarian Work

- ✓ **Gender Mainstreaming Specialists** ensure that gender perspectives are integrated into all areas of an organisation's work, especially in development and humanitarian projects.
- ✓ **Project Managers for Women's Empowerment** oversee projects designed to empower women and girls, often in development NGOs or agencies.

Health and Well-being

- ✓ **Reproductive Health Specialists** focus on women's reproductive rights, family planning, and related areas.
- ✓ **Counsellors for Gender-based Violence Survivors** provide support and therapy to survivors.

Economic Empowerment and Labour

- ✓ **Women's Entrepreneurship Advisors** support women in setting up and growing their businesses.
- ✓ **Gender Equality Specialists in Labour Organisations** work to ensure equal opportunities and fair treatment of women in the workforce.

Communication and Media

- ✓ **Gender-responsive Journalists** report on gender issues and rights violations and highlight stories of women and girls.
- ✓ **Media and Communication Specialists for Gender NGOs** manage communications for organisations working on gender equality.

Education and Training

- ✓ **Gender Equality Educators** conduct workshops and training sessions on gender sensitivity, women's rights, etc.
- ✓ **Curriculum Developers with a Focus on Gender** design educational materials that promote gender equality.

Arts and Culture

- ✓ **Artists and Writers Focused on Gender Issues** use various art forms to address, discuss, or highlight gender issues.
- ✓ **Curators for Gender-themed Exhibitions** organise exhibitions or events centred on gender equality themes.

Corporate and Private Sector

- ✓ **Diversity and Inclusion Managers** ensure gender equality in hiring, promotion, and workplace practices in businesses.
- ✓ **Corporate Social Responsibility (CSR) Professionals** focus on gender equality projects as part of a company's CSR initiatives.

These are just some of the many career options that can contribute towards improving gender quality, Goal 5 of the SDGs. Remember that as wicked problems, the goals are interlinked, and this list is by no means exhaustive, nor is it intended to be. It is designed to get you thinking about which areas interest you.

You may also find it helpful to look at roles included in a related SDG that interests you. The following websites will help you explore these and other roles in more detail:

- UK: https://www.prospects.ac.uk/job-profiles
- US: https://www.onetonline.org/ (use the occupational keyword search tool)
- Europe: https://eures.ec.europa.eu/index_en
- More about SDG 5: https://sdgs.un.org/goals/goal5
- Use https://www.careeralchemy.co.uk/understanding-job-market.html to help you compare jobs and understand key labour market information.

CONSOLIDATING YOUR LEARNING FROM SDG 5 – GENDER EQUALITY

What is your most significant light bulb moment of SDG 5?

* * * *

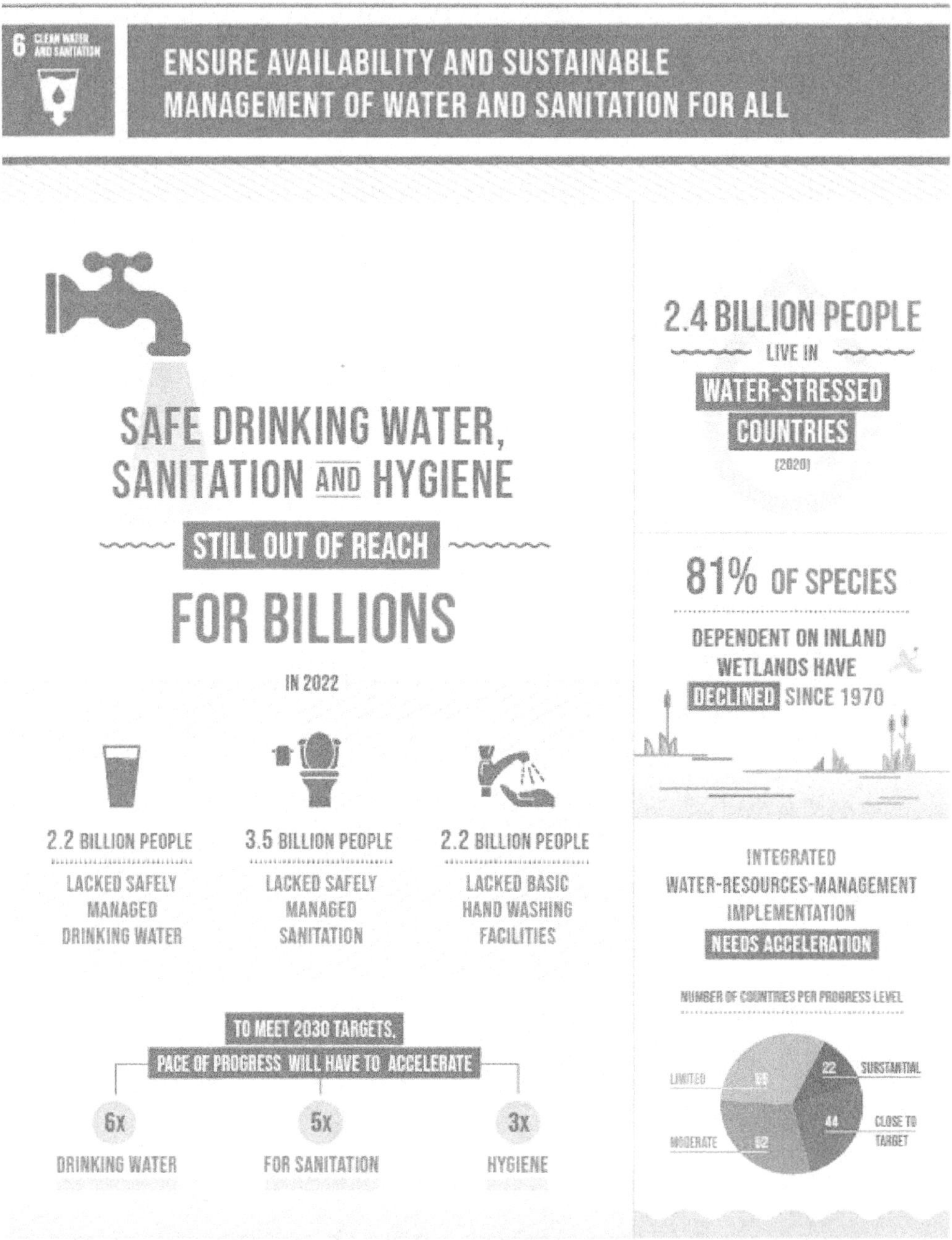

THE SUSTAINABLE DEVELOPMENT GOALS REPORT 2023: SPECIAL EDITION- UNSTATS.UN.ORG/SDGS/REPORT/2023/

6 CLEAN WATER AND SANITATION

SDG 6: CLEAN WATER AND SANITATION

"Ensure availability and sustainable management of water and sanitation for all."

SDG Goal 6 is centred on ensuring the availability and sustainable management of water and sanitation for all. Addressing the global water crisis requires expertise from various disciplines, and the career options related to Goal 6 span technical, policymaking, advocacy, and research roles. Access to clean water and sanitation is a fundamental human right.

Key factors which prevent an individual from having access to clean water and sanitation include:

- **Economic Barriers:** many people, especially in low-income countries, can't afford the costs associated with connecting to public water systems or building and maintaining private sanitation facilities.
- **Inadequate Infrastructure:** some regions lack the necessary water delivery and waste disposal infrastructure, especially in rural or rapidly growing urban areas.
- **Physical Geography:** in some regions, the physical geography, such as arid conditions, mountainous terrain, or remote locations, makes it difficult to source and distribute clean water.

- **Water Scarcity:** overuse of water resources, poor management, or prolonged drought conditions can lead to scarcity of freshwater.
- **Conflict and Instability:** wars or civil unrest can damage or disrupt water infrastructure, and communities might be forced to flee their homes, leaving behind established water and sanitation systems.
- **Environmental Pollution:** pollution from industrial, agricultural, or household sources can contaminate local water supplies.
- **Climate Change:** changes in climate patterns can lead to increased droughts, floods, or changes in water table levels, impacting the availability and quality of water sources.
- **Governance and Corruption:** weak governance, lack of political will, or corruption can hinder investments in water and sanitation projects, leading to mismanagement or diversion of resources.
- **Cultural and Social Norms:** some communities may have cultural or traditional practices related to water collection or sanitation that aren't aligned with best practices for health and hygiene.
- **Land Ownership Issues:** in some cases, disputes over land ownership or rights can prevent individuals from accessing water sources or building sanitation facilities on the land they occupy.
- **Rapid Urbanization:** the rapid growth of urban centres can lead to informal settlements or slums that lack formal infrastructure for clean water and sanitation.
- **Lack of Knowledge or Education:** people may not be aware of the importance of clean water, sanitation, and hygiene practices, or they might not have the information needed to build and maintain sanitation facilities properly.
- **Gender Inequality:** in some cultures, women, who often bear the responsibility for fetching water, face systemic barriers or safety risks that limit their ability to access clean and safe water sources.

KEY JOB ROLES RELATED TO GOAL 6:

Water Resources Engineering and Management

- ✓ **Hydrologists** study the distribution, movement, and properties of water.
- ✓ **Water Resources Engineers** design and maintain water infrastructure, such as dams, treatment facilities, and drainage systems.
- ✓ **Water Quality Specialists** monitor and ensure water quality meets health and environmental standards.

Sanitation and Wastewater Management

- ✓ **Sanitation Engineers** specialise in designing and implementing sanitation solutions, especially in challenging environments.
- ✓ **Wastewater Treatment Operators** manage the operations of wastewater treatment plants.
- ✓ **Wastewater Engineers** design systems to treat and repurpose wastewater.

Water Policy and Governance

- ✓ **Water Policy Analysts** research and recommend water use, rights, and management policies.
- ✓ **Water Rights Lawyers** advocate for equitable water rights and navigate water-related legal challenges.
- ✓ **Regulatory Compliance Specialists** ensure water and sanitation projects comply with local, national, or international regulations.

Research and Academia

- ✓ **Academic Researchers in Water Sciences** focus on studying various aspects of water, from its chemistry to its socio-economic implications.

- ✓ **Climate Scientists** investigate the implications of climate change on water resources.

Conservation and Sustainability

- ✓ **Water Conservationists** advocate for and implement measures to reduce water waste.
- ✓ **Watershed Managers** oversee the conservation and use of water within specific watershed areas.

Public Health and Hygiene

- ✓ **Public Health Specialists** focus on waterborne diseases and sanitation-related health issues.
- ✓ **Hygiene Promotion Officers** conduct campaigns to promote good hygiene practices, often in developing or crisis-hit regions.

Advocacy and Development

- ✓ **Water and Sanitation Project Managers** oversee development projects to improve water and sanitation access.
- ✓ **Water Advocacy Specialists** work for NGOs or international organisations to champion water and sanitation rights and access.

Technology and Innovation

- ✓ **Water Tech Developers** design or implement technology solutions for water treatment, conservation, or purification.
- ✓ **Desalination Specialists** focus on processes that remove salts and minerals from seawater or brackish water.

Community and Ground-level Implementation

- ✓ **Community Water and Sanitation Facilitators** work directly with communities, especially in rural or underserved areas, to establish and maintain water and sanitation systems.
- ✓ **Water and Sanitation Trainers** provide training on the maintenance and use of water and sanitation solutions.

Economic and Finance

- ✓ **Water Economists** analyse the economic implications of water use, distribution, and conservation.
- ✓ **Water Project Finance Specialists** work on funding and financing mechanisms for water and sanitation projects.

These are just some of the many career options that can contribute towards improving access to clean water and sanitation, Goal 6 of the SDGs. Remember that as wicked problems, the goals are interlinked, and this list is by no means exhaustive, nor is it intended to be. It is designed to get you thinking about which areas interest you.

You may also find it helpful to look at roles included in a related SDG that interests you. The following websites will help you explore these and other roles in more detail:

- UK: https://www.prospects.ac.uk/job-profiles
- US: https://www.onetonline.org/ (use the occupational keyword search tool)
- Europe: https://eures.ec.europa.eu/index_en
- More about SDG 6: https://sdgs.un.org/goals/goal6
- Use https://www.careeralchemy.co.uk/understanding-job-market.html to help you compare jobs and understand key labour market information.

CONSOLIDATING YOUR LEARNING FROM SDG 6 – CLEAN WATER AND SANITATION

What is your most significant light bulb moment of SDG 6?

* * * *

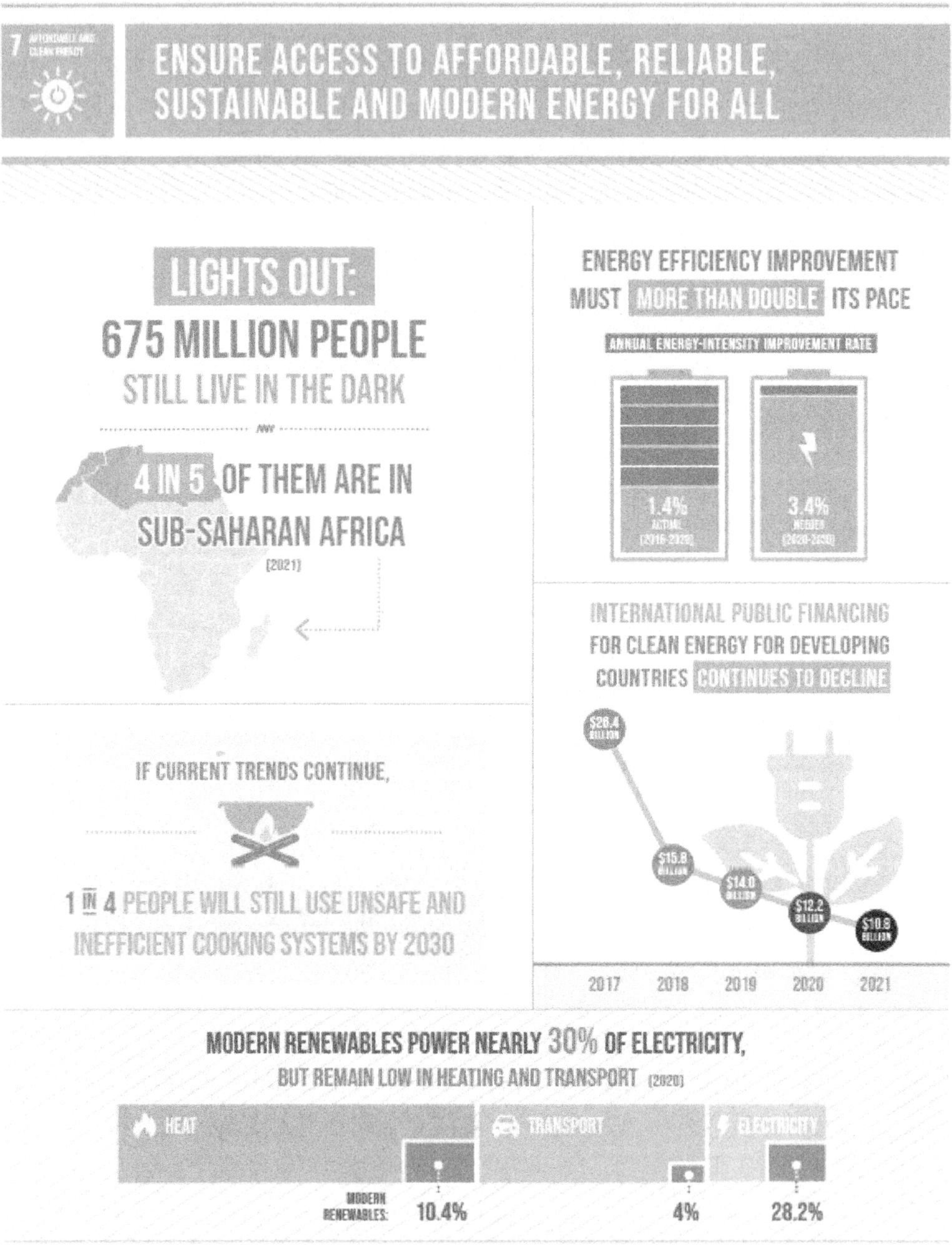

THE SUSTAINABLE DEVELOPMENT GOALS REPORT 2023: SPECIAL EDITION- UNSTATS.UN.ORG/SDGS/REPORT/2023/

SDG 7: AFFORDABLE AND CLEAN ENERGY

"Ensure access to affordable, reliable, sustainable. and modern energy for all."

SDG Goal 7 is focused on ensuring access to affordable, reliable, sustainable, and modern energy for all. Access to affordable and clean energy is crucial for sustainable development, economic progress, and improved living standards. Transition to cleaner and more sustainable energy sources is a global priority, leading to diverse career opportunities in both the public and private sectors.

Key factors which prevent an individual from having access to affordable and clean energy include:

- **Economic Barriers:** the initial investment required for renewable energy infrastructure, such as solar panels or wind turbines, can be high, preventing many from adopting them.
- **Infrastructure Challenges:** many regions, especially rural or remote areas, lack the infrastructure to deliver or distribute modern energy services.
- **Lack of Awareness or Knowledge:** individuals might not be informed about the benefits, operational methods, or maintenance of renewable energy systems.
- **Policy and Regulatory Barriers:** in some regions, the absence of supportive policies, subsidies, or incentives can hinder the adoption of clean energy solutions.

- **Monopoly of Traditional Energy Sources:** dependence on fossil fuels, supported by powerful stakeholders and established supply chains, can suppress the growth of cleaner energy alternatives.
- **Technological Limitations:** some renewable energy technologies might not be as developed or efficient in certain conditions, limiting their practicality or appeal.
- **Geographical Constraints:** not all regions have equal access to renewable energy resources. For instance, areas with little sunlight may find solar energy less viable, while calm regions might not benefit from wind energy.
- **Lack of Financing and Investment:** many developing countries face challenges in securing financing for large-scale renewable energy projects or infrastructure development.
- **Cultural and Social Factors:** traditional ways of life or societal resistance to change can deter communities from adopting newer energy technologies.
- **Supply Chain Challenges:** the production, transport, and installation of renewable energy technologies require a specific supply chain, which might not be established or optimised in some regions.
- **Land and Resource Conflicts:** implementing large-scale renewable energy projects, such as hydropower plants or wind farms, might lead to land acquisition disputes or concerns over environmental impact.
- **Technical Expertise:** there might be a shortage of trained professionals or technicians to install, maintain, or repair renewable energy systems in certain regions.
- **Intermittency and Reliability Issues:** some renewable energy sources, like solar and wind, are intermittent and may require backup systems or energy storage solutions, adding to costs and complexity.

- **High Dependency on Biomass:** in many developing countries, a significant portion of the population relies on traditional biomass (like wood or dung) for cooking and heating, which is often neither clean nor efficient.

KEY JOB ROLES RELATED TO GOAL 7:

Renewable Energy Engineering and Development

✓ **Solar Energy Engineers** design, implement, and manage solar energy projects.

✓ **Wind Energy Engineers** work on designing, installing, and optimising wind turbines.

✓ **Bioenergy/Biomass Specialists** focus on deriving energy from organic materials.

✓ **Hydroelectric Engineers** work on capturing energy from water sources, such as dams.

Energy Policy and Planning

✓ **Energy Policy Analysts** research and recommend policies to promote sustainable energy.

✓ **Energy Planners** design strategies for cities, countries, or organisations to transition to more sustainable energy sources.

Energy Efficiency

✓ **Energy Efficiency Consultants** advise organisations or homeowners on how to reduce energy consumption.

✓ **Energy Auditors** evaluate energy use patterns and recommend ways to improve efficiency.

✓ **Building Scientists** specialise in creating energy-efficient building designs.

Research and Development (R&D)

- ✓ **Clean Energy Researchers** develop new technologies or methods to harness sustainable energy.
- ✓ **Battery and Storage Researchers** focus on enhancing energy storage solutions, crucial for renewables.

Energy Finance and Economics

- ✓ **Energy Economists** analyse the economic dimensions of energy production and consumption.
- ✓ **Renewable Energy Financiers** develop financial models and instruments to support renewable energy projects.

Grid Management and Energy Distribution

- ✓ **Smart Grid Engineers** develop and manage digitalised grids that can handle renewable energy inputs efficiently.
- ✓ **Transmission Engineers** work on the infrastructure to transmit energy from production sites to consumption points.

Advocacy and Nonprofits

- ✓ **Sustainable Energy Advocates** lobby for policies and initiatives that promote renewable energy.
- ✓ **Project Managers for Energy NGOs** lead initiatives that aim to provide sustainable energy in underserved regions.

Energy Access and Rural Development

- ✓ **Off-grid Energy Solutions Specialists** design and implement energy solutions for regions without grid access.
- ✓ **Rural Energy Consultants** focus on energy solutions tailored for rural communities.

Energy Education and Training

- ✓ **Energy Educators/Trainers** teach about sustainable energy technologies, policies, and practices.

- ✓ **Community Outreach Specialists** promote sustainable energy practices and awareness at the community level.

Energy Regulation and Compliance

- ✓ **Regulatory Affairs Specialists** ensure energy projects comply with local, national, or international regulations.
- ✓ **Environmental Compliance Officers** ensure energy projects minimise environmental harm.

Energy Entrepreneurship

- ✓ **Start-up Founders in Clean Energy** launch and run businesses that offer innovative energy solutions.
- ✓ **Sustainable Energy Product Developers** create products that help in energy conservation or harnessing renewable energy.

These are just some of the many career options that can contribute towards improving access to affordable and clean energy, SDG 7. Remember that as wicked problems, the goals are interlinked, and this list is by no means exhaustive, nor is it intended to be. It is designed to get you thinking about which areas interest you.

You may also find it helpful to look at roles included in a related SDG that interests you. The following websites will help you explore these and other roles in more detail:

- UK: https://www.prospects.ac.uk/job-profiles
- US: https://www.onetonline.org/ (use the occupational keyword search tool)
- Europe: https://eures.ec.europa.eu/index_en
- More about SDG 7: https://sdgs.un.org/goals/goal7
- Use https://www.careeralchemy.co.uk/understanding-job-market.html to help you compare jobs and understand key labour market information.

CONSOLIDATING YOUR LEARNING FROM SDG 7 – AFFORDABLE AND CLEAN ENERGY

What is your most significant light bulb moment of SDG 7?

* * * *

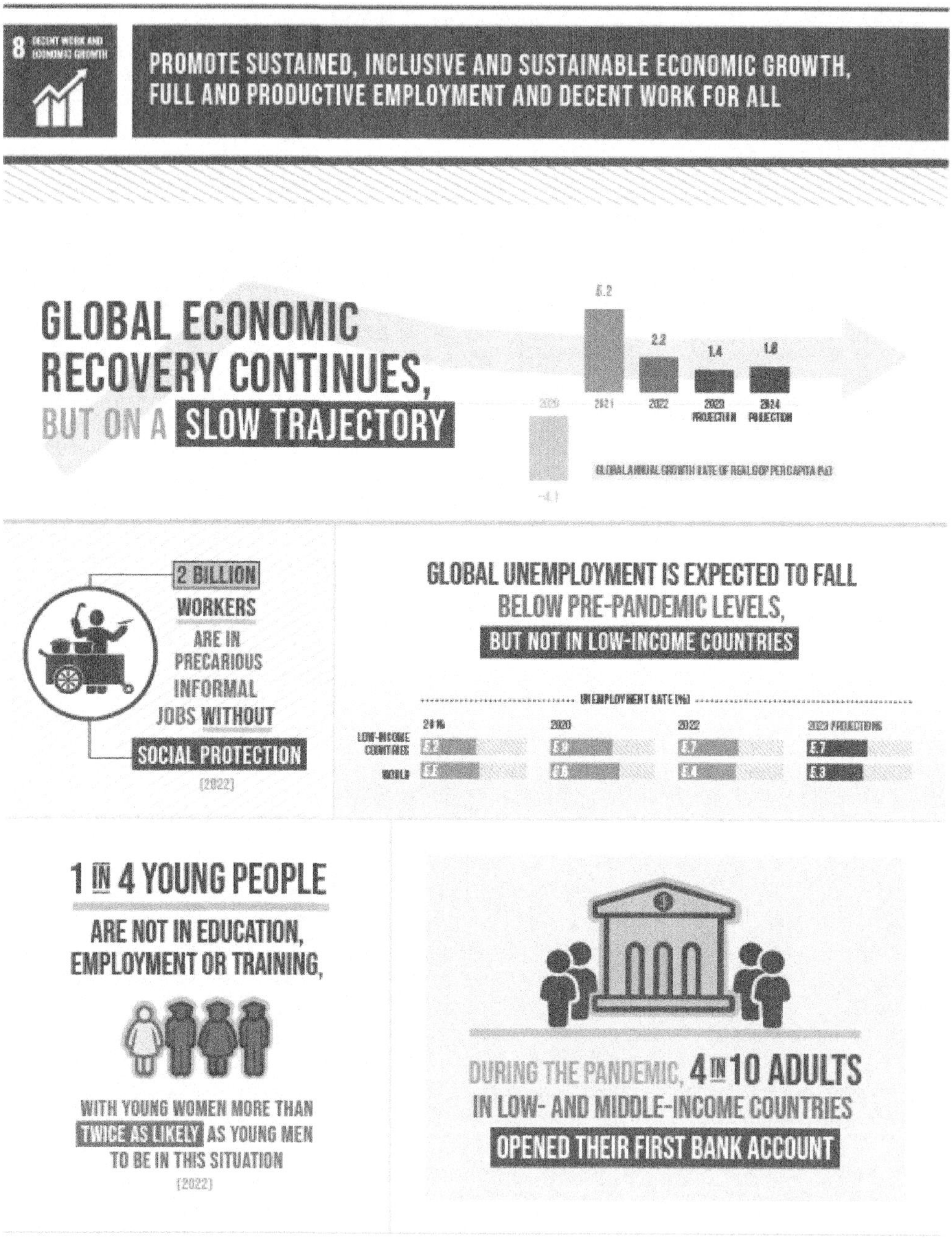

THE SUSTAINABLE DEVELOPMENT GOALS REPORT 2023: SPECIAL EDITION- UNSTATS.UN.ORG/SDGS/REPORT/2023/

8 DECENT WORK AND ECONOMIC GROWTH

SDG 8: DECENT WORK & ECONOMIC GROWTH

"Promote sustained, inclusive, and sustainable economic growth, full and productive employment, and decent work for all."

SDG 8 is dedicated to promoting sustained, inclusive, and sustainable economic growth, full and productive employment, and decent work for all. Gaining decent, full-time employment is crucial for an individual's economic well-being, self-worth, and integration into society. This goal encompasses a wide range of topics, from job creation and entrepreneurship to labour rights and workplace safety.

Key factors which prevent an individual from gaining decent, full-time employment include:

✓ **Lack of Education or Skills:** not having the necessary qualifications, training, or skills that meet the job market's demands can be a significant barrier.

✓ **Economic Downturns:** recessions or economic crises can lead to job cuts, reduced hiring, or even company closures.

✓ **Discrimination:** age, gender, race, disability, religion, or other forms of discrimination can limit employment opportunities for certain individuals or groups.

✓ **Health Issues:** physical or mental health challenges can prevent individuals from working full-time or taking certain types of jobs.

- ✓ **Limited Access to Job Opportunities:** living in a region with limited job opportunities, especially in rural or economically depressed areas, can be a hindrance.
- ✓ **Lack of Experience:** especially for new graduates or those re-entering the workforce, lack of prior work experience can deter employers.
- ✓ **Mismatch of Skills:** even if someone has qualifications, they might not match the specific needs of the available jobs.
- ✓ **Criminal Record:** having a criminal history can be a barrier in many professions, especially if it's not expunged or if employers don't offer second chances.
- ✓ **Informal Economy:** in some regions, the informal sector dominates, making it hard to find formal, full-time employment with benefits and legal protections.
- ✓ **Lack of Professional Networks:** often, job opportunities arise from professional or personal networks. Those without such connections may find it harder to access job openings.
- ✓ **Technological Displacement:** automation, digital transformation, and AI can displace jobs in certain sectors, pushing workers to retrain or shift industries.
- ✓ **Cultural or Social Norms:** in some societies, cultural or social expectations might limit employment opportunities for certain groups, such as women or minorities.
- ✓ **Restrictions on Movement:** in certain geopolitical contexts, individuals might be restricted from moving freely to regions with better job opportunities.
- ✓ **Immigration Status:** in many countries, non-citizens or those without the right work permits face significant barriers to full-time employment.

- ✓ **Lack of Access to Childcare:** parents, especially single parents, might find it challenging to secure full-time employment if they don't have reliable childcare.
- ✓ **Overqualification:** sometimes, individuals with higher education or advanced skills might be considered overqualified for available positions, making employers hesitant to hire them.
- ✓ **Job Market Saturation:** in certain fields or professions, there might be more qualified candidates than available positions.

KEY JOB ROLES RELATED TO GOAL 8:

Economic Development and Policy

- ✓ **Economic Policy Analysts** examine economic trends and suggest policies for sustainable growth.
- ✓ **Development Economists** study the factors promoting economic growth in developing nations.
- ✓ **Trade and Investment Officers** facilitate international trade and foreign investment.

Entrepreneurship and SME Development

- ✓ **Entrepreneurship Trainers** offer skills training to budding entrepreneurs.
- ✓ **SME (Small and Medium Enterprises) Consultants** advise SMEs on business strategies, funding, and expansion.
- ✓ **Business Incubator/Accelerator Managers** support start-ups and new businesses to grow.

Labour Rights and Relations

- ✓ **Labour Rights Advocates** campaign for workers' rights and fair labour practices.

✓ **Union Organizers or Representatives** advocate for the rights and interests of union members.

✓ **Labour Mediators** resolve disputes between employers and employees.

Workplace Safety and Standards

✓ **Occupational Health and Safety Specialists** ensure workplace environments are safe and adhere to regulations.

✓ **Compliance Officers** monitor and ensure companies adhere to labour laws and standards.

Employment Programs and Initiatives

✓ **Job Placement Officers** assist individuals in finding suitable employment.

✓ **Vocational Trainers** provide training in specific trades or job-related skills.

✓ **Youth Employment Program Coordinators** design and manage programs targeting job creation for young individuals.

Research and Academia

✓ **Labour Economists** study labour markets, employment trends, and wage structures.

✓ **Academic Researchers in Sustainable Growth** explore economic models and strategies that promote sustainable and inclusive growth.

Sustainable Tourism

✓ **Sustainable Tourism Consultants** advise on developing tourism that benefits local economies without harming the environment or culture.

✓ **Eco-tourism Operators** organise and promote travel to natural areas that conserve the environment and support local communities.

Financial Inclusion

- ✓ **Microfinance Officers** provide financial services to underserved populations.
- ✓ **Financial Literacy Educators** teach individuals to manage their finances, save, and invest.

Green Jobs and the Green Economy

- ✓ **Green Energy Job Trainers** equip workers with skills needed for the green energy sector.
- ✓ **Sustainability Consultants** advise businesses on transitioning to more sustainable models.
- ✓ **Green Product Entrepreneurs** develop and market eco-friendly products.

International Organisations and NGOs

- ✓ **Program Managers for Economic Development** oversee projects aimed at promoting economic growth and employment in underserved regions.
- ✓ **Field Officers** implement on-ground activities related to employment generation, skills training, and more.

These are just some of the many career options that can contribute towards improving access to decent, full-time work, SDG 8. Remember that as wicked problems, the goals are interlinked, and this list is by no means exhaustive, nor is it intended to be. It is designed to get you thinking about which areas interest you.

You may also find it helpful to look at roles included in a related SDG that interests you. The following websites will help you explore these and other roles in more detail:

- UK: https://www.prospects.ac.uk/job-profiles
- US: https://www.onetonline.org/ (use the occupational keyword search tool)
- Europe: https://eures.ec.europa.eu/index_en
- More about SDG 8: https://sdgs.un.org/goals/goal8
- Use https://www.careeralchemy.co.uk/understanding-job-market.html to help you compare jobs and understand key labour market information.

CONSOLIDATING YOUR LEARNING FROM SDG 8 – DECENT WORK AND ECONOMIC GROWTH

What is your most significant light bulb moment of SDG 8?

* * * *

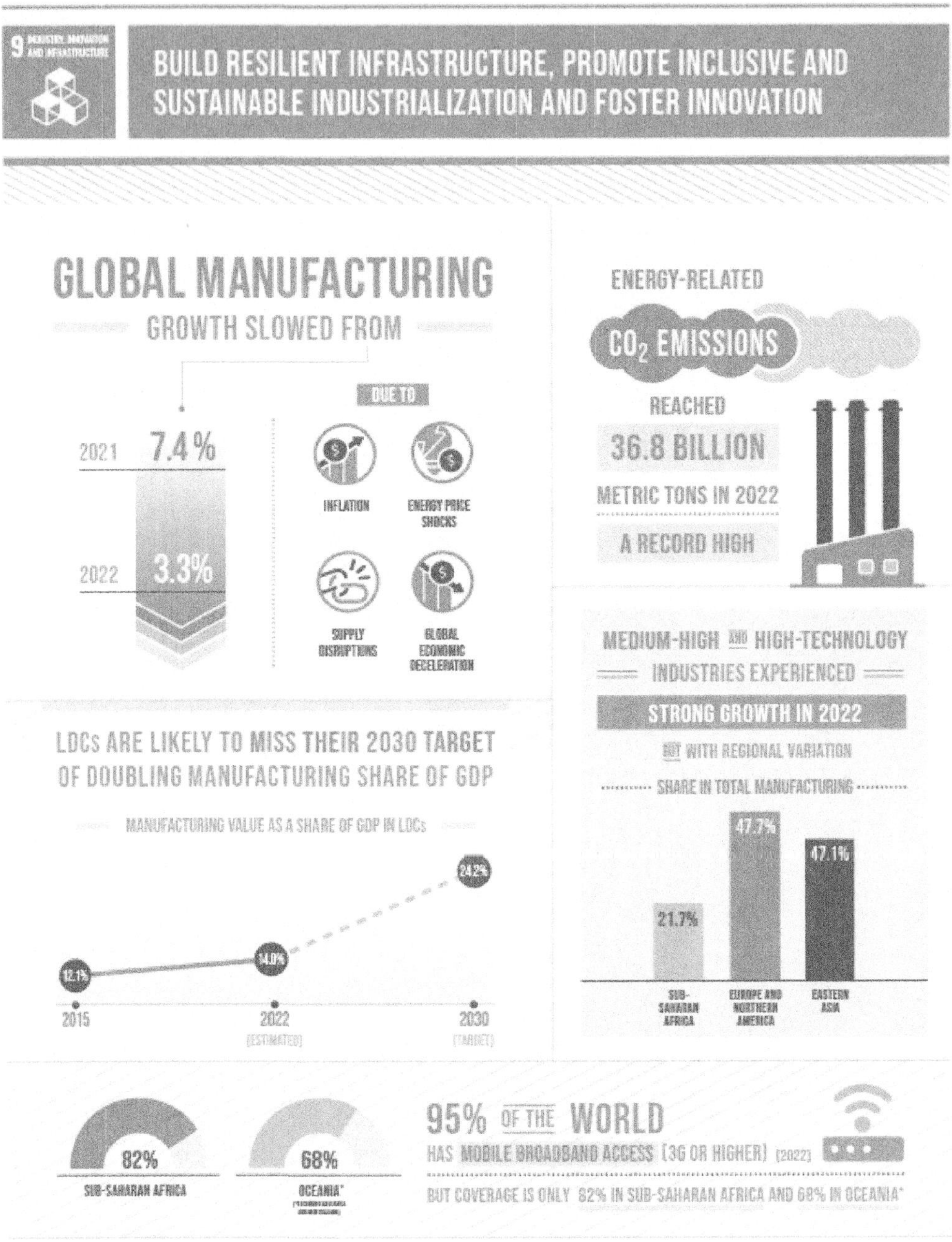

THE SUSTAINABLE DEVELOPMENT GOALS REPORT 2023: SPECIAL EDITION- UNSTATS.UN.ORG/SDGS/REPORT/2023/

SDG 9: INDUSTRY, INNOVATION, & INFRASTRUCTURE

"Build resilient infrastructure, promote inclusive and sustainable industrialisation and foster innovation."

SDG Goal 9 focuses on building resilient infrastructure, promoting inclusive and sustainable industrialisation, and fostering innovation. This goal touches on critical areas of modern society, including transport, telecommunication, research & development, and manufacturing.

Key factors that impede the creation of resilient infrastructure, promote inclusive and sustainable industrialisation and foster innovation:

- **Rapid Urbanization:** unplanned and rapid urbanisation can lead to overcrowded cities, inadequate infrastructure, and strained resources.
- **Lack of Funding:** many cities, especially in developing nations, face financial constraints that hinder investments in sustainable infrastructure and services.
- **Inadequate Infrastructure:** ageing or insufficient infrastructure can hinder the provision of basic services like water, sanitation, and transport.
- **Urban Sprawl:** uncontrolled expansion of cities can lead to increased transportation costs, loss of green spaces, and habitat destruction.

- **Pollution:** insufficient regulations and enforcement can result in high levels of air, water, and soil pollution.
- **Climate Vulnerability:** many cities, especially coastal ones, are vulnerable to the impacts of climate change, including rising sea levels, heat waves, and extreme weather events.
- **Inefficient Transportation:** over-reliance on private vehicles, coupled with inadequate public transport systems, can lead to traffic congestion and increased emissions.
- **Inadequate Housing:** the rapid growth of informal settlements or slums often means that many urban residents live in conditions lacking basic services or security.
- **Inequality:** socio-economic disparities within cities can lead to unequal access to services, opportunities, and decision-making.
- **Lack of Green Spaces:** urban areas might not prioritise or have the resources to maintain parks, gardens, or other recreational areas, affecting residents' well-being.
- **Water Scarcity:** many cities face challenges in ensuring a consistent, clean water supply due to over-extraction, pollution, and climate variability.
- **Waste Management Challenges:** inefficient waste management systems can lead to pollution, health issues, and environmental degradation.
- **Limited Stakeholder Engagement:** without active participation from all community members, including marginalised groups, planning might not reflect everyone's needs.
- **Short-term Planning:** politicians and decision-makers might prioritise short-term gains over long-term sustainability due to election cycles or other pressures.

- **Corruption:** corruption can divert resources from essential services and sustainable initiatives.
- **Cultural Resistance:** some communities might resist changes or innovations due to cultural, historical, or traditional beliefs and practices.
- **Lack of Technical Expertise:** cities might lack the technical know-how or capacity to plan and implement sustainable initiatives effectively.
- **Land Use Conflicts:** conflicting interests and priorities for land use (e.g., development vs. conservation) can hinder sustainable urban planning.
- **Energy Inefficiency:** older buildings and infrastructure might not meet modern energy efficiency standards, leading to excessive energy consumption.
- **Economic Reliance on Non-Sustainable Industries:** cities dependent on industries that are not environmentally friendly might resist transitions to greener alternatives due to economic concerns.

KEY JOB ROLES RELATED TO GOAL 9:

Infrastructure Development and Management

✓ **Civil Engineers** plan, design, and oversee the construction of essential infrastructure such as roads, bridges, and buildings.

✓ **Urban Planners** shape the development of urban areas, ensuring they are sustainable and meet the needs of their populations.

✓ **Transportation Engineers** specialise in designing and maintaining transportation systems, such as roads, railways, airports, and harbours.

Sustainable Industrialisation

- ✓ **Industrial Engineers** focus on improving production processes to be more efficient and sustainable.
- ✓ **Environmental Engineers** develop solutions to environmental problems, often related to industrial processes.
- ✓ **Manufacturing Consultants** help industries adopt sustainable and efficient manufacturing practices.

Research & Development (R&D)

- ✓ **R&D Managers** oversee research and development departments or projects.
- ✓ **Innovation Strategists** help companies or governments design and implement strategies for innovation.
- ✓ **Technology Developers** work on creating new technologies or enhancing existing ones for various industries.

Information and Communication Technologies (ICT)

- ✓ **Telecommunications Engineers** develop and maintain the infrastructure required for modern communications.
- ✓ **Network Administrators and Architects** design, implement and manage communication networks.
- ✓ **ICT Policy Analysts** study and recommend policies to foster the growth and equitable distribution of ICT.

Innovation Hubs and Incubation Centres

- ✓ **Business Incubator Managers** oversee programs that support startups and innovative businesses.
- ✓ **Innovation Hub Coordinators** facilitate collaborative spaces for tech developers, entrepreneurs, and researchers.

Financial & Investment

- ✓ **Infrastructure Finance Specialists** focus on financial models to support infrastructure projects.

- ✓ **Industrial Economists** analyse the economic dimensions of industries and recommend growth strategies.

Policy and Regulation

- ✓ **Infrastructure Policy Analysts** research and recommend infrastructure development and maintenance policies.
- ✓ **Industrial Policymakers** shape policies that guide industrial growth in a sustainable and inclusive manner.

Sustainability and Resilience

- ✓ **Resilience Planners** help cities and communities develop in ways that make them resilient to challenges like climate change or economic shocks.
- ✓ **Sustainable Design Engineers** specialise in creating infrastructure and products with minimal environmental impact.

Advanced Manufacturing & Industry 4.0

- ✓ **Automation Engineers** design and implement automated systems in manufacturing.
- ✓ **Robotics Specialists** develop and deploy robots in industrial settings.
- ✓ **Data Analysts for the Industry** use data to optimise industrial processes and predict trends.

Advocacy & Development Organisations

- ✓ **Program Managers for Infrastructure Projects** oversee large-scale projects aimed at improving infrastructure in underserved areas.
- ✓ **Industrial Development Advocates** campaign for equitable industrial growth and sustainable practices.

These are just some of the many career options that can contribute towards building resilient infrastructure, promoting inclusive and sustainable industrialisation, and fostering innovation, SDG 9. Remember that as wicked problems, the goals are interlinked, and this list is by no means exhaustive, nor is it intended to be. It is designed to get you thinking about which areas interest you.

You may also find it helpful to look at roles included in a related SDG that interests you. The following websites will help you explore these and other roles in more detail:

- UK: https://www.prospects.ac.uk/job-profiles
- US: https://www.onetonline.org/ (use the occupational keyword search tool)
- Europe: https://eures.ec.europa.eu/index_en
- More about SDG 9: https://sdgs.un.org/goals/goal9
- Use https://www.careeralchemy.co.uk/understanding-job-market.html to help you compare jobs and understand key labour market information.

CONSOLIDATING YOUR LEARNING FROM SDG 9 – INDUSTRY, INNOVATION, AND INFRASTRUCTURE

What is your most significant light bulb moment of SDG 9?

* * * *

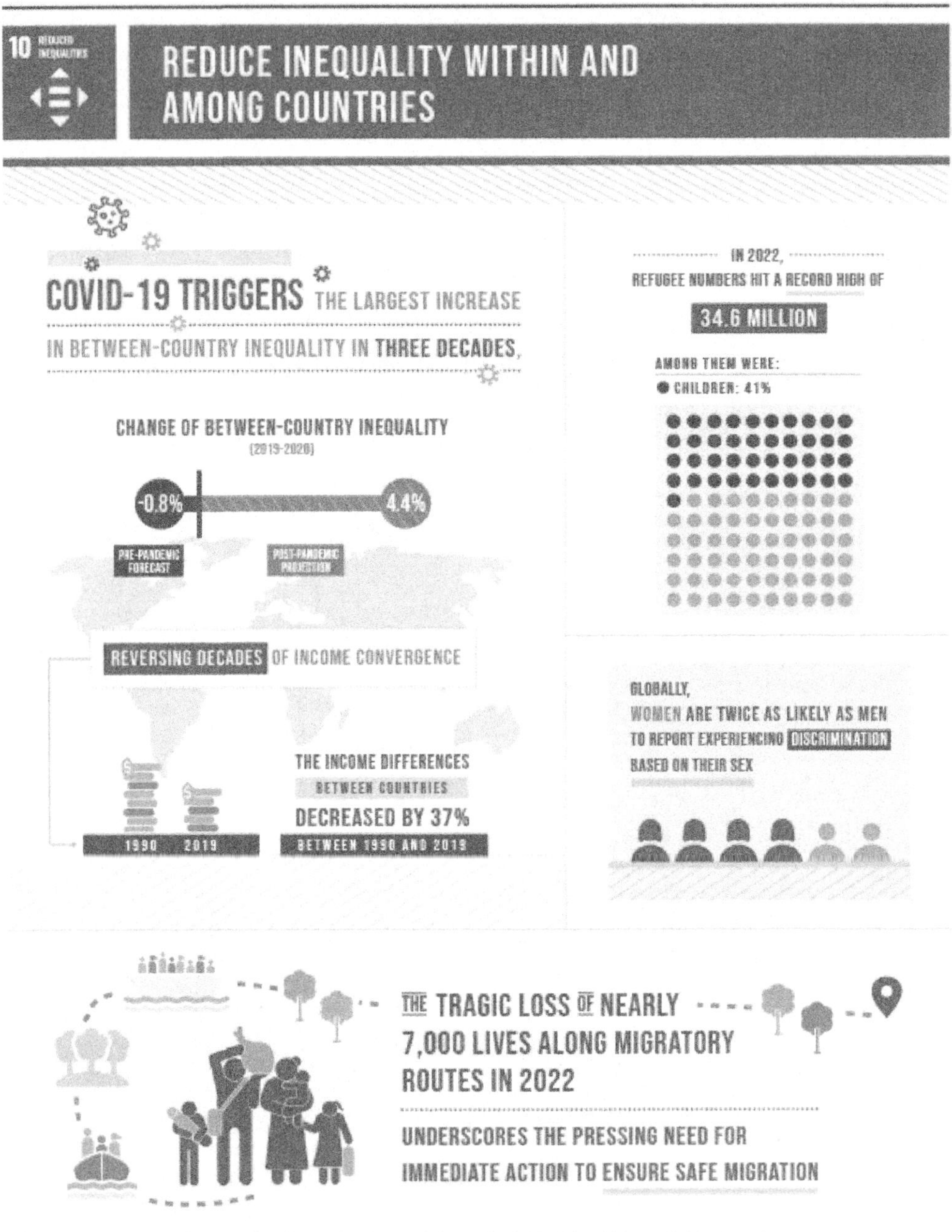

THE SUSTAINABLE DEVELOPMENT GOALS REPORT 2023: SPECIAL EDITION- UNSTATS.UN.ORG/SDGS/REPORT/2023/

SDG 10: REDUCED INEQUALITIES

"Reduce inequality within and among countries."

SDG Goal 10 focuses on reducing inequality within and among countries. It seeks to address issues related to income inequality, discrimination, migration, and the policies and practices that either exacerbate or alleviate disparities. The career options associated with this goal span multiple sectors and professions.

Key factors which are needed to reduce inequalities, within and among, countries include:

- **Historical Exploitation and Colonialism:** past colonisation and exploitation have left many nations economically disadvantaged, with lingering effects on their development and wealth distribution.
- **Unfair Trade Practices:** global trade rules and practices might favour developed countries, making it challenging for developing nations to compete on an equal footing.
- **Economic Policies:** policies prioritising the interests of the wealthy or prominent corporations can exacerbate income and wealth disparities.
- **Lack of Access to Quality Education:** disparities in educational opportunities and quality often perpetuate generational cycles of poverty and inequality.

- **Discrimination and Bias:** discrimination based on race, gender, ethnicity, religion, or other factors can limit opportunities and access to resources for certain groups.
- **Inefficient Tax Systems:** regressive tax systems, where the wealthy aren't taxed proportionally to their income, can perpetuate wealth disparities.
- **Corruption:** corruption diverts resources away from public services and welfare, often impacting marginalised communities the most.
- **Restricted Access to Healthcare:** limited or unequal access to healthcare means that not everyone has the same chance of living a healthy, productive life.
- **Unequal Access to Technology:** the digital divide can exacerbate educational and economic disparities, especially in the modern, tech-driven world.
- **Limited Representation:** if certain groups are underrepresented in decision-making processes or political arenas, their interests might be overlooked.
- **Labour Market Discrimination:** disparities in wages and employment opportunities, especially for women or minority groups, contribute to income inequalities.
- **Inheritance and Intergenerational Wealth:** wealth passed down through generations can perpetuate economic disparities.
- **Geographical Disparities:** inequalities can be pronounced between urban and rural areas or among different regions within a country.
- **Land Ownership Disparities:** in many nations, land ownership is concentrated among a few, leading to imbalances in wealth and power.
- **Global Financial Systems**: the structure and regulation of global financial markets can sometimes favour wealthy nations and

multinational corporations, limiting opportunities for developing countries.

- **Debt Burdens:** heavy debt burdens on developing nations can restrict their ability to invest in development and welfare, perpetuating inequalities.
- **Cultural and Social Norms:** in some societies, cultural norms might limit opportunities or rights for certain groups, such as women or certain castes or tribes.
- **Armed Conflict and Instability:** wars and conflicts disrupt economic activities, displace populations, and often hit the most vulnerable the hardest.
- **Limited Access to Capital:** without access to financial services or capital, entrepreneurs, and small businesses, particularly in developing countries, might struggle to grow and compete.
- **Environmental Degradation:** climate change and environmental degradation can disproportionately affect vulnerable populations, especially those in poorer nations or in regions reliant on agriculture.

KEY JOB ROLES RELATED TO GOAL 10:

Policy Analysis and Advocacy

✓ **Equality and Inclusion Policy Analysts** research and recommend policies to address various forms of inequality.

✓ **Human Rights Advocates** work to protect and promote the rights of marginalised and vulnerable groups.

Economic Development and Finance

✓ **Development Economists** focus on policies and strategies that can promote inclusive economic growth.

- ✓ **Financial Inclusion Specialists** advocate for and implement strategies to bring banking and financial services to underserved populations.

Social Work and Community Development

- ✓ **Community Development Workers** work on the ground to improve conditions and opportunities for marginalised communities.
- ✓ **Social Workers** support individuals and groups facing social, emotional, or economic challenges.

Legal Professions

- ✓ **Human Rights Lawyers** advocate for the rights of individuals and groups, often representing marginalised populations.
- ✓ **Immigration Lawyers** assist individuals in navigating the complexities of immigration policies and laws.

Researchers and Academics

- ✓ **Social Scientists** study the causes, impacts, and solutions to social inequalities.
- ✓ **Migration and Diaspora Researchers** focus on patterns, causes, and effects of migration, both internal and international.

International Organisations and NGOs

- ✓ **Program Managers for Inequality Projects** oversee initiatives aimed at reducing inequalities in various contexts.
- ✓ **Gender Equality Officers** focus on issues related to gender disparities in various sectors.

Public Health

- ✓ **Health Equity Researchers** study disparities in health outcomes and access to healthcare.
- ✓ **Public Health Advocates** promote policies and practices that ensure equal access to healthcare services.

Education

- ✓ **Educational Policy Makers** develop policies that ensure equitable access to quality education for all.
- ✓ **Diversity and Inclusion Officers in Academic Institutions** work to promote an inclusive educational environment.

Media and Communications

- ✓ **Journalists focusing on Inequality** report on issues related to disparities, bringing attention to them.
- ✓ **Documentary Filmmakers** produce content highlighting various inequalities and efforts to address them.

Business and Corporate World

- ✓ **Corporate Social Responsibility** (**CSR**) **Professionals** manage and implement initiatives aimed at addressing inequalities.
- ✓ **Diversity, Equity, and Inclusion** (**DEI**) **Consultants** advise organisations on how to foster more inclusive environments and practices.

Migration and Refugees

- ✓ **Refugee Support Workers** directly support refugees, helping them integrate into new communities.
- ✓ **Migration Policy Analysts** research and shape policies related to migration and integration.

These are just some of the many career options that can contribute towards SDG 10. As in the last SDG section, as wicked problems, the goals are interlinked, and this list is by no means exhaustive, nor is it intended to be. It is designed to get you thinking about which areas interest you.

You may also find it helpful to look at roles included in a related SDG that interests you. The following websites will help you explore these and other roles in more detail:

- UK: https://www.prospects.ac.uk/job-profiles
- US: https://www.onetonline.org/ (use the occupational keyword search tool)
- Europe: https://eures.ec.europa.eu/index_en
- More about SDG 10: https://sdgs.un.org/goals/goal10
- Use https://www.careeralchemy.co.uk/understanding-job-market.html to help you compare jobs and understand key labour market information.

Remember, the key to finding your ultimate concern is to find an intersection between who you are, what you can offer, what attracts you, and opportunities to make a positive difference.

CONSOLIDATING YOUR LEARNING FROM SDG 10 – REDUCED INEQUALITIES

What is your most significant light bulb moment about SDG 10?

* * * *

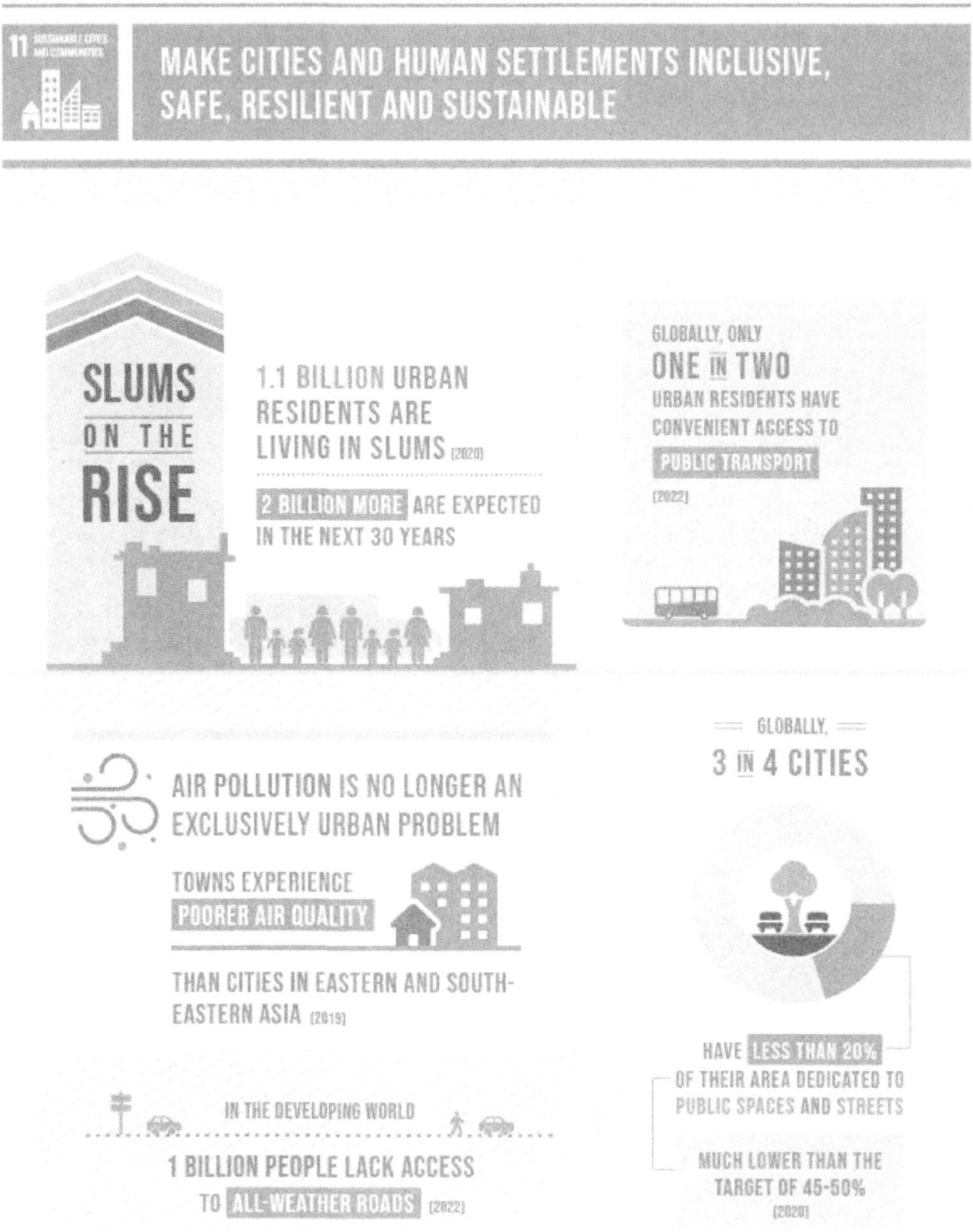

THE SUSTAINABLE DEVELOPMENT GOALS REPORT 2023: SPECIAL EDITION- UNSTATS.UN.ORG/SDGS/REPORT/2023/

SDG 11: SUSTAINABLE CITIES AND COMMUNITIES

"Make cities and human settlements inclusive, safe, resilient and sustainable."

SDG Goal 11 is dedicated to making cities and human settlements inclusive, safe, resilient, and sustainable. It addresses various urban challenges, from housing and transport to cultural heritage and environmental impact.

Key factors which prevent the creation of sustainable cities and communities include:

- **Rapid Urbanization:** unplanned and rapid urbanisation can lead to overcrowded cities, inadequate infrastructure, and strained resources.
- **Lack of Funding:** many cities, especially in developing nations, face financial constraints that hinder investments in sustainable infrastructure and services.
- **Inadequate Infrastructure:** ageing or insufficient infrastructure can hinder the provision of basic services like water, sanitation, and transport.
- **Urban Sprawl:** uncontrolled expansion of cities can lead to increased transportation costs, loss of green spaces, and habitat destruction.
- **Pollution:** insufficient regulations and enforcement can result in high levels of air, water, and soil pollution.

- **Climate Vulnerability:** many cities, especially coastal ones, are vulnerable to the impacts of climate change, including rising sea levels, heat waves, and extreme weather events.
- **Inefficient Transportation:** overreliance on private vehicles and inadequate public transport systems can lead to traffic congestion and increased emissions.
- **Inadequate Housing:** the rapid growth of informal settlements or slums often means that many urban residents live in conditions lacking basic services or security.
- **Inequality:** socio-economic disparities within cities can lead to unequal access to services, opportunities, and decision-making.
- **Lack of Green Spaces:** urban areas might not prioritise or have the resources to maintain parks, gardens, or other recreational areas, affecting residents' well-being.
- **Water Scarcity:** many cities face challenges in ensuring a consistent, clean water supply due to over-extraction, pollution, and climate variability.
- **Waste Management Challenges:** inefficient waste management systems can lead to pollution, health issues, and environmental degradation.
- **Limited Stakeholder Engagement:** without active participation from all community members, including marginalised groups, planning might not reflect everyone's needs.
- **Short-term Planning:** politicians and decision-makers might prioritise short-term gains over long-term sustainability due to election cycles or other pressures.
- **Corruption:** can divert resources from essential services and sustainable initiatives.

- **Cultural Resistance:** some communities might resist changes or innovations due to cultural, historical, or traditional beliefs and practices.
- **Lack of Technical Expertise:** cities might lack the technical know-how or capacity to plan and implement sustainable initiatives effectively.
- **Land Use Conflicts:** conflicting interests and priorities for land use (e.g., development vs. conservation) can hinder sustainable urban planning.
- **Energy Inefficiency:** older buildings and infrastructure might not meet modern energy efficiency standards, leading to excessive energy consumption.
- **Economic Reliance on Non-Sustainable Industries:** cities dependent on industries that are not environmentally friendly might resist transitions to greener alternatives due to economic concerns.

KEY JOB ROLES RELATED TO GOAL 11:

Urban Planning and Design

- ✓ **Urban Planners** design and manage the growth of cities to ensure sustainability and inclusivity.
- ✓ **Landscape Architects** plan and design outdoor spaces, including public areas, green spaces, and parks.
- ✓ **Transportation Planners** focus specifically on designing effective, sustainable transportation systems for urban areas.

Housing and Development

- ✓ **Urban Development Specialists** work on large-scale projects to develop or redevelop urban areas.

- ✓ **Affordable Housing Advocates/Developers** promote and develop housing solutions that are affordable and sustainable.
- ✓ **Slum Upgrading Specialists** work on projects to improve living conditions in informal settlements.

Transportation and Mobility

- ✓ **Transport Engineers** design, develop, and maintain sustainable transportation infrastructure.
- ✓ **Mobility Consultants** advise cities on solutions for public transport, walkability, and cycling.

Environmental and Sustainability

- ✓ **Urban Environmentalists** focus on urban environmental challenges such as air quality, urban heat islands, and green infrastructure.
- ✓ **Sustainable Infrastructure Engineers** develop infrastructure that minimises environmental impact.
- ✓ **Climate Resilience Planners** help cities prepare for and adapt to the impacts of climate change.

Cultural Heritage Preservation

- ✓ **Historic Preservationists** work to protect and restore historically significant urban sites.
- ✓ **Cultural Resource Managers** handle the protection, management, and promotion of cultural resources in urban areas.

Safety and Disaster Management

- ✓ **Urban Disaster Risk Reduction Specialists** develop strategies to reduce the risk of natural disasters in urban settings.
- ✓ **Emergency Management Professionals** plan for and respond to emergencies in urban areas.

Community and Social Engagement

- ✓ **Community Organizers** work directly with communities to advocate for their needs and rights in the urban planning process.

- ✓ **Public Engagement Specialists** design and implement strategies for public participation in urban planning and development.

Research and Policy

- ✓ **Urban Researchers** study urbanisation patterns, challenges, and solutions.
- ✓ **Urban policymakers** shape policies related to housing, transportation, environment, and other urban-related issues.

Smart Cities and Technology

- ✓ **Smart City Planners** integrate technology solutions to improve urban services and infrastructure.
- ✓ **Urban Data Scientists** analyse data to inform urban planning and policy decisions.

Public Health in Urban Settings

- ✓ **Urban Health Specialists** address public health challenges specific to urban environments.
- ✓ **Environmental Health Professionals** focus on health impacts related to environmental factors in urban settings.

International Organisations and NGOs

- ✓ **Urban Development Program Managers** oversee urban development projects, often in a global or regional context.
- ✓ **Habitat and Settlement Advisors** provide expertise on human settlement issues, often in developing countries.

These are just some of the many career options that can contribute towards developing sustainable cities and communities, SDG 11. Remember that as wicked problems, the goals are interlinked, and this list is by no means exhaustive, nor is it intended to be. It is designed to get you thinking about which areas interest you.

You may also find it helpful to look at roles included in a related SDG that interests you. The following websites will help you explore these and other roles in more detail:

- UK: https://www.prospects.ac.uk/job-profiles
- US: https://www.onetonline.org/ (use the occupational keyword search tool)
- Europe: https://eures.ec.europa.eu/index_en
- More about SDG 11: https://sdgs.un.org/goals/goal11
- Use https://www.careeralchemy.co.uk/understanding-job-market.html to help you compare jobs and understand key labour market information.

CONSOLIDATING YOUR LEARNING FROM SDG 11 – SUSTAINABLE CITIES AND COMMUNITIES

What is your most significant light bulb moment of SDG 11?

* * * *

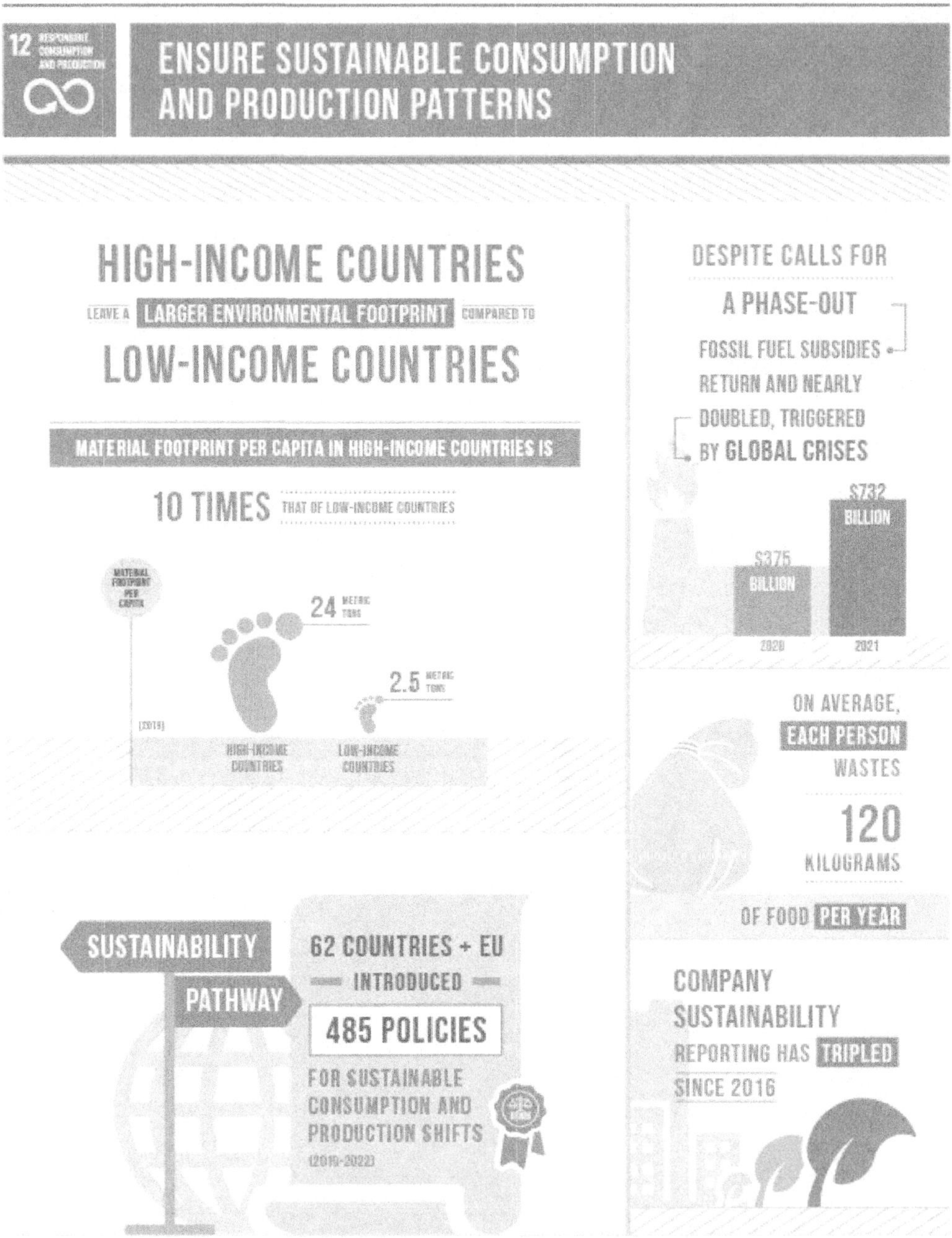

THE SUSTAINABLE DEVELOPMENT GOALS REPORT 2023: SPECIAL EDITION- UNSTATS.UN.ORG/SDGS/REPORT/2023/

SDG 12: RESPONSIBLE CONSUMPTION AND PRODUCTION

"Ensure sustainable consumption and production patterns."

SDG Goal 12 focuses on ensuring sustainable consumption and production patterns. It emphasises efficient resource use, waste reduction, and the integration of sustainability into business and consumer practices.

Key factors which act as barriers to responsible consumption and production include:

- **Consumerism Culture:** many societies value consumerism, leading to overconsumption and wasteful habits.
- **Economic Growth Models:** traditional economic models prioritise growth and increased production, sometimes without adequate consideration of sustainability.
- **Lack of Awareness:** many consumers aren't aware of the environmental and social impacts of their consumption choices.
- **Supply Chain Complexities:** globalised supply chains can make it hard for consumers and businesses to determine the sustainability of products.
- **Short Product Lifespans:** planned obsolescence and fast fashion contribute to a culture of disposability.

- **Inadequate Recycling Infrastructure:** without efficient systems for waste collection, recycling, and upcycling, much waste goes to landfills.
- **Lack of Eco-friendly Alternatives:** in some markets, sustainable products aren't readily available or are more expensive than non-sustainable counterparts.
- **Limited Regulations:** absence of strong regulatory frameworks can lead to unchecked pollution, waste, and unsustainable resource extraction.
- **Externalized Costs:** the actual environmental and social costs of production are often not included in product prices, making unsustainable products appear cheaper.
- **Lack of Incentives for Businesses:** without financial or regulatory incentives, businesses might not prioritise sustainable production.
- **Misleading Advertising:** greenwashing, or misleading consumers about the environmental benefits of a product, can make it difficult for consumers to make informed choices.
- **High Initial Costs:** while sustainable technologies (like solar panels) often save money in the long run, their initial investment can be a deterrent.
- **Cultural and Social Norms:** in some societies, consumption patterns are deeply rooted in cultural or social practices, making change challenging.
- **Information Overload:** while there's a lot of information about sustainable consumption, it can be overwhelming or confusing for consumers to decipher.
- **Global Inequities:** developed countries often consume far more resources per capita than developing countries, making it challenging to address consumption patterns globally.

- **Fragmented Production Systems:** without a holistic view of production systems, inefficiencies and wasteful practices can go unnoticed.
- **Inefficient Resource Use:** due to technological or economic reasons, industries might not always use resources optimally.
- **Competing Interests:** sometimes, there's a conflict between sustainability goals and other objectives, like job creation or economic growth.
- **Resistance to Change:** established industries, especially those linked to non-renewable resources, might resist transitioning to sustainable practices.
- **Over-reliance on Non-renewable Resources:** continued dependence on fossil fuels and other non-renewable resources hampers the shift towards sustainable production.

KEY JOB ROLES RELATED TO GOAL 12:

Sustainability in Business

- ✓ **Corporate Sustainability Officers** develop and implement sustainability strategies for businesses.
- ✓ **Supply Chain Sustainability Specialists** ensure that production and distribution processes are sustainable.
- ✓ **Sustainable Procurement Officers** ensure that goods and services procured meet sustainability criteria.

Waste Management

- ✓ **Recycling Coordinators** manage and optimise recycling operations.
- ✓ **Waste Management Specialists** develop waste reduction, collection, and disposal strategies.

- ✓ **Circular Economy Consultants** advise businesses on how to operate in a way that regenerates resources.

Product Design and Development

- ✓ **Sustainable Product Designers** design products to be long-lasting, repairable, and recyclable.
- ✓ **Life Cycle Assessment (LCA) Analysts** assess the environmental impact of products throughout their life cycle.

Consumer Behaviour and Education

- ✓ **Sustainability Educators** teach sustainable consumption practices in schools, colleges, or community programs.
- ✓ **Consumer Behaviour Researchers** study how consumers make choices and how they can be influenced towards sustainable consumption.

Agriculture and Food Production

- ✓ **Sustainable Agriculture Specialists** advise on sustainable farming practices that minimise waste.
- ✓ **Food Waste Reduction Coordinators** work with retailers, restaurants, and consumers to reduce food wastage.

Policy and Regulation

- ✓ **Sustainability Policy Analysts** research and recommend policies related to sustainable consumption and production.
- ✓ **Regulatory Affairs Specialists** ensure compliance with sustainability and waste management regulations.

Research and Academia

- ✓ **Sustainable Production Researchers** investigate new methods and technologies for sustainable production.
- ✓ **Consumer Sustainability Researchers** study sustainable consumption patterns and challenges.

Eco-labelling and Certification

- ✓ **Certification Auditors** verify if products and services meet sustainability criteria.
- ✓ **Eco-labelling Consultants** advise businesses on achieving certifications like Fair Trade, Organic, or Energy Star.

Environmentally Friendly Technologies

- ✓ **Green Tech Developers** invent and improve technologies that promote sustainability, like biodegradable materials.
- ✓ **Sustainable Energy Consultants** advise businesses and governments on using sustainable energy sources in production.

Advocacy & Development Organisations

- ✓ **Sustainability Advocates** raise awareness and push for changes in policy or business practices.
- ✓ **Development Workers** focusing on SCP (Sustainable Consumption and Production) implement sustainability projects, especially in developing countries.

Communications and Marketing

- ✓ **Green Marketing Professionals** promote products or services with environmental benefits.
- ✓ **Sustainability Communications Specialists** handle internal or external communications on sustainability initiatives.

These are just some of the many career options that can contribute towards developing responsible consumption and production, SDG 12. Remember that as wicked problems, the goals are interlinked, and this list is by no means exhaustive, nor is it intended to be. It is designed to get you thinking about which areas interest you.

You may also find it helpful to look at roles included in a related SDG that interests you. The following websites will help you explore these and other roles in more detail:

- UK: https://www.prospects.ac.uk/job-profiles
- US: https://www.onetonline.org/ (use the occupational keyword search tool)
- Europe: https://eures.ec.europa.eu/index_en
- More about SDG 12: https://sdgs.un.org/goals/goal12
- Use https://www.careeralchemy.co.uk/understanding-job-market.html to help you compare jobs and understand key labour market information.

CONSOLIDATING YOUR LEARNING FROM SDG 12 – RESPONSIBLE PRODUCTION AND CONSUMPTION

What is your most significant light bulb moment of SDG 12?

* * * *

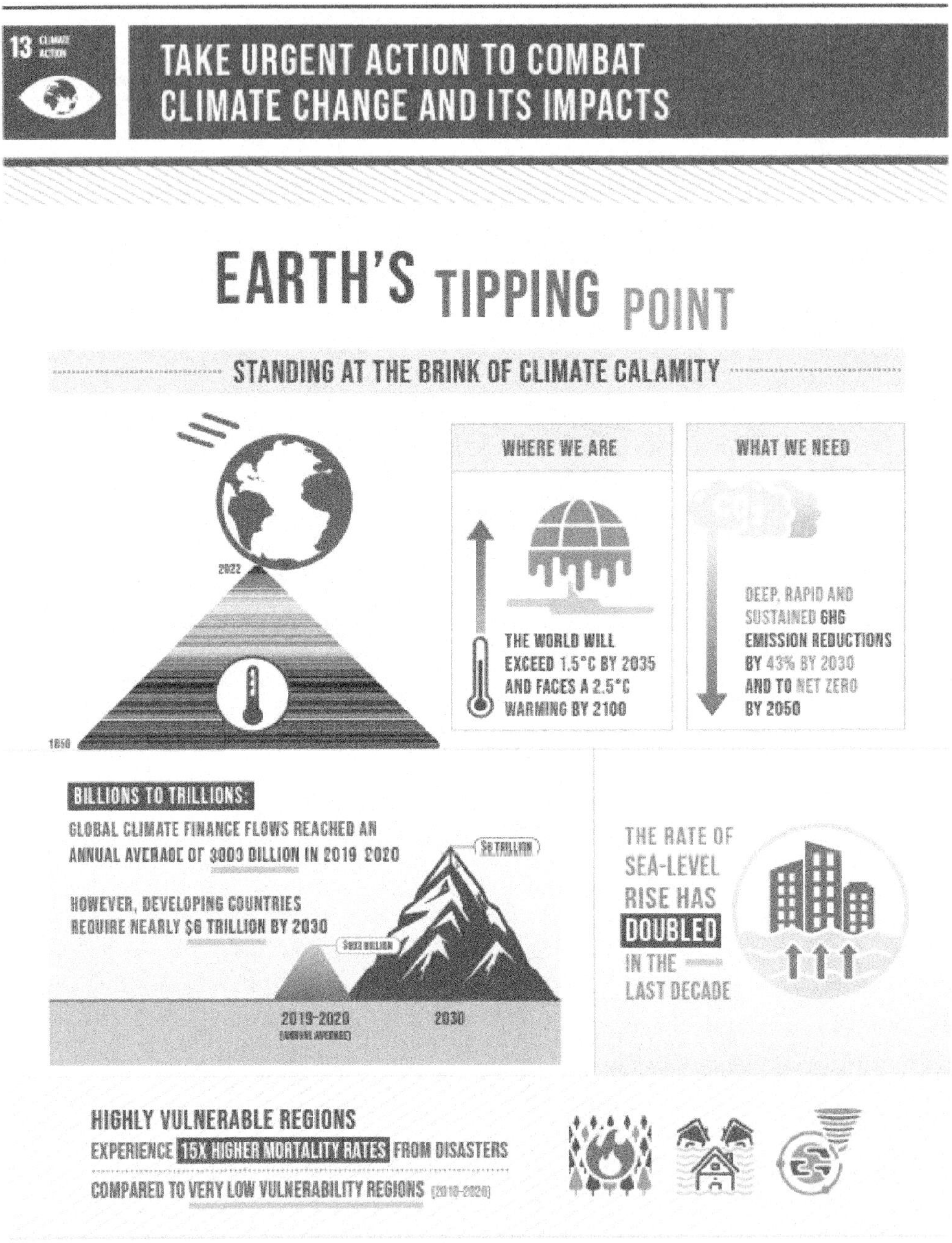

THE SUSTAINABLE DEVELOPMENT GOALS REPORT 2023: SPECIAL EDITION- UNSTATS.UN.ORG/SDGS/REPORT/2023/

13 CLIMATE ACTION

SDG 13: CLIMATE ACTION

"Take urgent action to combat climate change.
and its impacts."

SDG Goal 13 focuses on urgently combating climate change and its impacts. Addressing climate change is one of the most pressing challenges of our time and requires a multidisciplinary approach.

Key factors that prevent people from people acting quickly to combat climate change and its impacts include:

- **Lack of Awareness:** despite increasing information on climate change, many people remain unaware or only superficially informed about the specifics and severity of the issue.
- **Economic Interests:** fossil fuel industries and other sectors contributing to climate change often wield significant economic and political influence, resisting change that might affect their profits.
- **Short-term Thinking:** political and business leaders may prioritise immediate economic growth or election cycles over long-term sustainable planning.
- **Financial Constraints:** transitioning to greener technologies and infrastructures can require significant upfront investment, which can be a deterrent, especially for developing countries.
- **Information Dissemination:** there is a vast amount of misinformation or misleading narratives about climate change, often

propagated by interest groups or individuals denying its existence or human contribution.

- **Technological Barriers:** while green technologies have advanced, they might not be accessible or feasible for all regions or sectors.
- **Institutional Barriers:** inadequate institutional frameworks or governance structures can impede coordinated climate action.
- **Cultural and Behavioural Inertia:** long-standing cultural habits or lifestyles centred around high consumption can be hard to change.
- **Geopolitical Considerations:** climate change solutions require global cooperation, but geopolitical tensions can hinder collaborative efforts.
- **Equity Concerns:** developing countries might feel they're being asked to forgo development or bear undue burdens, given that developed countries historically contributed more to the problem.
- **Cognitive Dissonance:** people might recognise the threat of climate change but feel overwhelmed or powerless, leading to inaction.
- **Regulatory and Policy Inertia:** existing policies or regulatory structures might be slow to adapt to the needs of climate action.
- **Infrastructure Lock-in:** existing infrastructure, such as urban design or energy systems, can lock societies into carbon-intensive patterns.
- **Fragmented Stakeholder Interests:** different stakeholders, from businesses to governments to NGOs, might have differing priorities or approaches, complicating consensus-building.
- **Fear of Economic Disruption:** concerns about job losses in traditional industries or economic downturns can delay the transition to sustainable practices.
- **Public Scepticism:** despite scientific consensus, segments of the public remain sceptical about climate change, its causes, or its severity.

- **Delay in Observable Effects:** some impacts of climate change are long-term, leading to a perception that there's more time to act than there actually is.
- **Competing Crises:** other immediate crises, such as economic downturns, pandemics, or geopolitical conflicts, might overshadow climate concerns.
- **Lack of Political Will:** in some regions, there may be a lack of political will or leadership to address climate change proactively.
- **Path Dependency:** societies might continue on established paths because of the costs or complexities associated with changing directions.

KEY JOB ROLES RELATED TO GOAL 13:

Climate Science & Research

✓ **Climatologists** study climate patterns and variations.

✓ **Atmospheric Scientists** research the atmosphere to understand and forecast weather and climate patterns.

✓ **Oceanographers** study ocean processes and their relationship to climate.

Environmental Policy & Advocacy

✓ **Climate Policy Analysts** research, develop and implement climate-related policies at various levels of governance.

✓ **Environmental Advocates** lobby for policy change and create awareness about climate change issues.

✓ **Climate Diplomats** work on international agreements like the Paris Agreement.

Renewable Energy

- ✓ **Wind Energy Engineers** design and oversee the construction of wind energy projects.
- ✓ **Solar Energy Technicians** install and maintain solar panels.
- ✓ **Renewable Energy Consultants** advise governments, businesses, and NGOs on renewable energy strategies.

Carbon Management

- ✓ **Carbon Traders** deal with carbon credit trading under cap-and-trade systems.
- ✓ **Carbon Footprint Analysts** measure the carbon footprint of organisations, products, or services.
- ✓ **Greenhouse Gas Emission Managers** oversee and reduce GHG emissions in organisations.

Adaptation & Resilience

- ✓ **Climate Resilience Planners** develop strategies to make cities and communities resilient to climate change impacts.
- ✓ **Disaster Risk Reduction Specialists** plan and implement measures to reduce risks from natural disasters exacerbated by climate change.

Environmental Education & Communication

- ✓ **Environmental Educators** teach the public and students about climate change.
- ✓ **Climate Journalists** cover news and stories related to climate change and its impacts.
- ✓ **Environmental Filmmakers** produce documentaries and other content on climate-related topics.

Conservation

- ✓ **Conservation Scientists** research and implement strategies to conserve natural habitats impacted by climate change.

- ✓ **Wildlife Biologists** study wildlife and their adaptation or vulnerabilities to changing climates.

Sustainable Agriculture

- ✓ **Agronomists** research and implement farming practices that are resilient to changing climate conditions.
- ✓ **Agroecology Specialists** promote agricultural systems that are both sustainable and resilient to climate change.

Green Architecture and Building

- ✓ **Green Architects** design buildings that are energy-efficient and climate-resilient.
- ✓ **Sustainable Construction Managers** oversee the construction of green buildings.

Sustainable Transport

- ✓ **Sustainable Transport Planners** develop transportation systems that minimise carbon emissions.
- ✓ **Electric Vehicle Engineers** work on the development and improvement of electric vehicles.

Technology & Innovation

- ✓ **Climate Tech Entrepreneurs** launch startups that offer solutions to climate-related challenges.
- ✓ **Climate Modelers** use computer models to forecast future climatic changes.

Conservation Finance & Economics

- ✓ **Environmental Economists** study the economics of environmental conservation and climate action.
- ✓ **Conservation Finance Specialists** design financial instruments and mechanisms to support conservation efforts.

These are just some of the many career options that can contribute towards developing responsible consumption and production, SDG 13. Remember that as wicked problems, the goals are interlinked, and this list is by no means exhaustive, nor is it intended to be. It is designed to get you thinking about which areas interest you.

You may also find it helpful to look at roles included in a related SDG that interests you. The following websites will help you explore these and other roles in more detail:

- UK: https://www.prospects.ac.uk/job-profiles
- US: https://www.onetonline.org/ (use the occupational keyword search tool)
- Europe: https://eures.ec.europa.eu/index_en
- More about SDG 13: https://sdgs.un.org/goals/goal13
- Use https://www.careeralchemy.co.uk/understanding-job-market.html to help you compare jobs and understand key labour market information.

CONSOLIDATING YOUR LEARNING FROM SDG 13 – CLIMATE ACTION

What is your most significant light bulb moment of SDG 13?

* * * *

14 LIFE BELOW WATER

CONSERVE AND SUSTAINABLY USE THE OCEANS, SEA AND MARINE RESOURCES FOR SUSTAINABLE DEVELOPMENT

THE SUSTAINABLE DEVELOPMENT GOALS REPORT 2023: SPECIAL EDITION- UNSTATS.UN.ORG/SDGS/REPORT/2023/

SDG 14: LIFE BELOW WATER

"Conserve and sustainably use the oceans and seas, and marine resources for sustainable development."

SDG Goal 14 pertains to conserving and sustainably using the oceans, seas, and marine resources for sustainable development. This goal encompasses a variety of targets, from marine pollution reduction to sustainable fisheries management.

Key factors that delay the conservation and sustainable use of oceans, seas and marine resources for sustainable development include:

- **Overfishing:** many fisheries worldwide are exploited beyond their sustainable limits, leading to declining fish stocks.
- **Illegal, Unreported, and Unregulated** (**IUU**) **Fishing:** this contributes to overfishing, environmental degradation, and the loss of billions of dollars in revenue.
- **Marine Pollution:** around 12-14 million tonnes of plastic enter the oceans each year, harming marine life, impacting coastal economies, and entering the food chain.
- **Lack of Effective Governance and Regulation:** the vastness and shared nature of the oceans make regulation and governance challenging.

- **Climate Change:** rising sea temperatures, ocean acidification, and other impacts of climate change are profoundly altering marine ecosystems.
- **Destructive Fishing Practices:** methods like bottom trawling can cause significant harm to marine habitats.
- **Economic Prioritization:** marine resources are often seen first and foremost as economic assets, with short-term gains prioritised over long-term sustainability.
- **Lack of Awareness:** public understanding of marine conservation issues can be limited, reducing pressure on policymakers and industries to act.
- **Marine Habitat Destruction:** coastal development, pollution, and certain fishing practices can destroy crucial habitats such as mangroves, coral reefs, and seagrass beds.
- **Shipping and Maritime Activities:** oil spills, ship groundings, and anchor damage can harm marine environments.
- **Unsustainable Tourism:** coral damage, waste, and other impacts from tourism can degrade marine environments.
- **Competing Stakeholder Interests:** marine areas often have multiple stakeholders, from fishing industries to conservation groups, with competing interests.
- **Insufficient Scientific Knowledge:** the oceans remain one of the least explored and understood parts of our planet, making sustainable management more challenging.
- **Fragmented Jurisdiction:** international waters, or the high seas, are areas beyond national jurisdiction, complicating conservation efforts.
- **Financial Constraints:** for many developing nations, marine conservation and sustainable management require financial resources and capacities they may not possess.

- **Globalization of Seafood Markets:** the global demand for seafood can drive overfishing and unsustainable practices in distant waters.
- **Deep-sea Mining Interests:** the potential for mineral extraction from the ocean floor can threaten deep-sea ecosystems.
- **Invasive Species:** transported by shipping and other means, invasive species can alter marine ecosystems and outcompete native species.
- **Cultural and Social Norms:** in some communities, traditions or practices might conflict with sustainable marine resource management.
- **Lack of Effective Monitoring and Enforcement:** the vast expanse of the world's oceans makes monitoring and enforcing regulations exceptionally challenging.

KEY JOB ROLES RELATED TO GOAL 14:

Marine Science & Research

✓ **Marine Biologists** study marine organisms, their behaviours, and interactions.

✓ **Oceanographers** investigate the physical and biological properties of oceans.

✓ **Marine Geologists** examine the ocean floor and coastal zones.

Conservation & Restoration

✓ **Marine Conservationists** focus on protecting marine species and their habitats.

✓ **Coral Reef Restorers** specialise in techniques to restore degraded coral reefs.

- ✓ **Mangrove Restoration Specialists** work on restoring vital mangrove ecosystems.

Marine Protected Areas (MPAs) & Management

- ✓ **MPA Managers** oversee marine protected areas to ensure conservation objectives are met.
- ✓ **Marine Spatial Planners** organise the use of marine spaces in sustainable ways.

Sustainable Fisheries

- ✓ **Fisheries Biologists** research fish populations to support sustainable fishing.
- ✓ **Fishery Managers** implement and oversee sustainable fishing practices and policies.
- ✓ **Aquaculture Specialists** develop and manage sustainable fish farming practices.

Marine Pollution Control

- ✓ **Marine Pollution Analysts** monitor and analyse pollutants in marine environments.
- ✓ **Plastic Pollution Specialists** focus specifically on reducing and managing plastic waste in oceans.

Environmental Policy & Advocacy

- ✓ **Marine Policy Analyst** develop, review, and implement policies related to marine resources.
- ✓ **Ocean Advocates** lobby for the protection of oceans, raise awareness, and influence policies.

Marine Education & Communication

- ✓ **Marine Educators** teach the public, especially younger generations, about marine ecosystems and conservation.
- ✓ **Marine Science Communicators** disseminate research findings and raise awareness about marine issues.

Eco-Tourism & Recreation

- ✓ **Marine Eco-Tourism Operators** offer sustainable tourism experiences that promote marine conservation.
- ✓ **Marine Naturalists** guide and educate tourists about marine wildlife and ecosystems.

Technology & Innovation

- ✓ **Marine Technologists** develop technologies for monitoring and conserving marine environments.
- ✓ **Innovators in Bioplastics/Biodegradables** work on sustainable alternatives to conventional plastics that often pollute oceans.

Economics & Business

- ✓ **Sustainable Seafood Certifiers** validate that seafood products are sustainably sourced.
- ✓ **Marine Resource Economists** analyse the economic value and implications of marine resources.

Legal & Regulatory Roles

- ✓ **Marine Law Attorneys** specialise in laws and regulations pertaining to the ocean, fisheries, and marine resources.
- ✓ **Maritime Border Negotiators** focus on border and territory negotiations related to oceanic zones.

These are just some of the many career options that can contribute towards developing sustainable life below water, SDG 14. Remember that as wicked problems, the goals are interlinked, and this list is by no means exhaustive, nor is it intended to be. It is designed to get you thinking about which areas interest you.

You may also find it helpful to look at roles included in a related SDG that interests you. The following websites will help you explore these and other roles in more detail:

- UK: https://www.prospects.ac.uk/job-profiles
- US: https://www.onetonline.org/ (use the occupational keyword search tool)
- Europe: https://eures.ec.europa.eu/index_en
- More about SDG 14: https://sdgs.un.org/goals/goal14
- Use https://www.careeralchemy.co.uk/understanding-job-market.html to help you compare jobs and understand key labour market information.

CONSOLIDATING YOUR LEARNING FROM SDG 14 – LIFE BELOW WATER

What is your most significant light bulb moment of SDG 14?

* * * *

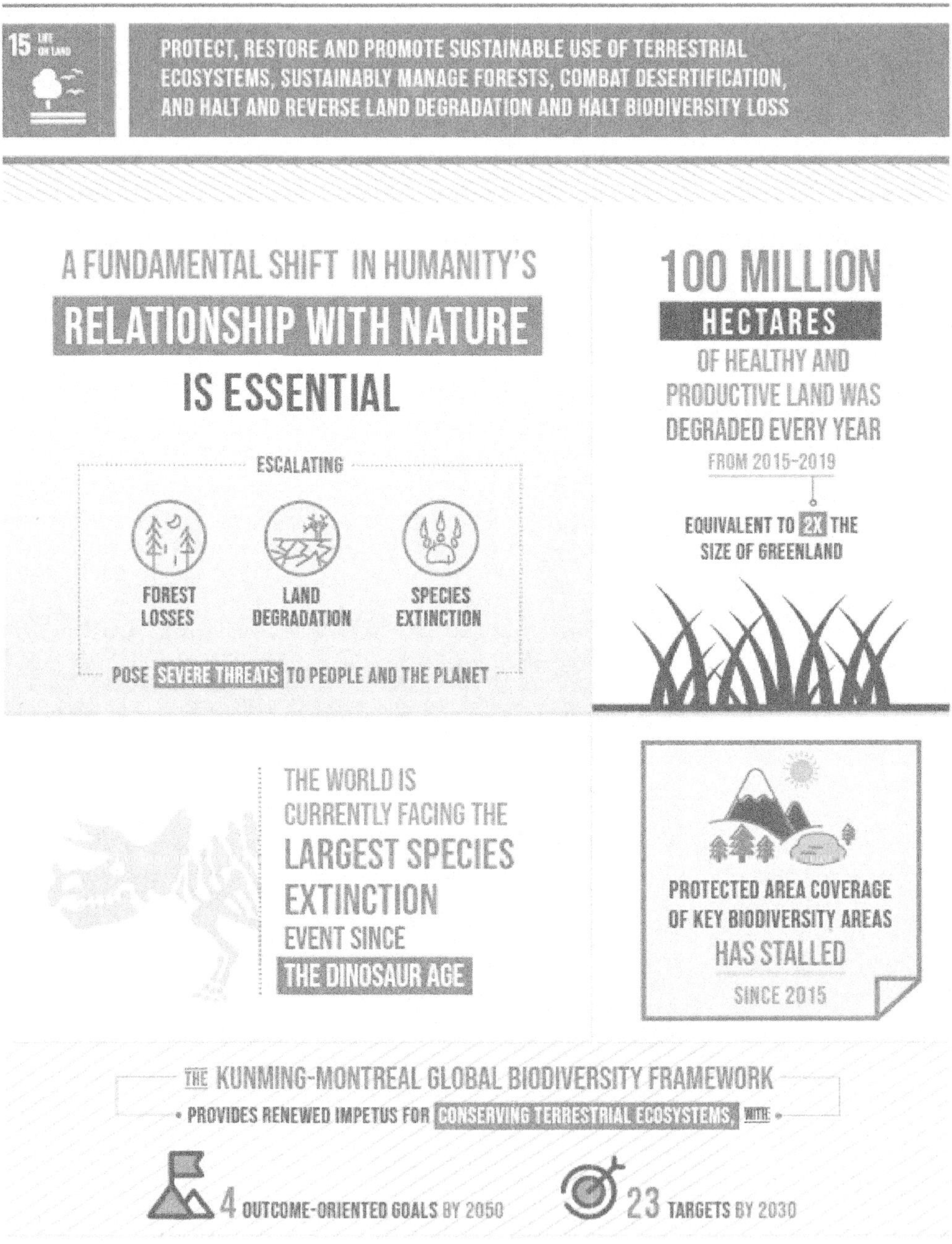

THE SUSTAINABLE DEVELOPMENT GOALS REPORT 2023: SPECIAL EDITION- UNSTATS.UN.ORG/SDGS/REPORT/2023/

SDG 15: LIFE ON LAND

"Protect, restore and promote sustainable use of terrestrial ecosystems, sustainably manage forests, combat desertification, and halt and reverse land degradation, and halt biodiversity loss."

SDG Goal 15 revolves around "Life on Land." Specifically, it's about protecting, restoring, and promoting the sustainable use of terrestrial ecosystems, managing forests sustainably, combating desertification, halting and reversing land degradation, and halting biodiversity loss.

Key factors that damage terrestrial ecosystems affect sustainable forest management and cause desertification, land degradation and biodiversity loss.

- **Deforestation:** converting forested areas to agriculture, urban development, or mining often leads to habitat loss and fragmentation.
- **Agricultural Expansion:** as the global population increases, the need for more food leads to the expansion of agricultural lands at the cost of natural habitats.
- **Overgrazing:** overstocking of domestic animals, especially in fragile ecosystems, can lead to soil erosion and degradation.
- **Unsustainable Land Use Practices:** slash-and-burn agriculture, non-sustainable logging, and other harmful practices degrade the land and its fertility.

- **Pollution:** Land contamination by pesticides, herbicides, chemical fertilisers, and other pollutants can harm terrestrial ecosystems.
- **Climate Change:** alters precipitation patterns, increases the frequency and intensity of droughts, wildfires, and storms, and shifts the natural habitats of many species.
- **Urbanization:** expanding cities consume vast tracts of land and create pollution, often at the expense of natural habitats.
- **Mining and Extraction Activities:** these can lead to deforestation, habitat fragmentation, soil erosion, and pollution.
- **Invasive Species:** non-native species can outcompete, prey on, or bring diseases to native species, altering ecosystem dynamics.
- **Over-exploitation:** overhunting, logging, and harvesting can reduce species populations to critical levels and disrupt ecosystems.
- **Infrastructure Development:** roads, dams, and other infrastructure can fragment habitats and create barriers to wildlife migration.
- **Land Tenure and Property Rights:** in many places, unclear land ownership or rights can lead to unsustainable exploitation of resources.
- **Lack of Awareness and Education:** people might not be aware of the consequences of their actions on the environment, leading to unintentional harm.
- **Economic Drivers:** policies prioritising short-term economic gains over long-term ecological sustainability can exacerbate environmental degradation.
- **Weak Regulatory Frameworks:** inefficient or poorly enforced environmental regulations can lead to unchecked damage to terrestrial ecosystems.

- **Trade and Globalization:** increased demand for certain commodities can lead to over-exploitation of resources in specific regions.
- **War and Conflict:** these can lead to resource exploitation, habitat destruction, and population displacements, all of which can affect ecosystems.
- **Loss of Traditional Knowledge:** indigenous and local knowledge about sustainable land management can be lost with modernisation.
- **Soil Erosion and Degradation:** unsustainable farming practices, deforestation, and overgrazing can degrade the soil quality and lead to desertification.
- **Water Management Practices:** unsustainable water use, diversion of water for agriculture or urban use, and damming can alter terrestrial ecosystems.

KEY JOB ROLES RELATED TO GOAL 15:

Conservation & Restoration

✓ **Conservation Biologists** study species and ecosystems to develop strategies for their protection.

✓ **Restoration Ecologists** work on restoring degraded ecosystems.

✓ **Wildlife Managers** oversee protected areas and develop strategies for species protection.

Forestry

✓ **Foresters** manage and conserve forests sustainably.

✓ **Agroforestry Specialists** integrate trees into agricultural landscapes for sustainable land use.

✓ **Silviculturists** specialise in the care and cultivation of forest trees.

Biodiversity & Wildlife Research

- ✓ **Wildlife Biologists** study animal species, their behaviours, and habitats.
- ✓ **Botanists** focus on plant species, their growth, and reproduction.
- ✓ **Ethnobotanists** study the relationship between plants and indigenous cultures.

Land Management & Planning

- ✓ **Land Use Planners** develop strategies for sustainable land use, ensuring a balance between development and conservation.
- ✓ **Range Managers** oversee natural grasslands and rangelands, often used for livestock.

Desertification & Land Degradation

- ✓ **Soil Conservationists** work on preventing soil erosion and maintaining soil health.
- ✓ **Desertification Specialists** develop strategies to prevent and reverse desertification.

Policy, Advocacy & Law

- ✓ **Environmental Policy Analysts** develop and assess policies related to terrestrial ecosystems.
- ✓ **Conservation Advocates** work with NGOs to promote policies and actions that support Goal 15.
- ✓ **Environmental Lawyers** represent and advise on legal issues related to the environment and land rights.

Education & Outreach

- ✓ **Environmental Educators** teach about terrestrial ecosystems, conservation, and sustainable land use.
- ✓ **Community Outreach Coordinators** engage communities in conservation efforts and sustainable practices.

Sustainable Agriculture

- ✓ **Agronomists** improve soil health and develop sustainable farming practices.
- ✓ **Permaculture Designers** design agricultural systems that mimic natural ecosystems.

Indigenous & Local Community Coordination

- ✓ **Indigenous Rights Advocates** support the rights of indigenous groups, who often play a key role in land stewardship.
- ✓ **Community Land Managers** work with local communities for sustainable land management.

Research & Academia

- ✓ **Ecological Researchers** investigate the dynamics and health of terrestrial ecosystems.
- ✓ **Environmental Economists** assess the economic value of biodiversity and ecosystem services.

Technology & Innovation

- ✓ **Geographic Information System (GIS) Specialists** use technology to map and analyse land use patterns and biodiversity.
- ✓ **Bioinformatics Specialists** use software and models to study biodiversity and predict ecological changes.

Private Sector & Business

- ✓ **Sustainable Supply Chain Managers** ensure that company supply chains do not harm ecosystems.
- ✓ **Corporate Sustainability Officers** integrate biodiversity and land conservation goals into business operations.

These are just some of the many career options that can contribute towards developing sustainable life on land, SDG 15. Remember that as wicked problems, the goals are interlinked, and this list is by no means exhaustive, nor is it intended to be. It is designed to get you thinking about which areas interest you.

You may also find it helpful to look at roles included in a related SDG that interests you. The following websites will help you explore these and other roles in more detail:

- UK: https://www.prospects.ac.uk/job-profiles
- US: https://www.onetonline.org/ (use the occupational keyword search tool)
- Europe: https://eures.ec.europa.eu/index_en
- More about SDG 15: https://sdgs.un.org/goals/goal15
- Use https://www.careeralchemy.co.uk/understanding-job-market.html to help you compare jobs and understand key labour market information.

CONSOLIDATING YOUR LEARNING FROM SDG 15 - LIFE ON LAND

What is your most significant light bulb moment of SDG 15?

* * * *

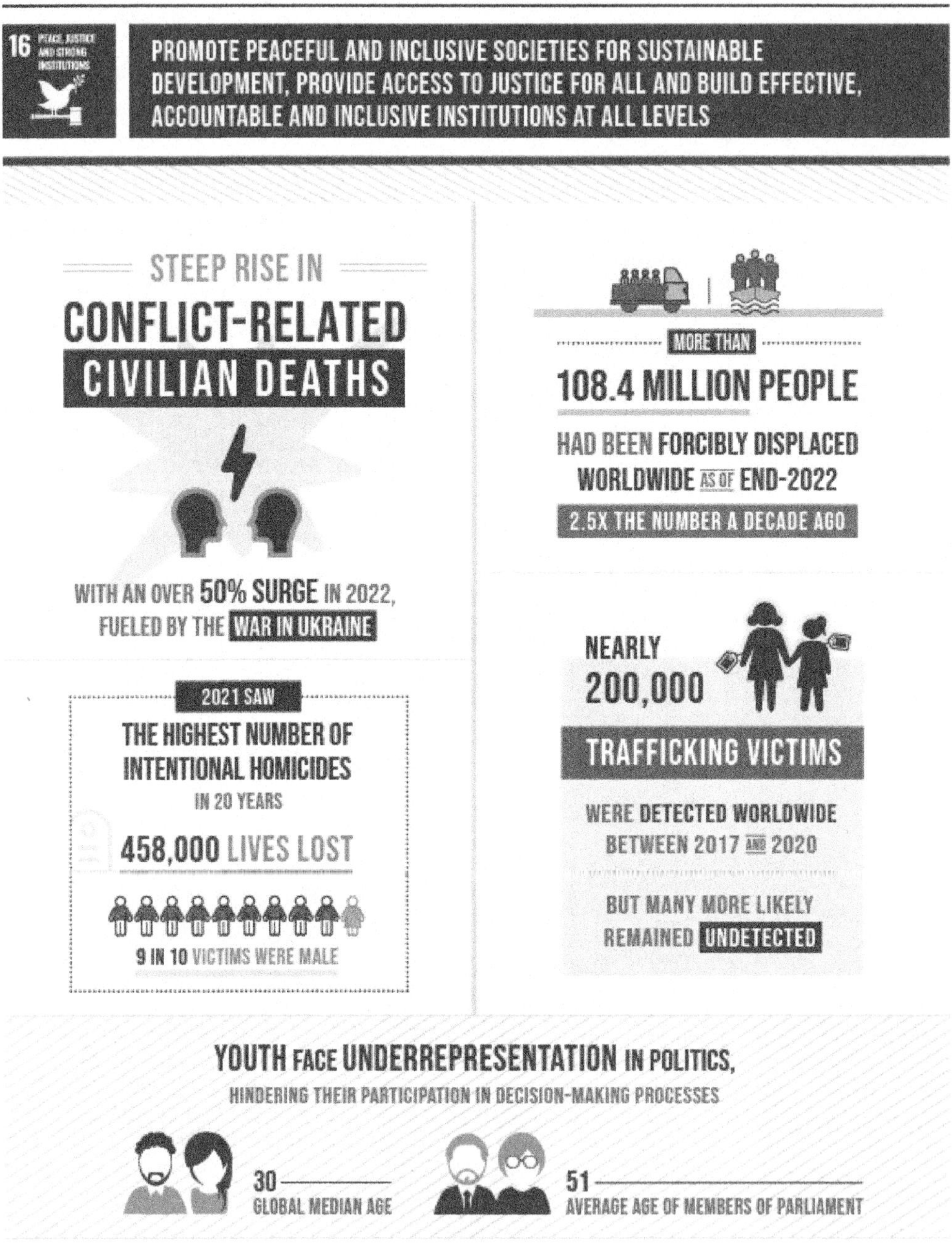

THE SUSTAINABLE DEVELOPMENT GOALS REPORT 2023: SPECIAL EDITION- UNSTATS.UN.ORG/SDGS/REPORT/2023/

16 PEACE, JUSTICE AND STRONG INSTITUTIONS

SDG 16: PEACE, JUSTICE AND STRONG INSTITUTIONS

"Promote peaceful and inclusive societies for sustainable development, provide access to justice for all and build effective, accountable and inclusive institutions at all levels."

SDG Goal 16 focuses on promoting peaceful and inclusive societies for sustainable development, providing access to justice for all, and building effective, accountable, inclusive institutions at all levels.

Key factors that inhibit the development of peaceful and inclusive societies prevent everyone from having access to justice, and enable institutions to be unaccountable and prejudiced, include:

- **Corruption:** the misuse of power for personal gain erodes trust in institutions and can perpetuate inequality and injustice.
- **Weak Rule of Law:** inefficient, outdated, or selectively enforced laws can perpetuate social injustices and allow crimes to go unpunished.
- **Lack of Judicial Independence:** courts that are influenced by political agendas, corrupt practices, or external pressures can't deliver impartial justice.
- **Economic Inequalities:** significant disparities in wealth and opportunity can lead to social unrest and perpetuate systemic biases.

- **Discrimination and Bigotry:** prejudices based on race, gender, religion, sexual orientation, or other factors can be institutionalised, leading to systemic injustices.
- **Inadequate Education:** without access to quality education, individuals may not fully understand their rights or the mechanisms to seek justice.
- **Political Instability:** frequent changes in leadership, coups, or other disruptions can hinder the development of stable and just institutions.
- **Authoritarian Regimes:** these can suppress dissent, limit freedoms, and rule without accountability.
- **Armed Conflicts and Violence:** wars, insurgencies, and frequent violent confrontations disrupt social order and can lead to human rights violations.
- **Limited Civic Participation:** when citizens aren't engaged or empowered to participate in decision-making, institutions may not reflect the will or needs of the people.
- **Weak Institutional Capacity:** underfunded, understaffed, or poorly organised institutions may struggle to fulfil their mandates effectively.
- **Impunity:** when wrongdoers, especially those in power, aren't held accountable, it erodes faith in the justice system and can lead to further violations.
- **Media Restrictions:** without a free press to expose wrongdoings and hold powers accountable, injustices might remain hidden.
- **Lack of Transparency:** governments or institutions that operate without transparency are more prone to corruption and less accountable to their citizens.
- **Social and Cultural Norms:** some societies may have norms or practices that inadvertently perpetuate biases or injustices.

- **Terrorism and Extremism:** these disrupt peace and often lead to heavy-handed state responses, which can further erode civil liberties and justice.
- **Migration and Displacement:** large movements of people can strain institutions and sometimes lead to xenophobia or discrimination against migrants.
- **Inadequate Access to Legal Services:** without affordable and accessible legal services, many can't seek redress for wrongs done to them.
- **Eroding Trust in Institutions:** when people don't trust their institutions, it becomes challenging to build peaceful societies, as citizens may resort to alternative, sometimes violent, means to address grievances.
- **External Interference:** sometimes, foreign powers or entities can influence domestic affairs, leading to internal strife or skewed justice.

KEY JOB ROLES RELATED TO GOAL 16:

Peace and Conflict Resolution

✓ **Peacebuilding Practitioners** work with communities to build and sustain peace.

✓ **Conflict Analysts** study conflicts to understand their roots and predict future conflicts.

✓ **Mediators and Negotiators** facilitate discussions to resolve conflicts at various levels.

Access to Justice

✓ **Human Rights Lawyers** advocate for the rights of individuals and communities.

- ✓ **Legal Aid Providers** offer legal assistance to those who cannot afford it.
- ✓ **Paralegals** work in various capacities to support legal proceedings and justice access.

Institutional Development

- ✓ **Institutional Reform Specialists** work with governments and organisations to enhance effectiveness and accountability.
- ✓ **Public Administration Experts** improve government processes, systems, and structures.
- ✓ **Election Monitors** ensure free and fair elections in various regions.

Civil Society & Advocacy

- ✓ **Civil Society Organizers** build and support non-governmental organisations (NGOs) and community groups.
- ✓ **Advocacy Specialists** campaign for policy changes, rights, or other societal issues.
- ✓ **Social Justice Advocates** work towards a more equitable and inclusive society.

Anti-Corruption & Transparency

- ✓ **Anti-Corruption Investigators** probe instances of corrupt practices in public and private sectors.
- ✓ **Transparency Advocates** push for more open and transparent governance and business practices.
- ✓ **Forensic Accountants** investigate financial discrepancies and fraud.

Child and Youth Protection & Empowerment

- ✓ **Child Protection Officers** safeguard children from harm and exploitation.
- ✓ **Youth Workers** engage and support young people, often focusing on empowerment and participation.

Law & Enforcement

- ✓ **Criminal Justice Professionals** work in various roles in the justice system, including judges, prosecutors, and defenders.
- ✓ **Law Enforcement Officials** ensure law and order while upholding human rights standards.
- ✓ **Prison Reform Advocates** work towards more humane and rehabilitative prison systems.

Research & Policy Analysis

- ✓ **Political Scientists** study the structure and operations of political entities.
- ✓ **Public Policy Analysts** examine policies to recommend improvements and ensure alignment with justice and peace goals.

Media & Journalism

- ✓ **Investigative Journalists** uncover and report on issues of public interest, including corruption, human rights violations, etc.
- ✓ **Media Advocacy Specialists** use media platforms to promote peace, justice, and strong institutions.

Education & Outreach

- ✓ **Peace Educators** teach peace and conflict studies, focusing on building understanding and resolving conflicts.
- ✓ **Civic Education Specialists** enhance public understanding of civic duties, rights, and responsibilities.

International Organisations & Diplomacy

- ✓ **Diplomats** represent their countries and work on relationships between nations.
- ✓ **International Development Workers** focus on projects that build strong institutions in developing countries.

Data & Technology

- ✓ **Data Analysts for Governance** analyse governance, crime, and justice data.
- ✓ **Civic Technologists** build technologies to enhance civic participation and government accountability.

These are just some of the many career options that can contribute towards developing peace, justice, and strong institutions, SDG 16. Remember that as wicked problems, the goals are interlinked, and this list is by no means exhaustive, nor is it intended to be. It is designed to get you thinking about which areas interest you.

You may also find it helpful to look at roles included in a related SDG that interests you. The following websites will help you explore these and other roles in more detail:

- UK: https://www.prospects.ac.uk/job-profiles
- US: https://www.onetonline.org/ (use the occupational keyword search tool)
- Europe: https://eures.ec.europa.eu/index_en
- More about SDG 16: https://sdgs.un.org/goals/goal16
- Use https://www.careeralchemy.co.uk/understanding-job-market.html to help you compare jobs and understand key labour market information.

CONSOLIDATING YOUR LEARNING FROM SDG 16 – PEACE, JUSTICE, AND STRONG INSTITUTIONS

What is your most significant light bulb moment of SDG 16?

****

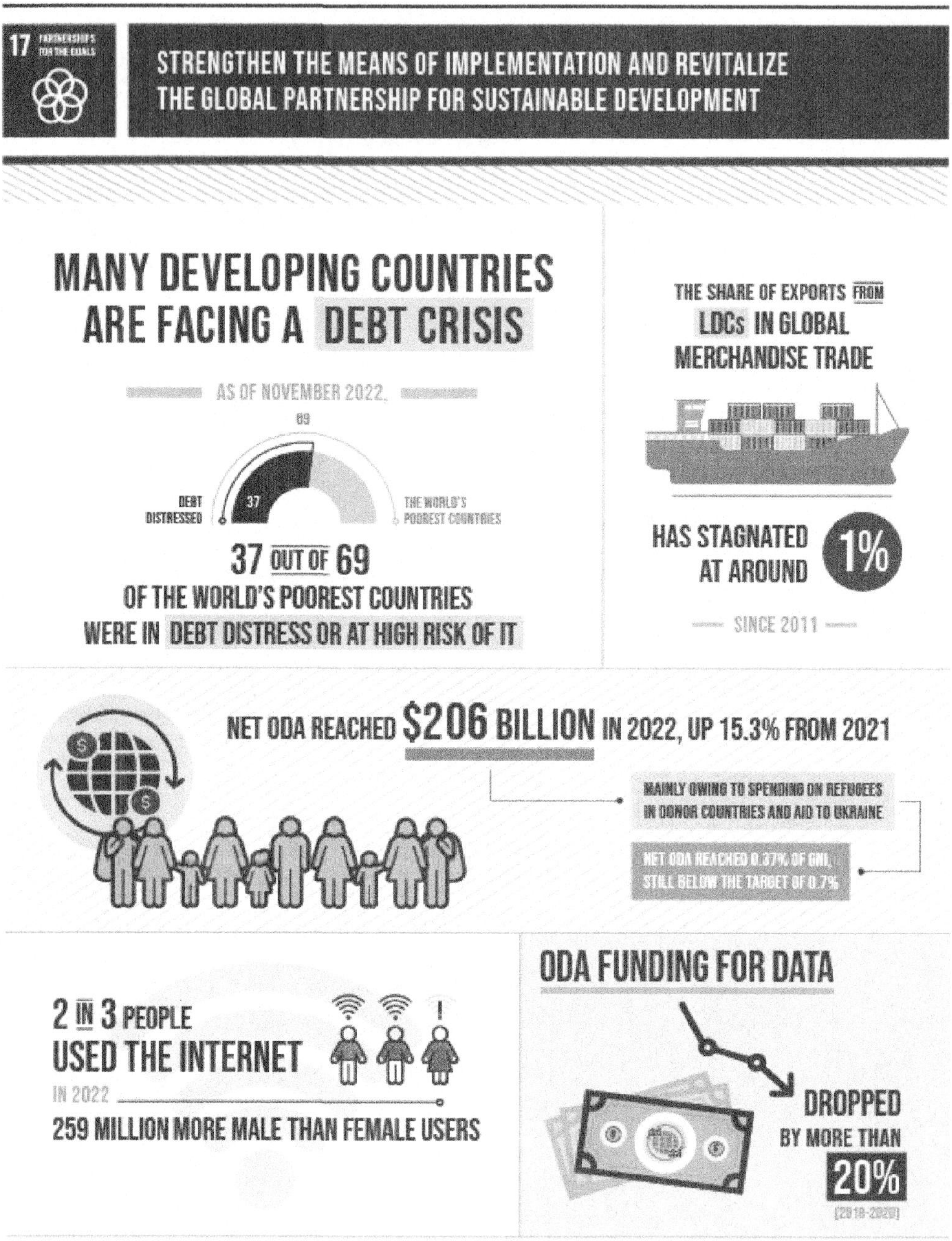

THE SUSTAINABLE DEVELOPMENT GOALS REPORT 2023: SPECIAL EDITION- UNSTATS.UN.ORG/SDGS/REPORT/2023/

17 PARTNERSHIPS FOR THE GOALS

SDG 17: PARTNERSHIPS FOR THE GOALS

"Strengthen the means of implementation and revitalise the Global Partnership for Sustainable Development."

SDG Goal 17 focuses on strengthening the means of implementation and revitalising the global partnership for sustainable development. This goal emphasises the importance of international collaboration, resource mobilisation, technology transfer, trade, policy coherence, and multi-stakeholder partnerships.

Key factors that inhibit the development of international collaboration, allocation of resources, technology transfer, trade, policy coherence and complex partnerships include:

- **Sovereignty Concerns:** nations might resist international collaboration if they perceive it as an infringement on their sovereignty or as outside interference.
- **Economic Disparities:** differences in economic development can lead to partnership imbalances, where richer countries might have more say or leverage.
- **Distrust and Historical Grievances:** past conflicts or disagreements can hamper present-day collaborations.
- **Protectionism:** countries might implement trade barriers to protect their domestic industries, hampering international trade.
- **Differing National Interests:** what's beneficial for one country might not be for another, leading to conflicts of interest.

- **Lack of Policy Coherence:** disjointed or conflicting policies within and between countries can make collaboration difficult.
- **Intellectual Property Concerns:** patents, copyrights, and proprietary technology issues can hinder technology transfer.
- **Political Instability:** nations undergoing political turmoil might not be reliable partners, discouraging collaboration.
- **Cultural and Normative Differences:** cultural norms, values, and practices variations can lead to misunderstandings or conflicts.
- **Inadequate Infrastructure:** in some cases, countries might lack the infrastructure to engage in technology transfer or resource allocation effectively.
- **Inconsistent Regulatory Frameworks:** differences in regulations, standards, and practices can hinder trade and technology transfer.
- **Short-term Focus:** political leaders might prioritise immediate domestic concerns over long-term international collaboration.
- **Geopolitical Rivalries:** strategic competitions between major powers can hamper international cooperation in areas of mutual concern.
- **Lack of Transparency and Accountability:** Trust can be eroded if countries or institutions don't operate transparently.
- **Financial Constraints:** economic downturns or budgetary constraints can limit a country's ability to contribute to international efforts.
- **Limited Capacity:** some nations might not have the institutional capacity or expertise to engage effectively in international collaborations.
- **Differing Priorities:** countries might prioritise different issues, making it hard to find common ground.
- **Populism and Nationalism:** a rise in populist or nationalist sentiments can lead to reduced international engagement.

- **Bureaucratic Hurdles:** red tape and bureaucratic inefficiencies can slow down or hinder collaboration efforts.
- **Lack of Political Will:** sometimes, the challenges lie not in external factors but in a sheer lack of will to collaborate or commit resources.

KEY JOB ROLES RELATED TO GOAL 17

International Development & Cooperation

✓ **International Development Specialists** work on projects that foster sustainable development globally.

✓ **Diplomats** facilitate relations between countries, promoting cooperation on development issues.

✓ **Development Finance Experts** focus on funding mechanisms to support development projects.

Trade & Economics

✓ **Trade Analysts** study global trade patterns and develop policies to promote fair trade.

✓ **Development Economists** research and design strategies to improve economic conditions in developing nations.

Technology & Innovation

✓ **Technology Transfer Specialists** facilitate the transfer of technologies between countries, especially to developing nations.

✓ **Innovation Policy Experts** design policies to foster innovation and technological development.

Data & Monitoring

✓ **Data Scientists** analyse data to monitor and assess progress on sustainable development goals.

- ✓ **Statisticians** collect and interpret data related to global challenges and solutions.
- ✓ **Monitoring & Evaluation Specialists** track the implementation and outcomes of development projects.

Partnership Building & Management

- ✓ **Partnership Managers** cultivate and manage relationships between different stakeholders, such as governments, NGOs, and private sector entities.
- ✓ **Multilateral Organisation Professionals** work for organisations like the UN, World Bank, or regional development banks to foster international collaboration.

Resource Mobilization & Fundraising

- ✓ **Grant Writers** identify and apply for funding opportunities for development projects.
- ✓ **Fundraising Specialists** mobilise resources for NGOs, agencies, or initiatives focused on sustainable development.

Policy & Advocacy

- ✓ **Policy Analysts** study and develop policies to foster global collaboration on sustainable development.
- ✓ **Global Advocacy Specialists** advocate for global cooperation, equitable policies, and sustainable development strategies.

Communications & Outreach

- ✓ **International Communication Specialists** facilitate communication between stakeholders from different countries or regions.
- ✓ **Public Relations Professionals** manage the image and messaging of organisations working on global partnership initiatives.

Education & Training

- ✓ **Capacity Building Trainers** educate professionals and communities to enhance their skills and knowledge for sustainable development.

- ✓ **Global Education Specialists** design curricula and programs that promote understanding of global challenges and cooperation.

Private Sector Collaboration

- ✓ **Corporate Sustainability Managers** drive sustainability initiatives and partnerships within corporations.
- ✓ **Supply Chain Sustainability Experts** ensure that business supply chains are sustainable and ethically managed.

Research & Academia

- ✓ **Sustainable Development Researchers** study various facets of sustainable development and global partnerships.
- ✓ **Academics in International Relations** teach and research the dynamics of international cooperation and global governance.

These are just some of the many career options that can contribute towards developing peace, justice, and strong institutions, SDG 17. Remember that as wicked problems, the goals are interlinked, and this list is by no means exhaustive, nor is it intended to be. It is designed to get you thinking about which areas interest you.

You may also find it helpful to look at roles included in a related SDG that interests you. The following websites will help you explore these and other roles in more detail:

- UK: https://www.prospects.ac.uk/job-profiles
- US: https://www.onetonline.org/ (use the occupational keyword search tool)
- Europe: https://eures.ec.europa.eu/index_en
- More about SDG 17: https://sdgs.un.org/goals/goal17
- Use https://www.careeralchemy.co.uk/understanding-job-market.html to help you compare jobs and understand key labour market information.

CONSOLIDATING YOUR LEARNING FROM SDG 17 – PARTNERSHIPS FOR THE GOALS

What is your most significant light bulb moment of SDG 17?

* * * *

MY INSPIRED CAREER AND LIFE PLANNER

THE WORLD'S WICKED PROBLEMS

Who am I already?

Who do I want to be or become?

What are my strengths, talents and skills? Where are they best served and most wanted?

Who do I want to spend my work time with?

What do I want to be known for?

What life do I want to live?

What fascinates me?

Where do I want to spend my work time?

What direction am I headed in? What's my goal?

ACKNOWLEDGEMENTS

This book is the result of my own journey to finding a career that makes my soul sing, fills my heart with joy, and keeps my brain engaged in something meaningful and intellectually satisfying so I can squeeze my own variety of juice out of life and live with zest and a deep sense of purpose.

I used to read the acknowledgments in other people's books and wonder why there were so many people involved, given there was just one author's name on the cover. Having gone through the process, I now understand why! So, it's my turn to say thank you from the bottom of my heart to everyone.

To my previous employers, whether before my own career crisis or after. The nudges you have given, whether good, bad, or downright ugly at times, have got me to this point, so thank you.

To those who have been on this writing journey with me, thank you. Those thanks start with Sunday Times No.1 best-selling author, international speaker, coach, and customer service expert, Michael Heppell, who helped me to find the motivation and persistence to ride what he calls the author coaster. If you are thinking of doing the same, you need to read his book, Write That Book, which will help you do the same - it's brilliant to coin a phrase!

To my fellow lady Alchemists (in first name alphabetical order, Adrienne Green, Desiree de Beer, Gail Molyneaux, Jane Brady, Kay Dobson-Bennet, and Sonja Batt), you have cheered every milestone and rallied around when I was at the bottom of the author coaster and its big dipper effects. Your support meant the world, and I will keep doing the same for you all, so you can get over the publishing line, too. Ladies, the best is yet to come, and I am privileged to have you as friends for life and to be sharing in your author journeys, too. Thanks to some of my closest friends and supporters who keep me energised and moving forwards, Cat Griffiths, Cathy Piquemal, Chris Morris Thornton, Helene McMurtrie (also my acupuncturist), Andrew Calvert (also my osteopath), Sonia Urbaniak, Clive King, Catherine Moyle, and Marie Claire for your support and encouragement as ever.

A motivated writer is all well and good, but a book needs words, and I hope you can hear the individual personalities of the 8 people who trusted me to tell their stories, including their own personal fears, challenges, and victories, and share their hopes. Vicki, Natalie, Meeta, Julia, Cathy, Chris, Mel and Steve, I am truly grateful for your trust in my ability to interpret each of your stories through life and work. I know your stories will inspire others to move forward - the various beta readers have confirmed that.

My sincere thanks to my fellow careers and employability professionals, Claire Johnson, Ciara Bomford, Professor Pete Robertson, Chris Webb, Gary Argent, Debbie Dymock, Lis McGuire, Liz Reece, Debbie Laaff, Bella Doswell, Anne Wilson, and Mark Saunders for saying yes when I asked you to review and sense-check the various chapters and appendices. Thank you, too, to my clients and other friends who have done the same. I really appreciate all your support and contribution. As you have seen, this book is rich in references throughout, with the aim of both anchoring the text from a theory and practice perspective and sharing resources for individuals to follow up on should they wish. As anyone who has written a book will tell you, copyright law is complex to ensure the work of others is quite rightly protected in the eyes of the law. I turned to Kath Foot for help with this. She and I have worked successfully together in the past on another careers-related project, and I knew she was the one I could trust to get in the metaphorical trenches and keep digging until we knew each and every reference, and its related content could be included. Kath, you are one in a million. Thank you for saying yes without hesitation.

For something to read well, it needs the skill of a helpful and savvy editor. So, I am extremely grateful to Natalie Plange, who has not only done a huge amount of editing and proofing for me but has also been so tolerant, patient, and helpful with ever-changing deadlines, as life either helped or hindered my ability to get words down on the page. She went through her own career change in the not-too-distant past, and her previous experience working in business marketing and communications meant that she instinctively understood my audience. Thank you for everything, Nat, and no, you can't edit this bit out!

The way words are laid out on a page makes a significant difference in how a reader engages with a book or otherwise. This is where Matthew Bird has come into his own, and I am grateful, Matt, for your diligence and attention to detail, though I suspect you may not want to see another light bulb for a while!

This book has been a special and significant kind of journey in my own development. So, to those who I have learned with on my way to becoming an accredited career and life coach, and continue to learn with, your wisdom and challenges have been worth their weight in gold. You have enabled me to trust in myself as a coach, develop my own theory and practice as reflected in this book. As a result, I have the most amazing life full of purposeful opportunities to spread the word about the value and importance of career guidance and coaching as a profession, and as the current President and Chair of the Board of the Career Development Institute, the UK body for the sector. Thanks must go to Jan Ellis for taking me on as a freelance associate of the CDI to look after members in Wales, a role I still very much value today.

The work we all do in this space is informed and sometimes heavily influenced by others whose work we read, and I am indebted to many authors of self-development and other related books. Those who have been particularly instrumental in forming my thinking include Po Bronson and his seminal book 'What Should I Do with My Life?', Parker J. Palmer and his book 'Let Your Life Speak', Matt Haig's 'The Midnight Library', and the work and writings of Joseph Campbell, Jean-Paul Sartre, Susan Jeffers, Shakti Gawain, Jack Canfield, Seth Godin, and Malcolm Gladwell.

The beginnings of my own book go back twenty-something years, and I have made several starts over the years, which have fallen by the wayside. Looking back, it was right they did, and the timing was wrong. As Michael Heppell references in the foreword, when the student is ready, the teacher appears. During lockdown, like many of us, I decided I needed to do a bit more learning and signed up to do a creative writing course with the Lifelong Learning Department of Aberystwyth University. As someone who loves learning and challenge (even if it is uncomfortable at times), shortly after, I signed up for another course, this time learning about how to podcast. My motivation in doing so was to share stories that would help others in their own career challenges and journey.

That course with those tutors gave me the skills and confidence to move forward and launch the ***Change Your Story*** podcast. Little did I know when I started that its real purpose was to collect many of the stories that would form the heart of this book. So, thank you, Kerry Ferguson and Ali Pierce, for your motivation and support and for helping me get to grips with the skills I needed.

I wrote this book to help you develop a sense of control and purpose so you can navigate your way and manage your working life effectively despite an increasingly uncertain and volatile world. To do this, I have included the work of many of the most astute, learned, and experienced academics and some of the most impactful organisations around the world. Thank you to each one of you who gave me permission to use your wisdom in this book and particularly Harvard Professor, Howard Gardner and Stanford Professor, Jennifer Aaker, who both sent messages of encouragement early on. I hope I have done all your work justice.

There is no point in writing a book for it to stay languishing in the dark recesses of a virtual or real bookshop. I am incredibly grateful to Jess at Jess Nian Photography, who somehow managed to capture what feels like my essence in the picture on the back cover. Jess, you have a real talent for understanding people and translating them into an image that conveys who they truly are - AI just can't do that authentically! Thanks must also go to Seb Waligorski for his first-class IT expertise and support over the last eight years whenever needed. I hope seeing your name here Seb will encourage you to finish your own book soon! I would also like to say thanks to my PR agent, Daisy Souster, the authentic and kind-hearted PR whizz originally behind the Captain Tom story, for doing what she does best - telling human stories in a way that captures the imagination and interest of others.

There are several others who I also need to mention: to the inimitable and stellar international educator of careers professionals, creative career coach, and author, Liane Hambly, thank you for all your help, support, and belief over the years; and thanks also to the remarkable Shelley Upton, whose own career illustrates perfectly how we can transform according to our interests and needs to do things that are of value to others. I am blessed to count you both as my friends and cheerleaders. Thank you both for saying yes when I asked you if you would host my virtual and face-to-face book launches.

As a proud Welsh woman, it was inevitable that there is a Welsh theme to some of the stories in the book, which we will also be celebrating at the launch. We are a small but mighty nation that is often wrongly overlooked and sidelined in the grand scheme of things. So, I am delighted that we will be celebrating the face-to-face launch of ***Change Your Story*** at Aberystwyth University with the help of someone who always has my back, the queen of conferencing, Lisa Massini. Aberystwyth University was where, in 2001, I first met someone who was to become my best boss and career mother, Dr Monica Jalloq, who saw something in this eager-eyed almost forty-year-old career changer who had a passion for helping people and wanted to make a difference. Aber Uni, as it is known to its friends, is the obvious place to celebrate, and I am grateful to the university and Arthur Dafis, their Communications and Public Affairs Office, and his colleagues for their support in spreading the story behind ***Change Your Story***. If reading this book has helped you, please share it with others and keep a look out for more helpful content by searching for #changeyourstory on LinkedIn, and other social media platforms.

Inevitably, my final thanks must go to my clients for choosing to trust and fully engage in my holistic career and life coaching approach. You should be so proud of the stories you have created for yourselves and your achievements. Thank you for teaching me so much and contributing along the way to what has become this book. Keep doing amazing things as you continue to write your own career stories.

Now that I have published my first book and my role on the Board comes to an end soon, it's finally time for some restorative, deadline-free downtime, no doubt much to the delight of my long-suffering family. As my soul mate and my biggest cheerleader of all, Rhys, my husband will be delighted, and so, I hope will be my children and grandchildren, to whom I have dedicated this book, as well as my two sons-in-law, Chris and Mike, and soon to be daughter in law, Phoebe. Thanks for bearing with me rambling on about it. It's finally time to take a break, crack open a bottle of something convivial to celebrate, and get out and about more. Our dachshunds will be delighted!!

Carolyn Parry
Ceredigion, Mid Wales
October 2023

REFERENCES

Please Note: For us to be able to make good choices, it is wise to ground our decisions in fact. The ideas, theories and data referenced in this book come from the work of many organisations and individuals. Their inclusion in these references does not imply their endorsement, but rather their willingness to be cited, where permission was needed, and provide a source of further reading for you to explore.

Introduction

www.thecdi.net. (n.d.). *New Career Development Framework*. [online] Available at: https://www.thecdi.net/New-Career-Development-Framework

Zak, P. (2013). *How Stories Change the Brain*. [online] Greater Good. Available at:
https://greatergood.berkeley.edu/article/item/how_stories_change_brain

Chapter 1

Guss, E. and Miller, M. (2008). *Ethics and Generational Differences: Interplay between Values and Ethical Business Decisions*. [online] Available at: http://spiritedwork.info/pdfs/GenDiffAndEthicalDecisionMaking.pdf [Accessed 9 Nov. 2023]

NERIS Analytics Limited (2023). *16 Personalities*. [online] 16personalities.com. Available at: https://www.16personalities.com/

Truity (2019). *Personality and Career Tests Online*. [online] Truity. Available at: https://www.truity.com/

Chapter 2

Angyal, A., Maslow, A., Murray, H.A., Bugental, J.F.T., Murphy, G. and Rogers, C. (1981). Humanistic Psychology. In: *Contemporary Theories and Systems in Psychology*. Springer, pp.507–515. doi:https://doi.org/10.1007/978-1-4684-3800-0_14

Harvard Second Generation Study (2010). *Harvard Second Generation Study*. [online] Harvard Study. Available at: https://www.adultdevelopmentstudy.org/

Life Values Inventory, Inc (2015). *Life Values Inventory - Values Clarification Program*. [online] Lifevaluesinventory.org. Available at: https://www.lifevaluesinventory.org/

Mogilner, C., Kamvar, S.D. and Aaker, J. (2010). The Shifting Meaning of Happiness. *Social Psychological and Personality Science*, [online] 2(4), pp.395–402. doi:https://doi.org/10.1177/1948550610393987

Waldinger, R. and Schulz, M. (2023). *The Good Life*. 1st ed. Rider

Chapter 3

Cambridge Dictionary (2019). *PERSONALITY | meaning in the Cambridge English Dictionary*. [online] Cambridge.org. Available at: https://dictionary.cambridge.org/dictionary/english/personality

dictionary.cambridge.org. (n.d.). *CHARACTER | Meaning in the Cambridge English Dictionary*. [online] Available at: https://dictionary.cambridge.org/dictionary/english/character

Dr Sally Caird (2013). *General Measure of Enterprising Tendency v2 - GET2*. [online] Get2test.net. Available at: http://www.get2test.net/

Eisenmann, T. (2013). *Entrepreneurship: A Working Definition*. [online] Harvard Business Review. Available at: https://store.hbr.org/product/what-psychological-safety-looks-like-in-a-hybrid-workplace/H06AWX

Francis-Devine, B. and Powell, A. (2023). *UK Labour Market Statistics UK Parliament.* [online] https://researchbriefings.files.parliament.uk . Available at: https://researchbriefings.files.parliament.uk/documents/CBP-9366/CBP-9366.pdf

Gardner, H. (1983). *Frames of mind: the Theory of Multiple Intelligences*. New York: Basic Books. https://www.multipleintelligencesoasis.org/resources

Gardner, H. (2020). *A Resurgence of Interest in Existential Intelligence: Why*

Now? [online] Howard Gardner. Available at: https://www.howardgardner.com/howards-blog/a-resurgence-of-interest-in-existential-intelligence-why-now

Irvine, S. (2022). *Women and the economy*. [online] Parliament.uk. Available at: https://researchbriefings.files.parliament.uk/documents/SN06838/SN06838.pdf

LinkedIn 2023 *Most In-Demand Skills: Learn the skills companies need most*. [online] Available at: https://www.linkedin.com/business/learning/blog/top-skills-and-courses/most-in-demand-skills

LinkedIn (2023). *Skills-First: Reimagining the Labour Market and Breaking Down Barriers European Highlights, May 2023*. https://economicgraph.linkedin.com/content/dam/me/economicgraph/en-emea/pdf/skills-first-report-european-highlights.pdf

ONS (2022). *Outcomes for disabled people in the UK - Office for National Statistics*. [online] www.ons.gov.uk. Available at: https://www.ons.gov.uk/peoplepopulationandcommunity/healthandsocialcare/disability/articles/outcomesfordisabledpeopleintheuk/2021

Peterson, C., and Seligman, M.E.P. (2004). *Character Strengths and Virtues: a Handbook and Classification*. Washington: American Psychological Association

PricewaterhouseCoopers (2023). *Skills First Report*. [online] PwC. Available at: https://www.pwc.com/gx/en/issues/upskilling/putting-skills-first-report.html [Accessed 10 Nov. 2023]

VIA Institute on Character (2020). *VIA Character Strengths Survey & Character Profile Reports*. [online] Viacharacter.org. Available at: https://www.viacharacter.org © Copyright 2004-2023, VIA Institute on Character. All Rights Reserved. Used with permission

Chapter 4

Coleman (2023). *4 Ways to Make Work More Meaningful.* [online] Harvard Business Review. Available at: https://store.hbr.org/product/4-ways-to-make-work-more-meaningful/h07te7?sku=H07TE7-PDF-ENG [Accessed 7 Nov. 2023]

Duckworth, A., Peterson, C., Matthews, M.D. and Kelly, D. (2007). *(PDF) Grit: Perseverance and Passion for Long-Term Goals.* [online] ResearchGate. Available at: https://www.researchgate.net/publication/6290064_Grit_Perseverance_and_Passion_for_Long-Term_Goals

Huskey, R. (2022). *Why does experiencing 'flow' feel so good? A communication scientist explains.* [online] The Conversation. Available at: https://theconversation.com/why-does-experiencing-flow-feel-so-good-a-communication-scientist-explains-173505

Inc, G. (2015). *Gallup Global Report: Where the Great Jobs Are.* [online] Gallup.com. Available at: https://www.gallup.com/services/186197/gallup-global-report-great-jobs-pdf.aspx#:~:text=This%20report%20uses%20employment%20and [Accessed 7 Nov. 2023]

International Labour Organization (2016). *What Is a Green Job?* [online] www.ilo.org. Available at: https://www.ilo.org/global/topics/green-jobs/news/WCMS_220248/lang--en/index.htm

Lievens, F., Harrison, S., Mussel, P. and Litman, J. (2021). Killing the Cat? A Review of Curiosity at Work. *Academy of Management Annals*, 16(1). doi:https://doi.org/10.5465/annals.2020.0203

Reeves, C., Islam, A. and Gentry, T. (2023). *The State of Health and Care of Older People, 2023.* [online] *ageuk.org.uk/state.* Age UK. Available at: https://www.ageuk.org.uk/globalassets/age-uk/documents/reports-and-publications/reports-and-briefings/health--wellbeing/age-uk-briefing-state-of-health-and-care-july-2023-abridged-version.pdf [Accessed 29 Oct. 2023]. Age UK is not part of, nor do they endorse this book

Vallerand, R.J. (2012). The Role of Passion in Sustainable Psychological Well-being. *Psychology of Well-Being: Theory, Research and Practice*, [online] 2(1), p.1. doi:https://doi.org/10.1186/2211-1522-2-1

Williams, K., Tomaney, J. and Reeves, R. (2019). *The Everyday Economy: why it matters and how to rebuild it*. [online] British Politics and Policy at LSE. Available at: https://blogs.lse.ac.uk/politicsandpolicy/the-everyday-economy/

Chapter 5

Asante, C. (2022). *Gen Z in the Workplace*. [online] www.kornferry.com. Available at: https://www.kornferry.com/insights/featured-topics/future-of-work/gen-z-in-the-workplace

Dan Buettner (2019). *Power 9 - Blue Zones*. [online] Blue Zones. Available at: https://www.bluezones.com/2016/11/power-9/ [Accessed 14 Oct. 2023]

Falk, S. (2023). *Understanding the Power of Intrinsic Motivation*. [online] Harvard Business Review. Available at: https://hbr.org/2023/03/understand-the-power-of-intrinsic-motivation

Forbes 30 under 30 Directory. (2021). *Forbes*. [online] Available at: https://www.forbes.com/30-under-30/directory/

Forbes. (n.d.). *Forbes 30 Under 30 2023*. [online] Available at: https://www.forbes.com/30-under-30/2023/

Greater Good. (2023). *Purpose Definition | What Is Purpose*. [online] Available at: https://greatergood.berkeley.edu/topic/purpose/definition

Jobs of Tomorrow: Large Language Models and Jobs WHITE PAPER SEPTEMBER 2023. (2021). World Economic Forum

Kharas, H.J., McArthur, J.W. and Ohno, I. (2020). *Leave No One behind: Time for Specifics on the Sustainable Development Goals*. Washington, D.C.: Brookings Institution Press

PwC (2022). *PwC's Global Workforce Hopes and Fears Survey 2022*. [online] PwC. Available at: https://www.pwc.com/gx/en/issues/workforce/hopes-

and-fears-2022.html [Accessed 14 Oct. 2023]

Rittel, H.W.J. and Webber, M.M. (1973). Dilemmas in a general theory of planning. *Policy Sciences*, [online] 4(2), pp.155–169. doi:https://doi.org/10.1007/bf01405730

Stewart, H. and al (2023). 'I Hope to Keep Going as Long as Possible': the Older People Returning to Work. *The Guardian*. [online] 16 Aug. Available at: https://www.theguardian.com/society/2023/aug/16/the-older-people-returning-to-work [Accessed 14 Oct. 2023]

UN DESA Publications. (2023). *World Social Report 2023: Leaving No One behind in an Ageing World*. [online] Available at: https://desapublications.un.org/publications/world-social-report-2023-leaving-no-one-behind-ageing-world

UNDP (2023). *Human Development Index*. [online] United Nations Development Programme. Available at: https://hdr.undp.org/data-center/human-development-index#/indicies/HDI

Wong, E. (2020). *What Is a Wicked Problem and How Can You Solve It?* [online] The Interaction Design Foundation. Available at: https://www.interaction-design.org/literature/article/wicked-problems-5-steps-to-help-you-tackle-wicked-problems-by-combining-systems-thinking-with-agile-methodology

https://www3.weforum.org/. (n.d.). *Insights and Tools*. [online] Available at: https://initiatives.weforum.org/reskilling-revolution/insights-tools [Accessed 10 Nov. 2023]

World Economic Forum in collaboration with PwC Putting Skills First: A Framework for Action MAY 2 0 23 . (n.d.). [online] World Economic Forum and PwC. Available at: https://www3.weforum.org/docs/WEF_CNES_Putting_Skills_First_2023.pdf

World Economic Forum. *https://www1.reskillingrevolution2030.org/skills-taxonomy/index.html*

Chapter 6

Allen, K. (2021). *The Psychology of Belonging*. London: Routledge, Taylor & Francis Group

Baumeister, R.F. and Leary, M.R. (1995). *APA PsycNet*. [online] psycnet.apa.org. Available at: https://psycnet.apa.org/record/1995-29052-001

Belbin | Engage and Develop the Talent Around You (2019). *Belbin*. [online] Belbin.com. Available at: https://www.belbin.com

Edmondson, A. and Mortensen, M. (2021). *What Psychological Safety Looks Like in a Hybrid Workplace*. [online] Harvard Business Review. Available at: https://store.hbr.org/product/what-psychological-safety-looks-like-in-a-hybrid-workplace/h06awx?sku=H06AWX-PDF-ENG

Edmondson, A.C. (2019). *The Fearless Organization: Creating Psychological Safety in the Workplace for learning, innovation, and Growth*. Hoboken, New Jersey: John Wiley & Sons, Inc.

GOV.UK. (2023). *Business Population Estimates for the UK and Regions 2023: Statistical Release*. [online] Available at: https://www.gov.uk/government/statistics/business-population-estimates-2023/business-population-estimates-for-the-uk-and-regions-2023-statistical-release#:~:text=At%20the%20start%20of%202023%3A [Accessed 15 Oct. 2023]

NCVO (2022). *UK Civil Society Almanac 2022*. [online] NCVO. Available at: https://www.ncvo.org.uk/news-and-insights/news-index/uk-civil-society-almanac-2022/#/

ONS (2023a). *EMP02: Public and Private Sector Employment - Office for National Statistics*. [online] www.ons.gov.uk. Available at: https://www.ons.gov.uk/employmentandlabourmarket/peopleinwork/employmentandemployeetypes/datasets/publicandprivatesectoremploymentemp02

ONS (2023b). *UK Standard Industrial Classification of Economic Activities -*

Office for National Statistics. [online] www.ons.gov.uk. Available at: https://www.ons.gov.uk/methodology/classificationsandstandards/ukstandardindustrialclassificationofeconomicactivities

Rybnicek, R., Bergner, S. and Gutschelhofer, A. (2019). How Individual Needs Influence Motivation effects: a Neuroscientific Study on McClelland's Need Theory. *Review of Managerial Science*, [online] 13(2), pp.443–482. doi:https://doi.org/10.1007/s11846-017-0252-1

Tabassum, N. and Fern, B. (2023). *Workforce*. [online] NCVO. Available at: https://www.ncvo.org.uk/news-and-insights/news-index/uk-civil-society-almanac-2023/workforce/ [Accessed 7 Nov. 2023]

Tracom (2019). *SOCIAL STYLE Model - TRACOM Group*. [online] TRACOM Group. Available at: https://tracom.com/social-style-training/model SOCIAL STYLE® is a registered trademark of The TRACOM Group and is used with permission. Learn more at www.tracom.com

Warwick Business School. (2020). *Putting theory into practice: David McClelland's Need Theory | News | Warwick Business School*. [online] Available at: https://www.wbs.ac.uk/news/putting-theory-into-practice-david-mcclellands-need-theory/

Watson, J.M. and Strayer, D.L. (2010). Supertaskers: Profiles in extraordinary multitasking ability. *Psychonomic Bulletin & Review*, [online] 17(4), pp.479–485. doi:https://doi.org/10.3758/PBR.17.4.479

Chapter 7

Auster, E. and Auster-Weiss, S. (2020). *Conquer Your To-Do List with This Simple Hack*. [online] Harvard Business Review. Available at: https://store.hbr.org/product/conquer-your-to-do-list-with-this-simple-hack/h05ree?sku=H05REE-PDF-ENG

Bawden, T. (2019). *Why women work better in warmer temperatures than men*. [online] inews.co.uk. Available at: https://inews.co.uk/news/science/why-women-work-better-in-warmer-temperatures-than-men-294149 [Accessed 7

Nov. 2023]

British Diversity Awards (n.d.). *THE WINNERS 2023*. [online] Bda2024. Available at: https://www.britishdiversityawards.com/the-winners-2023 [Accessed 31 Oct. 2023]

Business Balls (2021). *Pareto's 80-20 Rule Theory*. [online] Businessballs.com. Available at: https://www.businessballs.com/planning-workload-time-management-and-prioritisation/pareto-80-20-rule-theory/

CIPD (2022). *CIPD | Equality, Diversity, and Inclusion in the Workplace | Factsheets*. [online] CIPD. Available at: https://www.cipd.org/uk/knowledge/factsheets/diversity-factsheet/ with the permission of the publisher, the Chartered Institute of Personnel and Development in London (www.cipd.co.uk)

Citizens Advice (2023). *Duty to Make Reasonable Adjustments for Disabled People*. [online] www.citizensadvice.org.uk. Available at: https://www.citizensadvice.org.uk/law-and-courts/discrimination/check-what-type-of-discrimination-youve-experienced/duty-to-make-reasonable-adjustments-for-disabled-people/

Health and Safety Executive (2019). *Benefits and costs: Leading Health and Safety at Work*. [online] Hse.gov.uk. Available at: https://www.hse.gov.uk/leadership/benefits.htm

Indeed Career Guide (2022). *What Is the Covey Time Management Matrix? (And How to Use It) | Indeed.com*. [online] www.indeed.com. Available at: https://www.indeed.com/career-advice/career-development/covey-time-management-matrix

Chapter 8

Petruzzi, J. (2019). *Visualization and mental rehearsal*. [online] https://www.researchgate.net. Available at: https://www.researchgate.net/publication/332057157_Visualization_and_mental_rehearsal

Steffen, P.R., Hedges, D. and Matheson, R. (2022). The Brain Is Adaptive

Not Triune: How the Brain Responds to Threat, Challenge, and Change. *Frontiers in Psychiatry*, 13. doi:https://doi.org/10.3389/fpsyt.2022.802606

Chapter 9

Emmons, R. (2010). *Why gratitude is good.* [online] Greater Good. Available at: https://greatergood.berkeley.edu/article/item/why_gratitude_is_good Greater Good, the online magazine of the Greater Good Science Center at UC Berkeley

Greater Good (2023a). *Positive Emotions Open Our Mind. Greater Good.* Available at: https://greatergood.berkeley.edu/video/item/positive_emotions_open_our_mind Greater Good, the online magazine of the Greater Good Science Center at UC Berkeley

Greater Good. (2023b). *Gratitude Definition | What Is Gratitude.* [online] Available at: https://greatergood.berkeley.edu/topic/gratitude/definition Greater Good, the online magazine of the Greater Good Science Center at UC Berkeley

Linder, J.N. (2021). *Hacking the Brain's Negative Bias | Psychology Today United Kingdom.* [online] www.psychologytoday.com. Available at: https://www.psychologytoday.com/gb/blog/mindfulness-insights/202105/hacking-the-brains-negative-bias [Accessed 8 Nov. 2023]

McLeod, V. (2022). *Journalling for Well-Being.* [online] Vicki McLeod. Available at: https://vickimcleod.com/journalling-for-well-being/ [Accessed 9 Nov. 2023]

Mental Health UK. (2023). *Mental Health Awareness Week 2023.* [online] Available at: https://mentalhealth-uk.org/mental-health-awareness-week/

Neff, K.D. (2022). Self-Compassion: Theory, Method, Research, and Intervention. *Annual Review of Psychology*, 74(1), pp.193–218. doi:https://doi.org/10.1146/annurev-psych-032420-031047

Reflection App (2022). *Top Evidence-Based Benefits of Journaling for Mental Health | Reflection.app - Your guided journal for wellness and growth.* [online]

www.reflection.app. Available at: https://www.reflection.app/blog/benefits-of-journaling

Tully, S., Tao, H., Johnson, M., Lebron, M., Land, T., Armendariz, L., (September 24, 2023) "Gratitude Practice to Decrease Stress and Burnout in Acute-Care Health Professionals" OJIN: The Online Journal of Issues in Nursing Vol. 28, No. 3

UCL (2009). *How long does it take to form a habit?* [online] UCL News. Available at: https://www.ucl.ac.uk/news/2009/aug/how-long-does-it-take-form-habit

World Health Organization (2023). *Constitution of the World Health Organization*. [online] World Health Organization. Available at: https://www.who.int/about/accountability/governance/constitution

UN Sustainable Development Goals

EURES (2023). *EURES*. [online] eures.ec.europa.eu. Available at: https://eures.ec.europa.eu/index_en

National Center for O*NET Development (2023). *O*NET OnLine*. [online] Onetonline.org. Available at: https://www.onetonline.org/

ONS (2023). *Public sector employment, UK - Office for National Statistics*. [online] www.ons.gov.uk. Available at: https://www.ons.gov.uk/employmentandlabourmarket/peopleinwork/publicsectorpersonnel/bulletins/publicsectoremployment/june2023 [Accessed 22 Oct. 2023]

United Nations (1948). *Universal Declaration of Human Rights*. [online] United Nations. Available at: https://www.un.org/en/about-us/universal-declaration-of-human-rights

United Nations (2015). *The 17 Sustainable Development Goals*. [online] United Nations. Available at: https://sdgs.un.org/goals

United Nations (2023). *The Sustainable Development Goals Report 2023: Special Edition*. [online] unstats.un.org. Available at: https://unstats.un.org/sdgs/report/2023/

ABOUT THE AUTHOR

Carolyn Parry, FRSA, FHEA, RCDP, is a multi-award-winning and certified career and life coach, trainer, and TEDx speaker who is passionate about helping people identify and work towards achieving their potential.

She came to career development work in her late 30s as part of her own midlife crisis after a successful but unfulfilling seventeen-year management career in property, technology, and publishing. During her career she has worked in organisations as small as two people and as big as FTSE 250. Her existential career crisis led to her moving back to her Welsh roots from Sussex in 2001 and a decision to change career direction, aged 39.

She joined Aberystwyth University the same year to retrain as a university careers adviser. She worked there for almost 15 years supporting computer science, business, languages, information science, rural studies and law undergraduate and post graduate students in particular, and later while there, also began running staff training and development sesssions. In 2012, she was awarded a student-nominated Learning and Teaching Award for her passion and drive in supporting student employability. The following year, she received an Aberystwyth University Learning and Teaching Fellowship. In 2013, she became an Academic Champion of Enterprise and a University-wide Equality Champion. She was promoted to Deputy Director of the Careers Service in 2014 where she led on employer engagement before taking a secondment as Director of Student Development and Employability. Working with two other national trainers, she developed the

Association of Graduate Careers Advisory Services HE career coaching module for the AGCAS/Warwick Careers Education, Information and Guidance in HE qualification.

In 2015, aged 53, Carolyn took voluntary severance to set up Career Alchemy, her now award-winning career coaching and training practice. She invested some of her redundancy money in developing her all-age INSPiRED Career and Life Coaching framework, toolkit, and planner which has been used in this book. Designed to enable clients to create and develop purpose-led careers, Carolyn refined the framework further while working with the Careers team and students at the University of Northampton in 2016. The same year, she won the PRIME Cymru business start-up award, which she received from HRH King Charles, then the Prince of Wales, and was also shortlisted for a Wales Start-Up Awards.

In 2017, following nomination by a client, she received the Career Development Institute's prestigious UK Careers Adviser/Career Coach of the Year Award. She also won the contract to represent the Institute as their Project Associate for Wales, a role she still holds today.

In 2018, she became one of the £20,000 grant winners of the UK Government's Inclusive Economy Partnership. She used the award to fund a project with Unilever, which included commissioning specialists at Derby University's International Centre for Guidance Studies (iCeGS) to undertake action research to evaluate the effectiveness of the INSPiRED approach. Their research confirmed that INSPiRED significantly increases clarity of direction and an individual's confidence to their ability to get there.

In 2019, Carolyn received a second award from the then Prince of Wales, this time for business growth. INSPiRED remains at the heart of Carolyn's work with aspiring and established professionals who want to identify and change career direction. She works directly and via various public, private, and third-sector client organisations to help individuals identify and create happy and successful working lives.

A Fellow of the Royal Society of Arts, the Higher Education Academy, the International Enterprise Educators' Programme, and listed on the Professional Register of the CDI, Carolyn is also trained in various career development and therapeutic practices. Carolyn hosts her ***Change Your Story*** podcast, episodes from which have become some of the stories in this book. She frequently appears in the media and also as a podcast guest. She published her first book, ***Change Your Story***, in November 2023.

Carolyn is the current President and Chair of the Career Development Institute, having been elected by members to serve on the Board initially as President-Elect in 2020. She also serves on the Board of Antur Cymru, a £4M social enterprise, which helps Welsh businesses start and grow. Until recently, she was also a Trustee/Director on the Boards of Ceredigion Citizens Advice, part of the UK-wide network of Citizens Advice charities.

For more, please see Carolyn's profile on www.linkedin.com or follow her as @CareerAlchemist on X (formally Twitter).

To learn more about Career Alchemy and its coaching services, please visit www.careeralchemy.co.uk.

Printed in Great Britain
by Amazon

34869401R00264